# The US–China Rift and Its Impact on Globalisation

# Studies in Critical Social Sciences Book Series

Haymarket Books is proud to be working with Brill Academic Publishers (www.brill.nl) to republish the *Studies in Critical Social Sciences* book series in paperback editions. This peer-reviewed book series offers insights into our current reality by exploring the content and consequences of power relationships under capitalism, and by considering the spaces of opposition and resistance to these changes that have been defining our new age. Our full catalog of *SCSS* volumes can be viewed at https://www.haymarketbooks.org/series_collections/4-studies-in-critical-social-sciences.

*Series Editor*
**David Fasenfest** (York University, Canada)

*Editorial Board*
**Eduardo Bonilla-Silva** (Duke University)
**Chris Chase-Dunn** (University of California–Riverside)
**William Carroll** (University of Victoria)
**Raewyn Connell** (University of Sydney)
**Kimberlé W. Crenshaw** (University of California–LA and Columbia University)
**Heidi Gottfried** (Wayne State University)
**Alfredo Saad-Filho** (Queen's University, Belfast)
**Chizuko Ueno** (University of Tokyo)
**Sylvia Walby** (Lancaster University)
**Raju Das** (York University)

# The US–China Rift and Its Impact on Globalisation

Crisis, Strategy, Transitions

Raffaele Sciortino

Haymarket Books
Chicago, IL

First published in 2024 by Brill Academic Publishers, The Netherlands
© 2024 Koninklijke Brill NV, Leiden, The Netherlands

Published in paperback in 2025 by
Haymarket Books
P.O. Box 180165
Chicago, IL 60618
773-583-7884
www.haymarketbooks.org

ISBN: 979-8-88890-351-3

Distributed to the trade in the US through Consortium Book Sales and Distribution (www.cbsd.com) and internationally through Ingram Publisher Services International (www.ingramcontent.com).

This book was published with the generous support of Lannan Foundation, Wallace Action Fund, and the Marguerite Casey Foundation.

Special discounts are available for bulk purchases by organizations and institutions. Please call 773-583-7884 or email info@haymarketbooks.org for more information.

Cover design by Jamie Kerry and Ragina Johnson.

Printed in the United States.

Library of Congress Cataloging-in-Publication data is available.

You seem quite intelligent for an American

J.D. SALINGER, *For Esmè—with Love and Squalor*, 1950

# Contents

Acknowledgements IX
List of Illustrations XI

Introduction 1

1 **The Crisis inside Globalisation** 8
  1 Prologue: the Financial Imperialism of the Dollar 8
  2 Where Does Globalisation Go from Here? 20

2 **United States** 34
  1 Grand Strategy? 36

3 **China** 76
  1 Transition to What? 76
  2 The Agrarian Question 90
  3 Class Struggle and Capitalist Development 110
  4 A New Strategy 133
  5 China at a Crossroads 149
  6 Globalisation, the Chinese Way 172
  7 The Internationalisation of the Renminbi Yuan 194
  8 China's Geopolitics 215
  9 Imperialism and China: Concluding Remarks 229

**Epilogue** 244
  1 The Changing Pace of Decoupling 244
  2 Global Fallout 247
  3 Geopolitical Disconnections 254
  4 China: the Domestic Picture 258
  5 A Global Reformism? 261
  6 The Crisis to Come 263

Bibliography 269
Index 307

# Acknowledgements

I have been working on this book for three years, as part of an independent scholarship of critical political studies, mainly focused on capitalist globalisation, imperialism, Sino American relations, and neo-populism. The least that can be said is that the world has changed around us since. The Italian edition was published by the publishing house Asterios, Trieste, in fall 2022. I thank my friend Asterios Delithanassis for giving trust all these years and granting permission for the (condensed) English translation of this book and for reproducing the included figures and maps.

First and foremost, the idea for the book was conceived in dialogue with Robert Ferro, Stefano Vannicelli and Emiliana Armano, who also provided comments and suggestions on earlier drafts. Many other comrades and scholars have read and commented on the Italian edition or discussed it along the way: so, the list would inevitably be partial. I would like to express special appreciation to Elisabetta Grande, Guido Ortona, Stefano Lucarelli, Carmelo Buscema, Piero Pagliani, Dario Di Conzo, Fabio Ciabatti, Mimmo Porcaro, Carlo Formenti, Salvatore Engels-Di Mauro, Marco Briziarelli, Luca Bellocchio, Steve Wright, Nich Dyer-Witheford, Devi Sacchetto, Matteo Montaguti, Antonio Alia, Maurizio Pentenero, Gianluca Pittavino, Lorenzo Avellino, Porfido collective, Genova Citystrike collective, and Wildcat collective. Their feedback was in any case precious. I would also like to thank the Università della Calabria for the invitation to talk about the topic of the book for a "Giovanni Arrighi" seminar.

I could not have undertaken this journey without Rosanna Maccarone and Alvise Grammatica, who first gave the suggestion for an English version of this book and helped with their ongoing ideational and practical support. Special thanks also to Arianna Bove, who gave me the idea for the title. I extend my gratitude to Jon Wilcox for revising and copyediting this English translation: at short notice, he helped transform a coarse translation of the original Italian text into a scholarly work in English that stands on its own merit. Thanks should also go to the reviewers of the manuscript and the editorial board of Brill, in particular, David Fasenfest, the series editor, Jason Prevost, the editor for Social Sciences and International Relations, who both encouraged the translation, and Katie Short: they all gave me trust and were especially helpful for their precious editorial support.

I am also very grateful to all past and present scholars, who have contributed to the body of critical knowledge my study has been drawing on. In particular, I am grateful to Paolo Turco and Loren Goldner, with whom I had in the past the pleasure of discussing Marxist theory. I cannot fail to mention Lello Tuzio for the cover photo and the past discussions with him and other comrades on the "Chinese question". Finally, I would like to recognize everyone's contribution I have not mentioned, organisers and participants at a number of events, workshops and conferences, where the thinking about the US-China rift was further developed. Lastly, the silence of the mountains and Meo's miaows were the practical framework that made this book possible.

Of course, none of the mentioned persons and collectives bear responsibility for the views expressed in this book. Shortcomings are my responsibility only.

# Illustrations

### Figures

1.1  FDI inflows and the underlying trend, 1990–2018   23
1.2  The global value chain trade grew rapidly in the 1990s but stagnated after the 2008 global financial crisis   26
1.3  World global value chain participation   27
1.4  FDI, trade, GDP, and GVC trends, 1990–2019   30
1.5  Private capital formation in G20 developed economies, 1980–2019   31
1.6  The increase in global debt   32
2.1  Share of chip market by country/region, 2018   50
2.2  Trillions of dollars of federal surplus or deficit   68
2.3  US government debt held by foreign holders   69
2.4  US dollar share of world reserve currencies   70
2.5  US government debt held by the Federal Reserve   71
3.1  Rural population in China in poverty (2000–2020)   96
3.2  Strikes of various scales, 2011–2018   128
3.3  Foreign portfolio investment in Chinese stocks and bonds (trillions of renminbi)   143
3.4  China's trade deficit in semiconductors (USD billion)   152
3.5  China's debt to GDP   158
3.6  Uncommon prosperity: after booming, China's urban household income is slowing   165
3.7  Flow of Chinese vs. US foreign direct investment to Africa   178
3.8  China's tailored approach of exporting capital (country groups)   181
3.9  Long-run debt and commodity price trends in developing and emerging countries   183
3.10  Net difference in total trade in goods with US vs. China in the Indo-Pacific, 2019   187
3.11  Standard determinants of US dollar share of reserves   197
E.1  Trade decoupling trade interdependence between China and the United States is declining   248
E.2  Insecurities and investments. United States and China   250

### Maps

3.1  One Belt, One Road   174
3.2  China's 'Digital Silk Road'   177

3.3 Chinese share of total trade in goods from Comprehensive and Progressive Agreement for Trans-Pacific Partnership (CPTPP) countries, 2020   188

3.4 Gulf countries' share in China energy imports, by percentage, 2019   193

## Tables

1.1 What has shaped globalisation today? A timeline   9

# Introduction

> The living space of US conqueror is a band that goes around the earth.
> AMADEO BORDIGA, 1949

∴

Günther Anders once wrote that the power of an ideology lies not so much in the answers it gives as in the questions it stifles. In light of the emergence of a new dimension of historical dynamics—a dimension made all the more apparent, if only we do not let ourselves be dazzled by the media spectacle surrounding it, by the ongoing crisis of capitalist civilisation—we find ourselves confronted with unsettling questions. Questions that have been stifled by the exuberant political and cultural atmosphere accompanying the rise of globalisation over the past few decades. This change has been found outside the West, of course, but it has been arguably most palpable within Western societies, where dilemmas surrounding the relationship between the Western world and the rest of the globe are gradually breaking free from the constraints of 'post-democratic' hypocrisies.

The backdrop against which this study is presented is characterised by the imminent possibility of global economic upheavals and escalating tensions in international relations. These tensions have been laid bare by events such as the Ukrainian conflict, while on the horizon—the central theme of this book—looms a clash between the United States and China, driven by an ongoing rift. We face a growing state of chaos that extends beyond the realms of high politics and economics, increasingly seeping into the daily lives of hundreds of millions of people across the world.

This book endeavours to make a contribution to the pressing questions arising from the evolving context, which signifies a new *geistige situation der zeit*. It does so by building on previous studies that sought to contextualise the decade following the onset of so-called global financial crisis. An initial version of this work was published in Italian by Asterios in the late summer of 2022, titled *Stati Uniti e Cina allo scontro globale. Strutture, strategie, contingenze*. The present translation is a condensed edition intended for English-speaking readers, which includes a new chapter (Epilogue) covering developments in the year that has transpired since the original publication. The decision not to extensively revise the contents of the original text, beyond modifications required by the act of translation, allows readers to find elements that confirm previously outlined hypotheses and provides prompts for further exploration in light of developments that have unfolded since the book's inception.

The book is concerned with the root causes, current state, and future prospects of the deepening rift between the United States and China. The author attempts to trace the dynamics and turning points of the Sino-American relationship across various geo-economic and geopolitical dimensions. At the core of this inquiry lies the overarching question regarding the nature of this impending clash: is it primarily hegemonic, existential (for both parties?), or systemic? Let us take these in turn.

The interpretative framework employed is systemic, not applied in mechanistically 'structuralist' terms, but having recourse to a Marxist analytical toolkit that proceeds from the structure of contemporary global capitalism—as it has evolved since the resolution of the global crisis of the 1970s—to the strategies of pivotal state actors and vice versa. Central to this exploration is the interplay between the dynamics of global accumulation, geopolitical considerations, and the internal social and political dynamics within the United States and China. These dynamics, have, palpable repercussions on a global scale. That is to say, the trajectory of global capital unfolds on the level of the concrete dynamics of 'many capitals' (Marx), that is, within the context of the international division of labour, amid inter-capitalist competition and class struggles. The author's underlying conviction is that investigating the current US–China clash means confronting the constitutive nexus between internationalised capitalist reproduction (globalisation), the strengths and limitations of US hegemony founded on dollar-based finance imperialism, and China's asymmetrical and unstable position within the international division of labour.

Addressing this array of questions necessitates establishing a middle-range level of analysis. This level should enable us to revisit and thematise, after decades of relative theoretical and political neglect, the very essence of what imperialism represents today or has transformed into. Indeed, an analysis of the US–China relationship currently serves as both a path to and at a critical litmus test for any (Marxist) theory of imperialism rooted in the law of value and its adaptations within the world market. This represents the latent objective and perhaps heuristic value of the book. A realist geopolitical perspective is frequently employed but always within the broader context of the inherent contradictions of global capitalism—inter-bourgeois and class contradictions. This perspective helps elucidate the transition from a crisis of valorisation to a socio-political crisis and from inter-capitalist competition to an overt clash.

Geopolitics, therefore, is conceived as political economy, ultimately entailing class relations concentrated within the global interstate system during the stage of imperialism, whereby state and capital are strictly intertwined. This view moves beyond any instrumentalist or functionalist theories of the state. Furthermore, this work consistently draws upon the historical sociology characteristic of world-system approaches for comparative purposes, with particular attention to Giovanni Arrighi's (2007) recent reflections on China.[1] However, it attempts, albeit in a tentative manner, to transform this approach into a Marxist sociology that examines the specific features of China's shift towards capitalism and integration into the global market. This is done within the framework of a re-examined and reconstructed theory of imperialism, rather than within the framework of a theory of hegemonic successions, as in world-system approaches.

This systemic approach is put to the test by applying it to the current course and possible evolution of the US–China relationship, which is not merely conceived as a interaction between great powers but as the central axis of today's imperialistic configurations. It serves as a litmus test of their stability or crisis. The entire world system is at stake here, not merely two of its major components, even though they are the most significant. The crux of the matter today revolves around the head-on collision between these two heavyweights, which, at a deeper level, underscores the urgent need for a comprehensive restructuring of the capitalist interstate and class relations. At present, these relations appear to be spiralling into an uncharted crisis with no readily apparent resolution.

The book consists of three chapters. The first, titled "The Crisis inside Globalisation", takes as its starting point the global crisis that unfolded more than a decade ago and set in motion profound shifts in the international order. Within this chapter, we embark upon a genealogical exploration of global assemblages, commencing with the crisis of the Bretton Woods international monetary regime, marked by the dollar's departure from the gold standard in 1971. The exploration continues with the Sino-US rapprochement of 1972 and the resolution of the social upheaval initiated in the West during the so-called Long '68. The outcome of this complex historical trajectory was the emergence of a new form of imperialism, underpinned on international financial circuits dominated by the US dollar and characterised by a novel international division of labour. This paradigm shift allowed China to make a significant leap within

---

1 Giovanni Arrighi, *Adam Smith in Beijing: Lineages of the Twenty-First Century* (London: Verso, 2007).

an industrialisation process that had already commenced during the 'heroic' phase of 'socialist' accumulation, which, in reality, represented a unique form of primitive accumulation. Presently, globalisation finds itself at a critical juncture, marked by a slowdown but not yet at the threshold of full-scale deglobalisation. This slowdown signals a diminishing global accumulation, but it has not yet reached the point of a catastrophic downturn. Nevertheless, the asymmetrical relationship between the United States and China, which has been linchpin of globalisation thus far, has unquestionably entered a state of crisis. This is evident in the US's attempts to decouple the Chinese economy from the upper segments of the world market to which Beijing continues to strive to secure access. The fault lines of impending ruptures are already discernible, and they will become increasingly pronounced as the world economy grapples with the new crisis. The pace at which global disassembly unfolds and its trajectory are influenced by numerous variables, ultimately driven by the dynamics of global accumulation and class struggle. A shift to a more definitive course of deglobalisation will likely not occur without a major geopolitical crisis directly involving the Sino-US relationship.

The progression of the crisis is, in large part, determined by the nature and course of this impending clash. The subsequent two chapters of the book trace its root causes and potential trajectories within the framework of structural contradictions and deployed strategies. The book's objective is not to describe every single detail, a task beyond anyone, just as the sequence of topics is not strictly chronological. Rather, the two chapters have specific focuses.

The second chapter, devoted to the United States, explores the effort to outline a 'Grand Strategy' in response to the challenge posed, spanning the administrations of Trump and Biden. This chapter refrains from endorsing the argument of 'America in decline'. Rather, it acknowledges the role of the world hegemon, which still performs an indispensable ordering function on the international stage, as symbolised by the dollar's continued status as the quasi–world currency. However, this role has become increasingly burdensome and destabilising for global capitalism as a whole and the Chinese economy in particular. Meanwhile, the benefits of globalisation are growing increasingly problematic and divisive, even at the domestic level, as the domestic social and political crisis in the US demonstrates. Consequently, Washington faces immense difficulties in articulating a new Grand Strategy to address this historical phase, which possesses very different characteristics from the Cold War era. This predicament has also led to a heightened level of US assertiveness, irrespective of the political colour of the administration, resulting in comprehensive geopolitical activism. One prominent manifestation of this activism is the Ukrainian war, which will be analysed within the context of the reconfiguration of the strategic triangle involving Washington, Beijing, and Moscow.

The third chapter, dedicated to China, offers a concise overview of its distinctive path to capitalism, which commenced with a peasant democratic revolution. It encompasses various dimensions, including the agrarian question, the new development strategy, the dynamics of class struggle in both urban and rural settings, the emergence of the middle class, the external projection through initiatives like the 'New Silk Roads', the first steps towards internationalising the yuan, and the escalating diplomatic and military tensions with Washington. China's rising capitalism theoretically possesses significant room for both quantitative and qualitative development, even if this development can no longer take the heroic form of 'socialist accumulation' isolated from the global market. Instead, it is contingent on moving towards an internal social-democratic type of social compromise, renewing the nexus between economic-social growth and political stability on a more advanced foundation. Nonetheless, these development prospects are increasingly intertwined with the challenge of confronting the imperialist levy and successfully ascending the global value chains. This is necessary to fend off the concrete risks of regression or even disintegration, given the multifaceted internal challenges. Indeed, the asymmetry with the imperialist West remains structural, evident in various aspects such as Chinese capital exports, production structure, and monetary and financial assets.

In essence, the US–China rift is still in its nascent stages but inevitable. Neither of the two contenders can afford to back down: Washington is committed to preserving its hegemony, while Beijing's successful transition to modern capitalism, underpinned by relative surplus value and a social-democratic class compromise, hinges on its ability to reclaim manoeuvring space from Western imperialism. Hence, moving from structural perspectives to strategies, we encounter the inherent contradiction specific to this phase. Both China and the United States find themselves in the paradoxical situation of needing to preserve globalisation while simultaneously pursuing strategies that undermine it. Within this framework, the internal class struggle in both nations will act as an accelerator with global repercussions, albeit within a context vastly different from the cycle of mass worker struggles intertwined with anti-colonial and anti-Western uprisings of the 1960s and 1970s.

The relationship between the United States and China extends far beyond a mere geopolitical matter; it encapsulates the core contradictions of global capitalism. The trajectory of this clash fundamentally reflects the imperative for a comprehensive restructuring of capital relationships and, consequently, class dynamics, in order to address the profitability crisis that has thus far been mitigated by massive injections of liquidity. A US-led overhaul of production and finance, akin to the one witnessed in the 1970s and 1980s, without or prior to a full-scale confrontation with China, seems an unrealistic proposition today, especially considering the fear that Beijing might exploit such a scenario. Combining these two is a formidable challenge and would inevitably entail significant disruptions at all levels. Consequently, Washington is increasingly likely to sow global chaos without being able to present comprehensive solutions, as has largely been the case since World War II.

This leads to several crucial implications, summarised in Chap. 3.9, on the fabric of which this entire book is articulated.

First, it is evident that China's ascent does not currently represent a genuine hegemonic challenge. Such a challenge would require not only the decline of US power but also Beijing's ability to assume the specific imperialist role that Washington plays within the global capitalist system, a role for which Beijing remains significantly distant. No 'Chinese century' is on the horizon.

Second, China faces an existential challenge of its own: it must either achieve a significant leap in development or succumb to imperialist pressure, potentially jeopardising its hard-earned economic successes, the social compromise within its class structure, and the unity of its nation-state. The Chinese working class confronts a complex web of class and national factors, and its fate ultimately depends on the broader dynamics of the global class struggle. Neglecting this issue only serves to bolster the imperialist offensive against China.

Third, at the heart of the matter lies a systemic challenge. The United States does appear capable of safeguarding, for better or worse, its world hegemony (or at least dominance), albeit at a cost that undermines the foundations of globalisation—that is, the latest form of imperialism, which includes the hitherto beneficial intertwining with China. There is currently no vision for a new economic and geopolitical order. Chaos appears inevitable, and finding a non-destructive resolution for the working classes and the human species-being[2] necessitates a re-evaluation of the distinct configuration of contemporary imperialism. This re-evaluation would, at the very least, require a critical re-examination of the prevailing paradigm.

Fourth, it follows that the prospect of a new multipolar world order is highly uncertain, if not entirely improbable. Nevertheless, the multipolar perspective should be carefully considered as a global-scale form of reformism—a path

---

2   Karl Marx, *Economic and Philosophical Manuscripts* (1844), in *Early Writings*, translated by Rodney Livingstone and Gregor Benton (London: Penguin Books, 1974).

and position shaped by the dialectical interplay of state and social forces. However, one should harbour no illusions about its practical impact and ultimate feasibility.

Fifth, a likely trajectory appears to be one of systemic disintegration, leading to the fragmentation of the world market. This would not simply signify a cyclical oscillation between integration and fragmentation within the world political economy. Rather, it would suggest that the capitalist drive towards global integration and the socialisation of labour can no longer be contained within the framework of capitalist social relations. While this does not necessarily paint a rosy picture, it could potentially pave the way for a global struggle aimed at transitioning to a different social order, one where social reproduction is no longer subject to the dictates of competition and profit. Regardless of the course the international system takes, the final outcome will ultimately hinge on the agency of collective social forces, underscoring the indispensability of class analysis. This is especially pertinent in light of the emerging and intricate social and political phenomena of neo-populism, the declining trajectory of workers' movements, and the crisis of the Left in Western societies. Unless, that is, one is resigned to embracing destructive chaos and the consolation of identity politics and postmodern fragmentalism.

Readers will have the opportunity to assess the appropriateness of the analyses presented here, while also encountering issues and themes that the author has, at best, only touched upon. This study serves as an invitation for collective exploration of the frontiers and contentious matters that the trajectory of global capitalism invariably places on the agenda.

CHAPTER 1

# The Crisis inside Globalisation

## 1     Prologue: the Financial Imperialism of the Dollar

The relationship between the United States and China has played a fundamental role in the internationalisation of capital, at the levels of production, trade, and capital flow. This phenomenon, commonly referred to as globalisation, is not merely the result of political choice[1] but signifies a mighty leap in the constitution of the world market (*Weltmarkt*), a concept deeply rooted in Marxian economic thought. To gain a comprehensive understanding of what globalisation truly entails, it is essential to examine the nature and progression of this relationship.

### 1.1     *Genealogies of Globalisation*

Since the 1970s, there have been at least three fundamental processes that, in conjunction with the initial severe crisis in capitalist accumulation in the Western world since the conclusion of World War II, have coalesced to shape the frameworks underpinning globalisation. These processes have instigated a profound restructuring of the global capitalist system. Let us look at them (see Table 1.1).[2]

In the first place, we have the Long '68, in its dual dimension encompassing, on the one hand, various struggles within the metropolis, including the movements of mass workers in the Fordist factories, the emerging middle classes, youth activism, the women's rights movement, and the civil rights movement in the United States, and on the other, anti-colonial struggles, which were, in many ways, the catalyst for the aforementioned struggles within the developed world. These two dimensions, although distinct, converged around shared

---

1  For an overview of this topic, see Raffaele Sciortino, "Il dibattito sulla globalizzazione: dagli anni Novanta ai segnali di crisi" [The globalisation debate: From the 1990s to signs of crisis] (working paper, open access, Trieste, 2010), accessed 23 September 2023, https://www.asterios.it/catalogo/il-dibattito-sulla-globalizzazione-dagli-anni-novanta-ai-segnali-di-crisi.

2  I rephrase from Raffaele Sciortino, *I dieci anni che sconvolsero il mondo. Crisi globale e geopolitica dei neopopulismi* [The ten years that shocked the world: Global crisis and the geopolitics of neo-populisms] (Trieste: Asterios, 2019), available via https://www.researchgate.net/publication/352212013_I_DIECI_ANNI_CHE_SCONVOLSERO_IL_MONDO_Crisi_globale_e_geopolitica_dei_neopopulismi. The term 'assemblages' may serve to avoid subjectivist readings.

TABLE 1.1    What has shaped globalisation today? A timeline

| | |
|---|---|
| Long '68 | Social movements in the metropolis, anti-colonial struggles |
| 1971 | End of Bretton Woods regime |
| 1972 | Sino-American rapprochement |
| 1979–89 | Reaganism, Deng Xiaoping's Policy, end of bipolarism, end of the 'Third World' |

CREATED BY THE AUTHOR.

objectives—demanding broader social participation in the benefits of modernisation and seeking emancipation from subjugation to it. These grassroots movements exerted pressure to reconfigure the relationship between capital and labour within the metropolises and between imperialist powers and oppressed countries on the periphery. Even as these transformative dynamics unfolded, the United States, which had served as the linchpin of the international order during the 'Thirty Glorious Years' following World War II, found itself grappling with both external and internal crises, compounded by the disaster of the Vietnam War. Nevertheless, the Nixon/Kissinger administration was able to outline an imperialist strategy capable of turning strategic weakness into strength. In 1971 Washington terminated the post-war Bretton Woods international monetary regime by delinking the dollar from its fixed gold standard. This decision led to the establishment of a new global monetary standard centred on the fluctuating value of the dollar. Despite the inherent tendency of the dollar to depreciate due to mounting domestic and international deficits, it continued to function as a dominant means of payment and international reserve currency, underpinned by the enduring economic and military might of the United States. This resilience defied premature predictions of America's irreversible decline.[3] Furthermore, in 1972, diplomatic relations were initiated with China under Mao's leadership, following the tumultuous period of the Cultural Revolution. The Sino-American rapprochement, primarily a response to the growing global influence of the Soviet Union and its support for numerous anti-colonial movements, was a strategic manoeuvre by Nixon and

---

3   For an insightful, non-Marxist reading of these processes, see Michael Hudson, *Super Imperialism: The Economic Strategy of American Empire* (New York: Holt, Rinehart and Winston, 1972). Note that a new edition was published in 2002 by Pluto Press with the revised subtitle *The Origin and Fundamentals of US World Dominance*.

Kissinger to navigate a less painful exit from the quagmire of the Vietnam War, which was draining American resources and credibility.[4] This historic move brought China into the geopolitical arena, pitting it against Moscow after a decade of political estrangement, following the Sino-Soviet split of 1962. The initial phase of political dialogue between Washington and Beijing remained primarily centred on geopolitical considerations. However, starting in 1979, it acquired a geo-economic dimension with the advent of Deng Xiaoping's economic reforms and controlled opening to the global market.

The year 1979 marked a turning point in global strategic dynamics, driven not only by the initiation of Chinese reforms but also by two other significant events: the Russian invasion of Afghanistan, which turned out to be a trap orchestrated by the American administration to Moscow's detriment,[5] and the Iranian revolution, a profound rupture in the prevailing revolutionary political paradigms of the twentieth century. Amid these transformative events, the United States, through the Federal Reserve's dramatic escalation of interest rates—the infamous 'Volcker Shock'—and the consequent surge in the value of the dollar, positioned itself to attract capital on a global scale. This anti-inflationary interest-rate hike, in addition to decisively quelling labour movements in the West, had far-reaching consequences. It subjected Third World countries, which had shown signs of potentially establishing a new anti-Western economic order, to recurrent debt crises followed by the International Monetary Fund's imposition of structural adjustment plans. Meanwhile, it plunged the Soviet Union into a profound crisis, foreshadowing its eventual collapse a decade later. The Reagan era (1981–89), which concluded the Fordist social compromise and marked the definitive transition to the new post–Bretton Woods global financial architecture, also presaged the ultimate crisis of the Soviet bloc. This pivotal moment heralded the ascendancy of financialisation. Consequently, the United States emerged as the uncontested global hegemon, exporting 'democracy' and 'human rights' around the world in a series of interventions that spanned from the aggression against Iraq in 1991 to the bombing of Serbia in 1999, the invasion of Afghanistan, the second Gulf War in 2003, and subsequent actions in Libya, Syria, and beyond.

These, then, were the main building blocks that transformed the 1970s capitalist crisis into the foundation for the resurgence of world accumulation

---

4 Raffaele Sciortino, *Un passaggio oltre il bipolarismo. Il rapprochement sino-americano 1969–1972* [A transition beyond bipolarity: The Sino-American rapprochement 1969–1972] (Bologna: I libri di Emil, 2012).

5 Zbigniew Brzezinski, *The Grand Chessboard: American Primacy and its Geostrategic Imperatives* (New York: Basic Books, 1997).

known as globalisation, including the restructuring and reinforcement of US hegemony on a global scale. In parallel, the dollar's sphere of influence expanded to the entire world, debunking any declinist narratives regarding US dominance.

## 1.2 *Global Assemblies*

Let us break down the global architecture that has been created, starting with the geo-economic order, China's role within it, and the new social compact. These dimensions, together with their geopolitical implications, have formed the foundational pillars of the new financial imperialism centred around the US dollar.

The geo-economic order can be outlined by examining the intricate global interplay between countries with trade surpluses—the old European powers and, more importantly, emerging world factories, above all China, where Western multinational corporations have strategically relocated the medium and low segments of production chains—and the United States, which has played a pivotal role in this configuration. A significant portion of the trade surpluses generated by these manufacturing hubs has been channelled into the United States. This inflow of capital has taken several forms: it has been invested in the Treasury bond market, thereby sustaining the growth of both domestic and foreign US debt (as well as substantial military expenditures); it has been held as reserves in US dollars; or it has been reinvested in predominantly Anglo-Saxon stock and bond markets. The nexus between the US dollar and the global oil trade, stemming from an agreement between the Nixon administration and the Saudi royal house and later extended to the Organization of the Petroleum Exporting Countries or OPEC, further amplified this financial circuit. The revenues from the oil rent, which had swelled due to the price crisis of 1973 (to the detriment of Europe and Japan), were exchanged for US dollars, commonly known as petrodollars. These petrodollars have, in turn, flowed back into Wall Street, cementing the dollar's role as an international payment mechanism. Consequently, a new monetary and financial framework, often termed Bretton Woods II,[6] has underpinned the ongoing globalisation of production.

The contrasting US policy manoeuvres of 1971 and 1979, characterised by differing monetary approaches that have alternated over time, converged to

---

6 Michael P. Dooley, David Folkerts-Landau, and Peter Garber, "An Essay on the Revived Bretton Woods System" (NBER Working Paper 9971, National Bureau of Economic Research, Cambridge, MA, September 2003), accessed 23 September 2023, https://www.nber.org/papers/w9971.pdf.

produce a definitive outcome: the capture of value within an increasingly globalised production chain. This was made possible by the effective establishment, for the first time in the history of capitalism, of an international division of labour on a global scale. The surplus value generated by the Chinese working class, and not solely by China, flowed substantially to the West. It was either directly appropriated by multinational corporations, used to finance the US twin deficits, or channelled into the world capital market dominated by the dollar-based financial system. The US capital and consumer markets, largely supported by these debt and credit mechanisms, become indispensable not only to the Western world but also for the industrial development of emerging economies increasingly integrated into Western markets. *Our debt, your problem.* Running the empire through debt has become the paramount strategy of Yankee imperialist politics.

It was this complex system that marked the onset of what is commonly referred to as 'financialisation', which began with the proliferation of US dollar-based assets across global markets. These included Eurodollars, petrodollars, and various types of financial securities, all seeking returns on an unprecedented scale. The globalisation of value chains helped facilitate these financial flows, leading to the emergence of new configurations of capitalism that transcended traditional imperialist structures. This shift paved the way for the proliferation of increasingly sophisticated financial instruments, culminating in a pyramid of endlessly replicable securities, such as securitisation and derivatives. However, these securities were guaranteed only as a last resort and after a convoluted chain of intermediaries, all underpinned by a production network that extended to the entire globe.[7] This financialisation represented not only a global mechanism for capturing value but also a mode of financial regulation imposed on productive capital. It was an intricate interplay between bank credit and fictitious capital (in the Marxian sense). Interestingly, this interplay remained opaque even to market participants themselves until the eventual emergence of catastrophic consequences. As a result, it became increasingly interwoven and inextricable. Furthermore, this form of capital,

---

7  Tony Norfield, "Finance, the Rate of Profit and Imperialism" (paper delivered to the World Association for Political Economy conference, Paris, July 2012), accessed 23 September 2023, https://dokumen.tips/documents/public-debt-finance-and-imperialism.html; Guglielmo Carchedi and Michael Roberts, "The Economics of Modern Imperialism", *Historical Materialism* 29, no. 4 (2021): 23–69, https://doi.org/10.1163/1569206X-12341959; Michael J. Howell, *Capital Wars: The Rise of Global Liquidity* (London: Palgrave Macmillan, 2020); Carolina Alves, "Fictitious Capital, the Credit System, and the Particular Case of Governments Bonds in Marx", *New Political Economy* 28, no. 3 (2023): 398–415, https://doi.org/10.1080/13563467.2022.2130221.

which appeared as money simply begetting more money, exerted growing pressure towards the proletarianisation of ever-expanding human populations. It pushed the value of labour power below the levels required for reproduction,[8] contributed to the worsening environmental devastation, led to the prolonged use of factories beyond their depreciation, and intensified the commodification and erosion of both tangible and intangible social infrastructures. Finance, production, and social reproduction became locked in an increasingly incestuous embrace, marked by paroxysmal rhythms occasionally interrupted by economically, socially, and (geo)politically devastating shocks.

All of the aforementioned factors made possible the integration of the People's Republic of China into the framework of US-led globalisation. This integration was inherently asymmetrical, rooted in the inseparable connection between productive and financial globalisation on the one hand and China's opening to the global market on the other. In the Western imperialist sphere, the appropriation of surplus value generated by the Chinese and Asian labour force became a fundamental precondition for sustaining capitalist accumulation and maintaining social stability, often referred to as the 'neoliberal social compromise'.[9] Conversely, for China, Western nations became not only crucial in terms of quantity but also composition, serving as the primary destination for the export of low and, increasingly today, medium value-added final goods, which Chinese factories processed and assembled. This dynamic underscored China's significant dependence on the ultimate consumer market while simultaneously solidifying its two-way connection with the global dollar circuit. A portion of earnings from these exports had to be reinvested in US Treasury bonds or held as dollar reserves, serving as collateral for access—granted by Washington—to global markets. The reciprocal benefit was China's emergence from economic underdevelopment, a goal that was notably achieved over the course of forty years following its 'opening up'. This transformation was made possible not only through the infusion of foreign capital and technology but also, importantly, due to the socio-economic foundations laid during the prior phase of 'socialist accumulation'. It is crucial to acknowledge not only the residual areas of underdevelopment but also the fact that, during this period, Beijing had to relinquish any alternative model in favour of the export-led approach, leading to an increasingly substantial current account surplus. These are critical features that surfaced after the 2008 global financial crisis

---

8   John Smith, *Imperialism in the Twenty-First Century: Globalization, Super-Exploitation, and Capitalism's Final Crisis* (New York: Monthly Review Press, 2016).
9   Sam King, *Imperialism and the Development Myth: How Rich Countries Dominate in the Twenty-First Century* (Manchester: Manchester University Press, 2021).

and have since formed the basis for efforts to transition towards a 'new development model' aimed at greater autonomy from the West. This endeavour constitutes one of the primary factors driving the clash with the United States that is the subject of this book.

Lastly, there emerged the new social compact between capital and labour that characterised the era of so-called neoliberal capitalism, both in the Western world and, albeit in different terms, across the rest of the world. While China became the world's factory thanks to the partial proletarianisation—as we will explore, not entirely complete—of hundreds of millions of men and women, who toiled for meagre wages to the benefit of Western multinationals, the outsourcing of manufacturing led to the downsizing of entire industrial sectors in the United States and, to a lesser extent, in Europe. This transition favoured the rise of a 'cognitive' economy centred on high technology, finance, and services. Consequently, the productive and social position of the working class and the middle class underwent profound change. Throughout its ascendancy, globalisation managed to maintain a certain consensus—sometimes passive, sometimes active—due to the shifting composition of the working class. On one hand, the wage suppression resulting from outsourcing processes since the late 1970s was offset by the reduced cost of consumer goods produced in China. On the other hand, the livelihoods of families and individuals became increasingly tied to finance, facilitated by the open or creeping privatisation of pensions, healthcare, education, and, above all, consumer credit. Income thus became linked not only to market fluctuations but also to the self-discipline of workers, whose interests were supposedly no longer at odds with those of businesses. Simultaneously, old solidarities, particularly among generations, began to fray.

This situation was also made possible by the *strange* defeat of the preceding cycle of social and political struggles. This defeat was strange because, in reality, the revitalisation of capital in the West was able to derive strength from the social and political transformations it ushered in as well those brought about by the movements of Long '68. These movements had advocated for autonomy, challenged established (and ageing) institutions, and valorised individuality. The genius of the Western capitalist elite lay in connecting the reproduction of the working class's existence to market mechanisms while simultaneously liberating individuals from collective constraints. Financialisation thus became an integral part of social life, marking the decline of the political Left and historical workers' reformism. The hegemony of the new middle classes over a disoriented proletariat, which had previously emerged in the revolts of the 1960s and 1970s, become the cornerstone of the new neoliberal social compromise from the 1980s onwards. Both the 'right' and 'left' variants of this compromise—the yuppie variant of the 'animal spirits' of the market and the liberal-radical variant of the identity politics of 'new' subjects—shared fundamental principles, albeit with different emphases: absolute individual autonomy, meritocracy based on creative intelligence, a youth-centric postmodernist ethos, and network-based communities. Thus, the post-'68 neoliberal restructuring managed reconcile the irreconcilable: desire and money, individual autonomy and submission to the social being. This continued until today's era, characterised by capital's dominance over all aspects of life, elevating the individual only to plunge them—as Georg Lukàcs once wrote—into a vortex of impotence cloaked in extravagance. And while the characteristics of the social contract in the West underwent these transformations, the Global South, with its fading prospects of anti-imperialist emancipation, found itself straddling a spectrum stretching from impoverished nations to emerging economies. Consequently, here, too, the social and political landscapes were experiencing profoundly change, as were the terms of social and political emancipation for the working masses.

## 1.3 Geopolitics of the Dollar

Globalisation is thus a multilevel and multidimensional process that characterises an overarching phase of capitalist accumulation, rather than primarily a politics of the ruling class. Within this process, geo-economics converges with class dynamics and geopolitics, understood as a global politics or *Weltpolitik*, at the height of the new imperialism.

Undoubtedly, the linchpin of this new system is the United States, which has assumed a unique role as the guarantor of world order following the end of the US/USSR bipolar era. This role extends both in a political sense, where the US acts as a bulwark against any revolutionary threat that might imperil the foundations of the system, and in an economic sense, where it functions as the nation that intermittently tightens and reactivates the international liquidity cycle. This action compels all global actors to ensure the solvency of what has now become the world's large debtor for the sake of the system's resilience. However, this does not negate the existence of conflicts among different actors, expressed through proxy wars and imperialist aggressions, or the asymmetrical relations that render Washington the primary beneficiary (or predator) and the sole entity enjoying systemic geopolitical rent.

At the heart of this new 'Great Game' between financialisation and geopolitics is the global significance of the US dollar.[10] The dollar plays a dual

---

10  See, for a recent overview of the dollar system, "US Dollar Funding: An International Perspective" (report prepared by a Working Group chaired by Sally Davies and Christopher

role: first, as a system of payments that has become indispensable for facilitating the circulation of internationalised flows of value, and second, as a strategic instrument wielded by its issuing authority. This duality involves an increasingly contradictory interweaving in its function as unit of value at both the national and global levels. The full internationalisation of the dollar began after the end of bipolarism, although it had already replaced the British pound as the dominant global currency after World War II. After the war, the United States had emerged as the world's largest manufacturer and largest creditor. However, during the phase ushered in by the monetary events of the 1970s, it became the world's leading debtor. Despite this transformation, it managed to capture the streams of wealth generated along production chains that had become international. As structured since then (along the lines set out above), the global goods and capital market generates an escalating demand for liquidity in an abundant and universally accepted currency. This currency, thanks to the geopolitical 'collaterals' provided by the world hegemon—such as a military apparatus capable of global projection—can only be furnished and guaranteed by the United States. As a reserve currency, the dollar functions as a medium of exchange in international trade. It is also used as the standard denomination for various financial instruments, including bonds, bank loans, and various securities. Furthermore, it underlies government debt securities and shares traded on stock exchanges, as well as futures contracts on various commodities and as collateral for credit transactions in other currencies. The dollar's dominance in the international payments system transcends both its quantity and 'quality', extending well beyond the US share of global trade and industrial production. Additionally, due to its expansive market, the dollar is considered the classic 'safe haven' for financial investments during times of economic and geopolitical turmoil.

Without a doubt, this system benefits the United States across various dimensions. It ensures minimal costs, under normal circumstances, for both private and government debts—amounting to trillions of dollars that will never be fully repaid, as they are issued in the debtor's currency—sustaining the domestic market, 'normal' military expenditures (including digital investments), and social spending. Above all, it generates the financial credit that permits the exploitation of wealth worldwide. During critical situations, the dollar system facilitates the implementation of 'stimulus' packages, the unlimited printing of money (quantitative easing) to prop up Wall Street, and the

---

Kent, CGFS Papers 65, Bank for International Settlements, Basel, June 2020), accessed 13 September 2023, https://www.bis.org/publ/cgfs65.pdf.

extraordinary financing of military spending to bring recalcitrant actors back into line. Nonetheless, the strength and hegemony of the dollar system—unparalleled in the historical dynamics of world capitalism—also stem from its capacity to involve, however subordinately, a multitude of actors, regardless of their national affiliations. These actors traffic a mounting volume of dollar securities, disconnected from any corresponding real assets, in pursuit of future valorisation, exerting pressure on labour forces and natural resources on a global scale.

And it is precisely here that the monetary system intersects with the sphere of Washington's global strategy. All of this is facilitated by the control of information obtained through the majority of the world's monetary transactions. Over recent decades, the dollar has demonstrated an accordion-like flexibility as a global currency. Depending on the issue at hand and the prevailing adversary of the moment, dollar devaluation has been employed to unload debts and inflation onto the rest of the world, while dollar revaluation captures wealth flows, resulting in currency shocks, capital flight, and credit shortages in countries burdened by debt from the prior era of easy money. In both scenarios, the Federal Reserve has acted and continues to act as the operational hub of the financial-military complex, accommodating the shifting demands of Wall Street, US economic policy, and geopolitics. In doing so, it undermines or restricts the monetary sovereignty of other nations. Over time, monetary policy has been augmented with the use of sanctions—both primary (direct) and secondary (indirect)—either implemented or threatened. These measures are aimed at detaching entities from the dollar-centric payment system, thus severing their ties to the global trade and credit network, especially when such entities are perceived as a "threat to the national security, foreign policy or economy of the United States".[11] This practice has been increasingly employed in recent years, relying on Washington's assertion of extraterritorial jurisdiction over anyone using the dollar, falling within the purview of the US Treasury or classified under 'corrupt practices'. In response, a growing number of countries have formed a coalition of resentment against Washington's financial hegemony. This resentment also forms a central element in Beijing's perceptions, concerns, and policies.

It is important, however, to avoid misunderstandings and not overly emphasise the purely predatory nature of the dollar strategy. The dollar-centric

---

11   So reads the International Emergency Economic Powers Act, passed by the US Congress in 1977. To date, one in every ten countries in the world are under US sanctions. See Stuart Davis and Immanuel Ness (eds.), *Sanctions as War: Anti-Imperialist Perspectives on American Geo-Economic Strategy* (Leiden: Brill, 2022).

system primarily represents a structure that has evolved and solidified over the decades amid competitive dynamics between capitalist entities and class struggles within the framework of US global hegemony. Its function is to facilitate the international circuits of value production. Consequently, it is not simply a monetary and financial by-product, just as the US economy is not 'empty' of productive activities.[12] On the contrary, it continues to lead in numerous advanced technology sectors, closely linked to research and military production, spanning information and communication technologies (ICT), the healthcare industry, agribusiness, patents, and intellectual property. From a strictly capitalist perspective, the function of the dollar has been and remains effective and efficient, despite its inherent imbalances and asymmetries, in the sense that it extends the capital relationship on a global scale. This, of course, does not detract from the fact that this structure and its associated strategy have not been immune to a range of critical issues and contradictions. The 2008 financial crisis, in particular, brought these challenges to the forefront with unexpected and dramatic intensity.

## 1.4   The 2008 Global Crisis

Indeed, the 'balanced disequilibrium'[13] imposed since the 1970s has proven insufficient to prevent the growing contradiction between the ascent of the Chinese economy—characterised by a surge in domestic investments and wage growth—and the profitability dynamics in the imperialist West. This contradiction has become increasingly stifling, exacerbated by a decline in overall productivity that could no longer be compensated for beyond a certain point by the credit machine and indeed burdened by the enlarged bubble of fictitious capital. Thus, the limitations of the partial solution that globalisation had offered to address the crisis of the 1970s came to the forefront: (1) an only partial restructuring of production, still based on a combination of methods for extracting absolute and relative surplus value; and (2) a geographical diversification that, while it allowed for economic recovery in the West, it came at the cost of dramatic economic growth in East Asia, particularly in China, a growth that would prove challenging to contain in the long run within the cages of imperialist financialisation. These factors were ultimately behind the outbreak of the global crisis in 2008, marking the first significant shifts in the international order of globalisation. Simultaneously, within Western

---

12   An idea that Qiao Liang indulges in *Empire Arc: America and China at the Ends of Parabola* [in Chinese] (Hong Kong: Changjiang Literature Press, 2016).
13   Yanis Varoufakis, *The Global Minotaur: America, Europe and the Future of the Global Economy* (London: Zed Books, 2011).

countries, the crisis led to the unfreezing of social and political blocs, giving rise to the so-called populist (or, more accurately, neo-populist) moment,[14] characterised by a reaction to social polarisation, widespread personal debt, the destructuring of the working class, and the individualisation of social bonds.

What has all this left today, more than a decade after the outbreak of that crisis? There are at least three crucial points to make.

First: There is a pressing need for a substantial devaluation of both financial and fixed capital to pave the way for a profound restructuring of production. This restructuring should be oriented more decisively towards the extraction of relative surplus value, allowing for a genuine revival of accumulation. However, this imperative clashes with the prevailing approach of addressing the massive debt burden in the global economy by further expanding central bank money issuance and offloading the burden, on the part of the US, onto other nations. Thus, the need for a new standard of value remains unfulfilled to this day.

Second: Significant fault lines have developed in the Sino-US relationship, which has long been the central axis of globalisation. Beijing's deepening financial and technological interdependence with the United States runs counter to its aspirations to retain a greater share of profits for itself and achieve a more balanced development. This objective, driven by internal class dynamics, has drawn increased aggression from Washington, which seeks to reassert its grip on global value streams, thus setting the stage for an enduring confrontation.

That brings us to the third point. There is growing impatience among key players in the international system with the US levy on global value chains and the international disorder it causes. At the same time, Washington's role in the global order is not easily replaceable, at least in the short to medium term. While it is an increasingly costly role, no rival with the capacity to craft an alternative global order is on the horizon. Washington is unwilling to accept a multipolar order due (also) to internal reasons, while other global actors, notably China, cannot give up on securing a less disadvantageous position. This paradoxical situation could become increasingly explosive to the extent that, with the United States, globalisation is in danger of breaking down definitively, and without the United States, it is hard to see how it can hold up.

Thus, the systemic crisis of valorisation appears to be temporarily frozen.[15] The inability of global powers to proceed with creating a new order may point

---

14  Sciortino, *I dieci anni*, part 3.
15  Bruno Astarian and Robert Ferro, "Accouchement difficile—Épisode 3 : Peut-on mettre une crise au congélateur ?", *Hic Salta—Communisation* (April 2021), accessed 27 September 2023, http://www.hicsalta-communisation.com/accueil/accouchement-difficile-episode-3-peut-on-mettre-une-crise-au-congelateur.

to a genuine fear of the imperialist bourgeois elite. It may also suggest a nervousness about the profound economic, social, and political upheaval and certain bursting of the financial bubble that any comprehensive restructuring would entail. Such restructuring would involve leveraging new technologies to intensify work processes, potentially rendering much work redundant and deskilled, reshuffling management and control hierarchies, and even negatively impacting the role of the middle classes in the West. It is a transition rife with uncertainty, destined to intersect with the mounting disorder in the international order, and with no assurances that globalisation, from which all capitalist entities have selectively benefited thus far, will persist.

## 2   Where Does Globalisation Go from Here?

The COVID-19 crisis has significantly impacted an already fragile global economic system, which had been grappling with various challenges at the outset of 2020. These challenges included the US–China tariff war, the 2018 stock market crash (partially mitigated by Western central bank liquidity injections), signs of recession in countries like Japan and Germany, and extensive interventions by the US Federal Reserve in the repo market in late 2019. Additionally, on the socio-political front in the Western world, globalist elites were facing difficulties in dealing with the enduring 'populist moment'. While these issues were not particularly new, the pandemic accelerated pre-existing trends, particularly those related to the contraction of global trade, the restructuring of global supply chains, and the reduction of foreign investments.

The central question revolves around the fate of the economic cycle that commenced in the late 1970s. Specifically, it addresses whether deglobalisation has indeed begun and if Washington's economic and geopolitical confrontations with China are indicative of such a shift. Notably, since 2019, publications such as the *Economist* has been discussing the concept of 'slowbalisation', pointing to a reversal in key economic indicators compared to the pre-2008 period.[16] Why were the *Economist* writers not discussing 'deglobalisation' instead? This may be because the three fundamental processes characterising globalisation since the 1980s, according to prevailing technological economists' readings—namely, ICT, the logistics-driven transport revolution, and the expansion of the global market after the end of 'real socialism'—persist. Moreover, the global

---

16  For example, "The Steam Has Gone Out of Globalisation", *Economist*, 24 January 2019, accessed 23 September 2023, https://www.economist.com/leaders/2019/01/24/the-steam-has-gone-out-of-globalisation (subscription required).

value chains that these processes fostered, although undergoing reconfiguration,[17] appear to remain pivotal in the global production and circulation of goods, services, and capital.[18] To explore this further, we will analyse data from major international institutions, first focusing on trends in international trade, foreign investments, and global production chains. Subsequently, we will delve into the potential developments that could signify a shift from a deceleration to an actual reversal of globalisation.[19]

Following the peak reached prior to the 2008 financial crisis, which had seen impressive annual growth rates of around 7%, the subsequent collapse in 2009 marked the beginning of a decade characterised by weak growth in world trade (normally indexed as the sum total of imports and exports in relation to world gross domestic product or GDP)—averaging at approximately 3%, albeit with a brief upswing in 2017–18.[20] Even before the onset of the pandemic crisis, in 2019, world trade had seen a decline in its growth rate, almost reverting to levels below those recorded in 2008, though not in absolute terms.[21] It is worth noting that before the global financial crisis, world trade had surged to represent 30% of global economic output, effectively doubling over an exceptional thirty-year period. This expansion was driven significantly by China, which saw its foreign trade as a percentage of GDP rise to an impressive 60%, along with the extensive development of international supply chains and substantial trade flows, including intra-company trade among multinational corporations.

---

17  Susan Lund, James Manyika, Jonathan Woetzel, Jacques Bughin, Mekala Krishnan, Jeongmin Seong, and Mac Muir, *Globalization in Transition: The Future of Trade and Value Chains* (New York: McKinsey Global Institute, 2019), accessed 23 September 2023, https://www.mckinsey.com/featured-insights/innovation-and-growth/globalization-in-transition-the-future-of-trade-and-value-chains.
18  Pol Antràs, "De-Globalisation? Global Value Chains in the Post-COVID-19 Age" (NBER Working Paper 28115, National Bureau of Economic Research, Cambridge, MA, November 2020), accessed 24 September 2023, https://data.europa.eu/doi/10.2866/268938.
19  As will be seen below, this is not to embrace a simplistic, one-size-fits-all view of a 'flat' global capitalism. Instead, it acknowledges the intricate dynamics of world market, recognising the influence of the imperialist division of labour.
20  UNCTAD, *Trade and Development Report 2020—From Global Pandemic to Prosperity For All: Avoiding Another Lost Decade*, UNCTAD/TDR/2020 (22 September 2020), accessed 23 September 2023, https://unctad.org/system/files/official-document/tdr2020_en.pdf; Bernard Hoekman (ed.), *The Global Trade Slowdown: A New Normal?* (London: Centre for Economic Policy Research, 2015), accessed 23 September 2023, https://cepr.org/system/files/publication-files/60235-the_global_trade_slowdown_a_new_normal.pdf.
21  "Trade (% of GDP)", World Bank and Organisation for Economic Co-operation and Development (OECD) national accounts data, accessed 23 September 2023, https://data.worldbank.org/indicator/NE.TRD.GNFS.ZS.

While it is true that world trade witnessed a sharp downturn due to the pandemic crisis, with a 5.6% volume decrease in 2020 alone[22]—though this decline was less severe than the one experienced in 2009—trade has been on the rise since 2021, surpassing pre-pandemic levels, largely due to the strong performance of China and East Asia.[23] Nevertheless, the overall trajectory has been one of deceleration since the onset of the global crisis in 2008. This deceleration can be attributed to a combination of factors: short-term issues, such as the emergence of the pandemic and, prior to that, the initiation of the US trade war on China; cyclical factors tied to a decrease in aggregate demand; and structural changes, including the high degree of trade globalisation, the shift towards domestic priorities in the Chinese endeavour to rebalance its economy (with foreign trade falling to 40% of GDP, albeit still substantial), the restructuring of production chains, and, as we shall see, reduced levels of investment. While this represents a slowing trend, it has not yet, despite the lows in 2008–9 and 2020, manifested as a complete reversal of the previous growth trajectory.

When we examine foreign direct investment (FDI) flows between countries, which represent the crucial link between finance and global production, we can discern a distinct flattening in the growth trajectory over the past decade. By 2018, the percentage increase in FDI flows had reverted to levels not seen since the early-to-mid-1990s levels, an average annual growth rate of 1% compared to the 8% experienced between 2000 and 2008 and the extraordinary 20% observed before the turn of the century (see Figure 1.1). Following the slump after the 2008 financial crisis, there was a moderate increase in the mid-2010s, but the trend reversed again in 2018. That year, the United Nations Conference on Trade and Development (UNCTAD)[24] reported the third consecutive decline in global FDI, particularly stemming from the United States, which had initiated tax incentives under the Trump administration aimed at repatriating the profits of US multinationals. In 2017, the decline amounted to a staggering 23% year-on-year, shrinking from $2 trillion in 2015 to $1.43 trillion. By 2019, global FDI had only marginally recovered to $1.54 trillion, with

---

22   World Trade Organization, "World Trade Primed for Strong but Uneven Recovery after COVID-19 Pandemic Shock", news release 876, 31 March 2021, accessed 23 September 2023, https://www.wto.org/english/news_e/pres21_e/pr876_e.htm.

23   UNCTAD, *Global Trade Update*, UNCTAD/DITC/INF/2021/2 (May 2021), accessed 23 September 2023, https://unctad.org/system/files/official-document/ditcinf2021d2_en.pdf.

24   UNCTAD, *World Investment Report 2019—Special Economic Zones*, UNCTAD/WIR/2019 (12 June 2019), accessed 7 September 2023, https://unctad.org/publication/world-investment-report-2019.

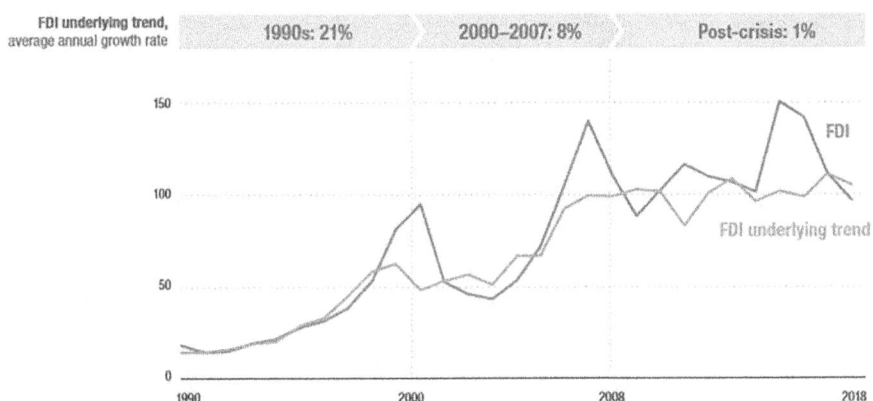

FIGURE 1.1   FDI inflows and the underlying trend, 1990–2018
(Indexed, 2010 = 100).
REPRODUCED FROM UNCTAD, *WORLD INVESTMENT REPORT 2019*, 15, FIG. I.11.
DATA FROM UNCTAD AND FDI/MNE DATABASE (WWW.UNCTAD.ORG/FDISTATISTICS).

a slight increase on the previous year. Concurrently, we witnessed a continuing disparity between the increasing flows directed by predominantly Western multinationals towards emerging countries on one side and the diminishing flows among Western countries on the other. The share of greenfield investments by Western countries in the world total dropped from approximately 80% to just over 50%, partly due to reduced returns on investments.[25]

Evidently, the trajectory of FDI has been significantly influenced by the pandemic crisis. In 2020, there was an annual overall decrease in FDI of 35%, which amounted to $1 trillion. This decline was less pronounced in emerging countries, largely due to Chinese investments, while developed countries, especially in Europe, experienced more substantial decreases than the United States. Asia, buoyed by the resilience of China and India, was the only region that saw FDI grow, albeit slightly. Nevertheless, 2020 marked the lowest overall FDI since 2005.[26]

---

25   UNCTAD, *World Investment Report 2019*; Simon J. Evenett and Johannes Fritz, *The 27th Global Trade Alert—Advancing Sustainable Development With FDI: Why Policy Must Be Reset* (London: Centre for Economic Policy Research, 2021), accessed 24 September 2023, https://www.globaltradealert.org/reports/75.

26   UNCTAD, *World Investment Report 2021—Investing in Sustainable Recovery*, UNCTAD/WIR/2021 (21 June 2021), accessed 24 September 2023, https://unctad.org/system/files/official-document/wir2021_en.pdf.

In terms of FDI capital inflows, the United States remained in the lead, although these inflows were declining, followed by China. Regarding FDI outflows, Japan ranked first, with the United States and China following closely behind. As a result, the Asia-Pacific region has transformed into a net exporter of private capital to the West since 2012. South–South investments (from 'emerging' to 'developing', according to mainstream terminology), primarily driven by China, had been increasing, but they still only accounted for approximately 30% of investments directed towards developing countries by Western multinational corporations. Furthermore, these developing countries have experienced a growth in net disbursements from FDI profits repatriating home since 2009, while FDI investments started to decline during the crisis.[27]

In a nutshell, FDI has been on a downward trend over the past decade, with a more pronounced decrease compared to the relatively resilient of global GDP and trade. Returns on profits, which serve as a somewhat vague indicator of profit rates, have generally declined, except in the case of China.[28] This decline has resulted in reduced reinvestment by foreign affiliates of multinational corporations. However, it is essential to note that overall FDI stocks have continued to grow. In 2021, global FDI increased by approximately 70% compared to the previous year (the peak of the pandemic crisis), reaching $1.6 trillion. The United States once again led both inward and outward flows, with Asia remaining the world's largest destination, accounting for 40% of the total. This confirmed the central role of the US–Asia axis, even though investments in manufacturing and supply chains remained relatively stable.[29] Additionally,

---

27   UNCTAD, *World Investment Report 2020—International Production Beyond the Pandemic*, UNCTAD/WIR/2020 (16 June 2020), accessed 24 September 2023, https://unctad.org/system/files/official-document/wir2020_en.pdf.

28   UNCTAD's *World Investment Report 2020* calculates a trajectory of returns from 3.7% in 1990 to 4.0% in 2000 to 7.0% in 2007. Since 2010, returns on foreign investments have started to decline.

29   OECD, "FDI in Figures" (October 2021), accessed 24 July 2022, https://www.oecd.org/investment/investment-policy/FDI-in-Figures-October-2021.pdf; UNCTAD, *Global Investment Trends Monitor, No. 40*, UNCTAD/DIAE/IA/INF/2021/3 (19 January 2022), accessed 24 September 2023, https://unctad.org/system/files/official-document/diaeianf2021d3_en.pdf; UNCTAD, "Global Foreign Direct Investment Rebounded Strongly in 2021, but the Recovery is Highly Uneven", 19 January 2022, accessed 24 September 2023, https://unctad.org/news/global-foreign-direct-investment-rebounded-strongly-2021-recovery-highly-uneven. This was then confirmed by OECD and UNCTAD, *World Investment Report 2022—International Tax Reforms and Sustainable Investment*, UNCTAD/WIR/2022 (9 June 2022), accessed 24 September 2023, https://unctad.org/system/files/official-document/wir2022_en.pdf. The rebound was possible thanks to the profits reaped by multinationals during the pandemic years, also fostered by government policies, but mainly channelled into M&A (mergers and acquisitions) transactions.

other types of international financial flows, such as financial funding by shadow banking, money markets flows, and private bonds (which have been on the rise and particularly volatile), have not ceased.[30] Thus, the overall landscape presents something of a chiaroscuro picture.

Turning to the third decisive component and a genuinely novel development in late twentieth-century globalisation, namely global value chains (as complementary to multinational corporations that dominated the mid-twentieth century), we can observe a similar pattern (see Figure 1.2).[31] After a tumultuous rise spanning decades, during which inter-firm trade within these chains accounted for 50% of world trade in 2008, there has been a deceleration in growth, and in some cases, even a slight decline over the decade following the global financial crisis, which was marked by stagnation and an almost flat trend in investment. This trend is particularly evident when viewed in relation to overall world trade.

Furthermore, this slowdown is confirmed by a more nuanced index that considers the ratio of intermediate goods in total world exports (see Figure 1.3).

However, compared to the other two general indices discussed here, global value chains also provide qualitative insights into the internationalisation of production, the real foundation of globalisation. First, these chains predominantly feature Western multinational corporations, whose control over supply chains has been strengthened due to digitisation, outsourcing, and the significance of intangible assets such as design, research, marketing, and logistics. In contrast to the post-war Fordism era, the international division of labour has been reconfigured. Peripheral countries have assumed subordinate positions, engaged in labour-intensive industrialisation primarily oriented towards the export of assembled products. With the partial exception of China, most of these countries remained at this level. In contrast, semi-peripheral 'newly industrialised' countries have managed to ascend partially up the value chain while maintaining their ties to Western monopoly capital.[32]

Second, throughout the ebb and flow of crises, this network has expanded globally, thanks in no small part to China's accession to the World Trade Organisation in 2001. Global integration, often quantified by economists

---

30  UNCTAD, *Trade and Development Report 2020*.
31  Guido Starosta, "Global Commodity Chains and the Marxian Law of Value", *Antipode* 42, no. 2 (2010): 433–65, https://doi.org/10.1111/j.1467-8330.2009.00753.x.
32  John Smith, "Imperialism and the Law of Value", *Global Discourse* 2, no. 1 (2011), accessed 17 September 2020, http://global-discourse.com/contents (website no longer functional).

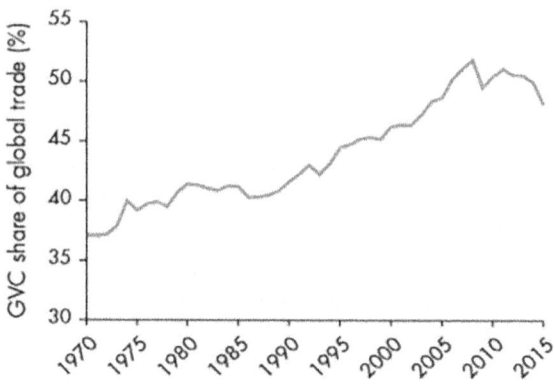

FIGURE 1.2  The global value chain trade grew rapidly in the 1990s but stagnated after the 2008 global financial crisis
REPRODUCED FROM WORLD BANK, *WORLD DEVELOPMENT REPORT 2020—TRADING FOR DEVELOPMENT IN THE AGE OF GLOBAL VALUE CHAINS* (WASHINGTON, DC: INTERNATIONAL BANK FOR RECONSTRUCTION AND DEVELOPMENT AND WORLD BANK, 2020), HTTPS://DOI.ORG/10.1596/978-1-4648-1457-0, 2, FIG. 0.1. DATA FROM EORA26 DATABASE; ALESSANDRO BORIN AND MICHELE MANCINI, "MEASURING WHAT MATTERS IN GLOBAL VALUE CHAINS AND VALUE-ADDED TRADE" (POLICY RESEARCH WORKING PAPER 8804, WORLD BANK, WASHINGTON, DC, 2019); ROBERT CHRISTOPHER JOHNSON AND GUILLERMO NOGUERA, "A PORTRAIT OF TRADE IN VALUE-ADDED OVER FOUR DECADES", *REVIEW OF ECONOMICS AND STATISTICS* 99, NO. 5 (2017): 896–911.

using the 'total reliance' indicator,[33] has notably increased due to the growing importance of Chinese intermediate products, upon which Germany and the United States, the two most influential global hubs, have become increasingly reliant. Lastly, global value chains, far from being 'flat' networks, increasingly tend to concentrate around three regional hubs: Germany, the United States, and China (which has overtaken Japan as the dominant hub in Asia). The first

---

33  Rebecca Baldwin and Richard Freeman, "Trade Conflict in the Age of COVID-19", *VoxEU* (policy portal of the Centre for Economic Policy Research), 22 May 2020, accessed 24 September 2023, https://voxeu.org/article/trade-conflict-age-covid-19.

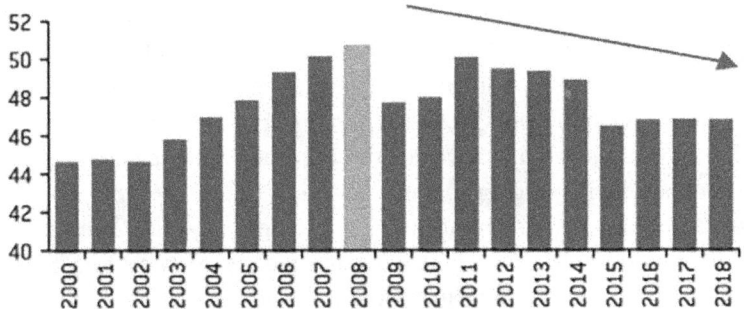

FIGURE 1.3   World global value chain participation (%)
Note: GVC participation is defined as the sum of imports of intermediates and exports of intermediates that are then used in the importing countries' exports, as a share of total exports.
REPRODUCED FROM ALICIA GARCÌA-HERRERO AND JUNYU TAN, "DEGLOBALISATION IN THE CONTEXT OF US-CHINA DECOUPLING", *POLICY CONTRIBUTION* 2020/21 (21 DECEMBER 2020), HTTPS://WWW.BRUEGEL.ORG/SITES/DEFAULT/FILES/WP_ATTACHMENTS/PC-21-2020-211220.PDF, 4, FIG. 4. DATA (2016–18) FROM UNCTAD-EORA AND NATIXIS.

two hubs, particularly for complex chains involving multiple border crossings of intermediate inputs, remain the primary ones. Their interconnectedness with Asian chains has significantly expanded over the past two decades, making them decisive for the international integration of production. However, the European hub centred around Germany maintains the highest degree of regional integration, four times greater than global connections. In contrast, the North American hub boasts the most extensive global interconnectedness.[34] China, meanwhile, has emerged as an Asian hub for simpler chains, primarily involving a single border crossing of semifinished goods, contributing decisively to enhancing intraregional integration within Asia. Moreover, simple global value chains now exhibit more intraregional trade than they did two decades ago, with less trade occurring between global hubs. This suggests that regionalisation, defined as the ratio of intraregional value chains, FDI, and trade[35] to the world total, should not, at least for the time being, be viewed

---

34   World Trade Organization, *Global Value Chain Development Report 2019—Technological Innovation, Supply Chain Trade and Workers in a Globalized World*, report no. 136044 (15 April 2019), accessed 24 September 2023, https://www.wto.org/english/res_e/publications_e/gvcd_report_19_e.htm.

35   According to a McKinsey Global Institute report, the share of intraregional trade is growing for Europe and the Asia-Pacific. See Lund et al., *Globalization in Transition*.

as a counterforce to globalisation but rather as a dynamic manifestation of it.[36] However, it should be noted that in the future, should ruptures occur in the world economic and geopolitical order, particularly between the United States and China, regionalisation processes could acquire a different systemic significance, representing competitive positioning among major global players within the context of an emerging deglobalisation.

A notable qualitative transformation is in progress as well: China is no longer exclusively the world's factory, serving as a means to export final products assembled from imported intermediate components (the share of which in Chinese exports has declined from 50% in the 1990s to around 30% in 2015).[37] Thanks to its ascent in international value chains, China has also begun exporting intermediate goods and services through simple and complex global value chains, positioning itself as a hub for supply and demand for numerous countries, not solely within Asia. This shift is a key factor behind its conflict with the United States, even though it does not directly challenge the imperialistic domination of Western capital rooted in monopoly centralisation.

Consequently, the internationalisation of production networks via global supply chains and the central role played by Chinese production platforms have become an entrenched reality that is challenging for the global capitalist system to disengage from. The bottlenecks in production and logistics that emerged during the pandemic crisis underscored the difficulty of unravelling these networks. However, while a slowdown in this dynamic along with an initial reconfiguration of supply chains has been observed in recent years, it has not yet escalated into a full-scale reversal. The advent of robotics and Industry 4.0 technologies has the potential, in theory, to encourage the reshoring of

---

36   Zhaohui Wang and Zhiqiang Sun, "From Globalization to Regionalization: The United States, China, and the Post-COVID-19 World Economic Order", *Journal of China Political Science* 26 (2021): 69–87, accessed 24 September 2023, https://www.researchgate.net/publication/346467025_From_Globalization_to_Regionalization_The_United_States_China_and_the_Post-Covid-19_World_Economic_Order. Intraregional FDI has accounted for approximately 50% of the total FDI stock since 2005. However, this figure drops to around 30% when considering that the investor often acts as a conduit for capital from non-regional sources. While intraregional FDI is growing, its pace is slower than the overall growth of global FDI, and Europe remains the primary recipient of these investments (UNCTAD, *World Investment Report 2021*).

37   World Bank, *World Development Report 2020*. This is particularly significant when viewed from the perspective of domestic value added as a proportion of the total value of products exported by a country. According to this criterion, compared to the classic trade balance criterion, the domestic value exported by China would be approximately half of what official figures suggest, and the trade deficit with the United States would appear smaller than reported.

production to Western countries by automating labour, including white-collar cognitive tasks. This automation could reduce costs in the West and make reshoring more economically viable.[38] Conversely, by cutting control and monitoring costs, as well as transaction and logistics costs, these technologies may also complement offshoring. Furthermore, digital innovations such as online platforms, e-commerce, automatic translation, and distributed manufacturing are facilitating the offshore exploitation of skilled cognitive labour, not limited to cheap manual labour. These innovations allow even small companies to participate in global supply chains and expand the export of services, data, and goods. In general, the high fixed costs associated with international supply networks make them resistant to quick replacement.

To date, multinational corporations have appeared inclined to pursue diversification, including geographical diversification, and replicate their supply sources rather than abandoning international, particularly supply chains, especially those involving China, or bringing production entirely back to their home countries.[39] Even the pandemic crisis did not significantly impact the scale or number of their international networks, although it did lead to reduced production intensity in the immediate aftermath. On the contrary, the subsequent economic rebound in 2021–22, starting in East Asia and then spreading to the United States and, to a lesser extent, Europe, reaffirmed the critical role of global supply chains, particularly those connected to China, which faced disruptions due to a sudden surge in demand.

The general fact remains, as we noted earlier, that the globalisation trends of FDI, trade, GDP, and GVC has been slowing down since well before the pandemic crisis (see Figure 1.4).

This globalisation trend is also evident in the policies pursued by Western states, which have gradually but consistently shifted towards protectionism. These policies include the US imposition of tariffs on imports from China, as well as the implementation of other tariff and non-tariff barriers, the stagnation of multilateral trade agreements, increased scrutiny and control of foreign acquisitions, and more stringent restrictions on FDI. Clearly, the catalyst for these processes was the global crisis of 2008. Collectively, these actions signal a broader deceleration in global capital accumulation, a phenomenon that also ultimately underlies various socio-political upheavals within Western societies over the past decade, from the rise in economic inequality to the crisis faced

---

38  Richard Baldwin, *The Globotics Upheaval: Globalization, Robotics and the Future of Work* (London: Weidenfeld & Nicolson, 2019).

39  World Bank, *World Development Report 2020*, 4. It should be noted that the empirical evidence on reshoring is limited.

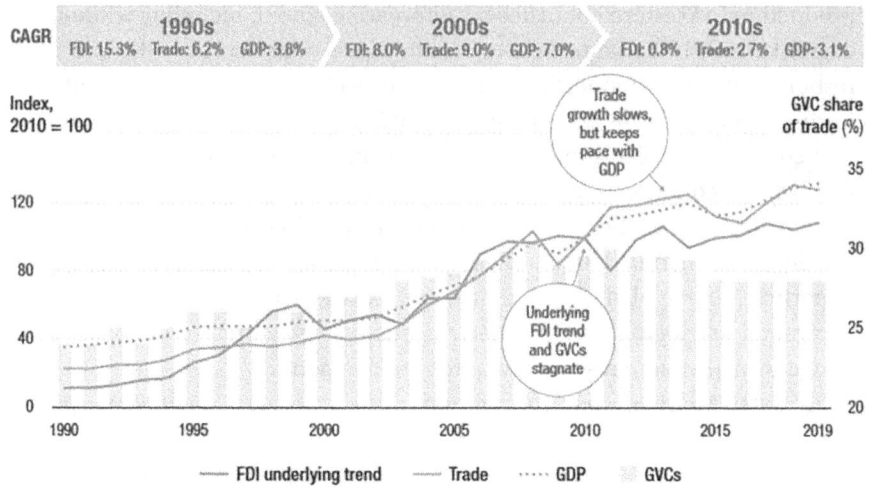

FIGURE 1.4   FDI, trade, GDP, and GVC trends, 1990–2019 (FDI, trade, and GDP indexed, 2010 = 100; GVCs, per cent)
*Note*: Trade is global exports of goods and services. GVC share of trade is proxied by the share of foreign value added in exports. The underlying FDI trend is an UNCTAD indicator capturing the long-term dynamics of FDI by netting out fluctuations driven by one-off transactions and volatile financial flows.
REPRODUCED FROM UNCTAD, *WORLD INVESTMENT REPORT 2020*, 123, FIG. IV.2. DATA FROM UNCTAD.

by the middle classes, as manifested in the emergence of neo-populism.[40] The decline in investments prior to the outbreak of the global financial crisis is a phenomenon observed worldwide, already known to experts in the field.[41] Although investments showed some signs of recovery after 2010, they never fully regained their pre-crisis levels (see Figure 1.5). Furthermore, total factor productivity in developed countries has been on a downward trajectory for some time, and this trend was exacerbated over the last decade due to the near-stagnation of Western economies. The slight overall economic recovery

---

40   Bruno Astarian and Robert Ferro, *Le ménage à trois de la lutte des classes : classe moyenne salariée, prolétariat et capital* (Toulouse: l'Asymétrie, 2019).
41   "Gross Capital Formation (% of GDP)", World Bank and OECD national accounts data, accessed 23 May 2022, https://data.worldbank.org/indicator/NE.GDI.TOTL.ZS.

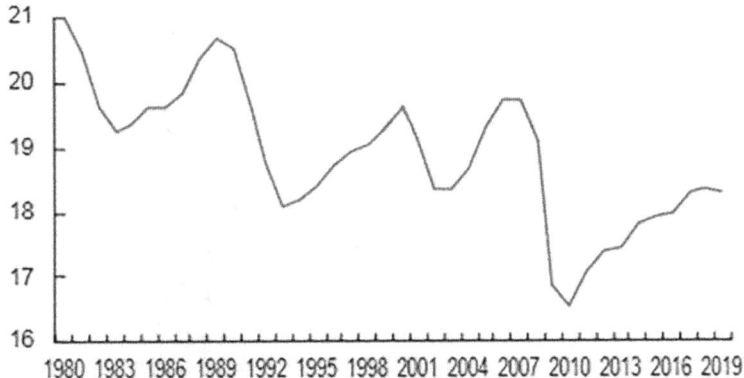

FIGURE 1.5    Private capital formation in G20 developed economies, 1980–2019 (percentage of GDP)
Note: G20 developed economies includes the Republic of Korea. Reproduced from UNCTAD, *Trade and Development Report 2020*, 16, fig. 1.10.
DATA FROM UNCTAD SECRETARIAT CALCULATIONS BASED ON UNITED NATIONS GLOBAL POLICY MODELS AND NATIONAL SOURCES.

in GDP, investment, and employment in 2017 did not bring about significant productivity gains.[42]

Even prior to the onset of the pandemic crisis, global economic growth was fragile, and the combined public and private investment as a proportion of GDP remained lower than pre-2007 levels.[43] The decline in productive investment, driven by diminishing profits,[44] was 'compensated' by the increased activity of central banks' easy money policies. However, this came at the cost of a global debt that soared to nearly $300 trillion by 2021, equivalent to 370% of world output. To put this in perspective, it was approximately half that amount, $164 trillion, in 2016 alone, or 225% of global GDP (see Figure 1.6). This leads to a pressing question: can the expansion of credit money and fictitious capital

---

42  "Coronavirus (COVID-19): Implications for Business", The Conference Board, 3 May 2021, accessed 24 September 2023, https://www.conference-board.org/topics/natural-disasters-pandemics/global-productivity.

43  Michael Roberts, "Profits Call the Tune", author's blog, 17 June 2021, accessed 25 September 2023, https://thenextrecession.wordpress.com/2021/06/17/profits-call-the-tune-2/.

44  Michael Roberts, "The Roaring Twenties Repeated?", author's blog, 18 April 2021, accessed 25 September 2023, https://thenextrecession.wordpress.com/2021/04/18/the-roaring-twenties-repeated/.

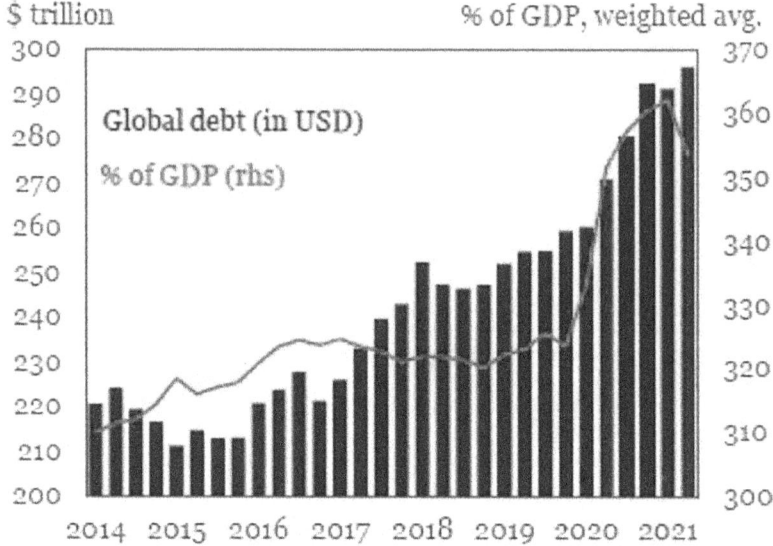

FIGURE 1.6　The increase in global debt
REPRODUCED FROM DHARA RANASINGHE, "GLOBAL DEBT IS FAST APPROACHING RECORD $300 TRILLION—IIF", REUTERS, 14 SEPTEMBER 2021, ACCESSED 25 SEPTEMBER 2023, HTTPS://WWW.REUTERS.COM/BUSINESS/GLOBAL-DEBT-IS-FAST-APPROACHING-RECORD-300-TRILLION-IIF-2021-09-14/. DATA FROM THE INSTITUTE OF INTERNATIONAL FINANCE, THE BANK FOR INTERNATIONAL SETTLEMENTS, THE INTERNATIONAL MONETARY FUND, AND NATIONAL SOURCES.

continue indefinitely as a pressure relief valve, or will it eventually trigger a devaluation and spark intense conflicts among global players as they seek to shift the resulting costs onto others?

In summary, while the overall slowdown in globalisation has not yet led to a concrete process of deglobalisation, the foundational factors that drove the prosperity of the 'neoliberal' golden years have weakened significantly. This weakening is primarily reflected in the sluggish dynamics of global capital accumulation. Consequently, the dollar's ability to serve as a pillar of the global monetary and financial order is waning, not because it can be readily replaced in the short to medium term, but because it has become a mechanism in an increasingly zero-sum game among major global players.

As globalisation has unfolded over the decades, its potential reversal or breakdown is intrinsically linked to the evolving relationships between the United States and China. This once-critical connection is now transforming into a growing rift with systemic implications. Washington is compelled to obstruct and reverse China's ascent, which, in the long run, could threaten the dominant position of the dollar within the imperialist framework. Meanwhile, China, driven by its unique capitalist trajectory, is gradually seeking a less subordinate position within the global market—neither aspiring to overthrow the existing order nor equipped to dominate it.

It is in this context of structural capitalist crisis and the 'spontaneous' reactions of social and state forces that the most visible indicators of an at-risk globalisation should be assessed. These signs, with uncertain outcomes, indicate a medium to long-term trend towards the disarticulation and potential reconfiguration of world capitalism. Such a process would undoubtedly involve social and geopolitical upheavals, as already evidenced by the ongoing Ukrainian crisis. In the course of this potentially catastrophic process, should world capitalism fail to recover, the alternative pathways of transitioning to a non-capitalist social order or witnessing the 'common ruin of the struggling classes' may emerge.

It is crucial—at the current level of contradictions—to recognise that so-called globalisation is not primarily or exclusively a policy that can be easily discarded without consequences. It represents the 'latest stage' (Lenin) in the evolution of the world market as a unified system of internationalised production and circulation. While it may not have exhausted its potential in the abstract, it also serves as harbinger of explosive contradictions that, under specific circumstances, could lead to its unravelling. A deep geopolitical crisis directly involving the United States and China is likely to be a telling sign of such impending developments.

CHAPTER 2

# United States

Amid a broader Western trend characterised by the defreezing of social and electoral blocs and the resurgence of nationalist policies in the aftermath of the global financial crisis, the United States has become a battleground for a new form of class struggle.[1] This struggle pits the 'local superclasses' against local working classes, with the former deeply entrenched in global hubs of economic activity and the latter dispersed across sparsely populated hinterlands. These working classes find themselves caught in a socio-political maelstrom lacking clear political reference points and representation. In this complex landscape, populism has emerged as a telling symptom rather than an external intruder in a supposedly healthy body politic. However, it is far from being a panacea for the deep-seated social crisis that continues to fester.

Within this context, Trumpism, while altering the priorities of the outgoing Obama administration's agenda for change, still responded to the same imperative of restructuring global dominance and addressing pressing domestic socio-economic concerns. Once a stronghold for the United States, globalisation has, amid stagnation, has begun to wane in its influence over China. Simultaneously, the dollar's supremacy has faced challenges. And factors like the economic burdens associated with global military engagements and the disenfranchisement and demoralisation of the middle and lower middle classes on the domestic front have further strained the status quo. These conditions have given rise to a quest for new means of global dominance, which are deemed necessary yet entail escalating costs verging on sustainability limits and uncertain returns. Hence, the pursuit of a revival of American supremacy, framed within a discourse of anti-globalisation and opposition to liberal elites. This revivalism seeks to address the grievances of those allegedly 'left behind', the 'losers' of de-industrialisation.[2] 'America First' became the rallying cry and alarm sounded by Trump, with the confrontation with and intention to decouple from China as a central component of this strategy. 'America First' embodied a populist message of sovereignty that, tapping into the genuine discontent of the 'deplorables' famously identified by Hillary Clinton, sought to

---

1 Michael Lind, *The New Class War* (London: Atlantic Books, 2020); Phil A. Neel, *Hinterland: America's New Landscape of Class and Conflict* (London: Reaktion Books, 2018).
2 Anne Case and Angus Deaton, *Death of Despair and the Future of Capitalism* (Princeton, NJ: Princeton University Press, 2020).

rebuild US global leadership on fresh grounds, primarily rooted in economic nationalism, often brought to the brink of confrontation with both China and European allies.

While the pandemic crisis briefly interrupted this transition on the domestic front, it became clear that the shift in US imperial policy was not solely a product of Biden's predecessor, as Biden himself had to acknowledge and adapt to this new arena of challenge for American imperialism. Trump's imprint on US policy could not be ignored by the incoming administration. On foreign policy, despite a visible effort to rekindle ties with European allies under the banner of a renewed Atlanticism, Biden has struggled to grant them the space and influence that Trump had either denied or clawed back, particularly in relations with Beijing and Moscow—this became evident in the context of the Ukraine crisis. Domestically, to counter the erosion of democratic principles[3] and promote social resilience among the American people, Biden has had to adopt the Trumpian premise that the costs should be borne by the rest of the world, all in the name of safeguarding the middle class. This was manifested in various industrial policy initiatives, including in 2022 a substantial $4 trillion stimulus package encompassing the American Rescue Plan, Infrastructure Law, Chips and Science Act, and Inflation Reduction Act. Curiously, this was sometimes misinterpreted by the political Left as a step towards a progressive Green New Deal, whereas its actual rationale was predominantly geopolitical, with a focus on countering China.[4]

The central question remains: can the actions of the US ruling class in pursuit of a social-national realignment against external adversaries succeed? Such a shift could temporarily quell growing internal turmoil. However, for this to be sustainable in the medium to long term, a coherent 'Grand Strategy' is essential. This strategy must be capable of thwarting and reversing China's

---

3 Salman Ahmed, Rozlyn Engel, Wendy Cutler, Douglas Lute, Daniel M. Price, David Gordon, Jennifer Harris (eds.) et al., *Making U.S. Foreign Policy Work Better for the Middle Class* (Washington, DC: Carnegie Endowment for International Peace, 2020), accessed 30 September 2023, https://carnegieendowment.org/files/USFP_FinalReport_final1.pdf.

4 This has interesting implications for the Anglo-Saxon radical Left (but not only) from whose political lexicon the concept of imperialism has largely faded. A comprehensive examination of the resurgence of workplace conflicts in the United States since October 2021, the wave of industrial actions collectively referred to as 'Striketober', falls beyond the scope of this discussion. The Striketober phenomenon marked the conclusion of the initial phase of neo-populism in the United States. For more insights into this subject, see Raffaele Sciortino, "Pandemic Crisis and Phase Changes", *Platforms, Populisms, Pandemics and Riots*, September 2020, accessed 2 October 2022, https://projectpppr.org/pandemics/pandemic-crisis-and-phase-changes.

ascent, reasserting US global hegemony, and ultimately rebuilding a united domestic front. But are the conditions necessary for such a strategy to succeed currently in place?

## 1     Grand Strategy?

Nothing is perhaps more indicative of the change taking place in US foreign policy than the apparent definitive choice by Washington, seizing the long-anticipated opportunity presented by the Ukrainian conflict, to pursue a dual-enemy strategy. This strategy envisions confronting Russia and China, if not simultaneously, then certainly within the framework of a protracted and encompassing conflict that would serve to reaffirm US global hegemony.[5] As of now, this may not necessarily entail direct armed confrontation, but it certainly involves an escalating military engagement. Importantly, these fronts are closely intertwined, with the weakening or potential disintegration of Russia being a pivotal instrument to undermine China's vital geopolitical support, isolating and encircling it in the process. This strategic shift conspicuously closes the geopolitical circle that began with the Sino-American rapprochement in the early 1970s.

While the trajectory of US power projection has become increasingly discernible, the intricacies of a Grand Strategy remain far from resolved. The Grand Strategy must synthesise the imperative to preserve the global dominance of the dollar and the 'free market' on one hand, with the more immediate politico-military necessities on the other. This synthesis is the quintessential characteristic of US geopolitics, in its various phases a close nexus between monopoly financial capital, driven by the relentless expansion of capital, and political power.[6] Internally, the United States has, at a conceptual level, become the exemplar society of capital. It is no coincidence that during two world wars, which marked the rise and consolidation of US supremacy, victory was not primarily achieved on the military battlefield. Moreover,

---

5  Zbigniew Brzezinski, *The Grand Chessboard: American Primacy and its Geostrategic Imperatives* (New York: Basic Books, 1997).
6  When I refer to geopolitics, I am drawing from the interpretations of Lenin and Luxemburg, who emphasise the interstate dynamics within the framework of imperialist capitalism. In this context, geopolitics is not limited to the conventional understanding of national power politics driven by factors such as geography or civilisation, which are typically treated as independent variables. Instead, it encompasses the complex interactions and power struggles among nations that characterise the stage of imperialist capitalism.

even during the Cold War, military setbacks did not undermine US effective hegemony, which rested on its ability to perpetually renew and reinvigorate this nexus in response to the shifting dynamics of imperialist capitalism.

Today, this synthesis can no longer be taken for granted. It hinges not only on strategic capabilities and resources but on objective conditions rooted in the dynamics of global capitalism—comprising accumulation, competition, and class struggle. This intricate framework is subject to manipulation, direction, or even bending under certain circumstances, but it cannot be fully controlled or disregarded. Consequently, designating China as the principal adversary, while necessary, is insufficient for Washington to rejuvenate its hegemony. This hegemony is not in a state of decline, as in being supplanted by a rising global rival, but it stands on uncertain ground regarding its ability to maintain order in a global capitalist system undergoing substantial turbulence. Thus, the sustainability of the hegemonic role hinges on Washington's ability to better grasp and decipher the hazy contours of the evolving landscape. In particular, this entails the capacity to respond to crises by reframing class conflicts and intercapitalist competition on a fresh foundation, ultimately reigniting global accumulation. Such a recalibration was achieved after World War II and again in the 1970s when, under altered conditions, a particular dollar strategy and geopolitics managed to coexist harmoniously. The looming question is whether history will repeat itself.

## 1.1     *The Problem*

The immediate challenge facing US imperialism, both on the international stage and in terms of domestic stability, lies in moving beyond the tactical measures taken thus far in dealing with China. While the Trump administration's efforts have led to "the development of a coherent and genuinely bipartisan policy toward Xi Jinping's China",[7] the results in terms of economic and geopolitical outcomes have been less than stellar. This suggests that relying solely on economic coercion against Beijing and diplomatic pressure on allies and third parties to choose sides is insufficient. It also highlights the complexity of formulating an effective strategy, which cannot be neatly planned but must emerge from the reconfiguration of multiple systemic factors.

Several factors contribute to the complexity of the current situation. First, there is the relative novelty of the confrontation, with the United States facing an adversary characterised by a unique blend of a millennia-old imperial

---

7   As stated by George Soros, Trump's arch-enemy, in "Will Trump Sell Out the U.S. on Huawei?", *Wall Street Journal*, 9 September 2019, accessed 28 October 2021, https://www.wsj.com/articles/will-trump-sell-out-the-u-s-on-huawei-11568068495 (subscription required).

tradition and an anti-imperialist history. While China's economic rise does not pose an immediate challenge to US global hegemony, such a confrontation has the potential to exacerbate existing tensions linked to the paradox of the current phase. With the United States maintaining its dominance, there's a risk of destabilising globalisation itself. However, in the absence of US dominance, it becomes exceedingly challenging to envision how the entire global order can remain intact. This encompasses various critical aspects: the international primacy of the dollar, the control of intricate global value chains, the potential realignment or disruption of international alliances, the erosion of Washington's soft power, the ever-expanding Pentagon budget, and the internal ramifications stemming from the confrontation with Beijing. The intricacies of this multifaceted scenario make it exceptionally difficult to disentangle and navigate effectively.

Second, there are several factors at play, including the strategic inertia of American imperialism rooted in a long history of unquestioned supremacy. This is compounded by exceptionalism reinforced in the post–Cold War era and a paradoxical revisionism regarding the existing international order. This 'dynamic' inertia may lead to the misconception that the current situation can be addressed through familiar diplomatic and military measures or through the modernisation of military capabilities. There is also a mechanistic fallacy that assumes there is always an existing strategy in geopolitics and that a naval hegemon like the United States, with no serious systemic rivals, will inevitably follow the same well-trodden path. While elements of these assumptions may still hold true, the complexity of contemporary challenges calls for a qualitative shift towards something new and different. This entails the ability to reshape the world by interpreting the potential advancements of capitalism rather than simply reaffirming existing arrangements.

## 1.2   *New Cold War?*

To grasp the altered dynamics of the current US–China confrontation, it is imperative to consider several key distinctions from the Cold War era. These disparities shed light on the uniqueness of the present situation, beyond the obvious fact that China today differs fundamentally from the Soviet Union. Although the ongoing conflict is portrayed as a clash of values between Western ideals of human rights, freedom, and democracy versus authoritarianism and control, these critical differences deserve attention.

First and foremost, the global integration of capitalist networks has progressed significantly, making it exceedingly challenging to establish clear divisions in the world market into relatively autonomous blocs (beyond current US attempts to decouple from China). This complicates any potential escalation of the current confrontation, rendering it riskier than during the Cold War. Second, the system of alliances is profoundly asymmetrical in favour of the United States, with China largely isolated on the geopolitical stage (only more so is a Russia presently in great difficulty)—unlike the Soviet Union, which had more substantial backing. However, it is crucial to note that the coherence of US alliances, both in Europe and Asia, faces a growing divide between the overt political-military subservience, as exemplified by the Ukrainian conflict (especially among European nations), and the economic interests of many US allies. This divergence implies that the continued existence of these alliances should not be taken for granted, especially in the event of an escalated clash with Beijing, given its severe economic repercussions. The costs associated with US protection have grown burdensome for its allies, who are essentially treated as vassals and tributaries. Finally, the United States today is far removed from the social cohesion that underpinned the pro–Cold War consensus. While this consensus endured despite being strained by the Vietnam War and the social unrest of the 1960s, eventually reconstituting itself in the Reagan era, it hinged on the promise of social advancement for the working and middle classes. This crucial factor is notably absent in contemporary America, which grapples with profound social polarisation that defies easy reconciliation. Concurrently, China is striving to solidify its internal cohesion, with limited success thus far.

These differences have spawned a host of paradoxical situations, where heightened capitalist global integration is at risk of devolving into the disintegration of the international system. Some analysts have noted that the roles seem almost reversed compared to the dynamics of the Cold War. The United States now appears as the rigid, ideologically driven superpower in distress, compelled to scale back its involvement in various geopolitical scenarios, seemingly bereft of fresh solutions aside from embarking on a perilous race to increase military expenditures. Conversely, China emerges as the pragmatic, adaptable power, steadily narrowing the gap in both domestic and international economic growth, favourably positioning itself on this evolving terrain.[8] While this juxtaposition requires nuance, it underscores the ongoing transformations in the configuration of global capitalism.

In this unfolding scenario, Washington increasingly finds itself compelled to elevate the level of confrontation rather than waiting for the rival power's 'spontaneous' economic weakening, as was the case during the Cold War. Failing immediate and drastic countermeasures, China's sustained rise could,

---

8   Kishore Mahbubani, *Has China Won? The Chinese Challenge to American Primacy* (New York: PublicAffairs, 2020).

over time, threaten the previously uncontested US dominance in East Asia, the region boasting the most promising growth prospects worldwide. The crux of the matter lies in the fact that, for many East Asian economies and beyond, there is no longer a direct correlation between the US diplomatic-military protection under the umbrella of the dollar and the potential for economic development. This is precisely why China, emblematic of a more autonomous trajectory separate from the imperialist West, has become an indispensable junction and a symbol of divergence for the US establishment, necessitating its removal at any cost, despite having little to no current prospect of replacing US hegemony. Consequently, globalisation no longer yields the dividends it once did for the United States.

## 1.3   From Trump ...

Over the post–Cold War decades, US policy towards China underwent three distinct phases. During the first phase, spanning the 1990s and early 2000s, the objective was to integrate China into the liberal international order while promoting its political liberalisation. This was seen as a long-term consequence of China's integration into international markets, and it was referred to as the strategy of engagement. In the second phase, commencing with Obama's 'Pivot to Asia', the challenge was to determine the extent to which China's economic growth should be accommodated, given its reluctance to make political concessions in line with Western expectations. China was perceived as moving towards a reshaping of international rules rather than conforming to them. Finally, during the Trump and subsequent Biden administrations, although they adopted different political styles, the imperative was to block and potentially reverse China's rise—marking the dawn of a new containment strategy.

The four years of the Trump presidency from 2016 to 2020 significantly disrupted the geopolitical equilibrium. Trump's approach openly introduced the notion of revitalising national unity to 'Make America Great Again'. Under the banner of long-term strategic competition,[9] this was coupled with direct economic confrontation with Beijing. Trump did not aim to embroil the United States in new, costly military conflicts. Instead, his approach emphasised the avoidance of such conflicts by leveraging the United States' formidable position outside of any multilateral frameworks. This approach sought to regain lost ground and, crucially, to relegate both adversaries and allies to their accustomed subservient roles through the instrument of coercive diplomacy.

---

9   The White House, *United States' Strategic Approach to the People's Republic of China*, May 2020, accessed 2 October 2023, https://trumpwhitehouse.archives.gov/wp-content/uploads/2020/05/U.S.-Strategic-Approach-to-The-Peoples-Republic-of-China-Report-5.24v1.pdf.

Importantly, this did not entail isolationism. On the contrary, it represented an effort to reconcile the imperative of reconstructing the domestic social front with the reaffirmation of US primacy worldwide, all while sidestepping overextension of military commitments—even if it meant forsaking the established liberal international order and tempering relations with the perennial adversary, Russia.

The Trumpist positions found some support on the strategic-military front, particularly among those who, following in the footsteps of Brzezinski,[10] were keenly aware of the impending intense geopolitical rivalries and sought to create a rift between Moscow and Beijing.[11] However, these positions faced significant challenges in gaining ascendancy. Despite their notably anti-Chinese stance, the neoconservatives and democratic interventionists, deeply entrenched within the Pentagon and the State Department, remained resolutely committed to a confrontational approach with both Russia and China. Their preferred method involved regime change strategies, inducing geopolitical instability, and pursuing a policy of containment. Ironically, Trump introduced a strategy akin to offshore balancing, reminiscent in some ways of Obama's initial but unfruitful attempts to reduce the United States' excessive military commitments, such as in the Middle East, Afghanistan, and Eastern Europe, in order to focus efforts on China and East Asia (the Pivot to Asia). Naturally, there were significant differences between the two approaches.

With Trump, the transformation of US strategy into a fully-fledged competition among major powers was definitively established. Consequently, China was increasingly portrayed as the primary culprit for the perceived failures of US policies over the preceding two decades. This was evident in the 2017 National Security Strategy and the 2018 National Defense Strategy, which boldly labelled Beijing as a revisionist power. This characterisation suggested that China aimed to gradually accumulate advantages, leading to a new international status quo without directly provoking a military response from the United States. China's goal was seen as establishing regional hegemony in the Indo-Pacific region initially, and global dominance in the future.[12]

---

10   Zbigniew Brzezinski, "Toward a Global Realignment", *The American Interest* 11, no. 6 (17 April 2016), accessed 2 October 2023, https://www.the-american-interest.com/2016/04/17/toward-a-global-realignment/.
11   Atlantic Council, *The Longer Telegram: Toward a New American China Strategy*, 2021, accessed 2 October 2023, https://www.atlanticcouncil.org/content-series/atlantic-council-strategy-paper-series/the-longer-telegram/.
12   The White House, *National Security Strategy of the United States of America*, December 2017, accessed 2 October 2023, https://trumpwhitehouse.archives.gov/wp-content/uploads/2017/12/NSS-Final-12-18-2017-0905.pdf; US Department of Defense, *Summary of*

The Trump administration primarily employed economic countermeasures as its key tools. This included initiating a trade war, imposing tariffs on a wide range of products imported from China, and repeatedly imposing sanctions on technological sectors crucial to China's economic modernisation, as identified in the 'Made in China 2025' plan. These actions were influenced by a combination of domestic and foreign policy considerations. Domestically, they were motivated by concerns such as the social consequences of relative de-industrialisation, hopes for reshoring some production and creating new industrial jobs, a growing anti-Chinese sentiment, and more. In terms of foreign policy, these measures were part of a broader strategy aimed at reasserting US supremacy and addressing mounting concerns about the supply of components for the military apparatus. The issue at hand was not solely the US trade deficit. In reality, a substantial portion of Chinese exports resulted from the assembly of components that contained added value from elsewhere. Moreover, to a significant albeit diminishing degree, these exports comprised products of foreign multinational corporations, which reaped the lion's share of profits. Instead, the primary concern revolved around China's pursuit of heightened economic autonomy through the acquisition of more advanced technological production capabilities.

It is no coincidence that in tandem with tariffs, the United States implemented a slew of other restrictions and controls, reflecting a multifaceted approach aimed at curtailing various aspects of its economic ties with China. These measures included the enactment of legislation such as the Foreign Investment Risk Review Modernization Act in 2018, regulations governing exports like the Export Control Reform Act of 2018, and new restrictions on the transfer of sensitive technologies to important Chinese companies included in an Entity List (e.g., Huawei,[13] SMIC, Xiaomi, etc.). Additionally, the United States extended its restrictions to companies from allied nations,[14] particularly focusing on disrupting the flow of Chinese digital products to the United States, and in the other direction, Chinese access to advanced US technologies (with

---

the 2018 National Defense Strategy of the United States of America, 2018, accessed 2 October 2023, https://dod.defense.gov/Portals/1/Documents/pubs/2018-National-Defense-Strategy-Summary.pdf.

[13] The boycott commenced in 2019 by targeting the sale of US-made semiconductors. In 2020, it was further expanded to encompass restrictions on the transfer of the machinery required for semiconductor production.

[14] US Chamber of Commerce—China Center, *Understanding U.S.-China Decoupling: Macro Trends and Industry Impacts*, 2021, accessed 2 October 2023, https://www.uschamber.com/sites/default/files/024001_us_china_decoupling_report_fin.pdf.

initiatives like the Clean Network Program in 2020).[15] Finally, an increasing number of Chinese companies were excluded from US stock exchange listings. In short, a series of presidential executive orders established the political and legal instruments to disrupt supply chains between the US and China, effectively initiating the process of decoupling and steering Washington towards a new techno-nationalist direction.

However, it is essential to note that the substantial shortcomings of these decoupling and reshoring efforts have underscored the absence of a comprehensive strategy suited to the evolving global landscape. On the trade front, the tariff war did contribute to a partial reduction in the US goods deficit with China between 2018 and 2019. Still, this reduction was accompanied by a shift in imports to other East Asian suppliers, particularly Vietnam. Consequently, the overall US trade deficit continued to grow. In 2020, during the final year of Trump's presidency, this deficit reached an all-time high of $916 billion. This was partially due to a significant decline in exports, only partially offset by improvements in services, such as digital, financial, and marketing. Combining both goods and services, the trade imbalance reached its highest level since 2008, amounting to $679 billion.[16] In the midst of the pandemic crisis, imports from China picked up and returned to the levels the Trump administration found when it came into office. Furthermore, despite efforts to encourage reshoring, there was little substantial success, at most resulting in a diversification of supply sources in favour of South East Asian countries and, to some extent, Mexico (nearshoring).[17] Following the tax reform introduced at the outset of the Trump administration in 2017, there was a temporary uptick in investment in capital goods within the United States. However, this increase in investment declined again during the height of the trade war,[18] causing domestic manufacturing output to remain essentially stagnant.

---

15  US Department of State, "The Clean Network", accessed 10 January 2021 https://www.state.gov/the-clean-network/ (page now archived).
16  Wolf Richter, "US Trade Deficit in 2020 Worst since 2008. ...", *Wolf Street*, 8 February 2021, accessed 2 October 2023, https://wolfstreet.com/2021/02/08/us-trade-deficit-in-2020-worst-since-2008-goods-deficit-worst-ever-despite-first-ever-petroleum-surplus-services-surplus-drops-again/.
17  Alan Beattie, "Coronavirus-Induced Reshoring Is Not Happening", *Financial Times*, 30 September 2020, accessed 17 January 2021, https://www.ft.com/content/e06be6a4-7551-4fdf-adfd-9b20feca353b (subscription required).
18  Enrica Di Stefano, "COVID-19 and Global Value Chains", Occasional Papers No. 618, Banca d'Italia, Rome, April 2021, accessed 2 October 2023, https://www.bancaditalia.it/pubblicazioni/qef/2021-0618/index.html.

It is in the realm of foreign direct investments between the US and China that the repercussions of Trump's actions have been immediately significant, resulting in a notable decline in both foreign direct investments and portfolio investments.[19] While the pandemic crisis of 2020 exacerbated this trend,[20] the post-pandemic recovery witnessed a renewed influx of US capital into China by banks and investment funds. Institutional investors also rushed to acquire private and state-owned Chinese equities and bonds.[21] Essentially, Beijing continued to attract US capital despite Washington's actions.[22]

On the diplomatic-military front, the Trump administration initiated a strategic reorientation that had varying outcomes. In the Middle East, the administration worked towards greater 'disengagement', completing the negotiation for the withdrawal of US troops from Afghanistan and attempting to shift focus away from regime change efforts in Syria. However, relations with Iran deteriorated, marked by the abandonment of the nuclear treaty negotiated by the Obama administration and the assassination of Qassim Suleimani in January 2020. Turning to East Asia, the US launched the Indo-Pacific Strategy in 2019,[23] a new name for the attempt to involve India, Japan, and Australia in a diplomatic-military containment strategy against China. This strategy sought to constrain China within its continental territory, limiting its autonomous access to the maritime routes of the Pacific and Indian Oceans. While the slogan 'free and open Indo-Pacific' (of which the US 'is and always will

---

19   Alicia Garcìa-Herrero and Junyu Tan, "Deglobalisation in the Context of US-China Decoupling", *Policy Contribution* 2020/21 (21 December 2020), Bruegel, accessed 2 October 2023, https://www.bruegel.org/policy-brief/deglobalisation-context-united-states-china-decoupling.

20   Organisation for Economic Co-operation and Development (OECD), "FDI in Figures" (October 2021), accessed 24 July 2022, https://www.oecd.org/investment/investment-policy/FDI-in-Figures-October-2021.pdf.

21   Hudson Lockett and Thomas Hale, "Global Investors Place Rmb1tr Bet on China", *Financial Times*, 14 December 2020, accessed 23 January 2021, https://www.ft.com/content/d9ac22d-90d8-4570-b89e-a99f1bd4829b.

22   Nicholas R. Lardy, "Foreign Investments into China are Accelerating", Peterson Institute for International Economics (PIIE) blog, 22 July 2021, accessed 2 October 2023, https://www.piie.com/blogs/china-economic-watch/foreign-investments-china-are-accelerating-despite-global-economic?utm_source=update-newsletter&utm_medium=email&utm_campaign=piie-insider&utm_term=2021-07-28. However, a reversal began in 2022 in response to the US central bank raising interest rates.

23   US Department of Defense, *Indo-Pacific Strategy Report: Preparedness, Partnerships, and Promoting a Networked Region*, 1 June 2019, accessed 2 October 2023, https://media.defense.gov/2019/Jul/01/2002152311/-1/-1/1/DEPARTMENT-OF-DEFENSE-INDO-PACIFIC-STRATEGY-REPORT-2019.PDF. The use of the phrase dates back to a 2007 speech by then Japanese prime minister Shinzo Abe.

be' a component[24]) gained currency during the Trump administration, it did not result on a fully developed strategic reorientation. At most, it signalled an intention to shift perspectives.[25]

In summary, Trump played a pivotal role in reshaping the US–China relationship by clearly indicating the direction in which Sino-US relations will evolve in the future. He underscored the inextricable link between international political economy and domestic considerations, highlighting that globalisation is not merely a battleground for intense competition but the focal point of a geopolitical clash, even if it entails questioning established norms and practices.

While the issue at hand has been identified, its complexity remains far from fully comprehended. It is not merely a matter of internal disagreements within the administration, such as the contention between proponents of a selective trade war and advocates of broad economic decoupling, or the divisions between those favouring new containment and the hawks pushing for regime change in Beijing. Instead, it revolves around the ongoing metamorphosis of global capitalism. The supremacy of the US dollar is at risk of becoming too 'rigid', particularly in the face of a Western economy struggling with dwindling growth prospects when compared to the vast economic potential in Asia. Yet, paradoxically, it remains indispensable for maintaining international liquidity and, consequently, the stability of the global economy.

Thus, Trump left behind a task that has only just begun, marked more by confusion than a well-defined strategy. The question regarding China, far from being resolved, has grown even more intricate. Moreover, it has strained Washington's relationships with its allies, fuelling their suspicions towards a hegemon increasingly perceived as unpredictable and unreliable, fixated on its own self-interests. This is not merely a transient issue of soft power, as some anti-Trump voices might contend. Trump was symptomatic of deeper issues, not the root cause.

## 1.4   ... to Biden

As such, upon assuming the presidency in January 2021, President Biden inherited a set of complex foreign policy challenges from the previous administration. These challenges were characterised by narrow margins for action, influenced both by the momentum accelerated, for better or worse, by Trump

---

24   US Department of State—Bureau of East Asian and Pacific Affairs, *A Free and Open Indo-Pacific: Advancing a Shared Vision*, 3 November 2019, accessed 2 October 2023, https://www.state.gov/a-free-and-open-indo-pacific-advancing-a-shared-vision/.
25   In May 2018, the US Pacific Command was renamed the US Indo-Pacific Command.

in the China dossier, and the deeply polarised political and social landscape domestically. Consequently, a concept of 'social geopolitics' emerged as a fundamental pillar, emphasising the idea that the United States had to be "strong at home to be strong abroad".[26] The Biden Doctrine, if one can really speak of a doctrine as such, thus started from the need to build a 'foreign policy for the middle class', a transposition of the 'Build Back Better' programme but at the geopolitical level. It aimed to break with the conventional compartmentalisation of foreign and domestic policies, recognising that there is no longer a clear demarcation between the two.[27]

This programme, ironically renamed 'America First Lite', needed to address concerns, some of which were valid, raised during the Trump era regarding the adverse effects of globalisation. However, it took a markedly different approach, seeking to avoid the divisive tactics that had exploited divisions within the middle class and had ultimately led to burnout. Biden's commitment, which began during his election campaign, was focused on expanding the welfare state while also pursuing a more nuanced approach to reshoring. The central problem identified was the competitiveness of the United States in the global marketplace. This issue was not dismissed but rather redefined in a way that would open up further only when the country was adequately prepared to confront new challenges. This preparation involved strengthening domestic infrastructure, restructuring supply chains, and setting global trade standards. These efforts also called for more targeted interventions aimed at generating clear, positive returns on the domestic social front. No longer was social well-being considered a mere by-product of world hegemony but rather an explicit goal, crucial for preventing the risky consolidation of the disconnect between society and the establishment.

For the Biden administration, the only way to confront China's ascent is head-on. Not because there is, let us stress again, an actual challenge to American hegemony posed by Beijing, but rather, China's rise signifies the critical test of Washington's hegemonic prowess at this advanced stage of global capitalism. In a world economy marked by decelerating growth, the challenge is to manage this confrontation without dismantling globalisation while simultaneously reaffirming the systemic importance of the US dollar and American financial leadership. Furthermore, this approach is motivated by the belief

---

26  Ahmed et al., *Making U.S. Foreign Policy Work Better*.
27  The White House, "Remarks by President Biden on America's Place in the World", 4 February 2021, accessed 2 October 2023, https://www.whitehouse.gov/briefing-room/speeches-remarks/2021/02/04/remarks-by-president-biden-on-americas-place-in-the-world.

that it is perhaps still feasible to cultivate an internal consensus, one that is not merely passive but actively supportive, regarding the United States' international role by framing it as a response to the perceived 'Chinese threat'. This perceived threat resonates across the political spectrum and various segments of society.

The overarching goal is to confront China from a position of strength, engaging simultaneously at three key levels: technological (shifting focus from predominantly trade to technology warfare), strategic-military (centred on the Indo-Pacific region and the alignment of China and Russia), and diplomatic (forging new alliances in pursuit of anti-Chinese containment).

## 1.5 *Selective Decoupling*

Until the outbreak of the conflict in Ukraine, the primary perception of the Chinese challenge in Washington was predominantly technological. The response to this challenge was envisioned as a multifaceted strategy, with the trade war representing just one dimension of it. According to the Biden administration, this strategy aimed to facilitate selective decoupling from China,[28] a process designed to undermine China's technological progress at its core while simultaneously reaffirming its subordinate economic role. The objective was to achieve this without disrupting the supply chains that are essential for the US market and not directly related to geopolitical rivalry.[29] The proactive dimension of this strategy aimed to revitalise the domestic manufacturing sector. It included measures such as the 'Buy American' programme, which offered corporate tax incentives and encouraged federal purchases of US-made products, making supply chains more 'resilient' through diversification and regionalisation, and providing subsidies for investments in high-tech industries, exemplified by the Endless Frontier Act of June 2021. These measures have been maintained despite the need to address growing domestic protectionist sentiments. However, the significance of trade balance indicators has diminished in comparison to the offensive against China's efforts to achieve greater autonomy in its supply chains, reducing dependence on the West. Disentangling from China's supply chains is a complex endeavour and may even yield counterproductive results. This complexity arises from the

---

28   Kathrin Hille, "The Great Uncoupling: One Supply Chain for China, One for Everywhere Else", *Financial Times*, 3 October 2020, accessed 2 October 2023, https://www.ft.com/content/40ebd786-a576-4dc2-ad38-b97f796b72a0.

29   US Department of State—Office of the Secretary of State, *The Elements of the China Challenge*, November 2020, revised December 2020, accessed 2 October 2023, https://www.state.gov/wp-content/uploads/2020/11/20-02832-Elements-of-China-Challenge-508.pdf.

fact that the United States wields control over the global economy through a diverse set of instruments that extend beyond exports, which are already substantial, especially concerning technological and financial services. In addition to tariffs and duties, economic sanctions are widely employed in Washington, regardless of the administration in power. These tools serve primarily to selectively influence the supply of high-tech components to Chinese industry, control the transfer of knowledge and advanced industrial processes, and manage the reverse dependence of the US industry on Chinese supplies.

In essence, this decoupling strategy focuses on technology, particularly digital innovation, as well as standards, data and knowledge access, and capital inflows into sensitive sectors. It is designed to target China's vulnerabilities in its pursuit of moving up the value chain through domestic technological innovation. However, paradoxically, it also reinforces China's dependence by obstructing its ascent and preserving the existing international division of labour, thereby ensuring China's reliance on dollar finance remains intact.

On the one hand, this helps shed light on President Biden's decision-making, which is largely consistent with the previous course of action. The Biden administration chose to maintain the tariffs on imports from China, initially implemented by President Trump, amounting to a total of $370 billion. However, it introduced a mechanism allowing for exemptions on a case-by-case basis, particularly when such exemptions serve the interests of American companies. Furthermore, the administration has continued to accuse China, albeit instrumentally and in alignment with previous rhetoric, of benefiting from economic growth 'at the expense of US workers and economic opportunities'.[30] On the other hand, there has been a notable escalation in sanctioning any potential transfers of technology and capital to a growing list of prominent Chinese companies, particularly those operating in the digital, telecommunications, and biotechnology sectors. These sanctions have been justified on the grounds of national security[31] or due to the belief that such transfers would

---

30   Office of the US Trade Representative—Executive Office of the President, "Remarks As Prepared for Delivery of Ambassador Katherine Tai Outlining the Biden-Harris Administration's 'New Approach to the U.S.-China Trade Relationship'", 4 October 2021, accessed 2 October 2023, https://ustr.gov/about-us/policy-offices/press-office/speeches-and-remarks/2021/october/remarks-prepared-delivery-ambassador-katherine-tai-outlining-biden-harris-administrations-new.

31   As per a presidential executive order of 3 June 2021 making permanent a law on wartime requisitions passed during the Korean War. See Executive Order 13959, "Addressing the Threat from Securities Investments that Finance Certain Companies of the People's Republic of China", accessed 3 October 2023, https://www.whitehouse.gov/briefing-room/presidential-actions/2021/06/03/executive-order-on-addressing-the-threat-from-securities-investments-that-finance-certain-companies-of-the-peoples-republic-of-china/.

be detrimental to the supply chain of critical products and materials. This comprehensive approach has involved measures such as including Chinese companies on the Commerce Department's Entity List, imposing investment restrictions through the Treasury Department's blacklist, and effectively excluding Chinese companies from being listed on US stock exchanges.[32] The overarching objective of this strategy is to undermine the highest value-added sectors of the Chinese industry. It does so by not only targeting the upstream supply of components but also by affecting all segments of the supply chain, effectively seeking to displace Chinese companies from the science and technology sector.

## 1.6  The Chip War

One of the primary focal points of this strategy is undeniably the semiconductor industry, a sector that lies at the heart of digital innovation for both input production and consumer goods. It serves as a formidable testing ground for President Biden's approach to selective decoupling. The semiconductor industry is one of the most globally integrated and research-intensive sectors worldwide, characterised by a lack of self-sufficiency in any single country or region along its entire supply chain. This industry comprises specialised segments, each dominated by a handful of highly concentrated companies, showcasing the ultimate example of the disintegration of the already vertically concentrated Fordist industrial model. As a result, there are a series of regional and national bottlenecks that can only be circumvented at significant costs, spanning across the four fundamental sectors of the overall supply chain:

1. Advanced design of integrated circuits (chips): This is where US companies still maintain dominance (see Figure 2.1).
2. Manufacturing (foundries): The most advanced semiconductor manufacturing for leading-edge chips, apart from a few niches hubs in the US, Netherlands, and Japan, is concentrated mainly in East Asia, particularly at Taiwan Semiconductor Manufacturing Company (TSMC) in Taiwan.
3. Assembly packaging.
4. Assembly testing: These stages are primarily located in China, Taiwan, and Singapore.[33]

---

32   Mikko Huopytari, Jacob Gunter, Carl Hayward, Max J. Zenglein, John Lee, Rebecca Arcesati, Caroline Meinhardt, Ester Cañada Amela, and Tom Groot Haar, *Decoupling: Severed Ties and Patchwork Globalisation*, Beijing: European Union Chamber of Commerce in China; Berlin: Mercator Institute for China Studies (MERICS), 14 January 2021, accessed 2 October 2023, https://merics.org/en/report/decoupling-severed-ties-and-patchwork-globalisation.

33   Semiconductor Industry Association, *2020 SIA Factbook*, April 2020, accessed 2 October 2023, https://www.semiconductors.org/wp-content/uploads/2020/04/2020-SIA-Factbook-FINAL_reduced-size.pdf; Congressional Research Service, *Semiconductors: U.S.*

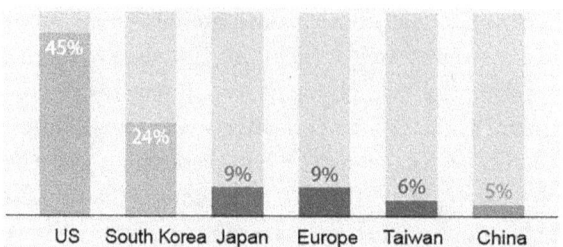

FIGURE 2.1  Share of chip market by country/region, 2018
REPRODUCED FROM HUOPYTARI ET AL., *DECOUPLING*, 13. DATA FROM THE SEMICONDUCTOR INDUSTRY ASSOCIATION, THE WORLD SEMICONDUCTOR TRADE STATISTICS, I GLOBAL, AND PWC.

In a nutshell, the United States controls the high-end and research segments of semiconductor development but relies on manufacturing facilities and external sales markets, which contribute to about half of the sector's global value. On the other hand, China plays a crucial role in the final assembly stages and represents the second-largest market for consumer electronics. However, with a delay of a decade or so and a capacity for circuits currently of only 14 nm, China remains highly dependent on external, especially Western, technology, and is the world's largest importer of such technology, surpassing even oil imports. It is this strategic vulnerability in China's semiconductor sector that Washington, beginning with the well-known Huawei incident, has sought to exploit to its advantage.

Indeed, the Biden administration has not only upheld but also expanded upon the measures initiated by the Trump administration. It has introduced a series of executive orders that, while aligning with broader policy priorities as previously discussed, have a specific focus on regulating and restricting the supply of cutting-edge technology. The objective is clear: to prevent China from manufacturing the latest generations of integrated circuits.[34] Concurrently,

---

*Industry, Global Competition, and Federal Policy*, 26 October 2020, accessed 2 October 2023, https://crsreports.congress.gov/product/pdf/R/R46581.

34  See Executive Order 14005 in favour of resilient and sustainable supply chains preferably located in the United States and Executive Order 14017 in relation to the 2021 supply crisis. "Ensuring the Future is Made in America with All of America's

there's an emphasis on bolstering domestic production capabilities, particularly in the field of foundries.[35] Over the decades of globalisation, the United States has witnessed a significant decline in its domestic production capacities, with its share in the global market dropping from almost half to a mere 12%.[36] This decline has been driven by competitive factors and concerns over an excessive reliance on foreign sources, particularly in the defence industry. To counteract this trend, the Biden administration has implemented a federal procurement and investment strategy, exemplified by the Endless Frontier Act, which aims to stimulate domestic production.[37] Furthermore, the administration has imposed more stringent trade regulations to address what it perceives as competitors' 'unfair practices'. It has also prioritised increased collaboration with allies, including joint productive investments in the United States.[38] All of these efforts converged in the bipartisan Chips and Science Act, which President Biden signed into law in August 2022. Laws like this represent the tools of a revitalised industrial-military policy through which Washington is enhancing its capabilities to regain full control of a critical supply chain,

Workers", EO 14005 (25 January 2021), accessed 2 October 2021, https://www.whitehouse.gov/briefing-room/statements-releases/2021/06/08/fact-sheet-biden-harris-administration-announces-supply-chain-disruptions-task-force-to-address-short-term-supply-chain-discontinuities/#:~:text=The%20Federal%20Acquisition%20Regulatory%20Council,in%20manufactured%20products%20or%20component; "America's Supply Chains", EO 14017 (24 February 2021), accessed 2 October 2021, https://www.whitehouse.gov/briefing-room/presidential-actions/2021/02/24/executive-order-on-americas-supply-chains/.

35  The White House, *Building Resilient Supply Chains, Revitalizing American Manufacturing, and Fostering Broad-Based Growth*, June 2021, accessed 3 January 2022, https://www.whitehouse.gov/wp-content/uploads/2021/06/100-day-supply-chain-review-report.pdf.

36  Antonio Varas, Raj Varadarajan, Jimmy Goodrich, and Falan Yinug, *Government Incentives and U.S. Competitiveness in Semiconductor Manufacturing* (Semiconductor Industry Association and Boston Consulting Group, September 2020), accessed 2 October 2023, https://www.semiconductors.org/wp-content/uploads/2020/09/Government-Incentives-and-US-Competitiveness-in-Semiconductor-Manufacturing-Sep-2020.pdf; William B. Bonvillian, "US Manufacturing Decline and the Rise of New Production Innovation Paradigms"(Paris: OECD, 2016), accessed 2 October 2023 https://www.oecd.org/innovation/us-manufacturing-decline-and-the-rise-of-new-production-innovation-paradigms.htm.

37  Tony Romm, "Senate Approves Sprawling $250 Billion Bill to Curtail China's Economic and Military Ambitions", *Washington Post*, 8 June 2021, accessed 2 October 2023, https://www.washingtonpost.com/us-policy/2021/06/08/senate-china-science-technology (subscription required).

38  For example, Intel's agreement with a reluctant TSMC to build a plant in Arizona. Pressure from Washington was also applied on Samsung in this direction.

particularly within the manufacturing segment. These initiatives are integral components of the broader infrastructure plan under the Biden presidency.[39] In response to these developments, major manufacturers in Silicon Valley have swiftly established the Semiconductors in America Coalition, a cross-sector alliance with a patriotic agenda aimed at securing funding from Congress to support these initiatives.

This discussion can certainly be extended to encompass other advanced sectors, ranging from artificial intelligence[40] to 5G networks and quantum computers. However, the fundamental challenge lies in the numerous obstacles and inherent contradictions associated with this path. Despite the pressure exerted on allies, it is highly unlikely, from a technical and industrial perspective, that Washington will achieve, in the short to medium term, a significant degree of self-sufficiency in these specialised sectors. Over many years, the United States has established strong dependencies on highly specialised suppliers, making any efforts to replace them with domestic alternatives a daunting task. Moreover, even if such a transition were successful, the economic costs incurred by companies would be substantial. Additionally, this approach of antagonising China carries the inherent risk of creating strategic dilemmas for allies, particularly those in Asia and the East, who find themselves increasingly caught between the United States and China. These allies are unlikely to entirely forsake the Chinese market, and their reluctance to do so is evident. Furthermore, given the uncertainty surrounding the outcomes of these efforts, combined with China's vulnerability to inflicted damage,[41] Beijing may be compelled to pursue an autonomous course of action, potentially yielding consequences that boomerang back on US efforts. It is worth noting that Washington's offensive stance may inadvertently bolster Chinese state-owned enterprises and drive private Chinese companies, which have been relatively open to the West, towards a more government-centric approach.

---

39   Chris Miller, *Chip War: The Fight for the World's Most Critical Technology* (New York; London: Simon & Schuster, 2022).

40   National Security Commission on Artificial Intelligence, *Final Report*, March 2021, accessed 2 October 2023, https://www.nscai.gov/wp-content/uploads/2021/03/Full-Report-Digital-1.pdf.

41   Which would be no small matter. See Matt Sheehan, "China Technology 2025: Fragile Tech Superpower", Macro Polo (Paulson Institute), 26 October 2020, accessed 2 October 2023, https://macropolo.org/analysis/china-technology-forecast-2025-fragile-tech-superpower.

This approach could marginalise foreign companies currently operating in the Chinese market.[42]

All these factors underscore the complexity and high costs associated with decoupling, even when implemented selectively. While damage to Beijing is all but guaranteed, for Washington the results could only be substantial if the confrontation extends beyond the technological sphere and has disastrous repercussions for globalisation as a whole.

### 1.7   Geopolitical Challenge: The Indo-Pacific

The withdrawal of US troops from Afghanistan in the summer of 2021, a decision made by President Biden but already in motion during the Trump administration, marked a clear shift in US geopolitical priorities towards East Asia. This shift represents more than a simple revival of the earlier 'Pivot to Asia' strategy under President Obama. The overarching strategic goal remains the preservation of US hegemony in the East Asian region, largely based on maintaining military control of the seas along two critical island chains. The first chain extends from Japan through Ryukyu, Taiwan, the Philippines, and Borneo, while the second chain links the Philippines, Volcano Islands, Bonin-Marine Islands, and Guam. This control effectively encircles the Chinese continental landmass, and in a crisis, it could enable the United States to constrain the Chinese navy in its ports, preventing attacks on Taiwan and East Asian bases, and potentially threatening a blockade of Chinese trade routes through the Straits of Malacca, Sunda, and Lombok.

However, with the Indo-Pacific Strategy,[43] the stakes have been raised considerably. On one hand, there has been a shift towards actual containment, involving operations like 'freedom of navigation' (FONOPs) to counter China's efforts to move its military presence away from the coasts and beyond the first island chain. On the other hand, the United States is not just focused on reshaping and expanding its military presence, which significantly outmatches China's capabilities in the region. The intensified pressure comes in the form of an effort to forge a genuine anti-Chinese alliance, known as the 'Quadrilateral Security Dialogue' or Quad. This initiative includes Japan, Australia, and India and aims to bolster the US system of regional alliances by enhancing the military capabilities of these partner nations and integrating them more closely

---

42   Hosuk Lee-Makiyama, "US Sanctions Against Chinese 5G: Inconsistencies and Paradoxical Outcomes", European Centre for International Political Economy, October 2021, accessed 2 October 2023, https://ecipe.org/blog/us-sanctions-against-chinese-5g/.

43   Kurt M. Campbell and Rush Doshi, "How America Can Shore Up Asian Order: A Strategy for Restoring Balance and Legitimacy", *Foreign Affairs*, 12 January 2021.

into an anti-Beijing coalition. The primary focus of this initiative is safeguarding the 'security' of regional waters, particularly with regard to Taiwan. It also encompasses technological and infrastructural cooperation, with the goal of countering China's 'New Silk Roads' strategy (covered in Chapter 3). These efforts involve alternative economic projects, especially in areas central to the ongoing technological rivalry, such as the semiconductor supply chain, the development of 5G networks, and the establishment of technological standards.[44] In essence, the selective decoupling strategy being planned by Washington is being projected into the Indo-Pacific region, offering allies an alternative to their deepening economic ties with the Chinese market over the years.

This explains the US efforts to engage India on multiple fronts. First, it is aimed at countering China's expansion along the Indian Ocean coastline towards the Middle East. Second, it seeks to diversify the supply chains of multinational corporations. India holds significant strategic value in both respects. As the largest purchaser of Middle Eastern oil after China, India can counterbalance China's influence in the region. Additionally, India offers a 'friendly' alternative for multinational investments, drawing them away from Chinese territory. The strengthened alliance between the United States and Japan is also notable, particularly in military terms. The primary shared objective is to prevent China from making any advances on Taiwan, and threatening Japan's control over the Senkaku/Diaoyu Islands, which China claims. Furthermore, with Japan's support, the United States aims to become a central partner for the countries in the Association of Southeast Asian Nations (ASEAN), both economically and militarily, to counter Chinese territorial claims in the South China Sea.

Would we then be witnessing the formation of an Asian counterpart to the North Atlantic Treaty Organization (NATO)? At present, this seems unlikely. While Japan possesses significant economic resources and has taken substantial steps towards naval rearmament and potential military nuclear capabilities, its vulnerabilities outweigh its objective potential for a significant resurgence in global politics. These vulnerabilities are rooted in both domestic and international factors. Domestically, Japan faces challenges such as demographic ageing (being the world's oldest country), reluctance among its population to engage in external commitments and military rearmament, and a complex historical legacy that includes imperialism. Internationally, Japan has ongoing

---

44   The White House, "Fact Sheet: Quad Leaders' Summit", 24 September 2021, accessed 2 October 2023, https://www.whitehouse.gov/briefing-room/statements-releases/2021/09/24/fact-sheet-quad-leaders-summit.

tensions with both North and South Korea, latent disputes with Russia, and deepening economic ties with the region, particularly China. These factors make it challenging for Japan to escape its role as a province heavily reliant on the United States. While Japan may have the capacity for greater international prominence, its society remains hesitant about pursuing direct confrontation with China or significant global leadership in the near term.

The situation becomes even more intricate when we consider India. India faces significant internal challenges, as evidenced by the struggles in managing the pandemic and ongoing farmer protests. These issues are deeply rooted in a society that has only partially modernised, and the Indian state's hold on unity is somewhat precarious. Moreover, India's geopolitical interests are complex and not easily subordinated to US directives. This complexity was evident during the Ukrainian conflict when Delhi resisted strong US pressure to sever economic and military ties with Moscow. India abstained from voting to condemn Russia's invasion at the United Nations and even chose to pay for discounted supplies of Russian oil in roubles. While historical tensions exist in India's relations with Beijing, particularly along the Himalayan border, and competition in the Asian geo-economic sphere is a possibility, it is a significant leap from this situation to being channelled into a rigid anti-Chinese alliance. Moreover, without India's participation, the Indo-Pacific Strategy of containing China would be challenging to sustain. It is worth noting that Washington has been emphasising economic cooperation with Delhi alongside its geopolitical objectives, particularly regarding securing supply chains currently connected to China and relocating them to 'friendly' countries, a concept sometimes referred to as 'friendshoring'.

To conclude on the future prospects of the Quad alliance, while Washington has taken initial diplomatic steps towards this loose coalition, it remains to be seen whether it will evolve into an effective anti-Chinese alliance. This uncertainty underscores the broader consistency of the entire US alliance system in the Asian-Eastern region.

For many countries in the region, aligning diplomatically with Washington is indeed a pragmatic choice. However, this alignment does not necessarily signify a commitment to taking sides in the strategic conflict with Beijing, particularly in the event of a war. Even within ASEAN, which is generally aligned with Washington's interests, and among US partners like South Korea,[45]

---

[45] Although the new, more pro-American, government in South Korea, led by the conservative People Power Party, has changed this approach somewhat.

there has been a reluctance to join the Quad alliance.⁴⁶ An illustrative example of this hesitation is how South East Asian nations have approached the Ukrainian conflict. In general, they perceive it as a war driven by NATO expansion amid 'great power' rivalries and hypocritical Western narratives, and they have no intention of getting entangled in it. The same reluctance is evident when it comes to anti-Chinese containment efforts, and there is a substantial gap between their position and the European countries firmly in line with Washington's strategic goals.

Despite this, the Biden administration made a renewed push in 2022 by introducing the Indo-Pacific Economic Framework. This initiative expands the Indo-Pacific Strategy into the economic domain to counter the Chinese Belt and Road Initiative. However, it is important to note that this is not the launch of a comprehensive free trade agreement; rather, it is a vague proposal for future negotiations. While it garnered non-binding support from almost all ASEAN countries and India, it raises questions about the initiative's actual substance. One key issue is the United States' unwillingness to guarantee Asian countries access to its domestic market and continuity in trade policies beyond changes in administration. Additionally, other aspects of the initiative, such as labour and environmental standards, are seen more as demands rather than offers.⁴⁷ As a result, the Indo-Pacific Economic Framework appears to be a feeble replacement for the defunct Trans-Pacific Partnership, with uncertain parameters. While it aims to serve US interests, it may come at a high political cost for Asian countries with uncertain economic benefits.⁴⁸

The fundamental issue here is that Washington has limited incentives to offer in terms of investment and alternative trade relations that would be more advantageous to its partners than what Beijing provides. The 'foreign policy for the middle class' is primarily geared towards delivering tangible benefits to the United States under the banner of 'America First'. The concept of establishing

---

46   Washington will "explore opportunities for the Quad to work together with ASEAN countries", according to The White House, *Indo-Pacific Strategy of the United States*, February 2022, accessed 2 October 2023, https://www.whitehouse.gov/wp-content/uploads/2022/02/U.S.-Indo-Pacific-Strategy.pdf.
47   Kentaro Iwamoto, "Indo-Pacific Economic Framework is not a FTA: 5 Things to Know", *Nikkei Asia*, 19 May 2022, accessed 2 October 2023, https://asia.nikkei.com/Politics/International-relations/Biden-s-Asia-policy/Indo-Pacific-Economic-Framework-is-not-an-FTA-5-things-to-know.
48   Mary Lovely, "US Re-engagement: Is a Framework That Builds out China Realistic?", *East Asian Forum Quarterly* 14, no. 1 (2022), accessed 2 October 2023, reproduced at https://www.piie.com/commentary/speeches-papers/us-re-engagement-framework-builds-out-china-realistic.

a 'democratic' supply chain in Asia for high-tech products that excludes China without reducing trade barriers is far easier said than done.

Given these challenging circumstances, the September 2021 agreement between the United States, United Kingdom, and Australia (AUKUS) for a trilateral partnership in the Indo-Pacific takes on significant importance. This agreement outlines plans for projecting naval forces into the region with an explicit anti-Chinese role, including activities such as patrolling with nuclear submarines and Canberra's procurement of specialised technology from the United States and United Kingdom (even at the expense of a major agreement with Paris, which faced some hiccups before acceptance). Consequently, while London's involvement—albeit with limited resources and influence in the region—has effectively brought it into the Quad, Canberra has steadfastly pursued an anti-Chinese stance[49] in both security and economic matters (such as banning Huawei and participating in the Quad semiconductor deal). This direction underscores the resurgence of the so-called Anglosphere, signifying the geopolitical alliance of Anglo-Saxon powers, as the central core of US global influence.

## 1.8    Taiwan

The complexities of these issues become even more apparent when considering the Taiwan matter, which has remained unresolved since the Sino-US rapprochement initiated by Nixon and Mao. The objective of maintaining Taiwan's de facto independence—while, at least thus far, adhering formally to the 'One China' policy—has evolved into a red line for Washington, persisting from the Trump administration into Biden's tenure. Consequently, Taiwan has become one of the focal points, if not the crux, of the US–China confrontation. Beijing, on the other hand, envisions reunification in the medium or long term. Beyond its political implications in terms of domestic legitimacy and international prestige, reunification would provide China direct access to the Pacific Ocean by breaking the maritime encirclement imposed by the United States. Presently, Taiwan functions as the United States' 'stationary aircraft carrier', strategically located just 150 km from the Chinese coastline. It serves as the linchpin of the first 'defensive' chain of islands encircling Beijing and constitutes a critical chokepoint for China's commercial and military maritime activities.

---

49   Even with the new defence treaty (the Mutual Access Agreement) signed with Tokyo in January 2022.

This is the primary arena where Washington exerts its pressure. Operating along the precarious line outlined by the Taiwan Relations Act of 1979—which allows for the provision of US arms to Taiwan without overtly violating the 'One China' principle—the Biden administration has intensified tensions, following the trajectory set by the Trump administration. This escalation has seen provocative actions, including fighter-bomber flights near the Chinese coast, missions by nuclear submarines in the strait separating the island from the mainland, the visible presence of military advisers, repeated presidential statements (subsequently denied but deeply concerning to Beijing) asserting US commitment to defend Taiwan in the event of a Chinese attack,[50] and an official visit by Democratic Congressional Leader Nancy Pelosi to Taiwan in the summer of 2022. Tokyo has increasingly supported this posture as well. Furthermore, under the umbrella of the 'Pacific Deterrence Initiative', the Pentagon's budget includes measures and initiatives aimed at bolstering Taiwan's asymmetric defence capabilities, including joint naval exercises.

Taiwan's significance is further underscored by the presence of semiconductor manufacturing facilities that are indispensable to the international value chain. This juncture is where Washington places significant emphasis as part of its anti-Chinese selective decoupling strategy. Consequently, there is substantial pressure on Taipei to restrict or impede the sale of components, the transfer of technology, and the migration of skilled labour to Chinese industry.

In essence, Washington has departed from its conservative stance of maintaining the de facto status quo in favour of a more assertive approach, employing the Taiwan issue as a simmering source of ongoing tensions and, ultimately, as leverage to provoke Beijing into potentially 'misguided' actions—akin to its approach in Ukraine with Russia. This is why Washington adheres to the policy of 'strategic ambiguity', refraining from explicitly indicating whether it would directly intervene in the event of a Chinese military attack. Such ambiguity affords the United States flexibility and manoeuvrability. While it appears to have gained dominance on the island, the 'local American party'[51] (specifically, the Democratic Progressive Party, which has been in power in Taiwan since 2016) has increasingly leaned towards formal independence from Beijing. It garners support from a social coalition centred around decidedly pro-Western middle-class groups and the youth—although the parallels with the Ukrainian

---

50  In a statement made on 19 August 2021, Biden went as far as to draw an analogy between Article 5 of the NATO treaty (which entails the obligation of military assistance in the event of an attack on an ally) and its application to Japan, South Korea, and Taiwan.

51  Alberto Bradanini, *Cina: l'irresistibile ascesa* (Rome: Sandro Teti, 2022).

scenario are only partial.⁵² For these multiple reasons, Taiwan possesses the potential to become the most likely flashpoint in a future Sino-US crisis. This is especially true at the military level, given Washington's decision to pursue the island's formal independence as a means to provoke a military response from Beijing, thereby instigating a crisis to thwart China's ascendancy. While we are not at that point yet, the Ukraine crisis has shown that making precise predictions about the timing of such events is best avoided.

### 1.9   *The Ukrainian Trap*

In the context of the Ukrainian conflict, Washington's dual front strategy—aimed at both countering China and Russia—seems to have taken an irreversible course. To understand the situation better, let's briefly recap some key events.⁵³ Following the dissolution of the Soviet Union, NATO expanded its presence to Russia's borders. In December 2001, during the George W. Bush administration, the United States withdrew from the Anti-Ballistic Missile Treaty, a significant treaty on strategic forces signed in 1972. Additionally, after the turbulent conflict in Chechnya during the 1990s, pro-Western 'colour revolutions' began in Georgia (2003), Ukraine (2004), and Kyrgyzstan (2005) in the early 2000s, with US involvement. The situation escalated further with Georgia's open conflict in 2008. Finally, Ukraine became a focal point. Destabilising Ukraine had been a long-standing objective for the United States for over fifteen years since the end of the Cold War. One needs only to reread Brzezinski's *The Grand Chessboard* (1997),⁵⁴ in which the plan to isolate Russia and prevent it from having even a limited sphere of influence in its neighbouring countries was outlined, with a timetable. The mobilisation of Maidan Square in 2014, orchestrated by US intelligence services, led to the overthrow of a Ukrainian government that had relatively friendly ties with Moscow. This was achieved through the efforts of a social coalition seeking European integration, centred around urban middle-class groups and politically dominated by fiercely anti-Russian nationalist forces. This event set in motion the ongoing proxy war in Ukraine.⁵⁵

---

52   China is not Russia, but the question remains: could the Taiwanese become, like the Ukrainians, cannon fodder for the Americans?.

53   See also Raffaele Sciortino, *I dieci anni che sconvolsero il mondo. Crisi globale e geopolitica dei neopopulismi* [The ten years that shocked the world: Global crisis and the geopolitics of neo-populisms] (Trieste: Asterios, 2019), available via https://www.researchgate.net/publication/352212013_I_DIECI_ANNI_CHE_SCONVOLSERO_IL_MONDO_Crisi_globale_e_geopolitica_dei_neopopulismi, 119–36.

54   Brzezinski, *Grand Chessboard*.

55   Just a few months after the withdrawal from Afghanistan, in November 2021, Washington entered into a strategic cooperation agreement with Kiev, essentially aligning Ukraine

The Ukrainian people, unwittingly drawn into this geopolitical game, have become pawns in US plans, while Moscow see this as an existential threat. For Russia, a Ukraine turned into a strategic weapons base on its border would profoundly impact the stability of nuclear deterrence. Consequently, Moscow *had to respond*. Washington now possesses the means to continually wear down its adversary. By activating financial and monetary measures to disengage Moscow from global financial networks, it can undermine the coherence of the Russian state, its economic structure, and its social fabric.

The obvious question arises: why is the United States retaliating with such force? On a tactical level, Washington has seized upon a long-prepared opportunity—having maintained a military presence on the ground since 2014—with the aim of prolonging the conflict as much as possible, thereby draining its adversary without the need for direct intervention.[56] Russia has accrued a considerable 'bill to pay' due to its strengthening under Putin's presidency, pursuit of strategic and economic independence (exemplified by the Eurasian Economic Union), establishment of strong economic ties with Germany, alignment with China, aspirations for a less dollar-centric global monetary order, and energy geopolitics (including its successful intervention in Syria to counter regime change and improved relations with the Organization of the Petroleum Exporting Countries). Furthermore, Moscow serves as a catalyst for tensions between the United States and less powerful entities that resist complete submission to dollar hegemony.

However, the issue is a strategic one. In the European theatre, Washington has consistently pursued a strategy of dual containment: Russia and Germany.[57]

---

with the United States in their geopolitical endeavours. NATO Secretary Stoltenberg stated that NATO had "began increasing support" to Ukraine "weeks, months before the Russian invasion" (*Il Fatto Quotidiano*, 16 June 2022, now archived).

56 Regarding the proletarian sectors of Ukrainian society, they do not appear to be demanding accountability for the country's destruction. Conversely, the Ukrainian ruling class seems to be driven by frustration over their inability to lease national resources to the West, a predicament attributed to Russia's interference. This contrasts with the ruling classes of other Eastern European countries, which have successfully forged such arrangements over time.

57 The White House, Memorandum of Conversation, 3 April 1949, accessed 3 October 2023, https://nsarchive2.gwu.edu/nsa/DOCUMENT/200008/. The Secretary of State Dean Acheson is reported to have said: "We see Japan and Germany as major power centres, neutralized now but inevitably reviving, lying between the USSR and the West. … From the Western point of view, we too realize the grave dangers of encouraging German revival. We believe however that the advantages of orienting Germany toward the West and countering Soviet moves justify a calculated risk." It is worth noting that the authenticity of this document has not been definitively established in the literature. William Burr, who edited the document in August 2000 for the US National Security Archive,

Moscow has been portrayed as an enemy or adversary, depending on the phase, to be *kept out* of Europe through isolation, while Berlin is considered an ally (or vassal?) to be *kept under* by highlighting the alleged Russian threat. This ultimately clarifies why the US deep state, in the face of Russia's expressed willingness—and Trump's desire—to improve relations, was neither willing nor capable of granting any substantial recognition to Moscow in terms of its defensive sphere of influence within the limited sphere of the former Soviet Union.[58] This approach, however, poses an increasingly significant challenge for the Pentagon, as it hinders the possibility of separating Moscow and Beijing, as advocated by figures like Kissinger and Brzezinski. Mackinder's cautionary perspective—whose geopolitical principles still guide US strategic thinking—emerges victorious: at any cost, prevent the formation of a 'Eurasian' alliance between Germany and Russia (to which China must be added today).[59] Such an alliance would pose a grave threat to the global supremacy of the US dollar.

### 1.10 *Dragging a (German-Centred) Europe against Russia and China*

In the interim, the (deserved) death knell for Europe's remaining aspirations of autonomy, which had already been diminished by the euro crisis, has sounded, albeit in the opposite direction.[60] To comprehensively assess this situation, particularly concerning Germany, both before and after the Ukrainian crisis, let's delve into the state of Europe's autonomy.

Following the turbulence triggered by the Trump administration, which ranged from imposing customs duties on select European products to disputes over military spending contributions, perceived unilateralism, and overt anti-German stances, President Biden swiftly embarked on an effort to mend the rift between the United States and the European Union. One of the primary concerns was the economic agreement on investments that Brussels

---

acknowledges the uncertainty surrounding its authenticity but adds: "Nevertheless, readers may find striking how much this document discloses about the main lines of Truman-Acheson national security policy, as well as U.S. policy beyond the Truman years".

58   Anatol Lieven, "Don't Kick the Can: Two Proposals for Upcoming Russia Talks", *Responsible Statecraft* (online magazine of the Quincy Institute for Responsible Statecraft), 7 January 2022, accessed 3 October 2023, https://responsiblestatecraft.org/2022/01/07/dont-kick-the-can-two-key-us-proposals-for-upcoming-russia-talks/.

59   Halford John Mackinder (1861–1947) was an English geographer, academic, and politician, generally regarded as a founding father of both geopolitics and geostrategy. His thought is still the 'bible' when it comes to the US strategic approach.

60   Raffaele Sciortino, "Chicken Game: Eurocrisis Again", *Insurgent Notes: Journal of Communist Theory and Practice*, 3 June 2012, accessed 3 October 2023, http://insurgentnotes.com/2012/06/chicken-game-eurocrisis-again/.

and Beijing had reached at the end of 2020, known as the Comprehensive Agreement on investments. This agreement, strongly championed by Germany under Chancellor Angela Merkel's leadership, had encountered significant roadblocks, partly due to pressure from Washington. In the initial months of his presidency, Biden managed to partially resolve some of these outstanding disputes. This led to agreements with Brussels on matters related to steel and aerospace, as well as plans for implementing a minimum global tax on the foreign earnings of multinational corporations. Although seemingly minor, this tax would permit Washington to incrementally raise federal taxes on domestic companies, thereby circumventing the proposed European digital tax. In the realm of military affairs, the new administration, as evidenced by the Pentagon's November 2021 Global Posture Review[61] and NATO's adoption of a new Strategic Concept 2030 at the 2022 Madrid summit,[62] demonstrated a renewed commitment to investing in the European geopolitical theatre. However, this commitment came at a cost to Europe, particularly Germany. A notable anti-Russian move came to the fore, marked by Washington's attempts to obstruct the commissioning of the Nord Stream 2 gas pipeline. This pipeline, intended to transport natural gas directly from Russia to Germany, faced significant impediments. Furthermore, both Nord Stream 1 and Nord Stream 2 pipelines suffered substantial damage due to an act of sabotage that occurred on 26 September 2022.[63]

Thanks to the Ukrainian conflict, Washington has not only thwarted the Nord Stream 2 gas pipeline but has also delivered a significant blow to the entirety of the EU's energy policy. This has pushed the EU towards disconnection from Russian energy supplies, and it has further complicated trade interconnections between Moscow and German industry, rendering them exceedingly challenging, if not impossible. This combination of factors, unless altered under changing circumstances, has the potential to undermine Germany's international competitiveness and place the very industrial fabric of Europe, with Germany at its core, at risk. Instead, it aligns with the United States'

---

61  US Department of Defense, "DoD Concludes 2021 Global Posture Review", news release, 29 November 2021, accessed 3 October 2023, https://www.defense.gov/News/Releases/Release/Article/2855801/dod-concludes-2021-global-posture-review/.
62  This document can be downloaded at https://www.nato.int/strategic-concept/index.html.
63  Anna Ringstrom and Terje Solsvik, "North Stream Leaks Confirmed as Sabotage, Sweden Says", Reuters, 18 November 2022, accessed 3 October 2023, https://www.reuters.com/world/europe/traces-explosives-found-nord-stream-pipelines-sweden-says-2022-11-18/.

objective of reshoring manufacturing to its domestic shores, as supported by the Congress Inflation Reduction Act.

Of paramount concern to the United States is the relationship between the European-German project and China. Washington's primary aim is to persuade Europe, particularly Berlin, that Beijing is already an adversary. This objective is pursued through various means, starting with diplomatic pressures and tangible actions, such as the Huawei 5G network deployment boycott initiated under the Trump administration. President Biden has continued along these lines, most notably with the bilateral initiative of the Trade and Technology Council, which seeks to reaffirm Western leadership in digital transformation.[64] However, it is important to note that we are still some distance away from revisiting projects like the Transatlantic Trade and Investment Partnership, the failed transatlantic trade treaty proposed during the Obama administration.

Nonetheless, a closer look reveals that the dual strategy of engaging both the Western and Eastern markets, from which the German (and European) economy has reaped substantial benefits, is gradually closing. Furthermore, in the medium to long term, Berlin must grapple with the potential economic and technological ascent of China, which, if achieved, could eventually limit German investment opportunities and access to markets.[65] This concern is already reflected in measures taken to safeguard 'technological sovereignty' against potential Chinese takeovers of German (and European) technology companies. While this is not an imminent threat, given the near-indispensable nature of Sino-German economic interdependence for German multinational corporations, it intensifies Washington's challenge of determining where and how to establish anti-Chinese boundaries for Berlin and the European Union. In contrast, anti-Russian boundaries appear to be the more straightforward path.

Exploring the underlying causes of the European ruling classes' swift and nearly complete alignment with Washington's directives on Ukraine (notwithstanding criticism amid some sectors of the industrial bourgeoisie, particularly in Germany), is beyond the scope of this discussion. The European Union currently appears united only in its hyper-mediated anti-Russian rhetoric and

---

64   European Commission, "EU-US Trade and Technology Council Inaugural Joint Statement", 29 September 2021, accessed 3 October 2023, https://ec.europa.eu/commission/presscorner/detail/en/STATEMENT_21_4951.

65   "Die Geschäftsgrundlage der deutschen industrie", German-Foreign-Policy.com, 18 October 2021, accessed 3 October 2023, https://www.german-foreign-policy.com/news/detail/8735/.

its unquestioning support for Atlanticism. This unity becomes more passive when it comes to conforming to US strategic interests during moments of international crisis orchestrated by Washington. In all other aspects, the EU is more divided than ever, as evidenced by the debates over anti-Russian sanctions and arms shipments to Ukraine. Any vague desire for political autonomy on the international stage, which today would mean achieving a position more independent of the US–China dynamic, appears to have vanished. Moreover, the EU's unity has been compromised by internal disputes well exploited by Eastern European countries with a pro-American stance, a fragmentation of the decision-making process, French delight in any setbacks suffered by Berlin, the weakening of German leadership following Merkel's departure, and more. However, the fundamental issue lies in the fact that the European Union is *not a single state*; it cannot replace the enduring political and military semi-sovereignty of its member states, a legacy that dates back to World War II. Furthermore, the process of Europeanisation, which has seen the expansion of European norms, institutions, and processes, has paradoxically weakened the autonomy of Germany and France because it has in reality advanced a form of globalisation with distinctly American traits. Europeanisation has ensnared France and Germany in the network of Eastern European countries that act as steadfast vassals of Washington and opportunistic beneficiaries of EU funding. The absence of a coherent class struggle has compounded these challenges. Ultimately, European fears, whether conscious or not, revolve around the belief that without appeasing Washington, the Western privilege of widespread prosperity may struggle against the growing demands of the East.[66]

In the short to medium term, Berlin, which is a prerequisite for any effective Europeanism, does not appear capable of imparting geopolitical substance to its global economic influence. This impasse cannot be resolved solely through geo-economic factors but would likely require a significant deterioration in the Ukrainian crisis, prompting a severe social reaction with potential neo-populist characteristics, oriented against the United States. Such a scenario could

---

66  It is not possible here to delve into the Marxist discourse of the late 1960s and early 1970s, which emerged in response to the dollar crisis leading to the 1971 dollar–gold inconvertibility. This debate revolved around the nature of the relationship between the United States and the European imperialist nations, as well as Japan. It featured notable discussions between figures like Martin Nicolaus and Ernest Mandel, and it played out in publications such as the *New Left Review* and the *Monthly Review*, among others. For our purposes here, we can simplify this complex discourse by referencing Nicolaus's characterisation of the European-Western countries as 'imperialised' imperialisms, signifying their subordinate status within the broader imperialist framework dominated by the United States.

undermine the relationship between the working classes and the current ruling class, which is firmly rooted in the framework of globalist Atlanticism, possibly rendering it irreparable. However, this prospect still appears distant at present.

### 1.11  *Lights and Shadows in Washington*

In the immediate term, Washington finds itself in a favourable geopolitical situation in Europe, but there are also reasons for concern in the future. First and foremost, it has successfully created a significant divide between Europe and Russia, one that may prove challenging to mend. In just a few weeks, it has managed to disrupt European energy policy and boost pro-NATO military spending. Additionally, it has paved the way for a similar approach towards Beijing, though it is important to note that the game is far from over, especially if Moscow achieves acceptable military progress in Ukraine. If that happens, the economic consequences of the Ukrainian crisis could become more apparent, potentially weakening the Atlanticist geopolitical consensus, particularly regarding sanctions. The extent to which Washington can control its European allies in this scenario remains to be seen. Another critical concern is the loss of American soft power among a substantial portion of European societies, which have had to bear the financial burdens of their governments' subservience to Atlanticism. This situation, on such a scale and to this degree, is unprecedented and raises questions about whether Biden's leadership is making Europeans nostalgic for the Trump era.

Second, the rest of the international system of states, representing 80% of the world's population, has been reluctant to embrace the Western narrative concerning the current crisis. These countries, from Asian to Latin American and African nations, are even less inclined to accept the sanctions imposed on Moscow. Furthermore, the global economic situation is deteriorating, especially with rising energy and food costs, and would only worsen with continued sanctions on Russia. This situation is causing headaches in Washington, as the Biden administration risks heading into the 2024 elections in a crisis of consensus on the domestic economic front.

The most significant source of tension on the horizon is undoubtedly the potential for further rapprochement between Moscow and Beijing. Washington has elevated the stakes, pushing Russia into a life-or-death struggle where no measures are off the table. Notably, the Ukrainian trap aims to weaken Russia, which has become increasingly crucial for China's geopolitical interests.[67] If

---

67  Zhang Yugui, "US Wages Economic War to Maintain Global Supremacy", *China Daily*, 1 April 2022, accessed 3 October 2023, http://www.chinadaily.com.cn/a/202204/01/WS6 246c83da310fd2b29e54bb2.html.

the Russian state were to collapse, it would pose a significant challenge for Beijing, potentially isolating and encircling it, making it harder for China to sustain its new economic and monetary course. This is why Beijing has, thus far, resisted US pressure to join the financial isolation imposed on Moscow or, at the very least, has refrained from actively supporting it. The uncertainties increase for the United States in this context, as Beijing is unlikely to concede on this front, either in substance or merely in appearance. The question arises: how will Washington respond under such circumstances? Furthermore, the swift move to freeze Russian dollar reserves has sparked and will continue to provoke serious concerns, if not second thoughts, among other state actors who are bound by the dollar-centric payment system and reliant on significant quantities of the greenback.

All these developments underscore the elevated tension within the global system. While we may not yet be on the brink of a geopolitical crisis of such magnitude that it triggers a process of true deglobalisation, the unfolding events foreshadow such a process and reveal the trajectory of world politics. A forthcoming global economic crisis will present Washington with a critical crossroads: either to persist with its current policies or to use the crisis as an impetus for comprehensive economic restructuring, with far-reaching implications in geopolitical terms. In either scenario, the central role of the dollar strategy remains pivotal.

### 1.12 *Dollar Fatigue*

Indeed, following the financial meltdown of 2008, the dollar did not undergo the collapse that the nature and trajectory of the subsequent global crisis might have suggested.[68] Additionally, no concrete measures were taken towards the multilateral reform of the international monetary and financial system, a reform that had been advocated by various international institutions[69] and countries like China[70] and Russia. While the credibility of the dollar-centric

---

68    Adam Tooze, *Crashed: How a Decade of Financial Crises Changed the World* (London: Penguin, 2018).

69    United Nations—Department of Economic and Social Affairs, *World Economic and Social Survey 2010: Retooling Global Development*, E/2010/50/Rev. 1, ST/ESA/330 (2010), accessed 3 October 2023, https://www.un.org/en/development/desa/policy/wess/wess_current/2010wess.pdf.

70    See the speech by China's then central bank governor Zhou Xiaochuan in March 2009 on the need for a reform of the international monetary system: "Zhou Xiaochuan 周小川, 'Reform The International Monetary System,' March 23, 2009", University of South California—USC US-China Institute, accessed 3 October 2023, https://china.usc.edu/zhou-xiaochuan-%E5%91%A8%E5%B0%8F%E5%B7%9D-reform-internatio nal-monetary-system-march-23-2009.

arrangement was shaken, both US actions and the absence of viable alternatives in the short to medium term contributed to a sort of freeze in the situation. This was exacerbated by the euro crisis of 2010–12, which effectively dashed the aspirations of the euro, a potential rival to the dollar. Nevertheless, monetary instability and the growing impatience of other global actors have been steadily mounting.

Furthermore, the underlying economic fundamentals of the US, particularly in terms of managing its twin debt (domestic and foreign), have not seen any improvement in the meantime.[71] A few key figures illustrate this (see Figure 2.2). In 2018, the federal debt stood at approximately $22 trillion, more than double what it was in 2008. By mid-2022, it had surged past the $30 trillion mark, equivalent to over 130% of the US gross domestic product (excluding a private domestic debt of over $30 trillion). A 2018 study by the Committee for a Responsible Federal Budget, validated by calculations from the Congressional Budget Office, projected that within a few years, debt servicing costs would approach nearly $1 trillion annually, surpassing both government health expenditures and eventually military spending as well.

Moreover, there is no indication of a turnaround on the horizon. The trade deficit with China has once again surged into negative territory, with a Chinese surplus for 2021 reaching nearly $400 billion, making it extremely difficult to establish a comprehensive strategic approach towards Beijing. Concurrently, government deficit spending has continued to rise, particularly since the onset of the pandemic crisis and the generous fiscal stimulus measures implemented by both the Trump and Biden administrations. These measures were financed by the massive liquidity issued by the Federal Reserve. While there was a relative decrease in expenditures in 2022 due to the diminishing federal response to the COVID-19 pandemic, it is expected to resume an upward trajectory thereafter.[72]

It is important to bear in mind that the dollar strategy hinges on precisely managing the dual US debt by transforming the world's demand for dollars into a potent force factor. This demand stems from the dollar's role as a reserve currency and international payment method, coupled with the United States' position as the global system's 'consumer of last resort'. This combination, along with its geopolitical influence, has allowed the US to maintain low interest rates for its burgeoning debts over the past decades. It has also enabled

---

71  See the real-time updated data at www.usdebtclock.org.
72  See figures at "Federal Deficit and Debt: October 2022", Peter G. Peterson Foundation, accessed 3 October 2023, https://www.pgpf.org/the-current-federal-budget-deficit/budget-deficit-october-2022.

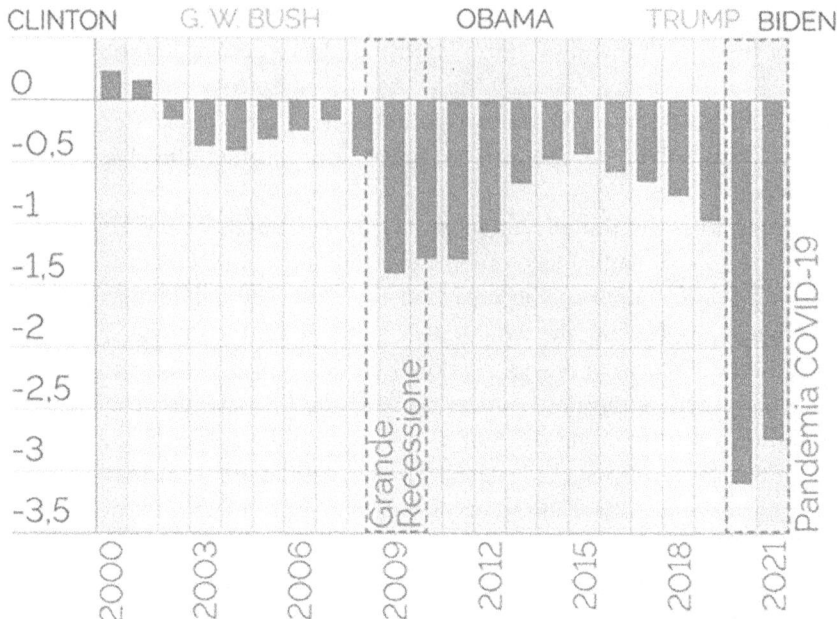

FIGURE 2.2  Trillions of dollars of federal surplus or deficit
REPRODUCED FROM ALBERTO GUIDI AND DAVIDE TENTORI, "L'ANNO DI BIDEN IN 13 GRAFICI", ISTITUTO PER GLI STUDI DI POLITICA INTERNAZIONALE (ISPI), 5 NOVEMBER 2021, ACCESSED 3 OCTOBER 2023, HTTPS://WWW.ISPIONLINE.IT/IT/PUBBLICAZIONE/LANNO-DI-BIDEN-13-GRAFICI-32268. DATA FROM THE FEDERAL RESERVE BANK OF ST. LOUIS.

Washington, following an oscillating 'accordion' pattern, to raise interest rates as needed by attracting capital from other parts of the world. This dynamic has led to the significant demand for US Treasury bonds from other central banks, with Japan and China leading the way. At its peak, this demand accounted for 35% of total foreign debt in the mid-2010s (see Figure 2.3). It also encompasses the reinvestment of petrodollars in the Wall Street stock exchange, among other factors.

Nonetheless, it is worth noting that in the aftermath of the 2008 financial crisis, many state-owned financial institutions began to diversify their reserves and bonds. Of particular significance is Beijing's decision to halt the increase in its holdings of dollars in various forms. This move was motivated by a desire to hedge against the dollar's volatility and was concurrent with a decrease in the trade surplus. The petrodollar circuit has also gradually become less important, though still crucial for pricing commodities in dollars.

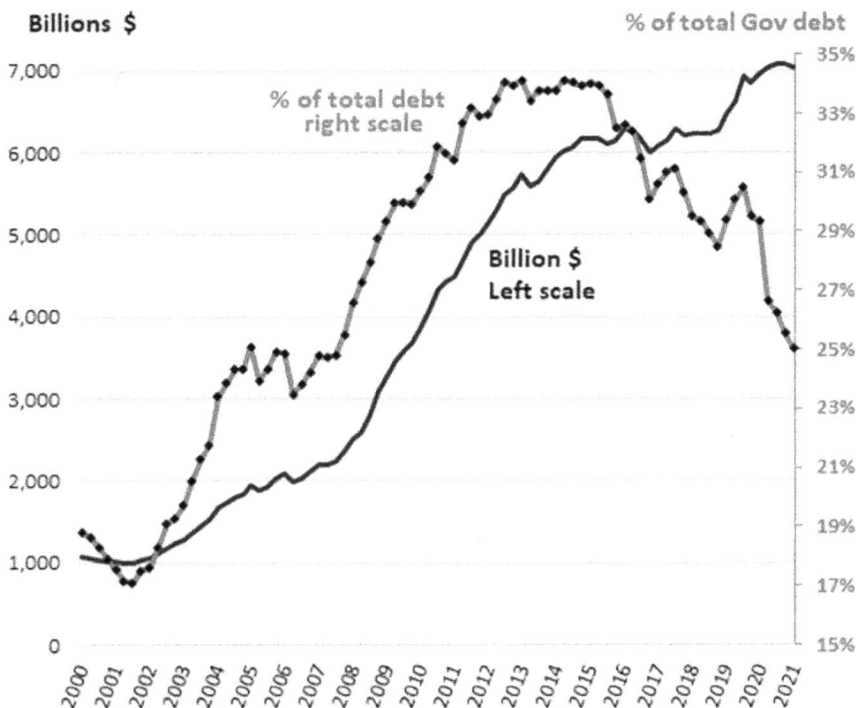

FIGURE 2.3  US government debt held by foreign holders (quarterly)
GRAPH MODIFIED FROM WOLF RICHTER, "WHO BOUGHT THE $4.7 TRILLION OF TREASURY SECURITIES ADDED SINCE MARCH 2020 TO THE INCREDIBLY SPIKING US NATIONAL DEBT?", WOLF STREET, 17 MAY 2021, ACCESSED 3 OCTOBER 2023, HTTPS://WOLFSTREET.COM/2021/05/17/WHO-BOUGHT-THE-4-7-TRILLION-OF-TREASURY-SECURITIES-ADDED-SINCE-MARCH-2020-TO-THE-INCREDIBLY-SPIKING-US-NATIONAL-DEBT/. DATA FROM THE US TREASURY DEPARTMENT (THE DOTTED LINE INDICATES THE PERCENTAGE OF US GOVERNMENT DEBT HELD BY FOREIGN ENTITIES; THE SOLID LINE INDICATES THE DOLLAR AMOUNT).

These significant developments are also evident when examining central banks' reserve currencies (see Figure 2.4). As of the end of 2021, dollar reserves accounted for 58.8% of the world's total (a similar share in 2022), marking the lowest point since 1995. To put this into perspective, in 2002, the dollar's share was 71%, and in 1977, it was as high as 85%, even when the era of inflationary pressures had already commenced.

However, it is important to emphasise that we are not currently in a de-dollarisation phase, whatever form that might take, nor does the dollar face a serious systemic rival in the medium term. The euro, which struggled to regain

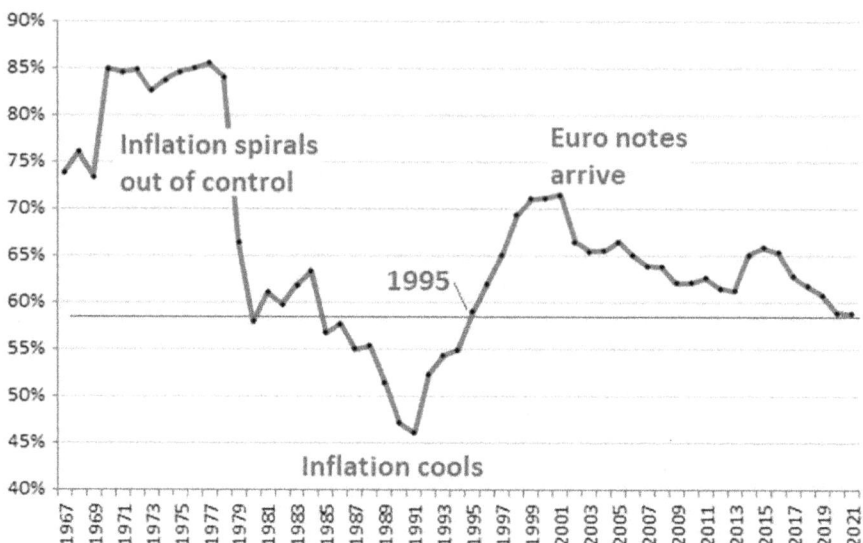

FIGURE 2.4  US dollar share of world reserve currencies (% allocated reserves, year-end)
GRAPH FROM WOLF RICHTER, "UPDATE ON US DOLLAR AS GLOBAL RESERVE CURRENCY AND THE IMPACT OF USD EXCHANGE RATES & INFLATION", *WOLF STREET*, 2 APRIL 2022, ACCESSED 3 OCTOBER 2023, HTTPS://WOLFSTREET.COM/2022/04/02/US-DOLLARS-STATUS-AS-GLOBAL-RESERVE-CURRENCY-DROPS-TO-26-YEAR-LOW-SLOWLY-BUT-SURELY/. DATA FROM THE IMF.

its footing after the euro crisis, accounts for only about 20% of the world's reserves. Moreover, the European Union is far from presenting a viable alternative to US hegemony. The Chinese renminbi yuan, as of today, also falls short of challenging the dollar's dominance, as we will explore further. Nonetheless, recent developments have begun to alter this landscape, driven by the emergence of a new economic cycle, increasingly complex geopolitical dynamics, and the strategies of global or regional players that are not (entirely) subservient to Washington. This shift warrants a closer examination of the potential consequences of an increasingly precarious global situation, which could lead to a gradual loss of US control, starting with the commodities market, and a future decline in global demand for dollars.

In the wake of the 2008 financial crisis, the US government—that is, the Federal Reserve Bank and the Treasury, with the Pentagon as the core of the American power structure—has increasingly relied on borrowing from itself and domestic financial institutions (see Figure 2.5). These domestic institutions have become the largest purchasers of US Treasury bonds, accounting

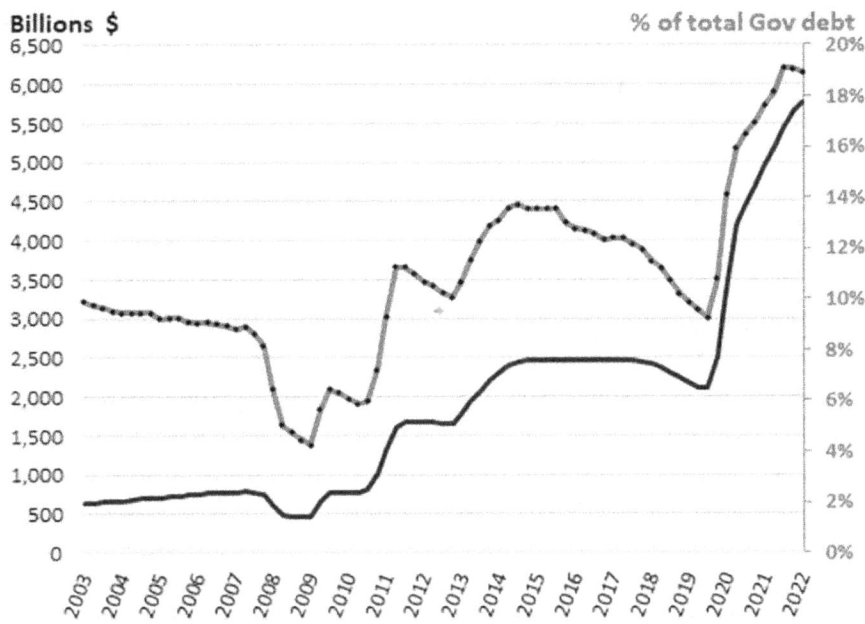

FIGURE 2.5    US government debt held by the Federal Reserve
Note: The dotted line indicates the percentage of US government debt held by the Federal Reserve; the solid line is the dollar amount.
REPRODUCED FROM WOLF RICHTER, "WHO BOUGHT THE INCREDIBLY SPIKING US GOVERNMENT DEBT, NOW $30.4 TRILLION IN TREASURY SECURITIES?", WOLF STREET, 19 MAY 2022, ACCESSED 3 OCTOBER 2023, HTTPS://WOLFSTREET.COM/2022/05/19/WHO-BOUGHT-THE-INCREDIBLY-SPIKING-US-GOVERNMENT-DEBT-NOW-30-4-TRILLION-IN-TREASURY-SECURITIES/. DATA FROM THE US TREASURY DEPARTMENT.

for three-quarters of the entire federal debt. This shift has been driven by the strategy known as quantitative easing, in which the Federal Reserve has maintained historically low interest rates. Simultaneously, it has accumulated Treasury bonds while injecting liquidity into financial markets. This policy has had the side effect of effectively devaluing dollar-denominated assets held by foreign entities.

Nonetheless, these limitations cannot be evaded indefinitely. Several indicators suggest this, one of which is the recent surge in inflation that has swept through the global economy in the aftermath of the pandemic crisis. While this inflationary wave cannot be attributed to a single cause, the massive liquidity injection in the West, especially during the initial two years of the COVID pandemic, undoubtedly contributed to its acceleration. This surge in price inflation is unprecedented since the early 1980s.[73] Consequently, the Federal Reserve has been compelled to shift its stance in 2022, moving away from the policy of quantitative easing and opting to increase interest rates. However, it seems that the Federal Reserve is chasing after the credit markets rather than anticipating their movements, which has created challenges for Wall Street and the ongoing economic recovery.[74] As the economic cycle inches closer to the possibility of a recession, there is a potential for a vicious circle to develop: addressing inflation requires raising interest rates, a move that could trigger a recession by causing the collapse of so-called zombie firms and deflating an overvalued stock market.[75]

Predicting the exact trajectory is fraught with uncertainty. One thing appears certain: the conclusion of the era of easy money is likely to burst multiple bubbles, both in the stock and bond markets, with ripple effects on the real economy. These effects could manifest through shifts in the real estate market, tighter bank credit, a surge in company and bank bankruptcies, and more. Washington may believe it can navigate these challenges without resorting to overly drastic measures. However, the potential price to pay is a protracted period of stagflation and a further delay in implementing a significant production restructuring.

One potential strategy, in theory, would be to pursue a drastic and rapid increase in interest rates, aiming to attract the world's wealth flows by revaluing the dollar and shifting the impending crisis onto others. This approach could be likened to the Volcker Shock of the early 1980s,[76] which marked the beginning of the Reagan era and the definitive crisis of so-called real socialism (and could potentially target China today). However, this option presents

---

73    Gary Clyde Hufbauer, Megan Hogan, and Yilin Wang, *For Inflation Relief, the United States Should Look to Trade Liberalization* (Policy Briefs 22–4, PIIE, March 2022), accessed 3 October 2023, https://www.piie.com/publications/policy-briefs/inflation-relief-uni ted-states-should-look-trade-liberalization.
74    During the first half of 2022, the S&P 500 index experienced a significant decline of 23%, and since the conclusion of November 2021, the Nasdaq index has plummeted by a substantial 33%.
75    Zombie firms, as the term suggests, manage to survive by servicing their debt obligations primarily due to the availability of cheap money.
76    In 1979 domestic inflation in the United States stood at around 12%, and by March 1980, it had surged to over 14%. Paul Volcker, who served as the Treasury Secretary during the Carter administration, responded by raising interest rates from 10.5% in July 1979 to 17.6% by April 1980, and eventually reaching 19.1% in June 1981. By the close of 1982, inflation had been effectively curbed, dropping to 4%. However, this accomplishment came after a recession that, on a Western country scale, contributed to the conclusion of a decade-long cycle of mass worker strikes and labour struggles.

several challenges in terms of feasibility and consequences. First, beyond the strictly economic implications, such a move would trigger social and political reactions to a recession and, possibly, a new financial collapse. Ruling politicians may not be adequately prepared for a robust internal clash, and the populist and anti-populist tactics employed thus far may not suffice to address the challenges. On the external front, capturing value from the rest of the world—essential for a restructuring aimed at bridging the gap between finance and productive enterprise and increasing the extraction of relative surplus value—would not be straightforward. Second, historical context matters. In the Reagan era, Washington's strategy was broadly accepted by Western bourgeoisies, with the consent of the most anti-proletarian part of the middle classes. It served as a lever to counter both the cycle of workers' struggles stemming from the Long '68 and the ambitions of countries in the so-called Third World. However, today's landscape is different. Western middle classes find themselves in a storm, marked by the rise of neo-populisms. Allied nations are increasingly dissatisfied and restless with their 'godfather' in Washington. Moreover, China's position has evolved. In the past, China was not a major player in the global economic and geopolitical arena. It was precisely the US geopolitical shift that allowed China to rise. However, today, Beijing is less inclined to play by US rules and less willing to be left holding the bag in the event of a new recession or financial crisis.

The nexus between geopolitics and the dollar—the core of the US hegemonic cycle in its historical phases[77]—has become more complex and even contradictory. The conventional recipes used thus far may not be well-suited to the new situation, as this chapter has highlighted. The escalating global chaos is unlikely to fill the gaps created by these challenges or prevent others from stepping in. China remains simultaneously more distant and closer than ever before.

### 1.13  *From Tactics to Strategy?*

The Biden administration's approach to the strategic challenge posed by US geopolitics, particularly in relation to Beijing, can be seen as a refinement of Trump's policy. However, it is important to note that this approach does not definitively solve the problem, and a well-prepared Grand Strategy remains elusive. Selectivity and greater incisiveness are unlikely to prevent Beijing from carving out a more autonomous space in the international division of labour

---

[77] That is, from World War II to the end of the Bretton Woods monetary regime in 1971, and from Bretton Woods II to the financial global crisis of 2008.

and shaping the world order to its advantage. The current challenges faced by the United States are not solely a result of insufficient economic and military resources, although it is essential to consider the growing economic weight and diminishing returns of military spending in terms of political effectiveness. It is also not merely a matter of 'imperial fatigue' waiting to be overcome by recovering internal energy and unity, especially in the absence of effective global rivals (no 'Chinese century' is on the horizon). Instead, the United States faces serious issues stemming from a systemic crisis of capitalist accumulation and the world order. Let us summarise these challenges.

1. Domestic challenges: The return to 'democratic normality' is superficial, and polarising dynamics persist. The Biden administration, already dealing with growing discontent over inflation, is in a transitional phase towards further political disarray, with or without Trumpism. Rebuilding an internal social bloc capable of sustaining the confrontation with China amid a lack of effective economic revival remains a pressing issue.
2. Alliances: Unlike the Cold War era of consolidated alliances, the United States now holds its allies in loose networks in Asia and increasingly burdensome ones in Europe. However, it struggles to provide economically advantageous and socio-politically sustainable global arrangements.
3. Strategic objectives: The US establishment's strategic objectives in the confrontation with China are uncertain. Is it aiming for regime change in Beijing? Does it anticipate a temporary downsizing of Chinese claims, inevitably leading to a revival, or a definitive solution involving the dismemberment of China's national and economic fabric? The escalation of the confrontation is challenging to manage since it is not possible to simply wait for China to economically and socially implode, as in the case of anti-Soviet containment.
4. Decisive options: As such, the United States faces a crucial decision—whether to halt China's rise, even at the risk of blocking and reversing globalisation. If this path is chosen, how will the United States bear the high costs of ending or disrupting globalisation, which has been the source of global value extraction since the world crisis in the 1970s? Moreover, how can it maintain the dominance of the dollar and the use of debt as instruments of global imperialism in a context of global upheaval?

The struggle Washington faces in developing a strategy that adapts to contemporary challenges is not a defect that can be easily corrected. While various factors at the national level[78] contribute to this struggle, such as decision-making

---

78  This is precisely the level at which two very different scholars, Giovanni Arrighi (in *Adam Smith in Beijing: Lineages of the Twenty-First Century*, London: Verso, 2007, 343) and, more

processes, self-referentiality of hegemony, and domestic political and economic constraints, the root of the issue lies in the broader current geopolitical landscape, which reflects the synthesis of imperialism within a world capitalist system. What we observe today is the exhaustion of the possibility of a coherent global strategy, something that only the United States could provide in the past. This exhaustion is symptomatic of the deep systemic crisis within world capitalism. This crisis is characterised by a world order that is no longer suitable, and it is pushing the boundaries in terms of surplus-value extraction, geopolitical hierarchies, and class relationships.

However, we have not yet, let us be clear, reached the final act of this crisis. Quite simply, certain capitalist actors have taken centre stage and are being drawn into global conflicts, contributing to the growing background chaos of a framework that will become increasingly turbulent. When the time comes, the current frozen state of the crisis will thaw. The economic crisis, which was only hinted at in 2008, will resurface with full force, likely originating from the centre of the world system. This will have devastating repercussions, even affecting the political balance of power, which has thus far only been shaken. At that point, we will see whether Washington can once again shift the costs onto the rest of the world, possibly through coercive cooperation with Europe and Japan, or whether this equation will prove to be impossible to solve.

This represents the genuine systemic challenge, and it is China that will come to symbolise it. The primary concern is not so much the potential decline of the United States but rather the potential for a new rearrangement of the world capitalist system or, conversely, a profound disintegration of it. Such a disintegration could reopen the possibility, although it may seem remote at present, of transitioning towards an entirely different societal organisation.[79] This is ultimately the significance of the conflict between the United States and China—nothing more, nothing less.

---

recently, Kishore Mahbubani, have, however, discussed the crucial question of why the United States is struggling to develop a new Grand Strategy.

[79] Sean Starrs, "American Economic Power Hasn't Declined—It Globalized!", *International Studies Quarterly* 57, no. 4 (2013): 817–30.

CHAPTER 3

# China

In the meantime, China is formulating its own strategic course—an unequivocally *national* strategy. This strategy is emblematic of China's position as a society with a form of capitalism that is lagging behind, having traversed a protracted and tumultuous phase of 'socialist' original accumulation as a transitional stage towards more contemporary economic and social structures. China's development, accelerated by mobilisations borne out of class struggle, necessitates an approach that, in an era of ultra-concentrated imperialism, diverges from the pursuit of unattainable self-sufficiency. Instead, it directly confronts the dynamics of the world market and geopolitics in search of a different configuration of globalisation.

## 1 Transition to What?

The fundamental question arising from China's current trajectory is: where is China headed? Inextricably linked to this inquiry is another: what characterises China's socio-economic structure, and what historical antecedents inform its evolution? When assessing this transition, one should not forget the historical underpinnings of China's remarkable yet imbalanced post-Maoist development. First, a radical peasant revolution, conducted under the banner of socialism established the political foundations for China's distinctive capitalist trajectory and the formation of a domestic market. This trajectory markedly differs from the trajectories stemming from the Western democratic revolutions. Second, the landscape of class struggle in the People's Republic of China, up to and beyond the Cultural Revolution, consistently provided a powerful impetus for unleashing latent collective and individual forces within Chinese society. Third, the swift emergence of a vigorous 'made by China' (not merely 'made in China') industrialisation endeavours to assert autonomy from the entanglements of US-led imperialist globalisation. This move holds significance for the working classes on both domestic and international fronts within the context of class struggle. In light of these multifaceted factors, we find ourselves at a pivotal juncture in China's unique trajectory of capitalism.

## 1.1  A Peasant Democratic Revolution

The Chinese revolution at its core was primarily a peasant-based national democratic revolution grounded in the agrarian landscape of a country boasting a population of over 500 million people. In the revolutionary theatre, the Chinese Communist Party (CCP) played the role of the 'Jacobin' leadership, in contrast to the 'Girondin' Chinese Nationalist Party (Kuomintang, aka Guomindang), which was unable to shoulder the agrarian question and the anti-imperialist struggle owing to its entanglement with foreign powers. It was indeed a 'peasant revolution', and not only in the sense of sociological classification, as the impoverished rural strata constituted the primary organised mass force on both political and military fronts. When I use the term 'Jacobin' it is important to note that it carries certain populist characteristics, which were particularly evident in Maoism. The CCP leadership's strategic objective, framed within the context of a 'new democracy' through the 'alliance of the four classes',[1] was primarily the liberation of the nation from the yoke of internal reactionary and external imperialist forces (Japanese occupation first, US pressure later). Socialism was envisioned as a subsequent process that would materialise after a more or less protracted period of industrialisation. This industrialisation process would ultimately tip the balance in favour of industrial workers over peasants, the two fundamental classes. While internal divisions within the party surfaced early on, regarding the methods and pace of implementing this perspective, as well concerning the alliance with Stalin's Soviet Union (which offered only lukewarm support for the Chinese revolution, and about which Mao harboured reservations), the basic assumption shared by the entire CCP was that the revolution was fundamentally a national endeavour. This perspective was first theorised and articulated within the communist movement in the mid-1920s by Stalin in the wake of the failed socialist revolutions in the West. The strategy of the Chinese revolutionaries was thus almost immediately[2] integrated into the framework of a progressive nationalisation of the international communist movement. This framework marked the political trajectory of the movement throughout the twentieth century, as the working classes grappled with the resilience of capitalism, which proved more enduring than anticipated in the West. In some cases, they even embarked on the mission of fostering national capitalism in countries oppressed or controlled by imperialism.

---

1  Those classes being the proletariat, peasantry, petty bourgeoisie, and national bourgeoisie.
2  Apart from, that is, the very brief phase between the founding of the CCP in 1921 and the defeat of the first Chinese Revolution in 1926–27.

With its inevitable peculiarities, the evolution of 'socialism' in China in its successive phases was a reaffirmation of this dialectic between capital and party-mediated labour and peasant movements. In China, much like in Russia, despite the differences in the nature of their respective revolutionary processes,[3] a national bourgeoisie capable of fulfilling its historical role did not emerge. Consequently, the development of national capitalism had to navigate a circuitous route through the intermediary role played by the working classes and their party organisation. Both Russia's and China's historical experiences shared the common feature of disguising the transition to capitalism as a transition to socialism. This concealment was not a calculated deception orchestrated from above but rather a consequence of what Marx referred to as the "illusion of an epoch".[4] This illusion was inevitable, given the active engagement of a working class unwilling to make heroic sacrifices only to be compelled to toil under the dominion of the 'bosses'. The secret of this 'romantic' period, as Italian communist thinker Amadeo Bordiga put it, during the phase of primitive capitalist accumulation through continuous class mobilisations in the name of socialism lies precisely in this powerful dialectic of social factors.

This was not for contingent reasons but historically determined. First, China's peculiar access in coerced stages to global capitalism, initially as a vulnerable target for plunder due to its perceived 'backwardness' by capitalist standards, was shaped by the "strict control of the world market"[5] and

---

3  In the Russian case, this process began with a successful political proletarian revolution spearheaded by a Marxist party, one element of the attempted 'assault on the heavens' in the heart of Europe between World War I and the early 1920s.
4  In part one of *The German Ideology*, written in 1845. See https://www.marxists.org/arch ive/marx/works/1845/german-ideology/cho1b.htm.
5  As stated by Leon Trotsky in *The Permanent Revolution* (1929), accessed 23 October 2021, https://www.marxists.org/archive/trotsky/1931/tpr/pr-index.htm. However, in his revolutionary impetuosity, Trotsky did not believe in the actual possibility of Marxism being adopted by the anti-colonialist and modernising 'petit-bourgeois democracy', as occurred in the Soviet Union and China for a not-so-short period. He believed at the outset that such a scenario would amount to a mere façade for a fragile bourgeois dictatorship. This perspective led him to underestimate the powerful forces emerging from economic and social formations beyond the confines of Europe, which, with the partial exception of Japan, did *not* follow the conventional trajectory of Western societies from feudalism to capitalism. During the early twentieth century, Russian revolutionary Marxism grappled with the question of the Asiatic mode of production, partly due to its confrontation with populism. However, the concept of combined and unequal development, as first formulated by Trotsky, was more commonly applied in the analysis of global capital configuration, particularly imperialism, rather than in exploring the interactions between different modes of production within a single economic and social framework. Those who did delve into this aspect, such as Georgi Plekhanov, often did so from a Menshevik perspective, which advocated a two-stages revolution. For example, at the Fourth (Unity) Congress of the Russian Social Democratic Workers' Party in

oppression of "a handful of very rich and privileged nations"⁶ over the rest of the world, which remained trapped in various stages of pre-capitalist or incomplete capitalist development. Second, this trajectory was also conditioned by the tenacious resistance offered, for better or worse, by the remnants of the Asiatic mode of production to the nascent forces of capitalism within the country. Unlike Western nations, which transitioned to capitalism through stages that included feudalism,⁷ China faced unique challenges. These challenges included the impediment to widespread dispossession of peasants from their land, as these peasants had achieved full possession of their parcels in the preceding centuries (though not necessarily capitalist or commercial ownership). Additionally, China's strong centralised state had to capacity to organise vital public works, which were essential for an agriculture system reliant on intensive labour rather than significant capital investment.⁸ This historical context contributed to a relative prosperity during the earlier centuries (until the eighteenth), particularly under the rule of first three Qing emperors.

---

Stockholm in 1906, Plekhanov evoked against Lenin the 'despotic' remnants of the Asiatic mode of production in Russia.

6   Vladimir Lenin, *Imperialism and the Split in Socialism* (1916), accessed 23 January 2022, https://www.marxists.org/archive/lenin/works/1916/oct/x01.htm.

7   The feudal system in China has never managed to consolidate itself due to the strength of a powerful central state. This central system, with its emphasis on a service nobility as opposed to a land and sword nobility (see Balasz below), repeatedly reasserted control after prolonged periods of disintegration. This resilience was largely due to the characteristics of a fragmented agricultural system that relied on collective infrastructure projects and could generate surpluses crucial for state centralisation. The attempt to impose a unilinear model of feudalism-capitalism onto China's historical reality, contrary to the Marxian scheme of 1859 that recognised the existence of the Asiatic mode of production (albeit insufficiently developed), can be traced back to the Stalinist political struggles of the 1920s and 1930s. These struggles aimed to justify the CCP's strategy of forming a democratic alliance with the Chinese 'national' bourgeoisie in opposition to 'Trotskyism'. This approach sought, more generally, to revive the Menshevik concept of a multi-stage revolution. This interpretation was later adopted and adapted by the 'populist' Mao, who positioned peasants as the leading class instead of the industrial proletariat, following the defeat of the Chinese revolution in 1926–27. The debate among Marxists on this subject is well documented, with notable contributions from, among others, Gianni Sofri, *Il modo di produzione asiatico* (Turin: Einaudi, 1969), and, with critical tones, Brendan O'Leary, *Asiatic Mode of Production: Oriental Despotism, Historical Materialism, and Indian History* (Oxford: Blackwell, 1989). Per the above citation, see Étienne Balasz, *Chinese Civilization and Bureaucracy: Variations on a Theme*, translated by H. M. Wright (New Haven, CT: Yale University Press, 1964).

8   Amadeo Bordiga, *Lotta di classi e di stati nel mondo dei popoli non bianchi* [Class and state struggles in the world of non-white peoples] (Naples: La Vecchia Talpa, 1972), first published in 1958; Ch'ao Ting Chi, *Key Economic Areas in Chinese History* (London: Routledge, 2019), first published in 1936.

However, as the endogenous limits of that development pattern[9] were met with increasing external colonialist pressures, this relative prosperity suffered catastrophic reversal, ultimately leading to the disintegration of imperial China in the nineteenth century. This period is often described as China's 'century of humiliations', although it did not involve or lead to the direct colonial conquest experienced by India,[10] and it came to an end with the 1949 revolution. It is crucial to note that the early signs of capitalism, such as commercial capital, merchant bourgeoisie, foreign trade, large, landed property, and technical advancements, all prerequisites for the establishment of the capitalist mode of production, *did* exist in late imperial China. Some historians even argue that these elements were present as early as the Song era (960–1279).[11] However, the absence of the necessary contextual conditions for the transition from mere industrious development to full-scale industrial capitalism—such as the extensive separation of peasants from land possession and the projection of sea power for colonial expansion—meant that these elements failed to coalesce into a self-sustaining endogenous transition before the intrusion of imperialism.[12]

In light of these considerations, the sprouts of capitalism that gradually emerged along the coast from the early twentieth century onwards, even in some limited areas with light industries,[13] should be viewed as enclaves of Western foreign capital rather than as manifestations of a burgeoning capitalist

---

9   Limits defined by historian Mark Elvin with the eloquent formula of the 'high-level equilibrium trap'. See Mark Elvin, "Why China Failed to Create an Endogenous Industrial Capitalism", *Theory and Society* 13, no. 3 (1984): 379–91, accessed 24 September 2023, https://www.jstor.org/stable/657457.

10  This is probably because India, unlike China, has never experienced the (relative) continuity of an highly centralised state. Paradoxically, at the time of its 'encounter' with the British in the eighteenth century, India appeared to be more 'modern' than China in certain respects. For example, India had greater autonomy among its commercial bourgeoisie, and this autonomy extended to its engagement in Indian Ocean trade with neighbouring Islamic entities. Additionally, certain regions in India featured a prevalence of private land ownership.

11  See Jacques Gernet, *A History of Chinese Civilization* (Cambridge: Cambridge University Press, 1995), originally published as *Le monde chinois* (Paris: Armand Colin, 1972). See also Balasz, *Chinese Civilization and Bureaucracy*; Akira Hayami, *Japan's Industrious Revolution: Economic and Social Transformations in the Early Modern Period* (Tokyo and London: Springer, 2015).

12  Kenneth Pomeranz, *The Great Divergence: China, Europe, and the Making of the Modern World Economy* (Princeton, NJ: Princeton University Press, 2000).

13  With the exception of the north-eastern regions occupied by Japan in the 1930s, where an original accumulation based on heavy industry was able to take hold precisely because of Japanese imperialist aims.

domestic market. Moreover, the large agrarian estates, which were closely connected to usurers and merchant capital associated with a comprador urban bourgeoisie, represented neither the remnants of an alleged feudal system nor the potential for a capitalist gentry. Instead, they were the result of the dissolution of central authority and the simultaneous increase in the monetisation of economic relations induced by foreign capital. These estates operated on the basis of land rent but lacked a capitalist mode of production, embodying a hybrid form of transition reminiscent of the Irish situation described by Marx in his notes for volume 3 of *Capital* regarding land rent.

To summarise, given these underlying conditions and in the absence of an ongoing anti-capitalist revolutionary process on a global scale—a continuous revolution with no rupture between the goal of achieving democratic reforms and the goal of socialism (as envisaged by Lenin in the context of a 'first imperialist war' (i.e. World War I) in which a 'backward' Russia would lean towards proletarian revolution in the West)—it became clear that such an uninterrupted revolution was unattainable in China from the beginning. This was the case regardless of the specific strategy adopted by the CCP under Mao, which differed significantly from Lenin's approach. Nonetheless, the 'second imperialist war' (World War II) did favour the Chinese revolutionary trajectory, just as it paved the way for the subsequent waves of anti-colonial struggles that took off shortly after. The 'Jacobin' party that seized power in China in 1949 had no choice but to grapple with the daunting task of laying the foundations for a distinctive form of national capitalist development through a process of primitive 'socialist' accumulation (socialist in the programmatic declarations of the time, but capitalist in the economic and social realities). This path was to be long and bumpy, with China facing international isolation that was only partially mitigated by selective Soviet assistance. The nation was burdened by dire social and economic conditions on all fronts and was under constant threat of US imperialist aggression, which materialised with the outbreak of the Korean War in the early 1950s. In China, socialism became synonymous with 'self-reliance' (*zili gensheng*)—all the more so after the Sino-Soviet split in the late 1950s—driven by the pursuit of state-led modernisation. Thus, the transition to a national-popular form of capitalism could commence.[14] But the

---

14   Chuang, a collective of communist thinkers, regards the People's Republic of China as a state developmentalist regime that does not neatly fit into any established mode of production, whether socialist or capitalist. As such, it dates the transition to capitalism to the end of the 1970s, coinciding with the advent of the Dengist era. This viewpoint not only challenges the conventional notion of a necessary phase of capitalist primitive accumulation but also suggests that the transition to capitalism can be attributed

crucial question was where to find the necessary material resources and social forces for the required process of primitive accumulation.

### 1.2    Overcoming Fragmentation

Beginning from a position of severe underdevelopment and fragmentation, in a nation ravaged by Japanese occupation and reduced to starvation, the Chinese revolution inevitably proceeded by implementing a radical redistribution of land to the 300 million impoverished peasants, constituting roughly 60–70% of the total population. This redistribution, especially prominent in the northern regions of the country where the revolutionary fervour had originated after 1945, resulted in the formal collective ownership of land by rural villages (while urban territories were nationalised). However, in reality, this led to an even greater fragmentation of cultivated land, surpassing the already high levels of parcel possession that had existed before. The slogan 'Land to the People' took on immense political significance as an expression of peasant mobilisation. From an economic standpoint, the emergence of extremely small family units rendered the task of resources consolidation nearly impossible. Concentrating resources was crucial not only for alleviating hunger but also for generating the surplus necessary to fuel industrialisation in the long term. The majority of agricultural produce, essential in defining effective property relations beyond the legal aspects,[15] was limited in quality and primarily allocated for self-consumption by peasants. Meanwhile, the portion channelled to the state at artificially low food prices served to sustain cities and provide for the modest needs of the urban working class. Given these conditions, effective 'socialist planning' or the socialisation of production was a distant dream, existing only on the formal level of eliminating individual private property. In the countryside, the primary form of cooperation was found in mutual aid groups established for essential collective tasks. In the cities, where a handful of factories still existed, the party could only manage to reorganise production with support from middle-class members, while laying the foundation for industrialisation was only possible with the aid of the Soviet Union.

---

to specific political decisions rather than inevitable historical forces. See "Sorghum & Steel: The Chinese Developmental Regime and the Forging of China", *Chuang* 1 (2016), accessed 25 September 2023, https://chuangcn.org/journal/one/sorghum-and-steel/; "Red Dust: The Transition to Capitalism in China", *Chuang* 2 (2019), accessed 25 September 2023, https://chuangcn.org/journal/two/red-dust/.

15    See Amadeo Bordiga, *Proprietà e capitale 1948–52* [Ownership and capital 1948–52] (Milan: Iskra, 1980).

Starting in the mid-1950s, the challenges of economic accumulation and industrialisation began to grow increasingly urgent, particularly in light of the significant pressure exerted by US imperialism, which reached a critical point with the Korean War (1950–53). This period saw a concerted effort from the authorities to drive specific changes in agricultural practices. Initially, the government promoted so-called collectivisation between 1953 and 1958. In reality, this involved encouraging the formation of agricultural cooperatives,[16] while still allowing individual families to maintain small plots of land for their use. Subsequently, in 1958, a more significant shift occurred with the establishment of communes. These communes represented a more extensive administrative grouping of cooperatives that extended beyond the village level. This move aimed to collectivise not only agricultural work but also other economic activities through production brigades, the basic accounting and farming units in the new 'people's commune' system. While this consolidated labour resources, it had the unintended consequence of impacting regional specialisation in the production of crops. Moreover, the basic unresolved issue remained: the limited role machinery played in the nascent national agricultural industry.

Against this backdrop, it was only a matter of time before the shortcomings of Maoist voluntarism became glaringly apparent, a fact that the party leadership had to confront in the wake of the devastating famine crisis of the early 1960s. In reality, rural areas were unable to generate a substantial surplus that would enable a real leap forward without risking politically destabilising consequences, such as an uncontrolled migration of peasants to urban centres.[17] Likewise, industry was unable to supply the countryside with the necessary capital goods, hindering any meaningful enhancement in productivity beyond the contributions of human labour.

All this should not, however, detract from the immense efforts as well as the peculiarities of the original Chinese style of economic accumulation. A vast majority of rural producers were able to retain their land without facing expropriation. The transfer of resources to the industrial sector during the initial phase was made possible due to the surplus generated by leveraging the legacy

---

16  In reviewing Karl Kautsky's *Die Agrarfrage*, Lenin issued the following warning: "The small farmers' associations are a link in economic progress; but they express a *transition to capitalism (Fortschritt zum Kapitalismus) and not toward collectivism*, as is often thought and asserted." See Vladimir Lenin, "Capitalism in Agriculture" (1899), reproduced at https://www.marxists.org/archive/lenin/works/1899/agriculture/index.htm, original emphasis.

17  Hence, as we shall see, the establishment of the *hukou* in 1958 to control the movement of the population.

of the pre-capitalist collectivist traditions. These traditions were revitalised through continuous political mobilisation of the peasant population, coupled with a judicious state policy of controlled pricing that favoured the urban centres.[18] As we delve further into the transition to the subsequent phase of industrialisation, starting with the Dengist reforms, it becomes evident that what occurred can be aptly described as a *semi-proletarianisation* of the peasantry.

The turbulent phase that followed the failure of the Mao-led Great Leap Forward (1958–62) and the aforementioned Great Chinese Famine (1959–61) witnessed, on the one hand, the restoration of a minimally sustainable equilibrium in the countryside, marked by the attainment of food self-sufficiency. This came at the cost of relinquishing some of the more collective forms of labour. Nevertheless, it did yield dividends in terms of infrastructure development and the maintenance of agricultural lands. On the other hand, this period saw the eruption of a furious political battle among different factions within the CCP. The Maoist faction successfully mobilised the youth in what became known as the Cultural Revolution, launched in 1966. This highly charged phase of political mobilisation, though predominantly centred in urban areas, with all the barely readable contradictions inherent to a post–Long '68 China, brought to the surface a fundamental question that could no longer be avoided. Could China, under the prevailing circumstances—heightened by the Maoist aspiration to encircle the city (i.e., imperialism) from the countryside (i.e., the Third World's anti-imperialist struggle) and relying solely on its own forces in fighting both US imperialism and Soviet revisionism—thrive without access to the resources of the global market, resources deemed essential for advancing 'socialist construction'? In tandem with these political dynamics, the significance of China's youth masses came to the forefront. Their quest for new directions and pursuit of individual recognition, politicised and channelled towards rural areas during the Cultural Revolution, played a pivotal role in garnering support for the shift towards economic de-collectivisation orchestrated by the post-Maoist party leadership.[19]

### 1.3 *From Sino-American Rapprochement to 'Reform and Opening Up'*
So, how could China break into the global market? As the Cultural Revolution came to an end in the early 1970s, a critical issue, officially termed the 'four

---

18  But by keeping workers' wages low, albeit with social guarantees, both to contain the gap between rural and urban classes and to redirect resources towards capital accumulation in industry.

19  Mao's aim was to encourage students to develop their talents in a policy of 'educating' the rural population, another classic populist trait.

modernisations' (agriculture, industry, science, and defence), became impossible for the CCP leadership to ignore. This posed a dilemma, given the international circumstances of the time: should China confront or compromise with what had long been considered its 'main enemy', US imperialism? Meanwhile, the United States was itself grappling with the challenge of devising an exit strategy from the quagmire in Vietnam. The role of the CCP as the linchpin of state unity and the laboratory for defining the national interest during different phases of the transition, albeit expressed in a language still steeped in revolutionary nationalism, becomes particularly prominent in this context. In the 1970s, the CCP explored two strategies to address China's precarious position, with international isolation having imposed unbearable costs in terms of both security and the difficulties arising from the aftermath of the Cultural Revolution.

1. In 1972 there was a diplomatic rapprochement with Washington, orchestrated under Mao's leadership. This move was part of an anti-Russian strategy and marked a significant shift in China's foreign policy.
2. Following Mao's era, the CCP initiated the economic policy of 'reform and opening up'. This policy aimed to extricate China from its internal turmoil, which had been exacerbated by the Cultural Revolution, and to adapt to the changing global economic landscape in the post-Mao era.

From a geopolitical perspective,[20] during the ongoing Vietnam War, the East Asian region was marked by the deteriorating relationship between Beijing and Moscow, reaching its climax with military border clashes in the summer of 1969. Simultaneously, the Nixon administration in the United States recognised the necessity of a shift in its Grand Strategy. The strategic manoeuvre executed by the Nixon-Kissinger duo was to utilise the 'China card' against Moscow as a means to extricate themselves from the complexities of the Vietnam conflict. As such, Washington was gearing up to relinquish its policy of containing *both* Russia and China in favour of a more measured approach, acknowledging the overextension of its commitments in East Asia. Beijing, for its part, was able to offer security assurances and foreign policy independence, honed during a decade of self-reliance on its own resources. This gave China the capacity for autonomous diplomatic actions, enabled by its unique position as a 'third party' within the strategic triangle involving the United States and the Soviet Union. Several factors contributed to China's geopolitical positioning: its central geographical location in Asia, the developmental potential of its large and

---

20   Raffaele Sciortino, *Un passaggio oltre il bipolarismo. Il rapprochement sino-americano 1969–1972* (Bologna: I libri di Emil, 2012).

populous nation, a modest yet functional nuclear arsenal since 1964, a historical legacy as a former great power eager to overcome the 'century of humiliations', and, not least, the unspent goodwill resulting from its revolutionary contributions that had given way to the anti-colonial wave across the Third World. The diplomatic acumen of the pragmatic Zhou Enlai did the rest.

Following the significant political realignment that occurred after Mao's death, characterised by this 'tacit alliance' with Washington, the inevitable challenge arose of gradually dismantling Maoism, including its economic and administrative facets.[21] However, the ideological façade of Maoism had to remain intact to uphold the legitimacy of the party's role as an essential institution for national unity and state cohesion. Hence, the political interactions between Washington and Beijing, initially rooted in geopolitics as an anti-USRR strategy, assumed a geo-economic dimension following the decisions made at the Third Plenum of the CCP in December 1978. This marked the strengthening of the Dengist agenda for internal reforms, aimed at decentralising and de-collectivising economic structures, accompanied by a cautious opening up to the global market.

Certainly, it is essential to understand that the progression of Dengist reforms was not a straightforward, top-down, linear trajectory. On the contrary, it was marked by its share of 'mistakes', moments of retrenchment, and internal party disputes. Moreover, one must consider the historical dialectic between central authority and local administrations, where the latter often found motivation to initiate economic 'experiments'. Successful experiments had the potential to be scaled up and adopted more broadly.[22] The process exploited the inherent strengths of the Chinese civil service, including its flexibility, pragmatism, and informality, often transcending ideological dogmas of the time. This complex blend, operating on the foundation of early capital accumulation, played a pivotal role in facilitating the necessary leap forward.

---

21   In 1971 Mao himself orchestrated the abrupt downfall of his once-presumed successor, Lin Biao, by staging a failed coup attempt. Following Mao's death in 1976, the remaining Maoist faction, now ominously referred to as the 'Gang of Four', was swiftly eliminated. Remarkably, these decisive measures encountered minimal opposition within the party's grassroots ranks. This attested to the fact that even the most dramatic shifts in leadership were primarily driven by the imperatives of advancing productive forces and safeguarding the nation—a set of principles that had already become deeply engrained during the 'heroic' phase of China's history. See Alexander F. Day, *The Peasant in Postsocialist China: History, Politics and Capitalism* (Cambridge: Cambridge University Press, 2013).

22   Isabella M. Weber, *How China Escaped Shock Therapy: The Market Reform Debate* (Milton Park, Routledge, 2021).

The primary arenas for these reforms were undoubtedly agriculture and industry. Initial reforms proceeded cautiously but left a profound impact on the social and economic landscape, along with a reconfiguration of the labour force. At the outset of these reforms, approximately 70% of the population still resided in rural areas. While stringent budget policies and tight credit controls were implemented to prevent destabilisation, especially following the gradual liberalisation of prices, there were brief moments when the situation seemed to teeter on the edge, notably in the late 1980s.

Within the framework of an economic reform model that did not correspondingly extend to political reforms, a pivotal shift occurred with the introduction of the household responsibility system in 1978, later formalised in 1982. This sanctioned the decentralisation of agricultural production, where family households were allocated cultivable plots exclusively for their use. These plots were distributed fairly evenly on a village scale, functioning as fiscally responsible economic management units. The early 1980s witnessed a remarkable surge of small-scale private activities in rural areas. This newfound dynamism was stimulated by a price reform that favoured rural regions, effectively reversing decades of price differentials that had previously favoured urban centres. It was a brief but significant golden age for petty commodity producers. Simultaneously, a phenomenon known as village and township enterprises began sprouting up rapidly, like mushrooms after rain. These were industrial plants located in rural areas, primarily engaged in sectors complementary to the resurgent agricultural and construction activities that were not adequately served by large state-owned industries. Initially owned and operated by local village administrations, these enterprises inherited the legacy of the Mao-era communes, which had aimed to integrate agricultural and industrial activities at the decentralised level. Up until the mid-1990s, these enterprises played a crucial role in facilitating the transition of a portion of the agricultural workforce, rendered 'surplus' due to the increasing commercialisation, from farming while enabling them to retain their ties to the countryside and land use rights. This, in turn, helped prevent an uncontrolled rural exodus before the burgeoning urban export industry took flight.[23] In fact, employment in this sector expanded from around 30 million initially to approximately 130 million by the mid-1990s, contributing to 25% of gross domestic product (GDP). However, starting from that point, the growth of this sector began to slow down

---

23   Hao Qi and Li Zhongjin, "Giovanni Arrighi in Beijing: Rethinking the Transformation of the Labor Supply in Rural China During the Reform Era" (working paper no. 455, Political Economy Research Institute, University of Massachusetts, Amherst, February 2018), https://doi.org/10.7275/27274276.

substantially, nearly stagnating. This was primarily due to intensified competition from urban and coastal companies in the domestic market, coupled with the impact of the Asian financial crisis of 1998.[24]

In the industrial sector, economic restructuring proceeded further and at a rapid pace during the 1980s and 1990s. It may suffice here to recall the more general aspects of the transformation, which are relatively well documented. They include:
- a shift towards favouring light industry over the previous emphasis on planned state-owned heavy industries;
- the emergence of a private industrial sector populated by small and medium-sized enterprises;
- the establishment of special economic zones along the coastal regions, offering highly favourable conditions to attract foreign investments deemed vital for technological modernisation;
- notable imports of machinery, equipment, and technology from abroad, although initially not fully balanced by exports, resulting in an exacerbated balance of payments deficit and increased external debt, reaching up to 10% of GDP by 1988;
- a consequent shift towards an export-oriented industry, with foreign trade accounting for a third and more of GDP; and
- a gradual transition to budget autonomy for both private and state-owned enterprises, the latter of which, in the process restructuring and consolidation, retained control over heavy sectors crucial for domestic accumulation.

It is evident that the combination of these processes significantly impacted the composition of the working class, both in terms of quantity and quality, as we will explore further. Concurrently, the de-collectivisation of agriculture laid the foundations for an expanding surplus of labour power in rural areas, setting in motion the internal migration that would fuel the growth of the industrial sector.

In overall terms, 'socialism with Chinese characteristics' underwent a transformation that opened up the nation to the global market and facilitated an extraordinary accumulation of capital that would have otherwise been unattainable. But China still had to pay a price for this transformation.

---

24  Wei Zou, "La metamorphose des enterprises rurales", *Perspectives chinois* 79 (September–October 2003): 18–31, accessed 25 September 2023, https://www.persee.fr/doc/perch_1 021-9013_2003_num_79_1_3142.

## 1.4 Chain Gang

The insertion of a transitional Chinese capitalism into the world market unfolded under conditions that were, to a large extent, not of its own choosing. The leap was necessitated by the looming threat of irreversible decline, akin to the economic and social collapses witnessed in the 'real socialism' countries of Eastern Europe. However, this insertion, spanning the first three decades and continuing until the outbreak of the global crisis in 2008, came with a significant caveat: China would assume a subordinate role within the intricate framework of a globalisation that meanwhile allowed the imperialist West to extricate itself from the crisis of the 1970s and enabled Washington to reconfigure and fortify its global hegemony, as previously discussed.[25]

The period of globalisation that followed, far from confined to a 'gone mad' financial sector, hinged on the interplay between countries with trade surpluses, notably China, the world's primary manufacturing hub, and the United States, whose role evolved into that of closing the circle of international liquidity flows. This arrangement led to an immense centralisation of global credit, coexisting with the internationalisation of industrial production, albeit within the destabilising intertwinement of investment credit, currency systems, and what Marx called 'fictitious capital'.[26] While China rapidly transformed itself into the world's factory, the United States experienced a transformation characterised by the downsizing of entire industrial sectors in favour of services, finance, and high-tech industries, causing a significant disruption to the composition of the Fordist working class.[27]

In return, China had to accept, and continues partly to do so, the international specialisation of its economy. It has been compelled to concentrate on exporting final goods with medium to low technological content, which its factories assemble using imported machinery and components from other nations. Notably, Japan and Germany have played pivotal roles in providing machinery, while the newly industrialised countries in East Asia have been vital sources of components. This has allowed China to navigate the path of development, albeit one marked by technological limitations and extensive growth restraints. Furthermore, China has had to grapple with significant and

---

25 Walden Bello and John Feffer, "Chain-Gang Economics", *Foreign Policy in Focus*, 30 October 2006, accessed 25 September 2023, https://fpif.org/chain-gang_economics/.
26 That is, any form of investment that is based upon the expectation of future returns. For example, bonds, stocks, derivatives, collateralised debt obligations, etc.
27 Bennett Harrison and Barry Bluestone, *The Deindustrialization of America: Plant Closings, Community Abandonment, and the Dismantling of Basic Industry* (New York: Basic Books, 1984).

potentially socially perilous imbalances, including the stark dualism between the industrial coastal regions and less developed inland areas, as well as the urban–rural divide. The latter has manifested though an 'excess' labour force in rural areas, temporarily managed, and, above all, a qualitative economic dependence on exports.

It is crucial to emphasise that this trajectory does not represent a departure from a supposed socialist system but rather the inevitable price China has had to pay to Western imperialism in order to lay the foundation for a transition to a higher stage of economic development. As China fully integrated into the global capitalist system, the class struggle in both the countryside and the factories assumed global significance too.

## 2  The Agrarian Question

The significance of the Chinese agrarian question extends far beyond the borders of the country and carries substantial implications for both capitalist development and class struggle in a nation that holds nearly 20% of the world's population while having access to only 10% of the world's arable land, which makes up just around 15% of the nation's total land area. This issue has global relevance and significance, as peasants are far from being inconsequential or transitional figures, especially in light of the 'new international division of labour' that has emerged since the 1970s. This division has witnessed, on the one hand, the process of dependent industrialisation in various parts of the former Third World and, on the other, a reconfiguration of the relationship between small-scale and large-scale agricultural production within new global chains.[28]

### 2.1  *Land and Revolution*

We have seen how the *nongmin*,[29] the peasant of the small family plot only partially integrated into the commodity economy, played a central role in driving the Chinese revolution. Their immense efforts served as the bedrock upon

---

28   Christian Berndt, "Uneven Development, Commodity Chains and the Agrarian Question", *Progress in Human Geography* (2018): 1–14, accessed 25 September 2023, https://journals.sagepub.com/pb-assets/cmscontent/PHG/Uneven_development-1520613548130.pdf; Henry Veltmeyer and Raúl Delgado Wise, "The Agrarian Question Today", in *Critical Development Studies: An Introduction* (Rugby, UK: Practical Action, 2018), 67–93.

29   The 'peasant' as distinct from the 'farmer' (*nongchangzhu*), the latter being a product and vector of capitalism's penetration into agriculture.

which Chinese industrialisation was built, evolving through a distinctive form of primitive accumulation. It is worth noting that this process did not involve the wholesale expropriation of rural labourers from the land, as seen the classic narrative of the genesis of European capitalism (which, it should be noted, also had exceptions). Moreover, Marx already warned that,

> the form of landed property with which the incipient capitalist mode of production is confronted does not suit it. It first creates for itself the form required by subordinating agriculture to capital. It thus transforms feudal landed property, clan property, small peasant property in mark communes—no matter how divergent their juristic forms may be—into the economic form corresponding to the requirements of this mode of production.[30]

This means that—contrary to what the Russian populists thought—no agrarian system inherently stands as an insurmountable barrier to the emergence of capitalism. Similarly, the development of capitalism within agriculture is a complex process, far less linear than industrial capitalism, which tends towards concentration and the dominance of big firms. Several factors contribute to this complexity. In the countryside, there are dense and enduring layers of premodern social relations that resemble 'geological stratifications'. Moreover, the technical and economic advantages of large-scale production do not always extend seamlessly to agriculture, as they do in industry, and where they do, it tends to be only within certain limits and under conditions that are not always present. Peasants and small farmers often engage in overwork and maintain low consumption levels, subjecting themselves to self-exploitation. The availability of arable land is often limited. The interests of rural areas tend to be subordinated to those of urban centres. There is frequently a reluctance to invest capital in land over the long term. Moreover, capital has a tendency to exploit or squander natural resources, such as land, without consideration for long-term sustainability. These factors collectively contribute to the persistence of small-scale agrarian production within the capitalist mode of production.[31]

The situation in China was further complicated by a unique set of circumstances. In the first two decades following the revolution, the country was

---

30  Karl Marx, *Capital*, Vol 3: *The Process of Capitalist Production as a Whole* (1894), pt. 6, chap. 37, reproduced at https://www.marxists.org/archive/marx/works/1894-c3/ch37.htm.

31  Amadeo Bordiga, *Mai la merce sfamerà l'uomo, 1953–4* [Never will the commodity feed man, 1953–4] (Milan: Iskra, 1974).

largely isolated from the global market. Additionally, there was a lack of capital available for investment in rural areas. Moreover, the political necessity for the CCP was to maintain its relationship with the peasant masses, which added another layer of complexity. Starting from a state of extreme fragmentation, the revolution in China, in the absence of international revolutionary developments in more advanced nations, had to be rooted in the task of modernising the country's socio-economic foundations at the grassroots level. Even the nationalisation of land, which was crucial in preventing the emergence and consolidation of absolute rent, could not, by itself, address the fundamental challenge of initiating the process of accumulation. This is because, as Lenin pointed out:

> Nationalisation ... means converting the land into the property of the state, and such a conversion does not in the least affect private farming on the land.[32]

It goes without saying that in the Chinese context, these were not even conventional 'farms' integrated into the domestic market circuit due to the disruptions caused by the Japanese occupation and the civil war.

### 2.2   *Minimum Agrarian Capitalism*

Against this backdrop, while the initial Maoist phase fell short of overcoming agrarian fragmentation, it virtually managed to secure self-sufficiency in food production under exceptionally challenging circumstances. This was achieved despite internal struggles within the party and involved the revitalisation of collective agrarian practices and the establishment of the foundations for market exchange between rural and urban areas. This effort laid the groundwork for a domestic market, albeit one based on 'administered' prices. As discussed in the previous chapter, these developments paved the way for the subsequent Dengist reforms. In rural areas, progress towards agrarian capitalism was made by promoting commodification and facilitating exchanges between

---

32  Vladimir Lenin, "The Agrarian Question in Russia at the Close of the 19th Century" (1908), reproduced at https://www.marxists.org/archive/lenin/works/1908/agrquest/vii.htm. The sentence is preceded by an assertion: "There is nothing more erroneous than the opinion that the nationalisation of the land has anything in common with socialism, or even with equalised land tenure. Socialism, as we know, means the abolition of commodity economy. ... So long as exchange re mains [sic], it is ridiculous to talk of socialism." This, however, in no way detracts from the nationalisation of land as the most advanced democratic reform.

small family farmholders under land use contracts. Given the prevailing conditions, this transition from subsistence agriculture to a more market-oriented economy was almost an obligatory step. Simultaneously, the industrial sector pushed for expanded accumulation by taking advantage of increased access to the global market and the need for additional labour power. In essence, this initiated a gradual transformation of Chinese agriculture *into* a capitalist system, albeit in less concentrated forms. It also marked the transition of the industrial sector *within* capitalism. The process unfolded gradually, with many ambiguities, as key indicators of agrarian capitalism remained limited for some time (some to this day). These indicators encompassed commodity exchange of agricultural products, crop specialisation, the presence of wage earners, the use of machinery, productivity gains, the market as the primary or exclusive source of input and income, and the formation and differentiation between rent and profit. Most significantly, the separation of peasants from the land remained largely only sketched out.

Nonetheless, this initial phase of rural reforms, lasting until the mid-1980s, constituted a golden era for peasants. Their incomes rose sharply as agricultural products become more and more commodified. It is no coincidence that the CCP, having in this way recovered a connection with the peasant class that had eroded in the 1960s, managed to weather the 1989 crisis—the Tiananmen Square protests, to which the rural populace remained largely indifferent. The CCP, functioning as a quasi-'peasant party', focused on preserving the urban–rural balance.[33] However, this came at a significant cost. Over time, agricultural productivity growth began to wane, even though initial increases in production and peasant incomes were robust. In the short term, an abrupt surge in agricultural prices occurred, initially justified by the need to set minimum price levels but ultimately posing a grave risk due to the onset of a broader inflationary trend in the late 1980s. These inevitable negative consequences became particularly pronounced in the 1990s. Agricultural output began to decline, as petty commodity production reached its limits despite small-scale mechanisation. Underemployment became apparent within the agricultural labour force, coinciding with the stagnation or decline of village and township enterprises. This period also witnesses a surge in internal migration to urban areas and coastal regions. The collective services of the prior phase largely

---

33  "Gleaning the Welfare Fields: Rural Struggles in China since 1959", *Chuang* 1 (2016), accessed 25 September 2023, https://chuangcn.org/journal/one/gleaning-the-welfare-fields/.

disappeared,[34] while the balance of prices and incomes shifted back in favour of the cities. Taxation burdens returned, with rural areas shouldering up to four times the tax load borne by urban areas. Finally, incentives for product marketing led to a decline in cereal cultivation, which was less profitable but essential for food self-sufficiency and price stability.[35]

The countryside has undeniably become an essential reservoir to meet the ever-growing demand for industrial labour power, characterised by very low reproductive costs. However, the dark side of these reforms has become increasingly apparent, and since the 1990s, it has even manifested in brutal forms. An extensive body of literature and filmography[36] has emerged documenting and denunciating[37] the abuses suffered by peasants and the massive migration to urban areas. Two key factors significantly impacted the conditions of peasants during this period. First, the negative consequences of the 1994 national taxation reform cannot be understated. This reform dramatically shifted the burden of public expenditures onto local authorities, creating a breeding ground for predatory taxation by local governments targeting the rural population. Coupled with declining rural incomes and the privatisation of village and township enterprises, this situation led to a significant upsurge in internal migration to regions focused on building up export sectors. The second factor contributing to social polarisation was the expropriation of agricultural land necessary for the rampant urbanisation and the emergence of an urban housing market.[38] Corruption and speculation were the root causes of peasant discontent, leading to resentment and protests. Throughout the 1990s, rural struggles primarily revolved around local-scale corruption and

---

34   Barry Naughton, *The Chinese Economy: Transitions and Growth* (Cambridge, MA; London: MIT Press, 2007), chap. 11.
35   Yuxuan Li, Weifeng Zhang, Lin Ma, Liang Wu, Jianbo Shen, William J. Davies, Oene Oenema, Fusuo Zhang, Zhengxia Dou, "An Analysis of China's Grain Production: Looking Back and Looking Forward", *Food and Energy Security* 3, no. 1 (2014): 19–32, https://doi.org /10.1002/fes3.41; Zhun Xu, Wei Zhang, and Minqi Li, "China's Grain Production", *Monthly Review* 66, no. 1 (1 May 2014), accessed 25 September 2023, https://monthlyreview.org /2014/05/01/chinas-grain-production/.
36   The so-called 'sixth generation' of Chinese filmmakers.
37   Chen Guidi and Wu Chutao, *Will the Boat Sink the Water? The Life of China's Peasants* (New York: PublicAffairs, 2003).
38   Isabela Nogueira, João Victor Guimarães, and João Pedro Braga, "Inequalities and Capital Accumulation in China", *Brazilian Journal of Political Economy*, 39, no. 3 (2019): 449–69, https://doi.org/10.1590/0101-35172019-2929; Zhang Yulin, "Land Grabs in Contemporary China", *Chuang* blog, 6 January 2015, accessed 25 September 2023, https://chuangcn.org /2015/01/land-grabs-in-contemporary-china/, reposted from *Nao* journal, translated by Pancho Sanchez (originally published in Chinese in 2014).

the imposition of taxes well above the legal limit of 5% of peasant income. Additionally, these mobilisations often involved negotiations over land prices with local authorities. Some of these movements, characterised by an ideology rooted in popular religiosity and references to Maoism, even took on a violent character.[39] In response to these challenges, the central government took action. Initially, it launched anti-corruption campaigns within the CCP and allowed for the election of village committees. Subsequently, it passed a law permitting the refusal of compensation for land expropriations conducted through certificates of uncertain value. It is worth noting that China's long-standing history of differentiated responsibilities between local officials and the central government also played a role in shaping these events.

In essence, the rural reforms and their repercussions highlighted the extensive scope of the ongoing restructuring process while revealing its social and economic limitations. These limitations included the social backlash against aggressive land expropriations, only partial dispossession of peasants from their land, and the commodification of a still relatively small portion of agricultural output.

### 2.3 *The Three Rights to Land*

Consequently, the 2000s witnessed a concerted effort by the central government to rectify the most glaring and perilous 'distortions' stemming from post-reform agricultural development. These corrective measures aimed to restore a modicum of rural welfare, which been significantly eroded during the period of de-collectivisation, and to provide a more precise definition of land rights to stimulate agricultural productivity and promote the marketisation of agricultural products.

As part of President Hu Jintao's pursuit of the 'harmonious society' (*hexie shehui*) strategy, the Eleventh Five-Year Plan initiated the construction of a 'New Socialist Country'. This initiative aimed to address the imbalances that had emerged rural and urban areas through the establishment of a comprehensive social security system encompassing pensions, healthcare, and welfare programmes.[40] Another crucial policy measure was the complete abolition

---

39  Bruno Astarian, *Luttes de classes dans la Chine des réformes (1978–2009)* (La Bussière: Acratie, 2009); *Chuang*, "Gleaning"; Kathy Le Mons Walker, "'Gangster Capitalism' and Peasant Protest: The Last Twenty Years", *Journal of Peasant Studies* 33, no. 1 (2006): 1–33, https://doi.org/10.1080/03066150600624413.

40  Jude Howell and Jane Duckett, "Reassessing the Hu-Wen Era: A Golden Age or Lost Decade for Social Policy in China?", *China Quarterly* 237 (2019): 1–14, https://doi.org/10.1017/S0305741018001200.

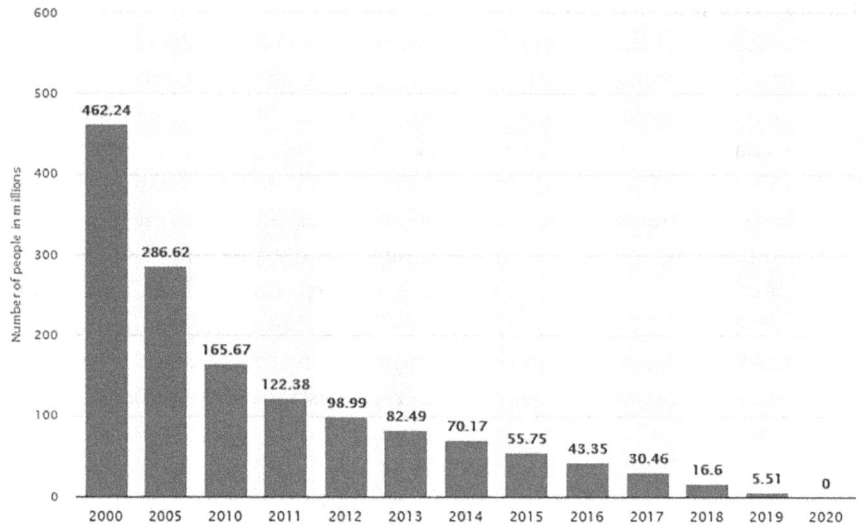

FIGURE 3.1　Rural population in China in poverty (2000–2020)
REPRODUCED FROM STATISTA, & SEPTEMBER 2023, ACCESSED 13 SEPTEMBER 2023, HTTPS://WWW.STATISTA.COM/STATISTICS/866620/NUMBER-OF-RURAL-RESIDENTS-LIVING-IN-POVERTY-IN-CHINA/. DATA FROM CHINA STATISTICAL YEARBOOK 2020, CHAPTER 6.35.

of land taxation, carried out between 2004 and 2006. This reform was also a response to the peasant mobilisations of the previous decade. Collectively, these measures, implemented within the framework of granting lasting land rights to peasants, resulted in progressively significant achievements in the fight against absolute poverty, a battle that was ultimately fully won under the leadership of Xi Jinping (see Figure 3.1).[41]

The road towards addressing land rights issues has been bumpier, marked by heated internal party debates over the highly sensitive matter of land ownership. Despite the hopes of the 'liberal' faction and of Western powers, a full-scale land privatisation policy was never fully realised, not even when it appeared imminent during the Seventeenth CCP Congress in 2008.[42] Concerns over the almost certain social upheaval that would follow, particularly the

---

41  Mylène Gaulard, *Karl Marx à Pékin : Les racines de la crise en Chine capitaliste*, Paris: Demopolis, 2014, 52ff.
42  Angela Pascucci, *Potere e società in Cina. Storie di resistenza nella grande trasformazione* [Power and society in China: Stories of resistance in the Great Transformation] (Rome: Il Manifesto, 2013).

creation of a landless peasant population with an uncontrolled migration to urban areas (a seemingly greater worry than keeping the reproduction costs of this labour force down), outweighed the desire to expedite the formation of farms capable of competing in the market.

Thus, the decision was made to initially extend the validity of land use rights granted by the reform. These rights, initially set at fifteen years in 1984, were extended to thirty years in 2003 and eventually to indefinite terms in 2016. Starting in 2003, the strategy shifted towards providing legal certainty for land rights to incentivise rural investment and establish a market for land use rights without formally undermining village collective ownership. Various forms of transfer of so-called contractual rights were introduced, ranging from sale to rent to subletting. (In practice, it involved land usufruct with complete control over the product, as defined by the Property Law of 2007.) Subsequently, at the Eighteenth Congress of the CCP in 2013, a third system of 'management rights', distinct from use rights, was introduced. This allowed for economic transactions on land rights that could be transferred to outsiders, within a regulated market established in 2016. Various profit-sharing arrangements were established, involving small family farms, larger agribusinesses, and cooperatives. In this way, a complex system was created, known as the 'three land rights' (sanquan fenli),[43] with the aim of stimulating larger-scale agriculture by consolidating land through more concentrated and profitable economic units. This approach aimed to strike a balance between stimulating larger-scale agriculture and retaining the rights of a still significant peasantry, all while avoiding radical disruptions to the right to land. It represented a challenging and intricate process, but one that was necessary given the economic, political, and social complexities of a rapidly transforming nation.

## 2.4 *Which Agrarian Capitalism Today?*

As of today, the population actually residing in the countryside amounts to about 550 million, which accounts for 40% of the total population. However, it is worth noting that the officially registered population under the *hukou* system (on which, see sec. 3.2.6) reached about 780 million in 2019, indicating the presence of at least 230 million floating labourers, commonly referred to as rural migrants (*nongmingong*).[44] In recent years, there has been a significant

---

43 Chao Zhou, Yunjian Liang, and Anthony Fuller, "Tracing Agricultural Land Transfer in China: Some Legal and Policy Issues", *Land* 10 (2021): 1–16, https://doi.org/10.3390/land10010058.

44 Qian Forrest Zhang and Zhanping Hu, "Rural China under the COVID-19 Pandemic: Differentiated Impacts, Rural–Urban Inequality and Agro-industrialization", *Journal of Agrarian Change* 21, no. 3 (2021): 591–603, https://doi.org/10.1111/joac.12425.

decrease in the number of official residents, dropping from 900 million in 2006 to 820 million in 2015. This shift is even more pronounced in the agricultural labour force, which has dwindled to less than 25% of the total population, amounting to about 200 million individuals.[45] In the mid-2010s, it was still slightly under half of the population, but it exceeded 50% in the mid-1990s and over 70% in the early 1980s.

These general figures reflect the profound economic transformation that has occurred in China's rural areas. This transformation is characterised by the increasing commodification of both agricultural output and inputs, including machinery, fertilisers, and pesticides, with the aim of boosting productivity and competitiveness. Chinese farmers have shifted their focus to higher-value crops such as fruits and vegetables. However, the extreme fragmentation of rural land holdings, with an average of about half a hectare per household, remains a persistent challenge.[46] Most farms—though estimates vary among experts—are still household responsibility units where family members work independently and occasionally hire wage labour. These farmers sell a portion of their produce[47] and supplement their income with minimum rural welfare, as mentioned earlier, and more significantly, remittances from younger family members employed in the cities. This sizeable population of peasants poses a dilemma for the Chinese state's aspiration to transition to full agrarian capitalism. They neither can rely solely on the market, either as producers or consumers, without risking a deterioration of their living conditions, nor can they easily transform themselves into agrarian entrepreneurs or, conversely, be absorbed as uncontrolled wage labourers flooding into the cities. This complex situation presents both a challenge and an impediment to domestic capitalist development.[48]

Hence, we observe the emergence of several intermediate forms within this complex landscape. One is that of the farmer who, leveraging the three-rights system, enters into a contract to sell the entire product of his land plot to a

---

45  To which must be added a 10% of non-agricultural workers residing in rural villages.
46  Yu Sheng, Ligang Song, and Qing Yi, "Mechanisation Outsourcing and Agricultural Productivity for Small Farms: Implications for Rural Land Reform in China", in *China's New Sources of Economic Growth*, vol. 2: *Human Capital, Innovation and Technological Change*, edited by Ligang Song, Ross Garnaut, Cai Fang, and Lauren Johnston (Acton: Australian National University Press, 2017), 289–313.
47  Qian Forrest Zhang and John A. Donaldson, "The Rise of Agrarian Capitalism with Chinese Characteristics: Agricultural Modernization, Agribusiness and Collective Land Rights", *China Journal* 60 (2008): 25–47, http://dx.doi.org/10.1086/tcj.60.20647987.
48  Jan Douwe van der Ploeg and Jingzhong Ye (eds.), *China's Peasant Agriculture and Rural Society: Changing Paradigms of Farming* (London: Routledge, 2016).

medium-large urban enterprise. In doing so, the farmer effectively becomes an extension of this enterprise without surrendering overall control of the land, ensuring that he cannot be dispossessed of it. There are also hybrid forms that involve the transfer of land management rights to agricultural enterprises. These enterprises may rent land from entire villages, consolidate it, and determine the type of cultivation, all while employing resident peasants who receive both wages and a form of rent.

Regardless of the specific arrangements, this path leads to a critical step: the widespread transfer by farmers of land management rights, which encompass the economic utilisation of arable land. Over the last decade, land transfers have become a central mechanism for achieving economies of scale in agricultural production.

On a national scale, in recent years, approximately a quarter to a third of arable land has changed hands in various forms, such as mortgages, subcontracting, and more, primarily in the major plains and coastal regions.[49] Of course, this process has not been limited to the agricultural sector alone. Public expropriations (*zhengshou*), typically for expanding urban areas, have continued, especially with the increasing rates of urbanisation. However, these expropriations have taken on more regulated forms of compensation.[50] It has been estimated that since the 1990s, around 10 million hectares of land have been transferred through various means, involving approximately 130 million peasants from 1.5 million villages.[51] While these figures are remarkable, what is equally impressive is the Chinese state's ability to curb the more chaotic forms of land enclosures, proletarianisation, and urbanisation that to some extent characterised the initial phase of this transition.[52]

As a result of these ongoing processes, one of the most significant outcomes is that the average medium-large private firm, which typically cultivates an average of 200 mu (approximately thirteen hectares) and is often considered (not entirely correctly) the Chinese counterpart to Western agribusiness, now covers more than 20% of cultivable land, often acquiring the most desirable locations with fertile soil.[53] These are commonly referred to as 'dragon-headed

---

49 Zhou, Liang, and Fuller, "Tracing Agricultural Land".
50 Joel Andreas, Sunila S. Kale, Michael Levien, and Qian Forrest Zhang, "Rural Land Dispossession in China and India", *Journal of Peasant Studies* 47, no. 6 (2020): 1109–42, https://doi.org/10.1080/03066150.2020.1826452.
51 Zhang Yulin, "Land Grabs".
52 This led to the formation of so-called villages within cities (*chengzhongcun*), which, however, are not comparable to slums.
53 Burak Gürel, "Semi-private Landownership and Capitalist Agriculture in Contemporary China", Review of Radical Political Economics 51, no. 4 (2019): 650–69, https://doi.org/10.1177/0486613419849683; Shaohua Zhan, *The Land Question in China: Agrarian Capitalism, Industrious Revolution, and East Asian Development* (London: Routledge, 2019).

enterprises' (*longtou qiye*), each having the capacity to integrate thousands of small family businesses.[54] Their numbers have grown substantially, from just 20,000 in 2000 to over 100,000 in the mid-2010s, forming connections in various ways with over eighty million family units, accounting for roughly 40% of the total. Simultaneously, the state has attempted to curtail land dispossession for non-agricultural purposes while encouraging the formation of both competitive family farms, with the support of rural credit, and cooperatives consisting of several family units, particularly through the system of transfers. In 2017, the central government initiated the Agrarian Revitalisation Programme with the precise goal of integrating small-scale production based on modernised agriculture.

It would be interesting to dwell on the intricate channels through which these policies are implemented in rural areas, encompassing the complex interplay between local party cadres, entrepreneurial figures often called upon to assume party roles,[55] providers of credit, and varying degrees of grey areas or even criminal activities. While this framework certainly plays a pivotal role in delineating the realms of local conflicts, we will not delve into it in detail here. In broad terms, state agrarian policy has oscillated over the past two decades. The factional balance within the CCP at the end of the 1980s seemed to lean towards proponents of radical privatisation and the complete abolition of differentiated residence permits between urban and rural areas (on which, see below). However, the government's central stance has favoured a balance between the interests of private capital and small-scale production, aiming to enhance efficiency through gradual processes of guided concentration. This shift became particularly evident during the transition from the presidency of Hu Jintao (2002–13) to that of Xi Jinping (2013–).[56]

---

54  Shaohua Zhan, "The Land Question in 21st Century China: Four Camps and Five Scenarios", *New Left Review* 122 (Mar/Apr 2020): 115–33, accessed 25 September 2023, https://www.researchgate.net/publication/340730559_The_Land_Question_in_21st_Century_China_Four_Camps_and_Five_Scenarios.

55  The so-called party officials by invitation or, more flexibly, the policy of 'village leadership to the rich' (*furen zhicun*). That is, the election of affluent individuals within village committees. See Qian Forrest Zhang, "Class Differentiation in Rural China: Dynamics of Accumulation, Commodification and State Intervention", *Journal of Agrarian Change* 15, no. 3 (2015): 338–65, https://doi.org/10.1111/joac.12120.

56  Zhan, "The Land Question". It is worth noting that the conflict between Xi Jinping and Bo Xilai leading up to the leadership transition within the CCP in 2012 might have been influenced by differing views on how to modernise the countryside and the pace at which to proceed. Bo Xilai appeared to advocate for a more rapid privatisation approach, aiming

## 2.5 Land Rent

This balanced policy has thus far proved successful in preventing the eruption of uncontrollable contradictions. However, it has not been able to prevent the emergence of phenomena associated with capitalist land rent (*tudi caizheng*) as modern market relationships have taken hold in rural areas. While absolute rent was abolished during the early 'heroic' phase of land nationalisation and urban housing allocation, a hybrid form of land rent has resurfaced, particularly in the hands of individual economic actors, be they families or private companies, since the late 1970s reforms. The formalised land use rights transfer market has played a pivotal role in driving this phenomenon, leading to a significant surge in the 'land price' (effectively, the cost of land use concessions), which has multiplied two to fivefold over the past decade.[57] This trend has affected even the farmers themselves, who often struggle to make a decent living from their modest land plots. In some cases, when they migrate to cities and face limited prospects of returning to their villages, they are persuaded by large companies or property speculators to relinquish their land use rights in exchange for compensation. The escalating costs associated with these transactions, an inevitable result of the integration of agriculture into modern market relations, have intertwined with rising production costs for agricultural products and the relative balance, in terms of quality and quantity, among different crops. This has made cereals, essential for the country's food self-sufficiency, less profitable.

In summary, despite the absence of absolute rent and the price control functions of the state, which have generated remarkable economic results by maintaining very small agricultural production, an incipient and hybrid land market is today increasingly asserting itself, imposing a growing burden on society. This burden will be compounded by the consequences of unbridled land (and subsoil) use, including pollution, water scarcity, and environmental and health crises (e.g., the SARS and COVID-19 outbreaks). Moreover, due to structural and social factors, China cannot easily offset these costs by taking the full 'American way' (Lenin) and fully transitioning from peasant economy to highly productive agrarian capitalism. This complexity is further reflected in the nascent but incomplete process of class differentiation in the countryside, which we will explore in the following section.

---

to finance a modern welfare system that would replace peasant land use rights and the compulsory residency system (*hukou*).

57  Jin Zhang, "The State, Capital and Peasantry in the Agrarian Transition of China: The Case of Guangxi Sugarcane Sector" (PhD thesis, Wageningen University, 2019), https://doi.org/10.18174/471122.

### 2.6 Semi-proletarianisation and Ambivalences of the Hukou

The process of agricultural modernisation in China has given rise to increasing differentiation within the previously homogenous rural population, resulting in varying degrees of class distinctions. This transformation has occurred alongside a widening income gap between urban and rural areas, which has reached significant proportions (with urban incomes being three times higher than rural incomes). However, this differentiation did not manifest as a straightforward and widespread proletarianisation of the rural labour force but rather took on the form of what is termed 'semi-proletarianisation' in Chinese political-sociological discourse—a concept often overlooked in the West.[58]

Certainly, wage labour has begun to spread in rural areas, particularly in the context of the growth of medium and large-sized firms, as discussed earlier. However, except in limited areas where intensive or seasonal large-scale agriculture is practised, wage labour remains a minority phenomenon in rural China,[59] and its forms are somewhat hybrid. Moreover, a significant portion of the young labour force under the age of thirty-five, who could potentially engage in wage labour, has moved away from agriculture, and found employment in the retail trade or, to a large extent, migrated to urban centres.

The predominant source of activity and income within rural family units has become what is known as 'dual employment' since the early 2000s. In this arrangement, the older labour force typically remains in the countryside to manage small to very small family-based businesses, with more than half of their income derived from rural welfare programmes and, most importantly, remittances sent by family members who have migrated to urban areas for employment in industries.[60] Within this framework, there is often a division

---

58  Mark Selden and Jieh-min Wu, "Chinese State, Incomplete Proletarianization and Structures of Inequality in Two Epochs", *Asia-Pacific Journal: Japan Focus* 9, no. 5.1 (January 2011), article ID 3480, accessed 25 September 2023, https://apjjf.org/2011/9/5/Mark-Sel den/3480/article.html; Pun Ngai and Lu Huilin, "Unfinished Proletarianization: Self, Anger, and Class Action among the Second Generation of Peasant-Workers in Present-Day China", *Modern China* 36, no. 5 (2010): 493–519, https://doi.org/10.1177/0097700410373576.

59  At the beginning of the 2010s, according to Huang et al., agricultural wage labour stood at one tenth of family self-employment (unlike in India, where wage earners reached 45% of the labour force). Philip C. Huang, Gao Yuan, and Yusheng Peng, "Capitalization without Proletarianization in China's Agricultural Development", *Modern China* 38, no. 2 (2012): 139–73, https://doi.org/10.1177/0097700411435620. See also Zhun Xu, "The Development of Capitalist Agriculture in China", *Review of Radical Political Economics* 49, no. 4 (2017): 591–98, https://doi.org/10.1177/0486613417717046.

60  According to official statistics, the wage share of rural per capita income grew from 19% in 1985 to 41% in 2010. See Zhang, "Class Differentiation".

of labour along gender and generational lines within smallholder families, with unmarried young women working in factories while middle-aged parents engage in farming. Remittances are frequently used to invest capital in small-scale commodity production or the retail trade. In any case, the dependence of small-scale farmers on the market has increased in various ways. However, this has not taken the form of direct expropriation of the means of production and subsistence, whether through classical primitive accumulation, differentiation from below between peasants and farmers, or multinational agribusiness land grabs. The social reproduction of this labour force has remained at very low-cost levels, benefiting industrial accumulation. Nonetheless, it has not been fully commodified and, with state subsidies, serves as a minimal potential safeguard against the vulnerabilities imposed by the market.

Semi-proletarianisation, a phenomenon that has unfolded organically from the grassroots, has given rise to a unique category of individuals known as *bangong bannong*, which translates as 'half wage labourer, half peasant', and tends to straddle the line between being a proletarian in the city and a peasant in the village. This arrangement hinges on two key factors: the preservation, albeit diminishing, of a worker's access to land and the internal migration to urban areas for unstable blue-collar employment, a trend that gained momentum in the early 1990s. Access to land is governed by the system of compulsory residence registration, known as *hukou*, introduced as far back as 1958 during the Maoist era to curtail the possibility of mass rural-to-urban migration. The *hukou* system entitles rural residents to land rights at the family and village commune levels, as well as to social security benefits, which were expanded by the central government in the early 2000s. For rural migrants, the *hukou* system acted as a partial social safety net, particularly during economic upheavals like the 1997 Asian financial crisis and the 2008–9 global financial crisis when urban employers laid off workers, allowing these migrants to temporarily return to their villages while awaiting economic recovery. It served as a safety net (or shock absorber), albeit an increasingly precarious one, though still considered vital. This is because the countryside, due to rising productivity and the increasingly voracious consumption of land for construction and infrastructure, no longer offers opportunities to employ (even occasionally) large numbers of returning migrants, except at labour costs below the value of labour power. Additionally, the younger generation is less inclined to leave urban areas and delay the fulfilment of the promises that led them to migrate from rural regions in the first place.

On the other hand, an abrupt abolition of the *hukou* system would present the Chinese state with the overwhelming challenge of dealing with a massive rural population at risk of becoming 'redundant', possibly numbering in the hundreds of millions. Moreover, an outright abolition would be unfeasible for local governments, which would be tasked with immediately providing an acceptable level of social services to migrant workers, a daunting proposition. Consequently, the Chinese state has approached with great caution the idea of reforming a *hukou* system that is considered somewhat mature.[61] However, recognising the need for some degree of change, in 2016, the central government officially ended the separation between urban and rural *hukou*, although disparities in terms of available services remain significant. The state has also moved towards granting temporary urban permits with basic social services to certain segments of rural migrants. Simultaneously, it has simplified the process of changing residence from rural areas to medium-small towns (but not major cities). This serves two main purposes: redirecting population flows away from mega-cities to more decentralised locations where industry is being relocated, and generating demand for the housing sector, which has been susceptible to speculative bubbles. However, these measures do not consistently align with the preferences of affected individuals. Rural *hukou* appears to be more desirable than urban *hukou* for many in small and medium-sized towns, both in terms of benefits and the outlook of older migrants who, after years of demanding work, opt for a return to the village. They seek the freedom from employer pressures, the ownership of a small plot of land, and significantly lower living expenses.

The gradual and partial nature of the solutions implemented by the state nevertheless reflects the complex social balances at play, as well as the underlying contradiction between the imperative to enhance and stabilise wage and social conditions for the rural population, including migrants, and the necessity to draw upon an industrial reserve labour force that, though smaller and less compliant than before, remains far from depleted.

### 2.7  A New Phase

The evolving class dynamics in the Chinese countryside defy a linear categorisation, situated at the intersection of residual semi-capitalist agrarian relations, small-scale commodity production, and large-scale farming and livestock husbandry. The trajectory towards full agrarian capitalism is evident, yet it encounters formidable obstacles and enduring complexities along the way.

---

61  "Free to Move, Forced to Move: The Present State of the Hukou System", *Chuang* blog, 18 May 2020, accessed 25 September 2023, https://chuangcn.org/2020/05/free-to-move/; Kam Wing Chan and Li Zhang, "The *Hukou* System and Rural-Urban Migration in China: Processes and Changes", *China Quarterly* 160 (1999): 818–55, https://doi.org/10.1017/S0305741000001351.

Social stratification stemming from increasingly prominent capitalist relations is indisputable, but so is the persistence of hybrid conditions.

This complexity is reflected both in the recent Chinese discourse surrounding rural class structures and in the characteristics of peasant mobilisations over the past two decades. The academic and politically charged debate in China[62] has primarily revolved around the nature of ongoing agrarian transformations, questioning whether it heralds an essentially irreversible move towards capitalism resulting in the complete *de-peasantisation* of direct producers, as Lenin had articulated. In this context, two broadly contrasting interpretations have emerged, which, upon closer examination, are not entirely antithetical. The first perspective,[63] which has been extensively discussed here, emphasises the emergence of a Chinese agrarian capitalism that operates 'from below and above', thereby acknowledging the significant role played by the party-state. This interpretation posits that this form of capitalism does not necessarily manifest as large-scale enterprises employing wage labourers but rather begins in small-scale production as its breeding ground, alongside cooperative ventures and family farms oriented exclusively towards the market. This process is characterised by its complexity, retaining vestiges of semi-proletarianisation of the producer, as previously discussed. However, these analyses suggest that this semi-proletarianisation is gradually waning as a bona fide agricultural wage labourer begins to take shape (although this perspective may tend to overestimate its prevalence). The second strand of thought[64] instead highlights the concept of 'capitalisation without proletarianisation'. It underscores the continued significance of small-scale commodity production, which allows for the persistence of a peasant economy marked by autonomy and self-sufficiency, albeit in a diminished form and with minimal wage labour involvement. This perspective forms the basis for political proposals put forth by the 'populist' movement of the early 2000s. Faced with the setbacks of the previous decade and the looming threat of social unrest stemming from the potential total commodification of land, this movement sounded the alarm by emphasising the 'three-dimensional agrarian problem'

---

62  Henry Bernstein, "Some Reflections on Agrarian Change in China", *Journal of Agrarian Change* 15, no. 3 (2015): 454–77, https://doi.org/10.1111/joac.12116.

63  Yan Hairong and Chen Yiyuan, "Agrarian Capitalisation without Capitalism? Capitalist Dynamics from Above and Below in China", *Journal of Agrarian Change* 15, no. 3 (2015): 366–91, https://doi.org/10.1111/joac.12121; Zhang, "Class Differentiation".

64  Huang, Yuan, and Peng, "Capitalization without Proletarianization"; Philip C. C. Huang, *The Peasant Family and Rural Development in the Yangzi Delta, 1350–1988* (Stanford, CA: Stanford University Press, 1990).

(*san nong wenti*: peasants, villages, agriculture).[65] This movement advocates a kind of contemporary Chinese variation of the European pre- and anti-enclosure 'moral economy'.[66] Later on, this current was joined by the New Rural Reconstruction movement, which incorporated partially neo-Maoist features characteristic of the so-called Chinese New Left. This movement, concerned about the danger posed by a widespread rural exodus, champions projects aimed at preserving village communities through the establishment of peasant cooperatives, alternative small-scale markets, access to favourable credit, and cultural activities.[67] These initiatives are seen as alternatives, or at the very least, complements to central government policies in response to peasant discontent and mobilisation. As previously discussed, the Chinese state, according to these analyses, emerges as a player not entirely committed to the vision of integral capitalist agriculture. Instead, it is seen as a credible interlocutor for pro-peasant proposals, sometimes even being viewed through a quasi-'socialist' lens. The state has responded to these concerns with welfare programmes geared towards building a 'New Socialist Countryside' and has at least partially curbed rampant land grabs by local governments.

This intricate scenario is also mirrored in the patterns of mobilisation that have unfolded in rural areas since 2000.[68] The altered governmental approach towards rural regions, particularly the elimination of taxes, has brought about a shift in the landscape. Consequently, there has been a decline in the number of mobilisations. Additionally, as a reflection of this changing phase, many of these mobilisations revolve around negotiations regarding the pricing of land use rights transfers, often involving rural residents who have either already migrated away or are in the process of doing so. The demographic makeup of these mobilisations has also evolved, with a substantial presence of migrants

---

65  Wen Tiejun, "Centenary Reflections on the 'Three Dimensional Problem' of Rural China", translated by Petrus Liu, *Inter-Asia Cultural Studies* 2, no. 2 (2001): 287–95; interview with He Xuefeng in Angela Pascucci, *Potere e società in Cina*.

66  See Edward P. Thompson, "The Moral Economy of the English Crowd in the Eighteenth Century", *Past & Present* 50, no. 1 (1971): 76–136, https://doi.org/10.1093/past/50.1.76. This perspective, broadly speaking, aligns with the historiographical-political tradition of 'polanism'. In this context, it delves into the dynamics between society, the 'market', and capital, mirroring the themes explored by scholars like Braudel and Arrighi in works such as Arrighi's *Adam Smith in Beijing*.

67  Zhan, "The Land Question"; Sally Sargeson, "The Demise of China's Peasantry as a Class", *Asia-Pacific Journal: Japan Focus* 14, no. 13.1 (2016), article ID 4918, accessed 25 September 2023, https://apjjf.org/2016/13/Sargeson.html.

68  *Chuang*, "Gleaning"; Aufheben, "Class Conflicts in the Transformation of China", *Aufheben* journal, issue 16 (2008): 1–52, accessed 25 September 2023, https://libcom.org/article/class-conflicts-transformation-china; Astarian, *Luttes de classes*.

who are now urban workers or young individuals involved in small-scale businesses within their villages, or available for employment by private companies acquiring 'their' land. Conversely, there has been a surge in mobilisations related to environmental concerns in recent years, driven by the growing and increasingly intolerable issues of environmental degradation and pollution.

## 2.8  The Problem of Food Self-Sufficiency

The challenges associated with China's journey towards agrarian capitalism coalesce around a final yet highly significant issue: the nation's food self-sufficiency. This concern underscores the geopolitical dimension of the agrarian question, demonstrating its significance beyond domestic borders. Here, we will provide a brief overview of this complex matter.

Food self-sufficiency was consistently a pivotal objective during the peasant revolution, as well as the subsequent nationalist and anti-imperialist Maoist era.[69] Amid the Cold War backdrop, this strategy aimed to counteract the green revolution, a movement sponsored by Washington in the 1960s with anti-communist undertones. The green revolution primarily relied on the introduction of market-driven inputs and technologies (such as hybrid seeds, chemical fertilisers, and pesticides) to alter crop selection according to foreign market demand, ultimately favouring the agrarian middle class.[70]

China's unique version of the agricultural revolution in the 1960s and 1970s, which followed a devastating famine triggered by the Great Leap Forward, significantly increased yields per unit area, ultimately achieving food self-sufficiency. However, this trajectory encountered obstacles in relative terms, and by the late 1990s, it faced an absolute decline, especially in cereals production.[71] Official data indicates that cereal production decreased by as much as one-fifth between 1998 and 2003, from around 500 million to 400 million tonnes annually. This decline was partly influenced by international price mechanisms favouring more marketable crops.[72] In response, the central

---

69  Sigrid Schmalzer, "Toward a Transnational, Trans-1978 History of Food Politics in China: An Exploratory Paper", *The PRC History Review* 3, no. 1 (2018): 1–14, accessed 25 September 2023, http://prchistory.org/wp-content/uploads/2017/11/Schmalzer.pdf.

70  D. Narasimha Reddy, "The Agrarian Question and the Political Economy of Agrarian Change in India", R. S. Rao Memorial Lecture delivered to the University of Hyderabad, 17 June 2016; Jens Lerche, "Agrarian Crisis and Agrarian Questions in India", *Journal of Agrarian Change* 11, no. 1 (2011): 104–18, https://doi.org/10.1111/j.1471-0366.2010.00295.x.

71  Li et al., "Analysis of China's Grain Production"; Xu, Zhang, and Li, "China's Grain Production".

72  Zhang Hongzhou, "The U.S.-China Trade War: Is Food China's Most Powerful Weapon?", *Asia Policy* 15, no. 3 (2020): 59–86, http://dx.doi.org/10.1353/asp.2020.0044.

government implemented subsidies, incentives, and credit programmes to boost production, effectively raising it to approximately 600 million tonnes within a decade. Nevertheless, China has witnessed a significant increase in agricultural imports in recent years, particularly in soybeans, which are used for both human consumption and livestock feed. Soybean imports now constitute 85% of total domestic consumption, establishing China as the world's leading importer of agricultural raw materials, with imports originating from countries including Russia, Ukraine, Argentina, Brazil, and the United States.[73] Concurrently, the CCP has set a red line to avoid crossing in terms of arable land, after two decades of continuous erosion, with the total area falling from 130 million to no more than 120 million hectares.

Food self-sufficiency in China currently stands at approximately 85%, based on a consistent diet that includes cereals, meat, and vegetables.[74] However, this self-sufficiency could face significant risks in the near future, especially if changes in dietary habits continue to evolve. The ratio of cereals, meat, and fruit/vegetables in the Chinese diet has shifted from 8:1:1 to 5:2:3, indicating a more 'Western' dietary trend. To address this shift, the Chinese government initiated a plan in 2016 for the structural adjustment of national cultivation to rebalance crop types. In 2021, a law against food waste, known as the 'empty plate campaign', was passed, along with measures to counter uneducative advertising and the growing issue of youth obesity. To mitigate potential food supply risks, China has increasingly invested in agriculture abroad, with a total stock of $19 billion in 2018. These investments involve purchasing or leasing land in regions like Africa, Latin America, and Ukraine (prior to the current conflict). The primary objectives are to diversify sources of food imports and create buffers against financial speculation on food prices. However, this strategy comes with significant costs and geopolitical uncertainties.

Chinese agriculture has become more integrated into the global market. While it imports low-value cereals, it exports significant quantities of high-value intensive crops and fish products.[75] This integration exposes China to fluctuations in international prices and places it within the international agrarian

---

73  Thierry Pouch and Jean-Marc Chaumet, *La Chine au risque de la dépendance alimentaire* (Rennes: Presses universitaires de Rennes, 2017).
74  For comparison, Japan, South Korea, and Taiwan have achieved a food self-sufficiency rate of 40%, however in each case the rural population represents about one-fifth of the total urban population.
75  Zhang, "State, Capital and Peasantry".

regime established since the 1980s.[76] This regime relies on finance, increased use of fossil energy, biofuels, biotechnology, longer food supply chains, dominance by multinational corporations over state-driven projects, and a shift from staple food production to market-oriented products. It remains to be seen whether and how Chinese agriculture will be able to withstand these transformations and the resulting contradictions between growing domestic food demand with export-oriented production and ensuring both access to global markets and domestic food supply stability. The crisis in agricultural and mining commodity prices that preceded the outbreak of the 2008 financial crisis was certainly a warning. Moreover, instability in international food and energy markets, which re-emerged during the pandemic crisis[77] and the Ukrainian war, has contributed to rising inflation concerns.

Indeed, China's post-revolutionary achievements in the realm of food production are undeniable, marked by the eradication of hunger and the capacity to sustain a burgeoning urban populace. To illustrate this profound transformation, consider the remarkable growth in wheat production: from a mere 113 million tonnes in 1949, it soared to an impressive 571 million tonnes by 2011. Furthermore, the per capita share of wheat consumption surged from 209 kg to 425 kg during this period. Nonetheless, underlying this remarkable success story is a global trend that extends beyond China's borders—an unsettling pattern of diminishing agricultural yields and declining returns on input investments. This paradox stems from the simultaneous expansion of market-driven agricultural relations and integration into the global marketplace, which inexorably drives up land rents and commodity prices. China finds itself at a crossroads, navigating the challenges posed by these market forces while grappling with the enduring fragmentary nature of its agricultural structure, which imposes limits on productivity gains. Consequently, China is compelled to accelerate its path towards modernisation, marked by energy-intensive farming practices, increased separation of seeds and products, mounting soil degradation, droughts, and environmental pollution—side effects of agricultural industrialisation. Simultaneously, the nation must contend with the consequences of rising global prices, which could imperil Chinese food

---

76  Harriet Friedmann, "International Regimes of Food and Agriculture since 1870", in *Peasants and Peasant Societies: Selected Readings*, 2nd ed., edited by Teodor Shanin (Oxford: Basil Blackwell, 1987), 258–76 (1st ed., Harmondsworth: Penguin, 1971).

77  Michael Every and Michael Magdovitz, *Biblical, Lean, and Mean* (special report, Rabobank—RaboResearch Global Economics & Markets, Utrecht, 17 March 2021), accessed 25 September 2023 https://research.rabobank.com/markets/en/detail/publication-detail.html?id=291426 (login required).

self-sufficiency, jeopardise the resilience of small-scale agriculture, and escalate the costs of labour reproduction.

China's unique position sets it apart from more traditional cases of 'underdevelopment', such as those seen in Latin America or India.[78] It enjoys a greater capacity for regulation and, to some extent, planning, unburdened by the presence of extensive landed aristocracy or a powerful agrarian bourgeoisie focused solely on protecting its vested interests. Nevertheless, the Chinese state is not immune to the dilemmas inherent in a capitalist development model that transfers an increasing share of its costs onto society and the environment as it strives for incremental improvements at the individual farm level. The future stability of China's countryside can no longer be taken for granted, and the Western-style development path—whether resembling American or European agriculture with varying scales of ownership and substantial subsidies from imperialist states—is not a feasible option. The persistent connection between the migrant proletariat and the rural population, both undergoing differentiation along class lines, suggests a potential source of unpredictability. The interplay of these forces within China, characterised by an agrarian class struggle, could potentially resonate on a global scale, amplifying peasant movements that have gained momentum across regions from Latin America to Africa to India in recent decades.

## 3 Class Struggle and Capitalist Development

While discussing the socio-economic nature of China can be quite contentious—some still label it as 'socialism' despite its practical functioning as a 'mixed economy'[79]—it is worth noting that over the past decade, China has emerged as a hotspot for class struggle. This is especially significant because this has occurred in a historical phase in which such overt manifestations of

---

78  Ashok Gulati and Shenggen Fan, *The Dragon and the Elephant: Agricultural and Rural Reforms in China and India* (Baltimore, MD: John Hopkins University Press, 2007).

79  See Rémy Herrera and Zhiming Long, *La Chine est-elle capitaliste?* (Paris : Éditions Critiques, 2019). Samir Amin, in his article "China 2013", *Monthly Review* 64, no. 10 (March 2013), https://doi.org/10.14452/MR-064-10-2013-03_3, took an intermediate stance. He discussed the 'autonomy of the political', which was not framed in Maoist voluntarism but rather in a *realist* reassessment of Lenin's discourse on the New Economic Policy, a strategy Lenin considered in the context of world revolution. Due to space restraints, a comprehensive discussion of the recent debate, both Marxist and non-Marxist, on this subject cannot be provided here. The first chapter of this section (3.1) referred to the 'classical' Marxist debate on transition, which has evolved over time.

class struggle have largely disappeared in the rest of the world, particularly in Western countries.⁸⁰ The vigour of the struggles of the Chinese working classes, which are often recorded in official statistics under the grim heading of 'mass casualties', revolves around fundamental issues like land, labour rights, and, increasingly, concerns about the environment. These struggles did not suddenly emerge in the past decade, as our discussion on rural areas has already demonstrated. Instead, they have deep historical roots. Moreover, the context of the unresolved global crisis, these struggles carry immense political weight. They impact internal class dynamics within China and the relationship between the Chinese state and the working class. Furthermore, they have implications on a global scale, influencing the dynamics of class struggle worldwide.

We should resist overly simplistic perspectives on this complex picture. Workerist viewpoints that portray Chinese workers as solely exploited by Western multinational corporations and place the Chinese bourgeoisie in the same category are overly reductionist. Similarly, Third-Worldist perspectives that depict Chinese workers as inherently aligned with the Chinese state, either in opposition to or in the process of disengaging from the West, oversimplify the situation. In reality, the class contradictions within China and the contradictions between China and imperialism both exist and are deeply intertwined. Furthermore, the figure of the Chinese proletarian, particularly the *nongmingong*, embodies a unique aspect of semi-proletarianisation. This process has played a pivotal role in propelling Chinese capitalism forwards but has also contributed to the tempering of class contradictions within the country.

Considering this multifaceted reality, it might be surprising to some, but this thesis asserts that China can be considered a *democratic nation*. Let me clarify that this notion of democracy does not align with the contemporary Western model, which often seems to have lost its substance due to hollow institutional

---

80  This transition phase was succeeded by the initial stage of neo-populist mobilisation, wherein the declining middle classes took a prominent role, replacing the proletariat to a certain extent, although the latter remained involved. In the subsequent phase, marked by the onset of the pandemic crisis and the initial signs of a new economic crisis, a divergence between these two classes will re-emerge. This shift will elevate social issues, without immediately erasing the multifaceted nature of mobilisations. The interclass composition of these movements will persist, and the demand for sovereignty ('sovereignism') will resurface in various forms on both sides of the Atlantic. For more insights, see Raffaele Sciortino, "Pandemic Crisis and Phase Changes", *Platforms, Populisms, Pandemics and Riots*, September 2020, accessed 27 September 2023, https://projectpppr.org/pandemics/pandemic-crisis-and-phase-changes.

and procedural aspects.[81] Instead, I mean democratic as it pertains to the dialectical relationship between the working class and the state. In this context, various forms of proletarian resistance interact with a governing power that not only recognises the need for social compromise but also endeavours to channel this energy towards driving capitalist development forward.[82]

### 3.1 Prologue: Reforms and Democratic Mobilisation

In the latter half of the 1970s, China experienced a complex period marked by internal political struggles within the CCP, featuring ideological conflicts between the left and right factions. These political battles were closely intertwined with a surge in social mobilisations that began to articulate explicit democratic demands. This period marked the definitive departure from the Maoist path, which had already been significantly weakened. During the early part of the decade, China had seen a combination of youth mobilisations and workers' struggles that had managed to resist certain anti-egalitarian policies. For instance, they had opposed the introduction of productivity-based wage incentives in factories. However, as these workers' struggles waned, the focus of urban-based demands, including students, party technicians, and the aspiring middle class, shifted increasingly towards democratic claims. While these claims were not necessarily aimed at challenging the CCP's political monopoly, they did target what were considered the 'extremist' policies of the Cultural Revolution. This period saw the emergence of the April 5 Movement in 1976, which gained momentum during the public commemorations of the death of Zhou Enlai, a prominent right-wing politician. The movement centred its demands around the so-called 'five great freedoms', which were actively promoted by a counter-movement opposed to the more extreme forms of class struggle witnessed in previous years.

---

81   The objective here is not to obscure the inherently alienated nature of any form of democracy across various contexts, as it fundamentally represents the heightened expression of the inherent separateness ingrained within capitalist society. Instead, the aim is to highlight the distinct forms and levels of development within class contradictions that persist regardless. As long as the capitalist social structure endures, democracy serves as the dynamic mechanism through which the proletariat becomes integrated into the ongoing processes of value circulation, as articulated by Jacques Camatte.

82   For an analysis of episodes and evolutions within the class struggle in China since the 1990s, see Aufheben, "Class Conflicts"; Astarian, *Luttes de classes*; Elisabeth Perry and Mark Selden (eds.), *Chinese Society: Change, Conflict and Resistance* (London: Routledge, 2003); Editorial, "Unruhen in China", *Wildcat*, no. 80 (December 2007): 2–10; Ching Kwan Lee, *Against the Law: Labor Protests in China's Rustbelt and Sunbelt* (Berkeley: University Of California Press, 2007); Ralf Ruckus, *The Communist Road to Capitalism* (Oakland, CA: PM Press, 2021), which also contains a valuable bibliography on the subject.

After definitively sidelining the leftist faction within the CCP in the autumn of 1976, Deng Xiaoping's astute leadership allowed him to cautiously support political reforms by the autumn-winter of 1978. During this period of political fervour, the Democracy Wall Movement emerged. This movement, comprising not only youth but also some proletarian participants, provided a platform for the urban population to voice without fear of repression their growing dissatisfaction following a decade of political and social upheaval. It effectively served as a grassroots catalyst for the new reformist direction. Crucially, the Democracy Wall Movement included a substantial number of young 'rebels' who had returned to urban areas after being sent to the countryside during the Cultural Revolution. These individuals were characterised by their inclination to articulate and pursue their own demands, relative cultural sophistication, and aspirations for social advancement. They represented a Chinese variation of the post-1968 push in the West, which sought individual autonomy and self-expression.

This burgeoning energy, initially harnessed and directed during the early stages of reforms, was subsequently contained and dispersed over the course of a decade. However, a period of economic overheating in the late 1980s, characterised by double-digit inflation, and the aftermath of a credit crunch reignited discontent among urban classes. It was during this time, as Europe was on the brink of the final collapse of 'real socialism', that China experienced the brief but impactful Tiananmen Square protests in 1989. During these protests, the aspirations of workers for improved living conditions, along with their disappointment and concerns about the limited progress achieved through reforms, briefly intersected with the demands of young students for greater political freedom. Despite this overlap, the two groups quickly diverged. While the workers were primarily seeking an improvement in their economic situation within the framework of the new economic policies, the students were advocating for an acceleration of reforms at the political level, including an end to the CCP's political monopoly. The coexistence of students and workers, even though they were spatially separated within the vast square, did not lead to fusion or a solid alliance. On the contrary, "the student leaders do not want to involve the working class",[83] partly due to class differences and partly due to political calculations related to their interactions with the party and the government, from which they received some degree of support. This division in the struggle, coupled with the general indifference of the peasant population and the CCP's commitment to the Dengist line of safeguarding party and state

---

83   Ruckus, *Communist Road*, 109.

unity in the wake of events in Eastern Europe, ultimately led to the dissolution of the democracy movement.

Subsequently, China witnessed the decoupling of economic reforms from political reforms, a move that the CCP did not renounce while it accelerated economic reforms. Deng Xiaoping's celebrated visit to the southern regions of China in 1992 marked a pivotal moment in this regard. This visit solidified the path towards the complete removal of price controls, a comprehensive overhaul of the taxation system (resembling a kind of Chinese-style fiscal federalism), the reduction of numerous public subsidies, and a significant restructuring of the industrial manufacturing sector. This restructuring played a crucial role in reshaping the Chinese working class.

### 3.2 Restructuring and Workers' Struggles: the State-Owned Enterprise

One of the primary factors contributing to the restructuring of the working class was the termination of lifetime employment in connection with the divestment, restructuring, or privatisation of state-owned enterprises. This transformation adhered to the principle of 'leave the small companies, keep the big ones'. These state-owned enterprises, granted accounting autonomy under the Enterprise Law of 1994 and gradually subjected to commercial criteria since the 1990s, witnessed a significant reduction in their numbers over a decade, leading to the elimination of between fifty and sixty million jobs.[84] The state's strategy was centred on preserving the core of large, profitable companies that remained under single central control through the establishment of the Administration and Supervision Commission in 2003. These large enterprises, commonly referred to as state-owned enterprises, played a pivotal role in strategic sectors such as infrastructure, mining, telecommunications, and steel. They accounted for more than half of all employment within public enterprises. Meanwhile, smaller- and medium-sized enterprises were either forced to close down or privatised. The process of rationalisation and mergers, encouraged from the top, especially following the Asian crisis of 1997, resulted in the creation of approximately 150 to 200 large state-owned enterprises. These enterprises enabled the state to maintain control over pricing and strategic decision-making. This strategic position allowed China to navigate the challenges of full integration into the world market after its accession to the World Trade Organization in 2001. However, with a few exceptions, these Chinese state-owned enterprises were unable to reach the levels of major Western multinational corporations.

---

84  Naughton, *Chinese Economy*.

The transformation in labour dynamics was accompanied by the dissolution of the system of guarantees linked to the work unit (*danwei*) system that had been established during the Maoist era. Under this system, labour force selection was directly managed by labour offices, which served as the primary intermediaries between the CCP and workers. Workers under this system enjoyed permanent employment (in some cases, overemployment), albeit with low productivity rates, as well as access to various social services provided by the factory, including healthcare, housing, and retirement benefits. In the new economic landscape, the direct relationship with the workforce, often facilitated through collective agreements, transitioned to the newly established state-led enterprises. By the mid-2000s, the labour force had shrunk to approximately sixty million workers. Importantly, this transformation was not always characterised by uncontrolled divestments. Instead, there was often a measured approach to change, which included offering redundancy incentives (referred to as *maiduan*), providing various subsidies, and facilitating early retirement for older workers. Additionally, a segment of the workforce, known as *xiagang* (literally 'out-of-place'), was given the opportunity to temporarily leave their positions without severing ties with the company, along with access to support programmes. Furthermore, local authorities extended unemployment benefits to workers undergoing dismissal procedures, excluding sole traders and rural migrants. Simultaneously, the housing that had previously been allocated by the *danwei* system was offered for purchase to workers at favourable prices. To adapt to these changes, the 'one-family two-system' was introduced, allowing the older family member, typically male, to retain his job and *danwei*'s benefits, albeit at a modest wage. Meanwhile, the younger family member was encouraged to seek employment in sectors more directly exposed to the market, often offering higher wages. This family-based wage system, combined with other measures, facilitated the transition away from the previous system and led to a significant influx of younger labour force members migrating to urban areas to work in the new factories, particularly in the special economic zones established in the 1980s.

This explains why, amid a backdrop of concessions, repression, and resignation resulting from a *fait accompli* politics, resistance against the dismantling of the *danwei* system proved to be relatively weak. This was despite the substantial initial number of workers impacted by these changes, which gradually dwindled as millions of young individuals entered the new factories that were emerging. The economic recovery further diminished the strength of resistance.

In instances where resistance was more combative, it primarily took the form of defensive struggles aimed at preserving the bare minimum of living conditions. This was particularly evident in certain regions of north-eastern China, the heartland of heavy industry that had been partly established during the heroic phase of 'socialist construction' and influenced by Japanese occupation. Owing to its historically homogeneous and class-conscious composition, this region did not experience the transformation of old industrial plants into privatised or deregulated factories, which might have offset job losses. Instead, within a decade, it evolved into China's Rust Belt, marked by widespread lay-offs and an overall deterioration in living standards. Typically, resistance episodes did not extend beyond localised workplace protests regarding unpaid wages or compensation for dismissals. Although various forms of mobilisation were evident, they usually focused on exerting pressure within different levels of local hierarchies. Only in a few cases did these protests escalate beyond the local party and administrative authorities. The early 2000s witnessed the most intense struggles, particularly in Liaoyang, the Daqing oil fields, and Lanzhou. While these confrontations had limited immediate outcomes, they sounded alarm bells for the central government, contributing to the decision in 2003 to enhance central regulation of the state sector and initiating a shift in social policy. This shift, as part of the launch of the 'harmonious society' initiative, aimed to address some of the issues previously seen in rural areas.

### 3.3 The Chinese Enterprise in Upward Globalisation

Let us exclude the sector of village and township enterprises and collective enterprises owned by local authorities in this discussion. Both sectors played a role in the early stages of reforms, employing over a hundred million wage earners in small to medium-sized units, but they underwent significant restructuring through privatisation starting in the mid-1990s.

By the mid-1990s, private enterprises in coastal areas and special economic zones already represented 40% of industrial employment and contributed to 34% of the total industrial output.[85] These were typically small and medium-sized factories engaged in the production of low-value consumer goods. They were often established by former cadres of state-owned enterprises or with capital from the Chinese diaspora. Approximately a decade later, these enterprises contributed to 68% of the country's GDP, employing fifty-seven million formal and an estimated hundred million informal workers. Subsequently, the growth rate of employment in this sector began to slow down. Private enterprise capitalism in China is characterised by the predominance of small

---

85   Martin Hart-Landsberg and Paul Burkert, *China and Socialism: Market Reforms and Class Struggle* (New York: Monthly Review Press, 2005); Marie-Claire Bergère, *Capitalismes et capitalistes en Chine* (Paris: Perrin, 2007).

enterprises, with even the largest ones barely reaching the scale of European SMEs. These businesses are particularly susceptible to fluctuations in the international business cycle and rely heavily on local political support, especially for obtaining credit. They resemble a kind of productive *Mittelstand* and have managed to survive, albeit often with difficulty, thanks to their utilisation of labour power based primarily on wages below the value of labour's reproduction and the extraction of absolute surplus value. They are also closely linked to local power networks and family connections both within and beyond China's borders. This sector, despite its wild exploitation of labour, does not represent a bourgeoisie as the dominant class in the traditional sociological sense. Without state support, this highly fragmented sector, defined by its regional diversity, could easily face extinction in the event of a severe economic crisis.

The sector of Chinese joint ventures involving foreign participation has also seen significant growth, largely facilitated by this bourgeoisie class. Initially, in the early 1980s, many Chinese enterprises, having undergone the processes described earlier, began to act as subcontractors for foreign companies, particularly those operating through intermediaries in Hong Kong, Macao, and Taiwan. Subsequently, with the influx of foreign investments, mixed Chinese-foreign participation enterprises emerged, accounting for roughly 20% of the total number of enterprises. It is worth noting that these foreign investments, which amounted to a stock of $346 billion as of 2000 and experienced increasing inflows since 1992,[86] primarily came from the Chinese diaspora in East Asia, especially Hong Kong and Taiwan.[87] As a result, these companies were not initially direct subsidiaries of Western multinational corporations, at least until China's accession to the World Trade Organization. Instead, they were largely East Asian companies that transformed China into the 'world's factory' during the phase of upward globalisation.

China's distinctive role in the global division of labour was that of an assembly site for more advanced East Asian economies, which were already oriented towards direct exports to Western markets. This assembly work primarily involved final products, especially medium-low technology consumer goods destined for re-export to the West.[88] Within these supply chains, multinational

---

86  Yanrui Wu, *China's Economic Growth: A Miracle with Chinese Characteristics* (London; New York, RoutledgeCurzon, 2004).

87  It is challenging to determine the exact extent to which Chinese capital was used to circumvent tax regulations and controls while being funnelled into foreign markets.

88  This is known as export processing, on which see Ho-Fung Hung, "America's Head Servant? The PRC's Dilemma in the Global Crisis", *New Left Review* 60 (Nov/Dec 2009): 5–25, accessed 27 September 2023, https://newleftreview.org/issues/ii60/articles/ho-fung-hung-america-s-head-servant.

corporations exerted significant control over distribution and technology, ensuring a substantial transfer of value from China to the West.[89] Given this arrangement, the notion of China surpassing the US economy, often invoked to stoke Western anxieties about China's rise, was and remains neither in heaven nor on earth.[90]

This pattern of accumulation was inherently characterised by an emphasis on extensive rather than intensive growth, prioritising absolute over relative surplus value. Consequently, it featured lower average productivity indices compared to the Western world. This trade-off was the price to be paid for the technological advancements facilitated by collaboration with foreign capital, which, while significant, might not have been as revolutionary as commonly perceived. This partnership also contributed to the development of global value chains and a logistics network that remains unmatched by international capital to this day.[91] It was an inevitable price, given the foundations laid by the previous phase of 'socialist' accumulation. These foundations had ripple effects, notably in the creation of a relatively weak domestic market for consumer goods due to modest wage levels, leaving limited autonomy for technologically advanced investment goods, with only a fraction being produced domestically.

Moreover, the widening imbalances between various regions, often exacerbated by the competition among local governments for investment and credit, complicated the implementation of a centralised industrial policy. Nonetheless, these processes provided the groundwork for state-driven developmental endeavours. State intervention emerged as a crucial intermediary because a fully-fledged industrial bourgeoisie with its own capital was still in its nascent stages, lacking the ability to independently navigate the global

---

89   Minqi Li, "China: Imperialism or Semi-Periphery?", *Monthly Review* 73, no. 3 (Jul/Aug 2021), accessed 27 September 2023, https://monthlyreview.org/2021/07/01/china-imperialism-or-semi-periphery/.

90   Michael Beckley, "'China's Century?' Why America's Edge Will Endure", *International Security* 36, no. 3 (Winter 2011/12): 41–78.

91   In 2019, China played a significant role in the global trade landscape, contributing to 15% of the world's total exports. Additionally, it accounted for 17% of all imports into the United States, with a substantial portion comprising components and intermediate goods sourced by foreign multinational corporations operating within China. Furthermore, China represented 21% of imports from East Asian countries. See Mary E. Lovely, "The State of U.S.-China Relations Heading into 2021" (prepared statement for the hearing on US-China Relations at the Chinese Communist Party's Centennial held before the US-China Economic and Security Review Commission, 28 January 2021, PIIE), accessed 27 September 2023, https://www.piie.com/sites/default/files/documents/lovely2021-01-28testimony.pdf.

market. Nevertheless, the competitive advantage derived from a disciplined and educated labour force with low costs gradually proved insufficient to merely compete on the global stage without succumbing to Western imperialism's voracious appetite.

The critical question that arose, even before the eruption of the global crisis in 2008, was whether the class struggle of the proletariat, on one hand, and the evolving needs of Chinese capitalism, on the other, should accept this existing industrial pattern or actively advocate for its restructuring. In essence, it called into question the potential margins available for China to secure a more advantageous position, considering the imperialist dynamics inherent to the global market.

### 3.4  *The New Working Class*

Recent data indicates that China's rural migrant (*nongmingong*) population, officially registered as residents of villages, numbers at least 230 million individuals. These migrants are dispersed across major cities, as well as small and medium-sized towns throughout China.[92] It is worth noting that this figure is likely an underestimate, as migrant workers now constitute a majority of the Chinese proletariat and often comprise a significant portion of the population in industrial cities. They represent the urban, blue-collar side of a prolonged process of semi-proletarianisation that has been ongoing in rural areas for nearly four decades. The migration from rural to urban areas has occurred in successive waves (we are now at the third generation) and has given rise to a 'new' working class, which engages in precarious and informal employment, primarily in private or mixed enterprises, and frequently coexists with the 'old' working class that emerged during the earlier phase of state-led industrialisation and enjoyed some limited 'guarantees' of the old system.

The new working class's labour force quickly proved to be exploitable in various types of factories, including those that emerged in the 1990s and those relocated to China by Western corporations. This workforce possessed several characteristics that made it highly attractive to employers: it was accustomed to discipline and cooperative labour practices due to historical and recent experiences, had received a basic education,[93] came with low reproduction

---

92  Zhang and Hu, "Rural China"; Jenny Chan and Mark Selden, "The Labour Politics of China's Rural Migrant Workers", *Globalizations* 14, no. 2 (2017): 259–71, https://doi.org/10.1080/14747731.2016.1200263.

93  It is worth noting that China's literacy rate has exhibited significant progress over the years, evolving from less than 20% in 1950 to 65% in 1980, and subsequently reaching an impressive 95% by 2010.

costs compared to Western standards, and appeared nearly endless in terms of its size. Consequently, factories could sustain long working hours and maintain extremely high work speeds, with a continuous influx of new labourers to replace those who departed.[94] This arrangement allowed China to acquire advanced production facilities and technologies at an accelerated pace, a process that would have taken much longer without access to this vast labour reserve. Concurrently, Western multinational corporations made significant leaps in extracting surplus value on a global scale. While this dynamic successfully helped overcome the crisis of the 1970s, it also contributed to suppressing commodity prices within the basket of goods consumed by Western working classes for several decades, resulting in a reduction in their real wages. To give an idea of the very low costs of reproduction of the Chinese migrant labour force, it is enough to recall that, according to official data from the National Bureau of Statistics, in 2009 approximately 80% of migrants lacked access to social welfare coverage, including pensions, healthcare, and unemployment benefits. Although this figure saw modest improvement over the subsequent five years, it remained high.

This has undoubtedly been one of the primary 'comparative advantages' of Chinese capitalism, sustained over a significant period. It owes its longevity to the division between cost-effective social reproduction, partially anchored in the migrants' rural places of origin, and the productive activities directed by the *dagong* (boss) in urban centres. During this time, social needs were streamlined to the bare essentials, even as the dormitory living arrangements within factories, which unfortunately became hubs for continuous wage abuses, became the norm. This process of 'unfinished proletarianisation'[95] generated a pervasive feeling of being suspended between two worlds, a sense of incompleteness, and the notion of being only half a worker. This was the flip side of the incomplete dispossession experienced in the rural areas. It sustained the expectation among a significant portion of the first two migrant generations that they could eventually return to their villages with improved living conditions.

However, since the last decade, if not earlier, a decisive shift has taken place. The generation born after 1980, which largely received secondary education, began to perceive their situation differently. On one hand, they no longer viewed their work in factories producing goods for foreign markets as a transitory experience. On the other, they started forming attitudes and habits more

---

94   Anita Chan, *China's Workers under Assault* (London: Routledge, 2001); Pun Ngai, *Migrant Labour in China: Post-Socialist Transformations* (Cambridge: Polity Press, 2016).
95   Pun and Lu, "Unfinished Proletarianization".

aligned with urban life, including consumption patterns, media consumption, the pursuit of personal goals, diminished company loyalty, heightened awareness of their rights, and a greater willingness to take collective action in the workplace. These changes have naturally led to a loosening of ties with rural life, rendering urban residency less transitory. As a result, demands for adequate social services began to emerge, marking the beginning of a decline in the effectiveness of the *hukou* system as a means of regulation and control.

Several factors have collectively contributed to improving the conditions of migrant workers, including their wages and living standards. First, their growing numbers allowed them to exert substantial pressure on both employers and local authorities. Additionally, the trend towards permanent settlement, which local governments began to take seriously by addressing housing and providing minimal social services, played a pivotal role. Moreover, the fierce competition among cities and regions to attract this labour force during a period of robust economic growth enhanced the bargaining power of rural migrants. Some local administrations even introduced territorial minimum wage regulations as a sign of this changing dynamic.

In a dialectic relationship with these factors, the 2000s witnessed a rise in the number of mass accidents, particularly in factories located in coastal regions. These incidents often gave rise to spontaneous strikes, typically of short duration and primarily driven by wage-related issues such as delayed payments, fraudulent practices, and various forms of exploitation. These protests were usually limited to the specific company involved[96] and frequently spilled onto the streets rather than resulting in the occupation of the workplace. The primary aim of these actions was to exert pressure on authorities to intervene. Within this context, various forms of resistance emerged, encompassing limited direct actions, petition drives, and legal actions supported by NGOs staffed by activist lawyers. Many of these disputes found their way into the courts for resolution. At the conclusion of these conflicts, the ad-hoc worker committees were either short-lived or ended up affiliating with the official trade unions to monitor the agreements forged with the companies. While this period did not constitute a comprehensive wave of labour unrest, nor did it witness coordinated mobilisations between rural migrants and workers in the restructured state-owned industries, the mounting pressure from workers had a discernible impact. This occurred precisely when the central government under Hu Jintao was gearing up for moderate social reforms. The government's motivation was not only to safeguard social stability but also to encourage the manufacturing

---

96   So-called 'cellular activism', as defined by Lee in *Against the Law*.

industry to leverage the relatively modest increase in labour costs—resulting from both grassroots struggles and top-down reforms—as a means to enhance productivity and transition towards higher value-added production. Indeed, between 2001 and 2007, according to the International Labour Organization (ILO),[97] Chinese wages experienced an annual growth rate of 8%, reversing the trend of the previous decade. However, despite this increase in wages, savings rates remained exceptionally high, reflecting an ongoing domestic market imbalance that prioritised investment over consumption. Notably, the share of labour income in the overall economic output reached its lowest point in 2008, following fourteen years of continuous decline and the absence of a robust social safety net.

It was against this backdrop, just before the outbreak of the global financial crisis, that the Labour Contracts Act was enacted in August 2008. This legislation mandated employment contracts for new hires, imposed limitations on employee terminations for workers with over a decade of seniority, introduced regulatory enhancements such as mandatory monthly salary payments, and facilitated collective bargaining.[98] Predictably, this law was met with resistance from both Chinese and international businesses, marking a significant departure from the era of labour market precarity. It underscored the beginning of a shift in the balance of power and a transformation in the state's industrial and social policies. Consequently, the 'turning point' of Xi Jinping's China finds its origins in this evolving social and political climate.

### 3.5 Workers' Struggles in the Global Crisis

The onset of the global crisis in China during the winter of 2008–9 momentarily disrupted the recently adopted 'reformist' and moderately social-democratic path. The crisis led to a rapid increase in unemployment, affecting approximately twenty-five million migrant workers,[99] especially in the highly

---

97  ILO, *Global Wage Report 2008/9—Minimum Wages and Collective Bargaining: Towards Policy Coherence*, 2008, accessed 27 September 2022, https://www.ilo.org/wcmsp5/groups/public/---dgreports/---dcomm/documents/publication/wcms_100786.pdf.

98  Accompanying these changes, the Arbitration Law enacted in May 2008 allowed workers to pursue cases of abuse in court without the burden of incurring legal fees. See Beverly J. Silver and Lu Zhang, "China as an Emerging Epicenter of World Labor Unrest", in *China and the Transformation of Global Capitalism*, edited by Ho-Fung Hung (Baltimore, MD: John Hopkins University Press, 2009), 174–87.

99  As of 2009, China's working-age population was estimated to be approximately 780 million individuals, with around 300 million engaged in agriculture and more than 200 million in industry and construction. The remaining portion of the workforce was active in the tertiary sector. Among these figures, rural migrants accounted for approximately 230 million

industrialised east coast regions that were closely linked to foreign markets. During this period, rural villages served as a temporary refuge for many workers, aligning with the annual 'spring movement' (*chunyun*) when workers typically returned home for the Chinese New Year holiday. However, a significant number of rural migrants chose to return to the cities in search of employment, reflecting the altered composition and attitudes mentioned earlier.

In response to the crisis, the Chinese government launched a dramatic fiscal stimulus package amounting to $580 billion, aimed at countering the abrupt decline in exports. This stimulus included substantial investments in infrastructure and an expansionary monetary policy, which initially helped mitigate the crisis's impact and eventually revived the economy, albeit with the continuing risk of inflationary overheating. Nonetheless, this recovery also bolstered the de facto bargaining power of workers. While the sudden drop in export-oriented production had immediately triggered demands for the payment of overdue wages, starting in the spring of 2010 a wave of spontaneous mass strikes erupted in some multinational companies, particularly in the electronics and automobile industries. These strikes began at Foxconn in Shenzhen, where workers reacted to the suicides of very young colleagues, which were attributed to the harsh factory dormitory conditions.[100] The strike wave then spread to Honda in Foshan, Toyota,[101] and subsequently across the entire Pearl River Delta region.[102] Notably, it was the industrial province of Guangdong, renowned as China's manufacturing hub, that experienced strikes that were for the first time characterised by *proactive* wage demands, at least

---

people, with two-thirds of them employed in urban industrial and unskilled service sectors. See Tobias ten Brink, *Chinas Kapitalismus* (Frankfurt: Campus Verlag, 2013).

[100] Pun, *Migrant Labour*; Jenny Chan and Pun Ngai, "Suicide as Protest for the New Generation of Chinese Migrant Workers: Foxconn, Global Capital, and the State", *Asia-Pacific Journal: Japan Focus* 37, no. 2.10 (2010), article ID 3408, accessed 27 September 2023, https://apjjf.org/-Jenny-Chan/3408/article.html.

[101] Kan Wang, "Collective Awakening and Action of Chinese Workers: The 2010 Auto Workers' Strike and its Effects", *Sozial.Geschichte Online* 6 (2011): 9–27, accessed 27 September 2023, https://duepublico2.uni-due.de/servlets/MCRFileNodeServlet/duepublico_derivate_o 0029001/03_WangKan_Strike.pdf; Lance Carter, "Auto Industry Strikes in China", *Insurgent Notes*, October 2010, accessed 2 October 2022, http://insurgentnotes.com/2010/10/auto-industry-strikes-in-china/; Yan Lang, "Some Thoughts on Foxconn and the Honda Strike", *Radical Notes*, June 2010, accessed 2 October 2022, http://radicalnotes.org/2010/06/12/china-some-thoughts-on-foxconn-and-the-honda-strike/; Anita Chan, "Labor Unrest and the Role of Unions", *China Daily*, 18 June 2010.

[102] Hao Ren et al., "Factory Stories: On the Conditions and Struggles in Chinese Workplaces", 2012–15, accessed 2 October 2022, http://www.gongchao.org/en/factory-stories/.

until the spring of 2014 when a strike took place at the Taiwanese Yue Yuen factory in Dongguan.[103]

It is beyond the scope of this discussion to delve into the complete history of workers' mobilisations during these years.[104] However, these mobilisations were made possible by a confluence of factors, including harsh working conditions, a temporary labour scarcity during a period of strong accumulation, and the use of social media. Additionally, the composition of these workers, often young and well-educated, felt a sense of detachment from both traditional peasant and working-class conditions. These labour struggles yielded substantial wage increases and revealed an emerging trend towards the formation of spontaneous committees during these disputes. In some cases, these committees evolved into company-wide trade union units,[105] as seen at Foxconn in Shenzhen three years after the 2010 strike and in Honda plants. Notably, these developments occurred not through autonomous workers' organisation but rather through the election of representatives supported by the official union and endorsed by local authorities. It is worth mentioning that the central government and local authorities did not oppose these labour struggles in foreign multinational factories; in some cases, they even supported the drive for unionisation. This shift was foreshadowed by the 2008 Labour Law, an effort to channel these activities into the official union structure and reinstate them after the hiatus caused by the economic crisis. This was an attempt to establish a new regulation of industrial relations within the framework of a new national development strategy, as we will explore further.

The decade spanning from the mid-2000s to the mid-2010s represented a golden age for the coastal export industry. During this period, there was rapid accumulation and wage growth, and an embryonic capital–labour social compromise began to emerge with state endorsement. Within this context, rural migrant workers leveraged both legal activism, such as using arbitration in labour disputes, and the official trade union, to assert their rights.[106] Workers'

---

103  Stefan Schmalz, Brandon Sommer, and Xu Hui, "The Yue Yuen Strike: Industrial Transformation and Labour Unrest in the Pearl River Delta", *Globalizations* 14, no. 2 (2017): 1–13, https://doi.org/10.1080/14747731.2016.1203188.

104  But on this history, see Florian Butollo and Tobias ten Brink, "Challenging the Atomization of Discontent: Patterns of Migrant-Worker Protest in China during the Series of Strikes in 2010", *Critical Asian Studies* 44, no. 3 (2012): 419–40, https://doi.org/10.1080/14672715.2012.711978; Jenny Chan, "The Collective Resistance of China's Industrial Workers", in *Global Perspectives on Workers' and Labour Organizations*, edited by Maurizio Atzeni and Immanuel Ness (Singapore: Springer, 2018), 107–25.

105  Zhang Lu, *Arbeitskaempfe in Chinas Autofabriken* (Vienna; Berlin: Mandelbaum, 2018).

106  Chan and Selden, "Labour Politics".

increasing awareness of their rights, coupled with the legal support provided by democratic NGOs and militant lawyers, foreshadowed a form of 'free unionism' in anticipation of potential political liberalisation.[107] Regarding the capital–labour relationship, state-affiliated unions played a pivotal role. They were supported by the centralisation-oriented (or what would once be simply called 'conservative') wing of the CCP and sought to stem the haemorrhaging of union membership that occurred as state enterprises underwent restructuring. This development was subtly hinted at and carried out with great caution, as seen in the 2006 dispute over the unionisation of Walmart's Chinese factories.

In both scenarios, the possibility of allowing workforce unionisation varied among large state-owned enterprises, mixed enterprises, multinational corporations, and small to medium-sized private businesses, depending on the prevailing mode of exploitation associated with the extraction of absolute surplus value. In enterprises where absolute surplus value extraction is dominant, management often resists significant wage concessions and is reluctant to engage in comprehensive trade union negotiations. Conversely, enterprises with a higher capital composition, advanced technology, and more complex facilities are compelled by technical requirements to involve a skilled labour force in solving organisational challenges and enhancing productivity. This enables such enterprises to offer more substantial concessions in wage negotiations and fosters a collaborative relationship with the official trade union.

In this context, the trajectory and continued existence of trade unionism (*gonghuizhuyi*) in China will increasingly hinge on the path taken by Chinese capitalism. This path navigates between the constraints of the international division of labour and the Chinese state's efforts to pursue a strategy of intensive development, shifting away from a primary focus on export-oriented growth. Such a strategy, under specific conditions, not only accommodates a compatible albeit moderately contentious trade union movement but also employs it to incentivise companies to advance technologically and extract relative surplus value. These developments are essential for expanding the domestic market and consumption within China, as well as for China's ambitions to ascend the hierarchy of the world market.

Therefore, the critical questions that arise are as follows: to what extent can current global hierarchies shift in response to Chinese pressure, and what implications will this systemic crisis leave in its wake? These questions

---

107   Tim Pringle, "What do Labour NGOs in China Do?", *Asia Dialogue*, 17 October 2016, accessed 27 September 2023, https://theasiadialogue.com/2016/10/17/what-do-labour-ngos-in-china-do/.

transform into broader political inquiries, extending to the working class and its evolving relationship with the state and both Chinese and international capital.

## 3.6    Results and Trends

Nevertheless, the culmination of labour strikes in China's coastal regions around 2014–15 yielded significant gains in workers' bargaining power and a heightened sense of awareness.[108] These advances translated into a remarkable annual wage increase averaging 11% between 2009 and 2014,[109] accompanied by improvements in social benefits, extending their reach from urban centres to rural areas. According to ILO data, from 2006 to 2017, China emerged as the world's fastest-growing wage economy, underscoring the potent leverage that wages can exert.[110] On a broader scale, the rapid expansion of social inequalities that had persisted began to abate, leading to a reduction in disparities between urban and rural areas, different regions, and various sectors.[111]

China's industrial cities, unlike their Western counterparts, continue to host substantial manufacturing infrastructure, housing vast workforces equipped with formal education and tacit knowledge. These urban centres serve as crucial nodes within global supply chains. Even a partial disruption of these networks could trigger immediate repercussions on a global scale, as evidenced by the bottlenecks experienced amid pandemic measures from 2020 to 2022. Building on this backdrop, both the first and most recent generations of rural migrants began advocating for a fair share of wealth and a more secure, dignified way of life. However, developments in the realm of labour struggles and the conditions of the working class have not remained static, further evolving and shaping the landscape.

---

108    As well as a growing number of vocational school students employed as trainees.
109    Jonathan Woetzel, Yougang Chen, James Manyika, Erik Roth, Jeongmin Seong, and Jason Lee, *The China Effect on Global Innovation* (New York: McKinsey Global Institute, 2015).
110    As of 2020, data from China's National Bureau of Statistics indicates that the average annual wage for an entry-level worker has surged to 61,000 yuan, equivalent to nearly 9,000 euros. However, it should be noted that significant variances persist among sectors and regions, and the vast informal sector continues to exert downward pressure on these figures.
111    Nogueira, Guimarães, and Braga, "Inequalities and Capital Accumulation". Notably, as measured by the Gini index, relative social inequality in China has declined, now falling below levels observed in the United States. Over the initial fifteen years of the twenty-first century, the less affluent half of China's population witnessed an average per capita income increase of 7.5%, whereas in the United States, there was a decrease of 0.7%.

Regarding labour strikes, a significant shift has occurred since the peak in 2014–15, with a noticeable decrease in their frequency, dropping by at least half in the subsequent years (see Figure 3.2).[112] Strikes in the coastal regions, where the previous wave of labour actions had transpired, also declined. Instead, there has been a noticeable increase in disputes related to factory relocations since as early as 2014. This shift can be attributed to the response of private entrepreneurs, both Chinese and foreign, to heightened worker militancy in the preceding years. Many of them began relocating their manufacturing facilities to inland regions such as Henan and Chongqing, which offered lower labour costs and lacked a history of worker activism. Some even opted for offshore production or the automation of their processes. This dynamic, coupled with a relative deceleration in economic accumulation from the mid-2010s onwards, placed the industrial proletariat in a challenging position. Consequently, workers' demands shifted towards a defensive stance. Additionally, authorities, in certain instances, adopted repressive measures, while some employers reverted to traditional modes of labour exploitation. Wage growth slowed, and the share of labour income in GDP expanded at a more sluggish pace.

As a result, although coastal regions like Guangdong and Zhejiang had absorbed 65% of the total migrant labour force in 2011, this proportion had declined to 55% by 2017. Meanwhile, the inland regions saw an increase from 34% to over 40% in their share of the migrant labour force during the same period. Nevertheless, this spatial redistribution of capital quickly led to a corresponding redistribution of labour conflicts. In both absolute and relative terms, by 2018, labour disputes became more prevalent in the inland regions compared to the coastal areas, despite the general economic slowdown mentioned earlier.

It was against this backdrop that the pandemic crisis of early 2020 took place. The government's response took on an almost military character, necessitated by the inadequacies of the national healthcare system. According to the Chinese Centre for Disease Control and Prevention, without stringent measures to curb the virus's spread, China could have witnessed a staggering two hundred million infections and more than three million deaths. While the plausibility of these estimates may be debated, one pivotal factor must not be overlooked: the resolute reaction of the Chinese populace upon learning of the virus's transmission. This groundswell of public concern created immense pressure on the state leadership, compelling them to act decisively

---

112  Zhun Xu and Ying Chen, "Spatial Shift in China's Labour Struggles: Evidence and Implication", *Journal of Labor and Society* 22, no. 1 (2019): 129–38, https://doi.org/10.1111/wusa.12397.

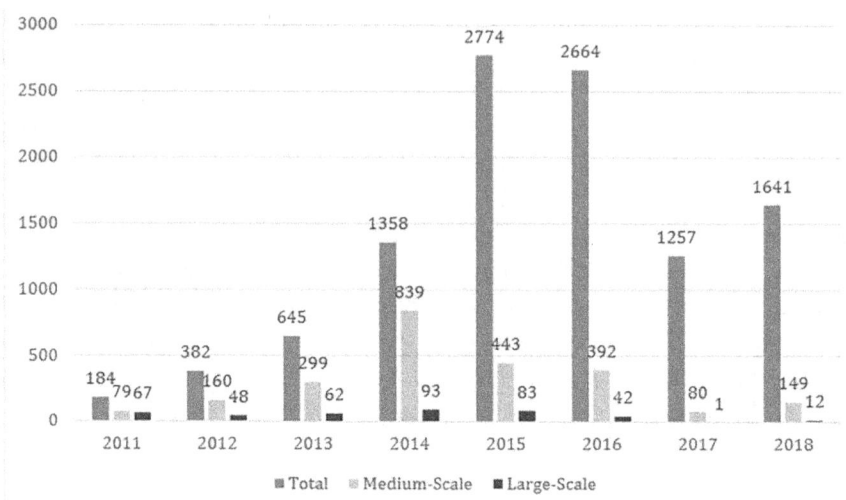

FIGURE 3.2  Strikes of various scales, 2011–2018
*Note*: Medium-scale refers to those involving 100–1,000 persons; large-scale strikes refer to those involving 1,000–10,000 persons. Reproduced from Xu and Chen, "Spatial Shift", fig. 1.
DATA FROM *CHINA LABOR BULLETIN*'S STRIKE MAP.

in the face of the perceived negligence and incompetence of local authorities. The bottom-up push was met with a corresponding top-down response, as the legitimacy of both the ruling party and the state hung in the balance. It constituted yet another manifestation of democratic dialectics, not in the conventional political sense but in terms of the material configuration of the relationship between the proletariat, the party, and the state. The 'people' exerted pressure on political power, prompting the latter to launch a campaign resembling a people's war against the virus. Simultaneously, the government sought to prevent the United States from exploiting the health crisis to undermine China's resilience. The population, in general, accepted the stringent measures implemented over the subsequent two years, partly because it saw the political and social turmoil caused by the virus in Western countries. This period led, perhaps more profoundly than ever before, to a transformation in people's perceptions of the West and, conversely, a bolstering of their confidence in their own system.[113]

---

113   It is important to clarify that we are not advocating against any measures to manage a pandemic emergency. This is not the scope of our discussion. It is worth noting, however,

When it comes to the overall working conditions, the data seem to indicate the emergence of a new wage and employment landscape since the mid-2010s.[114] Wage growth has started to exhibit signs of polarisation. Skilled workers with regular contracts in capital-intensive industries have experienced more significant wage increases, while the informal sector, which largely consists of unskilled labour-intensive services, has seen wage growth decelerate. Employment trends appear to mirror this shift. In 2018, overall employment did not register any growth for the first time, although there was a continued migration of workers from rural to urban areas, resulting in over 400 million urban workers. Conversely, agricultural employment in rural areas continued its decline. The construction sector, which reached a peak of 232 million employed in 2012, began to contract, with 218 million employed in 2017. Employment in the service sector, particularly in recent years, has increased, but this growth has mainly been in low-skilled roles without regular contracts and lower productivity. In several sectors, informal employment has surged while regular employment has decreased, leading to noticeable effects on wages.

Interpreting this data is not straightforward, as it paints a complex and nuanced picture. However, it does signal the onset of a new phase in economic development, at least as a partial trend. This phase is characterised by technological restructuring and a spatial redistribution of economic activities, as previously mentioned. The growth in employment in the high-tech industry is a manifestation of this trend, driven by state industrial initiatives, foreign investment flows, and facilitated by a large pool of graduates in technical and scientific disciplines. Conversely, unskilled industrial employment has started to decline in relative terms, partly due to automation and re-engineering efforts.

While it is challenging to predict future scenarios with certainty, questions arise about the effective margins China will have at its disposal to continue the apparent trajectory it has embarked upon. These questions extend beyond internal accumulation dynamics and encompass China's relationship with the global market's imperialist aspects. Furthermore, the potential repercussions

---

that there were social movements advocating for the relaxation of lockdown measures that gained momentum in mid-2022.

114  Scott Rozelle, Yiran Xia, Dimitris Friesen, Bronson Vanderjack, and Nourya Cohen, "Moving Beyond Lewis: Employment and Wage Trends in China's High- and Low-Skilled Industries and the Emergence of an Era of Polarization" (presidential address for the 2020 Association for Comparative Economic Studies Meetings), *Comparative Economic Studies* 62 (2020): 555–89, https://doi.org/10.1057/s41294-020-00137-w.

of this trajectory on various fronts should be considered: internal class relations, the urban–rural divide, disparities among different segments of the working class, the emerging middle classes, and the divide between successful youth and those who may be left behind.

### 3.7   From Democratic Class Struggle to ...

By way of a provisional summary, it could be said that while the inception of the Dengist reforms was marked by the upward surge of democratic aspirations from a middle class aspiring to a 'Chinese way', the closure of this cycle, four decades later, is defined by the democratic demands of a vastly different actor: the *new proletariat*. This newly formed and influential working class has emerged in just over three decades. This democratic class struggle has dual dimensions: first, it involves a fight against exploitation to enhance the workers' conditions within the existing capitalist framework (akin to trade unionist struggles); second, it exerts pressure on the state for a qualitative leap in national capitalist development in response to aggressive and domineering multinational capital.

The current landscape starkly contrasts with the earlier one, not only due to the transformed class dynamics arising from the initial phase of 'socialist' accumulation but also because of the altered conditions in global accumulation and geopolitics. Capital accumulation, especially in the West, has been sluggish, failing to fully recover from the 2008 crisis despite significant financial interventions. This slowdown is unlikely to offer China the same opportunities for overcoming its prior developmental backwardness. Conversely, Western imperialism has become increasingly assertive and anti-Chinese. Consequently, global geopolitics is pointing towards the dissolution of the three-decade-long mutually beneficial relationship between China and the United States.

The characterisation of the ongoing class struggle in China as democratic should not be misconstrued; rather, it underscores the real nature of class relations and the as-yet partially untapped, though not entirely straightforward, potential within them. The Chinese proletariat has evolved, and it is increasingly unwilling to tolerate extreme levels of exploitation. The young, highly productive, and underpaid working class is becoming scarce or, at the very least, less willing to endure unprecedented levels of exploitation. Up until now, major Chinese and foreign corporations operating in the global manufacturing hub have relied on the rapid turnover of labour, which allowed for the production of goods at exceptional rates, boosting profits and contributing to the suppression of wages for Western workers. The absolute surplus value extracted from the Chinese working class has effectively served as a means to extract relative surplus value from the Western working class.[115] However, this paradigm is beginning to falter, and the Chinese population is demanding something different and better: namely, wage increases, the establishment of a welfare state, and improved life opportunities both within and outside the factory. In essence, this is the kind of rebalancing towards domestic consumption that analysts often attribute to proletarian pressures and can be seen as a redefinition of the class compromise in a more (social) democratic direction.

This shift alone transforms the class struggle in China, which remains firmly entrenched within capitalist relations, into a global phenomenon. To address these demands, it becomes imperative for the Chinese state to challenge, at least partially, the inequality inherent in international exchange relations. This entails reducing transfers to the West, both in the form of financial investments in US debt securities and as a share of profits extracted by Western multinational corporations. Moving up the value chain becomes a crucial step for Beijing. Chinese capitalism has a vested interest in pursuing this path not only to prevent class conflicts from undermining its stability but also to establish a more self-reliant foundation for growth.

Hence, the old formula of extensive exploitation, aligned with a subordinate role in the international division of labour, no longer proves adequate. While Beijing had to make concessions to Western imperialism for the rapid industrialisation of the nation and its emergence from underdevelopment, China's ascent as a medium-sized capitalist power stands as the counterpoint to the setbacks suffered by Western working-class movements during the aftermath of the global upheavals of the Long '68. As a result, Western imperialism is now striving, and struggling, to impede China's progress. Beijing has come to realise that the previous development model, which relied on subordination to the United States, cannot be sustained indefinitely. Instead, it must prioritise boosting domestic accumulation through the modernisation of production technologies, the expansion of the domestic market, and economic engagement that counters Western strategies. Consequently, the torch has been passed, at least for the time being, to the Chinese state—as we will explore in the next chapter. Further steps in the class struggle are likely to unfold within a context of heightened disarray within global capitalism and, dialectically, increased entanglement with the dynamics of social class in the West.

Amid this complex landscape, the trajectory of democratic class struggle in China is likely to unfold in the near future, not as a resurgence of anti-capitalist sentiment, but through two intertwined yet ultimately distinct scenarios.

---

115  Astarian, *Luttes de classes*, 150–1.

The first scenario involves a potential global crisis that could lead to a slowdown in China's economic growth and a more contentious relationship with Washington. This would cast doubt on the current social pact and make its evolving, quasi-social-democratic character more uncertain. Such a resurgence of social conflict might also challenge the single party's and the state's control over the economy, potentially pushing for broader political and economic liberalisation. Western powers are eager to promote this path, as it would weaken China, their most formidable adversary in the current global order. It is also a goal shared by 'free unionism' with ties to the 'liberal' factions within the CCP, which prefer avoiding a direct, confrontational stance with the West.

The crucial point here is that this trajectory, while aiming for a Western-style democracy in its intentions, would necessitate China's integration into the club of developed, or more accurately, imperialist nations. Given the current configuration of world imperialism as increasingly centralised and predatory, this transition seems highly improbable.[116] Under existing conditions, such a development would actually weaken China and potentially lead to fragmentation. This outcome would provide US-dominated global capitalism with a few more decades of breathing room. Therefore, a complete liberal-democratic transformation for China in the near future appears unlikely. However, it is entirely plausible that both internal pressures and external manoeuvres may push for a relaxation of the state's control over capitalist accumulation and society.

Alternatively, the course of the class struggle in China could lead to a deepening of the existing class-based distinctions. In this scenario, the Chinese proletariat would continue to face the barriers imposed by Western imperialism, hindering the country's economic development and the improvement of workers' conditions. This class struggle would inevitably become intertwined with anti-imperialist nationalism, evolving not only into a trade unionist stance but also a political one. Initially, this convergence could align with certain factions within the CCP and the state apparatus that are unwilling to loosen their control over the country's economic development, as doing so could result in unimaginable social and political upheaval. Along this path, it is foreseeable that proletarian struggles would involve a fusion of class and

---

116  Just like Japan, albeit in a distinct historical phase, achieving such a transformation for China appears improbable. To be more specific, this transformation would likely necessitate a catastrophic world war against the United States, resulting in a decisive Chinese victory and the establishment of a completely new global order. This scenario, however, is highly challenging and fraught with difficulties. We will revisit this discussion in the concluding chapter.

national demands, which might, in the future, evolve towards an anti-capitalist movement, contingent upon a resurgence of class consciousness both within and beyond China's borders.

Balancing on this delicate precipice, the leadership of the CCP, under President Xi's guidance, faces a challenging trajectory in the present and even more so in the future. The leadership is wary of a direct confrontation with imperialism, yet it cannot, in the short to medium term, deviate significantly from its course as a capitalist nation and break free from subordination to dollar imperialism. Such a deviation would unleash a Pandora's box of contradictions and social conflicts that even the iron grip of the CCP might struggle to contain and direct. In summary, various factors, including the dynamics of class relations and social conflicts, appear to inexorably push China towards a collision course with US imperialism.

## 4  A New Strategy

As a result of the trajectory we have examined thus far, the Chinese party-state is faced with the dual challenge of forging a new social compromise with the working class, which has gained ground thanks to the notable successes of Chinese capitalism, and directing an intensifying market network towards a more technologically advanced and intensive form of development. This shift is imperative in light of the inevitable slowdown in gross growth rates, the profound transformation of the labour market due to social and demographic factors, and the need to reconfigure the relationship between urban and rural areas and between China and the rest of the world.

### 4.1  Background: Global Crisis

The global crisis of 2008–9 played a pivotal role in both slowing down the momentum for these reforms initially and then accelerating their urgency. It underscored the systemic nature of the challenge and the interdependence of China and the United States within the global economic framework. Initially, the two countries were compelled to cooperate in the aftermath of the subprime financial bubble's burst to avert a catastrophic global economic collapse. This cooperation prevented a complete decoupling of the Chinese and Western economies.

Washington continued to rely on Chinese and Asian credit to finance its massive domestic and external debt, keeping interest rates low to implement stimulus programmes and easy money policies like quantitative easing. Similarly, US multinationals benefited from offshore production. The global crisis hit the Chinese economy suddenly and severely, prompting Beijing to respond with a substantial economic stimulus package totalling approximately $580 billion. Concurrently, an expansionary monetary policy encouraged local governments to increase credit issuance. This swift action helped China recover from the drastic decline in exports but came at the cost of overheating the economy, potentially leading to speculative bubbles and financial insolvency cases.

China has grappled with the challenges inherent in its deep integration with the United States and the dollar-based financial system. This connection was forged through the accumulation of substantial reserves, including US government bonds, as a quasi-obligatory exchange for accessing Western markets for its export goods. However, it also meant dealing with the downsides, such as the difficulty of establishing an effective alternative economic model, even as the current account surpluses trended downward and dependence on Western technology persisted. Beijing was thrust into confronting the pressing issues of an increasingly disorderly international landscape earlier than expected. Previously, it had cautiously aimed to navigate global affairs with a de facto reformist approach, ultimately aimed at a relatively symmetrical multipolar world order over the long term.

These pressing questions loomed large: How sustainable is China's growth while remaining reliant on global demand, particularly from Western countries? How can the domestic market be rebalanced to become self-propelling? In essence, how can China transform itself into an alternative growth pole, both domestically and internationally? These pivotal questions marked the beginning of the geopolitical transition that unfolded after the 2008–9 global financial crisis. This transition set the stage for a course of (thus far) *controlled confrontation* with Washington. Essentially, a strong and successful China would continue to cooperate with the West but on its own terms. It would seek to rewrite the rules of the international system, retain a larger share of profits, internationalise its currency, pursue development rather than growth under Western norms, and promote new regional, if not global, hierarchies. Under the leadership of President Xi Jinping, China is navigating this transition— a journey that presents challenges and uncertainties but is simultaneously inevitable.

### 4.2    *Developmental State with Chinese Characteristics*
The debate within the CCP regarding China's economic model has remained contentious, primarily between two factions. The first faction advocates preserving the existing model, which has proven profitable and successful. This approach aligns with the Dengist principle of China's low-profile ascent,

aiming to avoid arousing opposition from the United States. Conversely, the second faction advocates a comprehensive technological leap.

The latter perspective has gained momentum not only due to China's successes in integrating into the global market but also because it recognises the indispensable role played by the CCP in mitigating the risks associated with integration by relinquishing important aspects of state planning. This is especially evident since the Asian financial crisis of 1997, during which China provided some support to the East Asian region facing the flight of Western speculative capital. It became clear that, even with adjustments, the state's control of the economy remained essential.

Several structural and political factors have played a significant role in shaping China's economic landscape throughout its history. These factors contribute to China's unique economic model. First, state ownership of large enterprises remains a prominent feature of the Chinese economy. While not negated by the Dengist reforms, state-owned enterprises have undergone processes of selection and consolidation. The state sector continues to contribute substantially to GDP, accounting for approximately 40% of it. Moreover, it plays a vital role in industrial output, making up between 30% and 50%, depending on the calculation method used. Furthermore, almost 20% of urban employment is associated with state-owned enterprises.[117] This level of state ownership provides the government with the ability to direct investments and regulate their pace. This control extends to sectors such as energy, infrastructure, capital goods, information and communication technologies (ICT), and armaments. The state's involvement in these areas has positive ramifications for small and medium-sized private enterprises. They benefit from lower input costs and reduced dependence on foreign sources, as well as from a more stable business cycle. This arrangement also diminishes the need for monopolistic practices among larger corporations.[118]

The Chinese government exercises control over credit through state-owned banks and enforces a centralised monetary policy governing interest rates and currency exchange rates. This approach has allowed for a gradual shift from an 'administrative' (dirigiste) form of state planning, which was largely theoretical, to a more practical form of macroeconomic management of industrial policy. This management style utilises tools like credit allocation, currency

---

117  Gang Chen, "Consolidating Leninist Control of State-Owned Enterprises: China's State Capitalism 2.0", in *China's Political Economy in the Xi Jinping Epoch: Domestic and Global Dimensions*, edited by Lowell Dittmer (Singapore: World Scientific, 2021), 43–60, https://doi.org/10.1142/9789811226588_0002.
118  Herrera and Long, *La Chine est-elle capitaliste?*.

regulation, interest-rate adjustments, and subsidies to businesses.[119] While this transformation corresponds with the proliferation of market relationships, it concurrently mitigates the adverse effects of unchecked domestic competition and the dangers of excessive reliance on external sources. Consequently, China has experienced a less 'financialised' accumulation process compared to Western economies. The country also exercises central control over its reserves and capital flows while relying heavily on state banks for credit.[120]

These elements have become even more critical with the opening of the banking system to private and international capital in 2005. This opening allowed state-owned enterprises to raise capital on stock exchanges and led to the emergence of a shadow banking system, which tends to operate beyond central control and occasionally serves as a vehicle for international speculation.[121]

On the political front, China's unique development path and the prevailing social dynamics have contributed to maintaining a relative level of state control over the economy. The Chinese state's character is not merely a variation of East Asian developmentalism. It *does* share certain commonalities with the industrialisation processes of nations like South Korea, Japan, Taiwan, and Singapore, such as state-led price controls, export support, the presence of large national enterprises, access to inexpensive bank credit, capital control, Taylorist work organisation combined with methods of absolute surplus value extraction, a disciplined and educated yet affordable workforce, and an emphasis on emulating Western technologies over autonomous innovation. However, there are also significant differences that set China apart.

One of the key distinctions is that China's industrialisation and modernisation resulted from a protracted social and political revolution. This revolution set China on a trajectory that often put it at odds with the geopolitical and geo-economic order dominated by the United States. Notably, the Chinese state operates as a party-state, meaning it is not merely a bureaucratic apparatus, whether efficient or plagued by clientelism. Instead, it functions as an entity deeply intertwined with its social base, acting as an effective mediation

---

119   Gerard DiPippo, Ilaria Mazzocco, Scott Kennedy, and Matthew P. Goodman, *Red Ink: Estimating Chinese Industrial Policy Spending in Comparative Perspective* (Washington, DC: Center for Strategic and International Studies, 2022), accessed 27 September 2023, https://www.csis.org/analysis/red-ink-estimating-chinese-industrial-policy-spending-comparative-perspective.

120   Michael J. Howell, *Capital Wars: The Rise of Global Liquidity* (London: Palgrave Macmillan, 2020), chap. 9.

121   As was the case in 2015 to 2016 when stock market property bubble burst, partially eroding Chinese foreign exchange reserves.

channel between the state, capital, and various social classes. It plays a pivotal role in bridging the urban–rural divide and in managing China's relationship with the outside world. Furthermore, the Chinese state is committed to safeguarding the nation's unity against any potential fragmentation processes. The political influence of the industrial proletariat and the peasantry has continuously exerted pressure on the state apparatus. They represent the social counterparts to China's broader reluctance to conform to US-dictated rules and its determination to assert its independence on the global stage.

Against this backdrop, Xi Jinping's ascent to the party leadership, fully endorsed during the Third Party Plenum in November 2013, marked a departure from Western-style liberalisation, as advocated in reports like the World Bank's *China 2030*.[122] His approach can be summarised as follows:

1. Continued state intervention: Xi's leadership recognises the continued importance of state intervention, along with the role of state-owned enterprises. These are viewed as levers for transitioning to labour-intensive exploitation, achieving technological advancement, and internationalising investment.
2. Gradual opening of capital markets: While there is no return to isolationism or a closed market, Xi's strategy involves a planned gradual opening up of the Chinese capital market. This includes steps like liberalising interest rates, encouraging foreign capital investment through the Shanghai Stock Exchange (which is set in the future to replace Hong Kong stock exchange), and cautiously moving towards partial currency convertibility.
3. Modernising agriculture: The involves modernising agriculture, moving away from small-scale farming without causing mass dispossession. This is in line with the goal of further urbanisation and gradually overcoming the *hukou* system, but only after establishing a comprehensive welfare system, including property taxation and measures to boost domestic consumption.
4. Channelling workers' struggles: Workers' struggles can be directed towards fostering innovation within enterprises. This approach leverages labour movements against foreign multinationals and encourages young people to engage in technological innovation and entrepreneurship.
5. Anti-corruption campaigns: On the domestic political front, resistance from party cadres and business leaders who might obstruct the efficient

---

122 World Bank—Development Research Center of the State Council, the People's Republic of China, *China 2030: Building a Modern, Harmonious, and Creative Society* (Washington, DC: World Bank, 2013), accessed 27 September 2023, https://www.worldbank.org/content/dam/Worldbank/document/China-2030-complete.pdf.

use of liquidity funding needs to be overcome. Anti-corruption campaigns serve to break this resistance and centralise party authority. This aspect has been labelled by Western media as an 'authoritarian turn' by Beijing's strongman.

The party-state must therefore pivot towards centralisation to pave the way for decisive strides, at least in intent, towards a fully developed capitalist model. This transformation must align with widespread domestic consensus and international recognition. This entails securing a competitive edge in the global market, a critical imperative for China to retain a larger portion of profits for domestic reinvestment while effectively countering the declining productivity trend brought about by the repercussions of the global financial crisis.[123] Moreover, this strategy involves improving key elements to advance up the value chain, such as emphasising selective large-scale investments, the acquisition of cutting-edge technologies, access to broader markets, including the domestic market, and prioritising the development of innovative and competitive capabilities across various sectors.

Xi Jinping's presidency has articulated this strategic vision, and we will now briefly outline its main components.

### 4.3 First Step: 'Made in China 2025'

In the wake of the global crisis, signs of a significant shift in Chinese industrial policy began to emerge. Initially, in 2010, with the launch of the 'Strategic Emerging Industries' project, which focused on cutting-edge technologies, and its subsequent inclusion in the Twelfth Five-Year Plan for 2011–15.[124]

In 2015 the ambitious 'Made in China 2025' initiative was introduced. This comprehensive plan involved substantial investments in the technological modernisation of ten strategically important industrial sectors. It was designed to position China as a dominant player in the global market, leveraging both technological and economic strengths. The ultimate aim was to create national champions capable of international competitiveness, driven by homegrown

---

123   Brandt et al. have observed that China's decline in productivity, measured as output per worker, has exceeded that of the global average. Loren Brandt, John Litwack, Elitza Mileva, Luhang Wang, Yifan Zhang, and Luan Zhao, "China's Productivity Slowdown and Future Growth Potential" (Policy Research Working Paper 9298, World Bank, Washington, DC, June 2020), accessed 23 October 2021, https://elibrary.worldbank.org/doi/epdf/10.1596/1813-9450-9298 (subscription required).

124   See Kucuk Ali Akkemik and Murat Yülek, "'Made in China 2025' and the Recent Industrial Policy in China", in *Designing Integrated Industrial Policies*, vol. 1: *For Inclusive Development in Asia*, edited by Shigeru Thomas Otsubo and Christian Samen Otchia (London: Routledge, 2020), chap. 11.

technology rather than relying solely on foreign acquisitions. The focus of this initiative was on setting, rather than merely adhering to, international trade standards. Central to this strategy was the concept of techno-nationalism, emphasising indigenous innovation and self-sufficiency in technology.[125] To achieve these objectives, China pursued external expansion through the acquisition of Western high-tech companies. Domestically, it sought to catch up with Western counterparts by harnessing the potential of its vast domestic market, a skilled workforce, established supply networks, and state-funded research investments.

One particularly significant aspect was the emphasis on research and innovation in digital telecommunications. China had already established some national champions and developed competitive technology, notably in areas such as 5G networks and submarine cables, which were integral to the development of digital payment systems. However, substantial dependence on US microprocessor production persisted, as we will explore in the following sections.[126] The same challenge applied to artificial intelligence, where China aimed to leverage its massive domestic user base and a well-established commercial ecosystem, while seeking to reduce reliance on GAFAM (Google, Apple, Facebook, Amazon, Microsoft) and other foreign tech giants.

The 'Made in China 2025' initiative drew its inspiration primarily from the manufacturing structure of Germany (as well as Japan), particularly the German 'digital Taylorist' Industry 4.0 strategy. This approach is quintessentially characterised by top-down industrial policy, featuring a web of interrelated interventions designed to bolster domestic firms. These measures include technology transfers from foreign companies, protective measures against competition, government subsidies at both central and local levels, investments, and the acquisition of technologically advanced foreign companies.[127]

---

125 Jost Wübbeke, Mirjam Meissner, Max J. Zenglein, Jaqueline Ives, and Björn Conrad, "Made in China 2025: The Making of a High-Tech Superpower and Consequences for Industrial Countries" (MERICS Papers on China No. 2, Berlin, MERICS, 12 August 2016), accessed 26 October 2021, https://merics.org/en/report/made-china-2025.
126 As of 2018, amid an ongoing trade war with the US, China's domestic production accounted for a mere 16% of microprocessors, a far cry from the ambitious target set by the 'Made in China 2025' plan, which aimed for a 70% share of the global market. To put this in perspective, this 16% represented only 4% of the world's total microprocessor production.
127 Max J. Zenglein and Anna Holzmann, "Evolving Made in China 2025. China's Industrial Policy in the Quest for Global Tech Leadership" (MERICS Papers on China No. 8, Berlin, MERICS, 2 July 2019), accessed 27 October 2021, https://merics.org/en/report/evolving-made-china-2025.

Unsurprisingly, this plan, closely intertwined with China's external ambitions during the 2010s, raised concerns among Western powers. They perceived that it represented an effort to break free from the previous development model centred on the asymmetric ties with imperialist finance and multinational corporations.

### 4.4   Second Step: Dual Circulation

The tariff war initiated by the Trump administration had a profound impact on the global economic and geopolitical landscape, as well as on the relationship between the United States and China. Washington's punitive stance, which has not been rescinded by the Biden administration, has actually accelerated China's drive towards greater technological and industrial autonomy. This strategic shift encompasses even the largest private companies, which, in isolation, might have been more inclined to compromise with Western markets.[128] It is worth noting that this development has triggered a significant shift in the Chinese debate, both in academia and in the public sphere, which has been relatively rare in recent decades. It has led to a polarisation between two opposing positions: the 'pessimists', who advocate for preparing for potential decoupling from the United States due to structural conflict, and the 'optimists', who caution against extreme reactions that could jeopardise China's continued rise.[129] During this debate, the concept of a 'new type of nationwide system', later embraced by Xi Jinping, emerged to underscore the indispensable role of the state in mobilising national resources.

Against this backdrop, the Fourteenth Five-Year Plan (2021–25) was formulated and launched in October 2020 during the Fifth Plenum of the Nineteenth CCP Congress. President Xi had already warned, in a speech a few months prior, about the emergence of a new global phase characterised by significant turbulence that would put China to the test.[130] In general, China's political elite

---

128   Dan Wang, "China's Sputnik Moment? How Washington Boosted Beijing's Quest for Tech Dominance", *Foreign Affairs*, 29 July 2021, accessed 23 October 2021, https://www.foreign affairs.com/united-states/chinas-sputnik-moment (subscription required).

129   Li Wei, "Towards Economic Decoupling? Mapping Chinese Discourse on the China–US Trade War", *Chinese Journal of International Politics* 12, no. 4 (2019): 519–56, https://doi.org/10.1093/cjip/poz017.

130   "Xi Jinping: Speech at the Symposium of Experts in Economic and Social Fields" (speech of 24 August 2020 delivered to a symposium of economist and sociologists on the Fourteenth Five-Year Plan), published in Chinese by Xinhua News Agency, translated by Etcetera Language Group and published in English by the Center for Security and Emerging Technology on 30 September 2020 at https://cset.georgetown.edu/publication/xi-jinping-speech-at-the-symposium-of-experts-in-economic-and-social-fields/.

believes that the US shift marked by the onset of the trade war is not a passing phase and necessitates a comprehensive response. This response centres on the dual circulation strategy as a new development pattern.

To prevent any misunderstandings that might draw comparisons with Maoist strategies, it is crucial to emphasise that China's current strategy is twofold. China is actively working to reduce its reliance on foreign countries by strengthening its value chains and stimulating domestic demand. However, rather than isolating itself from the international community, China seeks to expand its presence in global markets with the specific goal of becoming indispensable in critical international supply chains.[131] The primary innovation in this strategy is the emphasis on developing the domestic circle—a network of autonomous and controllable national supply chains. This involves increasing domestic production, encouraging domestic innovation, and driving higher domestic demand. China is not closing itself off from the world ("domestic and international dual circulation are mutually reinforcing"[132]); instead, it aims to shift the focal point of its development to its own production, distribution, and consumption circuits. This shift is intended to reduce dependence on foreign markets and technology while promoting products labelled as 'made by China' rather than just 'made in China'.

Expanding the domestic market is not solely about increasing demand for consumer goods but, more importantly, about boosting the production of capital goods that can engage with external networks from advantageous positions. This transformation entails a shift from simply assembling components to designing, producing in-house, and releasing machinery under Chinese brands.[133] Such a shift could mark the definitive departure from the 'world assembly line' model, which has relied on low wages and 'triangular trade' (importing semifinished products into China, transforming them into final products, and re-exporting them). Additionally, this shift could lead to increased private and collective consumption through social spending and a reduction in high saving rates, which have persisted due to the absence of a robust and widespread social safety net.

---

131 According to Xi, China is "strengthening the dependence of the international industrial chain on our country, [we are] taking strong countermeasures against attempts by foreign players to cut off supplies". Translated from an article by Xi Jinping dated 18 December 2020 at http://www.xinhuanet.com/politics/leaders/2020-12/18/c_1126879325.htm.
132 Xi Jinping, speech of 24 August 2020.
133 Florian Butollo, *The End of Cheap Labour? Industrial Transformation and "Social Upgrading" in China* (Frankfurt: Campus Verlag, 2014).

The dual circulation strategy is primarily centred on four key priority areas, each crucial for China's future development. First, there is a strong focus on ascending the technological hierarchy. China recognises that it currently occupies a position as a 'third-tier' manufacturing power, trailing behind Germany and the United States. To address this, the strategy emphasises indigenous innovation (*zizhu chuangxin*), shifting the emphasis from applied technology to basic research. The goal is to reduce dependence on international supply chains and strengthen reliance on domestic sources.[134] This objective is supported by the promotion of concentrated industrial activities in mega-urban areas, which serve as innovation hubs with access to well-suited labour markets.[135] The second priority revolves around increasing urbanisation rates. Currently standing at around 60%, with only 45% of residents having regular urban status, the aim is to elevate urbanisation levels to 75–80% within a fifteen-year timeframe. Achieving this goal involves reforming the *hukou* system to expand the domestic market. The third priority is to 'get the Chinese house in order', which entails establishing a modern social security system capable of overcoming the existing fragmentation and providing comprehensive coverage to citizens. Lastly, the fourth priority is to further stimulate renewable energy production, an area where China has made significant strides and aims to maintain its position as a global leader in this field.

### 4.5  New Regulation

The internal deliberations among China's elite regarding the implications and direction of the new approach have been extensive, with a focus on the methods to be employed—should there be more dirigisme or further market reforms?—and on determining the optimal degree of China's openness to the global economy. The government, at least up to this point, has chosen a middle path that is not merely a compromise but rather a balanced approach with a clear exit strategy.

On one hand, amid the global pandemic, China made decisions to further open its financial markets to the outside world between 2020 and 2021, based on the Foreign Investment Law of January 2020. These new regulations relaxed previous limitations on equity holdings, access to futures markets, and the

---

134  Kaidong Feng, Yin Li, and William Lazonick (eds.), "Transforming China's Industrial Innovation in the New Era", special feature, *China Review* 22, no. 1 (February 2022): 1–353; Yin Li, *China's Drive for the Technology Frontier: Indigenous Innovation in the High-Tech Industry* (London: Routledge, 2023).

135  A good example of this is the Greater Bay Area project (Hong Kong, Macau, and Guangdong Province).

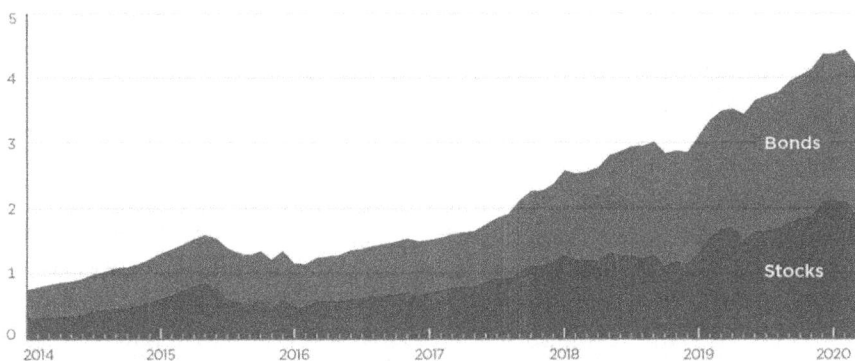

FIGURE 3.3  Foreign portfolio investment in Chinese stocks and bonds (trillions of renminbi)
REPRODUCED FROM NICHOLAS R. LARDY AND TIANLEI HUANG, "RISING FOREIGN INVESTMENT IN CHINESE STOCKS AND BONDS SHOWS DEEPENING FINANCIAL INTEGRATION", PIIE, 6 JULY 2020, HTTPS://WWW.PIIE.COM/RESEARCH/PIIE-CHARTS/RISING-FOREIGN-INVESTMENT-CHINESE-STOCKS-AND-BONDS-SHOWS-DEEPENING-FINANCIAL. DATA FROM THE PEOPLE'S BANK OF CHINA VIA WIND FINANCIAL INFORMATION.

trading of shares and Treasury bills. As a result, some of the largest US financial institutions seized these new opportunities to expand their operations in China during 2020 and 2021 (see Figure 3.3). They also gained access to private wealth management and insurance funds while being allowed to operate wholly-owned or majority-owned subsidiaries.

This, however, does not diminish the fact that in response to the growing restrictions placed on Chinese companies' access to US and European stock markets, as well as on corporate takeovers,[136] Beijing initiated a comprehensive set of countermeasures starting in 2020. One noteworthy development was the introduction of the Foreign Sanctions Act in June 2021.[137] Furthermore, it remains to be seen whether, in the geopolitical climate shaped by the Ukrainian conflict, the flow of foreign capital into China will continue or, as

---

136  Organisation for Economic Co-operation and Development (OECD), "OECD Business and Finance Outlook 2018—China's Belt and Road Initiative in the Global Trade, Investment and Finance Landscape", Paris, 2018, accessed 28 September 2023, https://www.oecd.org/finance/Chinas-Belt-and-Road-Initiative-in-the-global-trade-investment-and-finance-landscape.pdf.

137  Gibson Dunn, "China's 'Blocking Statute'—New Chinese Rules to Counter the Application of Extraterritorial Foreign Laws", 13 January 2021, accessed 28 September 2023, https://www.gibsondunn.com/wp-content/uploads/2021/01/chinas-blocking-statute-new-chinese-rules-to-counter-the-application-of-extraterritorial-foreign-laws.pdf.

some data suggests, experience a decisive reversal. In any case, the significance of the external aspect of dual circulation has been underscored.

Conversely, what garnered the most attention from Western observers was the remarkable series of measures introduced to regulate internal markets and, more broadly, societal relationships as part of this strategy. While analysing this shift in regulatory approach, it is essential to consider the underlying factors: the connection between the social equality[138] sought through recent years' class struggles and the urgent imperative to restructure Chinese capitalism. Chinese leadership has clearly recognised this connection, as evidenced by the assertion that "common prosperity is an essential requirement of socialism and a key feature of Chinese-style modernization".[139] The new development approach, aimed at curbing the "disorderly expansion of capital" within the context of an "international environment that has become increasingly complex and serious" (as articulated during the Sixth Plenum of the CCP in November 2021), also necessitates a reduction in economic inequalities. This has led to a regulatory crackdown, particularly targeting large private companies in the digital platform economy.

In October 2020, a cybersecurity campaign was initiated, involving fourteen ministries and state agencies, with the objective of restoring order in the digital technology sector. The following month, the State Administration for Market Regulation, which had previously undergone reorganisation in 2018, introduced new anti-monopoly regulations for the sector. Shortly before this, the Chinese regulatory authority had blocked an initial public offering (IPO) by Ant Group, the financial subsidiary of Alibaba, which happens to be China's largest e-commerce company.

The major digital corporations, which had rapidly achieved oligopolistic control over China's digital networks, had started focusing on data monetisation and user profiling by offering microcredit services. For example, Jack Ma's Alibaba saw its financial platform become even more profitable than its commercial activities. They also began issuing derivatives with microloans as underlying assets, reminiscent of the US subprime crisis. This move by the private sector had the potential to sideline commercial banks, thereby jeopardising state control over credit and interfering with the payment system. While

---

138  Since spring 2021, after the lockdowns following the pandemic crisis, minimum wage levels in many regions have been raised.
139  From Xi Jinping's speech on 17 August 2021 at a party meeting. See "Full Text: Xi Jinping's Speech on Boosting Common Prosperity", Caixin Global, 19 October 2021, accessed 12 January 2022, https://www.caixinglobal.com/2021-10-19/full-text-xi-jinpings-speech-on-boosting-common-prosperity-101788302.html.

this scenario is not unfamiliar in the West, it posed significant risks for the Chinese state, which could not afford the emergence of powerful private speculative finance. Consequently, Alipay was not only subjected to a substantial fine but also required to segregate its payment and lending activities by establishing a separate company with state capital participation. This newly formed entity would be responsible for managing the profiling data of the billions of users it had accumulated over the years.

In 2021, China implemented similar policy measures against other major network corporations. Didi, often referred to as the Chinese counterpart of Uber, was compelled to delist from the New York Stock Exchange. Concurrently, local and central authorities began the process of regulating the labour market within the gig economy, starting with Didi's taxi drivers. This segment of the economy, which is estimated to employ around seventy million workers, came under initial scrutiny. Furthermore, Tencent, the owner of WeChat with over a billion users, faced stricter controls on its applications to safeguard user privacy. The regulatory authority mandated the separation of Tencent's private payments company. Meituan, a meal delivery platform, received fines for engaging in monopolistic practices and was required to involve the official labour union in the company.

In essence, the central state in China aimed to curb the abuse of dominant market positions by Big Tech companies. This was to be achieved through the separation of various activities (sales, distribution, credit intermediation, and assessment), acceptance of state capital participation and oversight in these companies, and enabling smaller businesses to sell on multiple platforms to counteract monopolistic practices by the larger players. This approach could be seen as a genuine anti-monopoly legislation, which, if implemented in the West, might be hailed as democratic or criticised as 'populist'. However, when applied by China, it apparently reveals its 'authoritarian' face!

Simultaneously, digital sovereignty is not just being achieved through the transformation of the internet network, which involved establishing a 'Great Wall' against US operators and creating a protected market with 800 million users. It is also being accomplished by enhancing the rights of user-citizens when dealing with big businesses. In November 2021, one of the world's strictest privacy laws came into effect. Since 2022, there has been legislation regulating algorithms to restrict the use of filtering software. This should be considered alongside the data cybersecurity law in place since September 2021, which prohibits the transfer of data to countries lacking equally stringent regulations, effectively centralising data at the state level. Digital sovereignty and the territorialisation of the internet represent the flip side of a 'democratic' movement—a new agreement between the state and its citizens—in response to both domestic and foreign Big Tech companies.

These oligopolistic digital corporations epitomise a new industrial generation that has the potential to become a centre of independent power. They are resistant to state control while simultaneously promoting practices and content that encourage individual autonomy and the Western way of life. However, their excessive power, primarily in commercial applications, does not contribute significantly to closing the technological gap with the West, particularly in the hardware and microprocessor sectors. Consequently, the regulatory focus has shifted towards more significant scrutiny of big software companies than hardware manufacturers.

In addition to these regulatory measures, there have been significant policy shifts in terms of monetary and capital controls, such as the ban on cryptocurrency transactions. This action should be understood in the context of the digital yuan strategy and the internationalisation of the Chinese currency. Furthermore, when it comes to societal intervention, the government has implemented restrictions on young people playing video games and using certain social media platforms like TikTok. These activities, recognised for their addictive nature among young people, have come under scrutiny. Additionally, fines have been imposed on figures in showbusiness and web influencers, often referred to as 'pick-up artists', who are accused of promoting consumerist behaviour models.

Another area of state intervention related to the concept of common prosperity is education. The government has taken measures to curb the proliferation of private fee-paying courses, especially those conducted in English. Simultaneously, teachers have been encouraged to reduce the extracurricular study burden, which is exceptionally high in China's highly competitive educational environment, where educational qualifications are of paramount importance for social advancement.

The trend of regulatory interventionism appears set to continue, possibly extending to taxation, particularly in the real estate sector, as part of a broader effort to establish a sustainable welfare system. The measures outlined here provide a glimpse of the Chinese government's resolute commitment to impose limits on the unbridled capitalist practices that prevailed in previous decades. This transformation is, in essence, the 'Chinese way'—a path marked by numerous revolutionary and post-revolutionary shifts—as China transitions towards a form of capitalism characterised by domestic social-democratic principles and increased assertiveness on the international stage, particularly in its dealings with imperialism.

## 4.6 Not a Foregone Conclusion

To date, it remains challenging to fully assess the overall impact and degree of success of China's new strategy. Nevertheless, this strategy aligns with and stimulates a trend that is already evident in the broad contours of macroeconomic indicators.

First, in terms of import–export rebalancing, after the 2008–9 crisis, China's current account surplus gradually decreased, primarily due to a reduction in trade surpluses, moving from 10% in the 2000s to around 2% at the end of the 2010s. This reduction reflects both greater industrial self-sufficiency and the expansion of the domestic market.[140] The share of exports in GDP has also declined in recent years, falling below 20%—according to some estimates, even less—compared to an average of 35% in the previous decade,[141] below the average for the euro area and Japan and South Korea. This places China's trade intensity, which measures the sum of imports and exports as a percentage of total output, at around 30%, down from approximately 50% between 2008 and 2018.[142] While this decline can be attributed to factors such as the global financial crisis and the trade tensions with Washington, it is also a reflection of China's economic strategy shifting towards a more balanced approach.[143] However, it is important to note that the qualitative aspect of foreign trade, linked to foreign investment, remains crucial. Foreign-invested companies still contribute significantly to value-added in high-tech sectors and, more broadly, account for almost half of Chinese exports.[144]

---

140 OECD, "OECD Inter-Country Input-Output (ICIO) Tables", accessed 14 January 2022, https://www.oecd.org/sti/ind/inter-country-input-output-tables.htm.
141 Herrera and Long, *La Chine est-elle capitaliste?*.
142 Susan Lund, James Manyika, Jonathan Woetzel, Jacques Bughin, Mekala Krishnan, Jeongmin Seong, and Mac Muir, *Globalization in Transition: The Future of Trade and Value Chains* (New York: McKinsey Global Institute, 2019), accessed 23 September 2023, https://www.mckinsey.com/featured-insights/innovation-and-growth/globalization-in-transition-the-future-of-trade-and-value-chains.
143 Nonetheless, China has maintained its position as the global leader in total trade in goods since 2013. In 2021, with a GDP of $16.6 trillion, the combined value of imports and exports exceeded $6 trillion, accounting for approximately 17% of the world's total trade. China has held the title of the world's largest exporter since 2009. See Tianlei Huang and Nicholas R. Lardy, "China is Too Tied to the Global Economy to Risk Helping Russia", PIIE blog, 15 March 2022, accessed 28 September 2023, https://www.piie.com/blogs/realtime-economic-issues-watch/china-too-tied-global-economy-risk-helping-russia.
144 Italian Trade Agency, *Il mercato dei macchinari in Cina*, March 2020, accessed 28 September 2023, https://www.ucimu.it/fileadmin/public/Documenti_PDF/IL_MERCATO_DEI_MACCHINARI_IN_CINA_01.pdf.

Regarding the rebalancing between investment and final consumption, while the latter has been growing, investments remain relatively high. Just before the onset of the pandemic, domestic consumption had increased to over 50% of GDP, compared to about 30% for investments. The industrial sector still represented nearly 30% of the value produced, although it was surpassed by the tertiary sector starting in 2014. Both the global financial crisis and the pandemic, a decade later, led to an increase in fixed investments due to anti-cyclical infrastructure plans initiated by the government. These two variables should not be seen in opposition to each other. Final consumption is influenced by investments through the income channel, and it includes not only personal consumption, but also social consumption related to public services.

Finally, inter-regional rebalancing, particularly between the coastal areas and the interior regions, holds significant strategic importance in preventing a territorial divide. The global financial crisis triggered a dual process: the relocation of Chinese companies to Asian countries with lower labour costs and the development of industrial complexes in China's interior regions.[145] This shift has had initial repercussions, notably in terms of gradual wage adjustments due to emerging labour conflicts and the tendency of migrant workers to move closer to their hometowns.[146] Here it is important to emphasise that the industrialisation of inland regions is progressing, albeit to a limited extent, except for the Chongqing region. Moreover, this transformation has not led to a decline in industrial activities in the primary coastal regions.

In summary, the industrial transformation, driven by the party-state's strategy and influenced by dynamics in class struggle, is pushing for an overall reconfiguration across sectors, regions, and in relation to the West. However, the development of this new pattern remains uneven. The processes of automation and functional diversification coexist with widespread labour-intensive exploitation, while the emergence of skilled jobs is accompanied by a growing pool of deskilled jobs.[147] China finds itself at a crossroads, and the outcome of this transformative process is far from certain.

---

145   "The Changing Geography of Chinese Industry: Data Brief", *Chuang* blog, 5 August 2019, accessed 28 September 2023, https://chuangcn.org/2019/08/the-changing-geography-of-chinese-industry-data-brief/.
146   According to data from the National Bureau of Statistics, the number of migrant workers in the coastal provinces declined by 0.7% in 2019, while it increased by 3.0% in the western provinces.
147   Sam King, *Imperialism and the Development Myth: How Rich Countries Dominate in the Twenty-First Century* (Manchester: Manchester University Press, 2021), 219–57.

## 5 China at a Crossroads

In the midst of these changes, China's journey is beset with obstacles originating from both within the country, stemming from the unique contradictions of its distinct form of capitalism and social consensus, as well as from external factors. In this chapter, we will examine some of the key challenges, such as limited access to critical technologies essential for advancing up the value chains, declining productivity, mounting debt concerns, the precarious state of the real estate market, and the uncertain social standing of the middle classes. While our analysis is not exhaustive, it seeks to underscore the intricate and contradictory nature of the ongoing developments.

### 5.1 Access to Advanced Technology: the Case of Microprocessors

The central arena of contention between China and Washington undeniably revolves around China's quest for access to advanced technology and the competitive drive to shape technical standards.[148] This pursuit forms a critical component of China's broader 'New Silk Roads' strategy (see below) and aims to attain greater autonomy in the industrial sphere and eventually disengage to some extent from the dominance of the US dollar. In this complex landscape, strategy and tactics, long-term perspectives, and immediate contingencies become increasingly intertwined.

Nonetheless, the fundamental challenge remains that China's technological value chains have experienced substantial growth in recent decades, but they remain deeply interwoven with global supply networks. This translates into a continued reliance on the import of critical components, primarily from countries like the United States, Germany, and Japan. This reliance extends across various sectors, including those where China has made significant advancements such as robotics,[149] electric vehicles, artificial intelligence, and 5G networks, where Chinese brands dominate the domestic market. However, in sectors like advanced microprocessors, aircraft, and motor vehicles, China lacks competitive global brands and depends heavily on foreign manufacturers for these strategic technologies. These bottlenecks, though not numerous, hold

---

148 John Seaman, "China and the New Geopolitics of Technical Standardization", *Notes de l'Ifri* (publication of the French Institute of International Relations), 27 January 2020, accessed 28 September 2023, https://www.ifri.org/en/publications/notes-de-lifri/china-and-new-geopolitics-technical-standardization.

149 Hong Cheng, Ruixue Jia, Dandan Li, and Hongbin Li, "The Rise of Robots in China", *Journal of Economic Perspectives* 33, no. 2 (2019): 71–88, accessed 28 September 2023, https://pubs.aeaweb.org/doi/pdfplus/10.1257/jep.33.2.71.

paramount strategic importance in China's quest for access to vital technologies. The current state of Chinese research, which has surged in investment and is now the world's second-largest after the United States, has indeed resulted in a high number of patents. Nevertheless, according to experts, Chinese research is perceived as lagging behind that of the United States, primarily focusing on applied research and therefore insufficient to reverse the flow of technology imports from abroad.[150]

It is no coincidence that the Chinese political debate on these issues has pivoted around the imperative to shift the focus of research funding from the private sector—where, up to now, the majority of R&D investment has been driven primarily by considerations of immediate profitability—to state-sponsored research centres, thus fostering basic research through comprehensive projects. This underscores another critical issue: the existing imbalance, favouring private over public investment. This disparity has made effective strategic planning challenging, despite initiatives like 'Made in China 2025'. The problem persists, primarily because of the difficulty in concentrating market forces, which have been more loosely supervised than directly controlled by industrial policies.[151] As China crafts its economic strategy in response to US decoupling, it remains an open question whether the ongoing confrontation will drive China further towards self-sufficiency or instead result in chaos and regression before substantial progress is made in that direction.

The case of the microprocessor industry, the backbone of the digital economy, epitomises these challenges and is crucial for China's envisioned qualitative leap in its economy. As we discussed in the previous chapter, the US strategy of economic warfare against China has singled out this sector as its focal point. Now, let us delve into the Chinese dimension of this issue. In the globalised microprocessor industry, China has emerged as a dominant player, particularly in the final stages of assembly. Its output in this sector accounts for 16% of global production, with particular strengths in packaging, chip assembly and testing, and chips for artificial intelligence, optical equipment, and sensors. However, when it comes to manufacturing (foundries) and,

---

150  Alex He, "What Do China's High Patent Numbers Really Mean?", Centre for International Governance Innovation, 20 April 2021, accessed 28 September 2023, https://www.cigionl ine.org/articles/what-do-chinas-high-patent-numbers-really-mean/; Richard Hanania, "The Inevitable Rise of China: U.S. Options With Less Indo-Pacific Influence", *Defense Priorities*, 26 May 2021, accessed 28 September 2023, https://www.defensepriorities.org /explainers/the-inevitable-rise-of-china-us-options-with-less-indo-pacific-influence.

151  Carsten A. Holz, "Industrial Policies and the Changing Patterns of Investment in the Chinese Economy", *China Journal* 81 (2018), https://doi.org/10.1086/699877.

more crucially, chip design, China remains heavily reliant on the supply of foreign-made microprocessors, making it the world's largest importer of such technology.[152]

This dependence comes with a significant lag in technology advancement, estimated at approximately ten years. China's autonomous capacities currently do not extend beyond 14–16 nm circuits, a notable gap when compared to Taiwan's TSMC, which leads with 7 nm circuits for commercial use and has even lower threshold circuits in development. The vulnerabilities arising from this dependency are evident, especially in areas such as chip design and advanced machinery used in microprocessor production (see Figure 3.4).[153] This has already been illustrated by the struggles faced by Chinese companies like Huawei, as well as the US ban on selling ultraviolet lithography technology (controlled by the Dutch company ASML) to the leading Chinese company SMIC (Semiconductor Manufacturing International Corporation). This technology is critical for achieving circuits below the 10 nm threshold and has wide-ranging implications across sectors, particularly for artificial intelligence, which relies on advanced microprocessors to expand beyond mass consumption applications, including military applications.[154]

As mentioned earlier, in 2019, China's domestic production of microprocessors accounted for only 16% of its total consumption. The critical gap primarily lies in the advanced machinery required for microprocessor foundries, preventing them from establishing a strong presence in the high-end market segment. 'Made in China 2025' outlines ambitious goals for this sector, aiming to produce up to 70% of the country's microprocessor needs by 2025, ultimately meeting the highest international standards by 2030. Companies

---

152   In 2020, integrated circuits took the top spot among Chinese imports, totalling a staggering $350 billion. This amount significantly outstripped the second-highest import item, crude oil, which stood at $176 billion. See Filippo Fasulo, "Strategie Globali: Indo-Pacifico, mare loro?", ISPI, 22 September 2021, accessed 28 September 2023, https://www.ispionl ine.it/it/pubblicazione/strategie-globali-indo-pacifico-mare-loro-31743.
153   John Lee and Jan-Peter Kleinhans, "Mapping China's Semiconductor Ecosystem in Global Context: Strategic Dimensions and Conclusions", Berlin, MERICS and Stiftung Neue Verantwortung, 30 June 2021, accessed 28 September 2023, https://merics.org /en/report/mapping-chinas-semiconductor-ecosystem-global-context-strategic-dimensi ons-and-conclusions; John Lee and Jan-Peter Kleinhans, "Mapping China's Place in the Global Semiconductor Industry", MERICS, 14 September 2021, accessed 28 September 2023, https://merics.org/en/comment/mapping-chinas-place-global-semiconductor-industry.
154   Dieter Ernst, "Competing in Artificial Intelligence Chips: China's Challenge amid Technology War", Waterloo, ON, Canada, Centre for International Governance Innovation, 2020, accessed 28 September 2023, https://www.cigionline.org/publications/compet ing-artificial-intelligence-chips-chinas-challenge-amid-technology-war/.

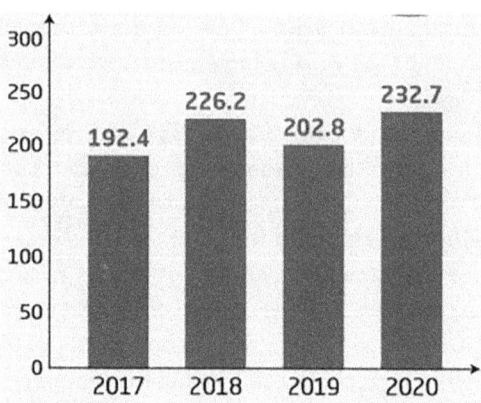

FIGURE 3.4 China's trade deficit in semiconductors (USD billion)
REPRODUCED FROM ALEXANDER BROWN, JACOB GUNTER, AND MAX J. ZENGLEIN, "COURSE CORRECTION: CHINA'S SHIFTING APPROACH TO GLOBALISATION" (MERICS CHINA MONITOR, BERLIN, MERICS, 19 OCTOBER 2021), ACCESSED 28 SEPTEMBER 2023, HTTPS://MERICS.ORG/SITES/DEFAULT/FILES/2021-10/MERICS-CHINAMONITOR_GLOBALIZATION_2021-10-13.PDF. DATA FROM THE GENERAL ADMINISTRATION OF CUSTOMS, QIANZHAN.

like SMIC are investing in foundries capable of designing integrated circuits for both high-end and medium-to-low-end markets to achieve these targets. However, the outlook remains uncertain, with potential bankruptcies looming if state investments fail to yield effective results in a fiercely competitive global market. Additionally, ongoing decoupling efforts by Washington may disrupt the supply chain.[155] Nevertheless, Beijing cannot afford to back down from this confrontation, especially given its increasing significance in the military

---

155 Matt Sheehan, "China Technology 2025: Fragile Tech Superpower", Macro Polo (Paulson Institute), 26 October 2020, accessed 29 September 2023, https://macropolo.org/analysis/china-technology-forecast-2025-fragile-tech-superpower.

domain.[156] China can rely on a rapidly expanding domestic market, which accounts for 25% of the global market, mirroring the United States' share.[157]

Furthermore, a substantial investment race has already erupted in this sector, with hundreds of billions of dollars at play. The prospect of a fragmented global supply network is compelling both corporations and governments to prioritise resilience and redundancy in supply chains to reduce foreign dependencies. However, this global drive may lead to rising costs, undermining returns on massive investments and resulting in potential overcapacity and intensified competition. Ultimately, China's attempts to ascend the global hierarchy are likely to become increasingly costly. At some point, surplus production will need to be managed, potentially at the expense of various competitors.

### 5.2  *The Productivity Issue*

China's economic and social achievements are indisputable, regardless of the metrics chosen to evaluate them. These successes encompass an increase in per capita GDP, reaching $10,500 according to World Bank data for 2021, and an absolute GDP of $16.6 trillion in 2021, equivalent to 17% of the global total.[158] Additionally, China has witnessed an increase in life expectancy, reaching 76.5 years in 2017, and has lifted approximately 700 million people out of absolute poverty. All of this has been achieved by a 'developing' nation that has transitioned into a middle-income status, as categorised in international economics. This transformation was made possible by China's revolutionary history and the fortuitous opportunity window that opened over the past three decades. The era of ascendant globalisation and a favourable geopolitical climate, during a unipolar moment for the United States that was preoccupied with other matters, facilitated China's integration into the global market. Despite the challenges, China managed to navigate this period without experiencing the political upheaval of the 1980s, which could have jeopardised its national unity. Some might attribute this to a combination of luck and political acumen, echoing Machiavellian principles.

---

156   As in the case of quantum computers research.
157   Antonio Varas, Raj Varadarajan, Ramiro Palma, Jimmy Goodrich, and Falan Yinug, "Strengthening the Global Semiconductor Supply Chain in an Uncertain Era", Boston Consulting Group, 1 April 2021, accessed 29 September 2023, https://www.bcg.com/publications/2021/strengthening-the-global-semiconductor-supply-chain.
158   For comparison, the United States boasts a per capita GDP of $68,300. To put this into perspective, World Bank data from 2019 revealed that China's GDP per capita was approximately one-fourth of the average for OECD countries.

However, the current transition presents a different set of challenges. Just as China was poised for a potential leap forward as a 'semi-peripheral' capitalist nation with significant growth prospects, it encountered its first major global economic crisis since the 1970s. The imperialist toll on the value produced in China, in various forms, became even more burdensome. This was exacerbated by an endogenous decline in profitability, as diminishing returns on invested capital signalled the gradual exhaustion of a cycle built on the extraction of absolute surplus value. Productivity stagnated, and the imperative for a revolutionary leap capable of overcoming these challenges was met with a less favourable global context, marked by diminishing accumulation in core countries, and the overt hostility of Washington on both commercial and technological fronts, as well as geopolitically.

The decline in productivity increments became notably evident after the global financial crisis, particularly when compared to Western economies. The World Bank attributes much of this decline to the deceleration in China's GDP growth.[159] According to the International Monetary Fund (IMF), China's 'total factor productivity' had only reached about a third of that seen in the United States, Japan, or Germany up to that point.[160] This productivity challenge was not solely linked to significant differences in productivity between private enterprises in the coastal provinces and those in the interior of China. State-owned enterprises also experienced declining efficiency, partly due to the financial burden imposed by the state's demand support policies implemented in response to the crisis. In essence, as the support for economic growth relied heavily on investments in traditional sectors like physical infrastructure and real estate, which could be used counter-cyclically, but did not bring about substantial productivity gains, the returns on capital gradually diminished.

Indeed, diminishing profitability of companies, especially in the industrial sector, became increasingly noticeable during the 2010s. Meticulous research by the Chuang[161] collective identifies three main phases of economic growth

---

159   Brandt et al., "China's Productivity Slowdown"; Karim Foda, "The Productivity Slump: A Summary of the Evidence", Washington, DC, Brookings Institution, 2016, accessed 13 January 2021, https://www.brookings.edu/wp-content/uploads/2016/08/productivity-evidence.pdf.

160   Alessia Amighini (ed.), *China after COVID-19: Economic Revival and Challenges to the World* (Milan: ISPI, 2021), accessed 29 September 2023, https://www.ispionline.it/en/publication/china-after-covid-19-economic-revival-and-challenges-world-30780.

161   "Measuring the Profitability of Chinese Industry: Data Brief", *Chuang* blog, 21 June 2020, accessed 29 September 2023, https://chuangcn.org/2020/06/measuring-profitability/. See also Zhang Yu and Zhao Feng, "Saggio del plusvalore, Composizione del Capitale e Saggio del Profitto nell'Industria Manifatturiera Cinese: 1978–2004", in *Il mistero del dragone. La dinamica economica della Cina*, edited by Joel Andreas, Kam Wing Chan, Zhao Feng,

following the Dengist reforms. The first phase, in the 1990s, involved the tumultuous restructuring of the planned economy, especially for state-owned heavy industry, resulting in declining profitability indices, at least until private enterprises gained full momentum. The second phase, from 2000 until the global recession in 2008–9, marked the completion of restructuring and the emergence of an export-led model with rapidly rising rates of surplus value extraction and profitability. This period was characterised by labour-intensive production, the relocation of foreign multinationals, and the intense exploitation of worker-farmers. Finally, the third phase, starting with the global crisis, witnessed a strong initial rebound in profitability during the 2010s, thanks to massive central monetary stimulus. However, this was followed by a decline, accompanied by a relative flattening of the economic growth curve, which became most pronounced just as the pandemic crisis emerged.

Over the past fifteen years, investment trends have generally followed a parallel trajectory, a pattern corroborated by various sources. Focusing on the most recent decade and a half, there has been a significant increase in total investment in fixed assets, including construction, with a peak in 2015–16, followed by a subsequent decline in the following years.[162] Between 2007, just before the outbreak of the global financial crisis, and 2020, infrastructure investment as a percentage of GDP dropped from 12% to 6%, while the growth rate decreased from 13.6% to 5.8% annually.

The economic landscape of the last decade has become more intricate and challenging to decipher. On one hand, substantial investments in construction, physical infrastructure, transportation, and industrial facilities initially led to an economic upturn, albeit short-lived. This period was accompanied by the initial signs of a real estate and stock market bubble. These, along with liquidity injections from central banks, temporarily masked underlying issues. On the other hand, factors such as rising wages due to labour disputes and emerging challenges in the global market have driven the need for a qualitative restructuring of production structures. This goes beyond mere quantitative expansion

---

Chloé Froissart, Hung Ho-Fung, Peter Nolan, Christine Peltier, Tim Pringle, and Zhang Yu (Trieste: Asterios, 2007), 216–40. Drawing on the Penn World Table (a set of national accounts data maintained by scholars in California and Gronigen), Roberts highlights the growing correlation between Chinese capital profitability and GDP growth. See Michael Roberts, "China's Crackdown on the Three Mountains", author's blog, 8 August 2021, accessed 29 September 2023, https://thenextrecession.wordpress.com/2021/08/08/chinas-crackdown-on-the-three-mountains/.

162  Alessia Amighini, "Cina: i freni alla corsa del Dragone" [China: The brakes on the dragon's race], ISPI, 5 August 2021, accessed 29 September, https://www.ispionline.it/it/pubblicazione/cina-i-freni-alla-corsa-del-dragone-31336.

in established sectors (i.e. beyond the growth in profit mass as profitability declines)[163] and involves a shift from labour-intensive to capital-intensive production with increased productivity, although not universally applied.

However, this transition occurs within the broader context of a relative decline in the manufacturing sector's share compared to services. The latter is known to be less prone to productivity gains. Additionally, the agricultural sector likely reached its economic limits under unchanged conditions, risking significant social unrest. These circumstances are enough to instil a sense of unease, especially considering the ominous signs accumulating in the global economy and the emergence of significant geopolitical conflicts, as exemplified by the situation in Ukraine. In a single word: the uncertainties wrought by globalisation.

### 5.3     Debt Conundrum

State fiscal stimulus in the early 2010s played a significant role in fostering another pertinent phenomenon: the escalating indebtedness of local governments, corporations, and households, particularly those of the emerging middle class. This surge in debt was the flip side of credit growing at twice the rate of GDP. It is widely recognised that this phenomenon disproportionately affected sectors like infrastructure, construction, and real estate. For instance, in 2009, immediately following the global crisis, the non-financial sector received loans equivalent to 32% of GDP, which then dropped to 20% in 2010. Apart from the intricacies related to the power dynamics between the state and private industry, along with varying bourgeois interests represented within the party-state—often leading to public subsidies for unprofitable investments—there were global economic recovery challenges and the complexities of an ongoing economic transition that underscored China's relative overcapacity. Consequently, China found itself grappling with an unprecedented level of debt while simultaneously witnessing the formation of speculative bubbles, ranging from real estate to the stock market.

However, this problem is not confined to a particular sector. China initially resorted to debt as a means to mitigate the adverse effects of the global crisis. Yet, it has since continued on this trajectory to finance high-tech investments, boost domestic consumption, promote its own brands' global competitiveness, support crucial external economic endeavours, and decrease its dependence on Western imperialism. Success in this endeavour would potentially enable China to manage its debt to some extent, thanks to the expansion of

---

163   Gaulard, *Karl Marx à Pékin*, 151ff.

capital reproduction. Conversely, if this process were to stagnate, it would give rise to internal turmoil—albeit slightly mitigated by the fact that the Chinese state has managed to avoid reliance on institutions such as the IMF, World Bank, Western banks, and states. A stalled process would essentially represent the successful transfer of the global fictitious capital bubble, engineered by Western imperialism, onto the shoulders of China.

It is also important to acknowledge that, thus far, the predictions—some might even call them wishful thinking—of a looming collapse of the Chinese economy by Western mainstream sources, a refrain that has persisted for over a decade, have failed to materialise. In fact, a substantial portion of domestic debt is interconnected through credit circuits, spanning various institutions at different levels, or involving transactions between local governments and state banks. Central government debt levels remain relatively low when compared to international standards. Household debt, relative to GDP, remains quite modest (standing at around 55% in 2022, up from 36% in 2013, with much of it tied to real estate mortgages) (see Figure 3.5).

Furthermore, China retains a firm grip on liquidity control through central authorities, while household savings are abundant and widespread. Moreover, foreign debt denominated in dollars is at relatively low levels, and China even holds the status of a net creditor in the global debt landscape (owning 6% of the world's credits, with the majority allocated to poorer nations). Not to be overlooked are China's massive reserves in dollars and euros, and the likelihood of Washington imposing a financial sanctions regime on Beijing, akin to what has occurred with Russia, does not seem imminent.

However, it should be noted that despite these mitigating factors, debt levels have risen significantly. Following a period of reduction between 2003 and 2008, rates of indebtedness have climbed, especially in the case of corporate debt (non-financial), which expanded from 2008 onwards to reach 150% of GDP by the present day. Public debt, on the other hand, has seen local debt consistently outpace central debt since 2010, exceeding 25% of GDP in 2020. In addition to this, there exists what is termed 'hidden debt' (estimated at approximately $1 trillion) that flows through specialised financial vehicles designed to circumvent central restrictions. When combined with the central government's debt of $3.6 trillion, total public debt in 2021 stood at around $15.5 trillion, nearly 90% of GDP (a significant increase from the approximately 50% recorded in 2013).[164]

---

164 Claudio Cesaroni, "Non solo Evergrande", ISPI, 18 November 2021, accessed 29 September 2021, https://www.ispionline.it/it/pubblicazione/non-solo-evergrande-32378.

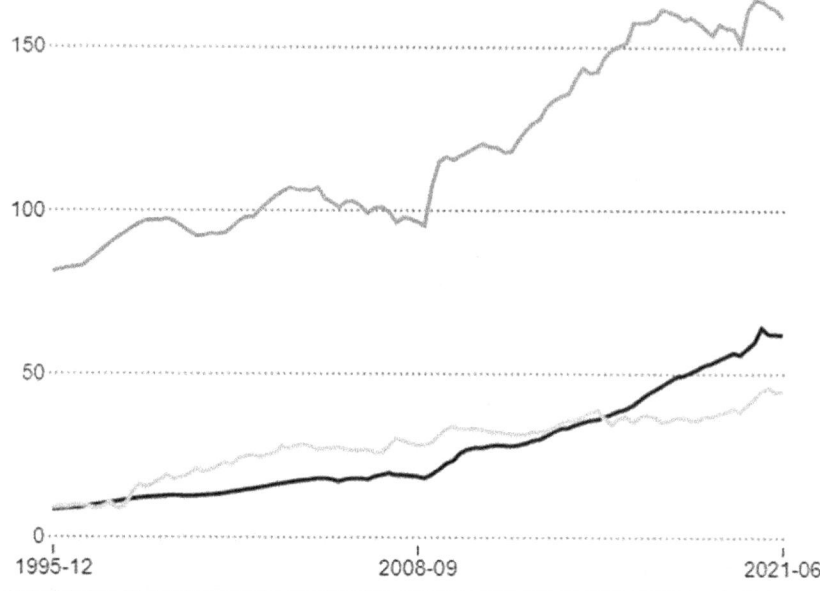

FIGURE 3.5   China's debt to GDP
*Note*: The debt of local governments is missing from the chart.
REPRODUCED FROM ROBERTS, "CHINA'S CRACKDOWN", UNPAGINATED. DATA FROM THE INSTITUTE OF INTERNATIONAL FINANCE.

There are two additional factors that bear significant relevance and potential risk, especially when viewed from a long-term perspective. First, the so-called shadow banking system, an unregulated financial network operating outside the purview of state-controlled circuits, has witnessed substantial growth in recent years. Estimates for China place shadow banking at nearly $13 trillion (a significant increase from $7 trillion in 2017).[165] This expansion is closely related to the second factor: the Chinese bond market. Comprising both government and private company bonds, this market has risen to become the third largest in the world, boasting a total worth of $13 trillion. More importantly, the share

---

165   Frank Tang, "China Estimates Shadow Banking Worth US$12.9 Trillion as it Moves to Clean Up High-Risk Sector", *South China Morning Post*, 7 December 2020, accessed 29 September 2023, https://www.scmp.com/economy/china-economy/article/3112892/china-estimates-shadow-banking-worth-us129-trillion-it-moves?module=hard_link&pgtype=article.

of foreign investors in this market has steadily increased in recent years, following its opening to them in 2016. Following the economic rebound of 2020, in the aftermath of the pandemic crisis when China led the way, the share of foreign investors surged notably, driven by expectations of recovery and a robust yuan.[166] Clearly, as China's financial market opens further to the global arena, it becomes increasingly exposed to international liquidity flows, dollar dependence, and potential geopolitical shifts—a situation reminiscent of that witnessed in 2015–16.

Confronting these inherent risks, the central government has repeatedly implemented measures to restrict credit, especially with the aim of reducing local governments' debt leverage. However, it must always tread a fine line between imposing restrictions and loosening them, depending on the prevailing economic conditions. This delicate balancing act also extends to controls and liberalisation concerning monetary and credit regulation. China's central bank retains control over central rates, reserve requirements, and loan volumes, yet it has partially deregulated local bank rates. Exchange rates have been progressively determined by the market, although they are closely managed through monetary policy measures (primarily open market operations, inter-bank rate setting, yuan sterilisation, and short-term repo operations). Additionally, while institutions for managing non-performing loans, such as Asset Management China (AMC), have long been in place, the government has initiated several measures. These include new rules for debt restructuring and a reform of local government budgets aimed at restricting the use of special financial vehicles.[167] All of these actions have contributed to slowing the growth of both government and corporate lending since 2016, albeit at the cost of curbing economic growth.

In response to the pandemic emergency, state interventions between March 2020 and March 2021 were significant, although less aggressive than those seen in 2009. Consequently, there was yet another brief surge in construction, stock market indices, and exports (though not as pronounced as imports), but this came at the cost of abandoning the debt-reduction efforts made in previous years. As a result, overall indebtedness increased by 22% during this period, a noteworthy contrast to the 8.5% increase in the United States and the 14% rise in the euro area. This trend mirrored a global phenomenon where central banks worldwide acted as lenders of first resort and/or 'bad banks' for the

---

166  Hudson Lockett and Thomas Hale, "Global Investors Place Rmb1tr Bet on China", *Financial Times*, 14 December 2020, accessed 13 January 2021, https://www.ft.com/content/d9ac2 22d-90d8-4570-b89e-a99f1bd4829b.
167  Brandt et al., "China's Productivity Slowdown".

financial and production systems, amassing more than $26 trillion in the last two years. In China, the total debt—encompassing households, corporations, and the public sector—surpassed $46 trillion by March 2021, equivalent to 287% of the country's GDP.[168] While these figures are always subject to some degree of uncertainty, this represented a substantial acceleration in debt accumulation. So far, this has not led to a severe general debt crisis, thanks to continued economic growth, although it has slowed down due to declining investments, and state credit controls implemented through four major banking institutions. Nevertheless, the dynamics in this arena have evolved significantly, with a redistribution of financial assets resulting in their share falling to less than 50% of the total, while regional banks have seen their influence grow.

In light of these developments, it is no coincidence that Xi Jinping issued a warning about the pursuit of "genuine rather than inflated GDP growth". This includes both the absorption of adverse effects from previous stimulus policies and the avoidance of large inflows and withdrawals of foreign investment in the capital market.[169]

### 5.4   Real Estate Bubble?

The escalating indebtedness across various sectors of the Chinese economy has become closely intertwined with the emergence of price bubbles, notably the real estate bubble that first materialised in the early 2010s. Subsequently, the Chinese state intervened by directing this bubble towards the stock market. This redirection was prompted by an initial, although restrained, opening of China's capital account to foreign investors, a relaxation of financial regulations (pertaining to margin trading and initial bids), and, starting in 2013, the establishment of the first offshore trading centres for the Chinese renminbi yuan. In 2014, the fluctuation band of the yuan was doubled. The stock market bubble, which was characterised by a 30% loss of its value in the mid-2010s, did eventually burst. This was not solely due to endogenous factors but was also influenced by external reasons. The real estate bubble, however, experienced a resurgence, propelled by fiscal stimulus measures, a sustained demand

---

168   Amanda Lee, "China Debt: How Big Is It and Who Owns It?", *South China Morning Post*, 19 May 2020, accessed 29 September 2023, https://www.scmp.com/economy/china-economy/article/3084979/china-debt-how-big-it-who-owns-it-and-what-next.

169   Xi Jinping, "Understanding the New Development Stage, Applying the New Development Philosophy, and Creating a New Development Dynamic", *Qiushi Journal* (English edition), speech of 12 July 2021, reproduced at https://www.chinadaily.com.cn/a/202107/12/WS6 0ec3e56a310efa1bd6614fb.html, accessed 29 September 2023. Xi goes on to say that "we have enabled the market to play the decisive role in resource allocation and given better play to the role of the government".

for urban housing, and the inflow of capital from overseas. These factors came into sharp focus in 2021 with the Evergrande crisis. To gain insight into the current state of the housing market and the role of the state in this context, it is instructive to conduct a brief analysis of the Evergrande situation.[170]

The Chinese real estate market initially began to flourish in 1988 when private home ownership was legally recognised, with land granted by the state for a period of seventy years. Following the redemption of previously state-owned flats in the 1990s and a subsequent full-scale marketisation, the market grew further through low-interest mortgages. The result was an increase in the number of households that owned homes, with over 90% of the more than 270 million regular resident households in urban areas becoming homeowners. Home ownership has become a substantial part of the assets held by the Chinese population, comprising nearly 80% of their total wealth. Mortgages make up approximately 70% of household debt, and multiple home ownership has become a means for small- to medium-sized savers to store their wealth.

The rising demand for residential properties has consistently driven an increase in real estate prices, especially in major coastal cities. At present, the per capita residential space in China meets European standards, averaging around 40 sqm. This trend has been further propelled by credit policies, leading to the construction and real estate sector's remarkable growth, which constituted 13% of GDP in 2019 (a significant leap from 5% in 1995). This sector now represents nearly 30% of the total loans in the banking system, contributes to around 25% of household consumption, and provides employment for about 20% of urban workers.

Moreover, the financialisation of real estate has become increasingly evident. Banks frequently employ real estate loans as primary collateral for their activities, and this practice is also adopted by companies that secure land use rights. Concurrently, the construction of luxury housing and commercial properties has often taken precedence over the development of urban housing. The result has been overinvestment, leading to approximately a hundred million unoccupied housing units, primarily in first- and second-tier cities, where vacancy rates reach as high as 20%.

Significantly, real estate construction has evolved into the primary revenue source for local governments, especially after the mid-1990s tax reforms. These governments generate funds by selling land use rights, equivalent to approximately 7% of GDP, to both private and state-owned builders who secure

---

170   Mylène Gaulard, "Changes in the Chinese Property Market: An Indicator of the Difficulties Faced by Local Authorities", translated by Will Thornely, *China Perspectives* 2 (2013): 3–14, https://doi.org/10.4000/chinaperspectives.6143.

financing at low rates, primarily from commercial banks or the shadow banking system. Consequently, these transactions have accounted for up to 40% of local government revenues, further escalating land prices. With a lack of real estate taxation and high levels of debt, this is how money has been raised to fund the ever-growing cost of public services.

These intricacies echo processes that are well documented in Western economies. However, in China, which is at a less mature stage of capitalist development, distinguishing between investments intended to meet genuine social needs—a critical aspect of expanded social reproduction, even as urban sprawl takes precedence over rural areas and living spaces become more vertically structured[171]—and purely speculative investments can sometimes be challenging.

The surge in real estate prices during the 2010s was a by-product of these complex processes, which the central state sought to manage. Consequently, there were persistent shifts between accommodative monetary policies and credit constraints. In 2008–9, low-interest rates, employed as an anti-cyclical tool, fuelled a substantial investment boom in the real estate sector, leading to exponential price escalations. However, during the second half of 2010, tightening measures were introduced. From 2014 to 2015, there was another surge in real estate credit, marked by annual growth rates of 20% (in contrast to 6% for the manufacturing sector), which persisted until 2018. In 2016, the central bank lowered the minimum required mortgage down payment for first-home purchases to 20%, increasing to 30% for second homes and beyond.[172] Consequently, property prices have doubled or even tripled over the course of a decade, particularly in the most expensive coastal cities.

The average house price-to-income ratio has also increased significantly, rising from fifteen in 2014 to over forty in cities such as Beijing, Shanghai, and Shenzhen.[173] However, in recent years, and especially in the aftermath of the COVID-19 pandemic, the issue of speculative oversupply has unveiled the other side of the coin: a discernible downward trend in property prices and diminishing sales. It is within this context that the second-largest company in the

---

171 Amadeo Bordiga, "Spazio contro cemento", in *Drammi gialli e sinistri della moderna decadenza sociale* [Mystery dramas of modern social decadence] (Milan: Iskra, 1978).
172 "China Eases Mortgage Down Payment to 20% for First Homes", US-China Business Council, accessed 29 September 2023, https://www.uschina.org/china-hub/china-eases-mortgage-down-payment-20-first-homes, reproduced from Bloomberg, original article posted 2 February 2016.
173 Kenneth Rogoff and Yuanchen Yang, "Peak China Housing" (NBER Working Paper 27697, National Bureau of Economic Research, Cambridge, MA, August 2020), accessed 29 September 2023, http://www.nber.org/papers/w27697.

sector, Evergrande, found itself in mid-2021, grappling with $300 billion of debt that was challenging to repay. This debt was partly comprised of advances from small buyers (1.2 million households) for homes that were either under construction or merely planned. Additionally, it included junk bonds sold to both domestic and international investors, as well as its own employees, allured by high dividends (ranging from 7% to 9%) distributed in line with a classic Ponzi scheme.

Consequently, the government found itself compelled to infuse liquidity through the central bank into the banking system. This action was taken both to avert a potential domino effect across the financial sector and to incentivise Evergrande to complete its housing projects. The government's approach was to facilitate Evergrande in unwinding its assets without resorting to a conventional bailout. However, it is essential to note that, precisely to clamp down on such speculative activities, Beijing had implemented the 'three red lines' policy in 2020. This policy set three financial limits for companies operating in the real estate sector: a 70% cap on financial liabilities relative to assets, a 100% limit on net debt over net worth, and a requirement for available liquidity to cover short-term debt. Beijing's objective was not only to compel companies to deleverage and transfer losses to speculative investors but also to utilise the Evergrande case as an example for the entire sector. The central government had substantial capacity to mitigate the economic repercussions of such situations, and to date, no systemic fallout has occurred. Consequently, the comparison between Evergrande and Lehman Brothers, which was briefly circulating in the Western press, seems unfounded. Central authorities appeared determined to temper speculative property investments, even at the cost of declining property prices. Xi Jinping underscored this when he stated, "housing is for living, not for speculation". Clearly, a central goal is to redirect credit towards more strategic and technologically advanced sectors.

As part of the ongoing regulatory adjustments, the crackdown on real estate speculation was accompanied by plans, in October 2021, to implement a comprehensive wealth tax. This tax was intended to apply to both residential and non-residential properties, whereas presently only real estate transactions are taxed. Rural properties would be exempt, and local authorities would gain an alternative revenue source.[174] However, discussions regarding a wealth tax

---

174   Jane Cai, "Property Tax Concerns for China's Homeowners, Buyers amid Xi Jinping's Common Prosperity Drive", *South China Morning Post*, 23 November 2021, accessed 29 September 2023, https://www.scmp.com/economy/china-economy/article/3156951/property-tax-concerns-chinas-homeowners-buyers-amid-xi.

have been ongoing since 2014,¹⁷⁵ and after some experimental trials in designated areas, any substantial decisions have been postponed.¹⁷⁶ On this front, progress appears to be at a standstill.

This issue is fundamentally significant. As capitalist dynamics advance, land rent, which was nationalised by the revolution to safeguard small agriculture and foster an unburdened industrial take-off, tends to re-emerge in the hybrid guise of land use rights. These land use rights then develop a life of their own within the realm of real estate and financial speculation. As commodification expands and housing fully transforms into a commodity for consumption, it imposes a substantial levy on profits. This situation is exacerbated by wage pressures stemming from limited consumption demand among wage earners. The Chinese state can and must mitigate the most detrimental consequences of this phenomenon, but it cannot entirely eliminate them. Balancing the effects of increasing rent in the real estate sector, without causing the sector to collapse—given its role as a significant driver of economic growth—and without putting the banking system at serious risk, necessitates a decisive redirection of the housing industry towards social demand. This redirection should encompass even the most vulnerable segments of the urban proletariat, who, if granted urban *hukou* (household registration), would experience higher wages and the possibility of homeownership, facilitating their full integration into the 'internal circulation' of the economy. It is evident that everything is interconnected. Any social pact in social-democratic terms aligns with the pursuit of moving up the international value chain by minimising imperialist value extraction. This move is essential to achieve a more equitable wealth distribution, which, based on recent data, appears to have slowed down the upward trajectory of previous years (see Figure 3.6).

### 5.5   *Middle Classes*

Mainstream perspectives in the West regarding the expansion of Chinese middle classes have been tainted, or at least were tarnished until the pandemic, by a dual viewpoint. On one hand, there is the notion of China opening up as a substantial consumer market for Western products. On the other hand, there is the idea of a 'democratisation' of the country's institutions driven by

---

175   Ruihan Huang and Joshua Henderson, "Is There a Method Behind China's Tech Crackdown Madness?", Macro Polo (Paulson Institute), 21 October 2021, accessed 29 September 2023, https://macropolo.org/china-tech-crackdown-software-hardware/?rp=m.

176   "China Will Not Expand Its Property Tax Trial This Year", *Bloomberg News*, 16 March 2022, accessed 29 September 2023, https://www.bloomberg.com/news/articles/2022-03-16/china-will-not-expand-its-property-tax-trial-this-year-l0tex2zh.

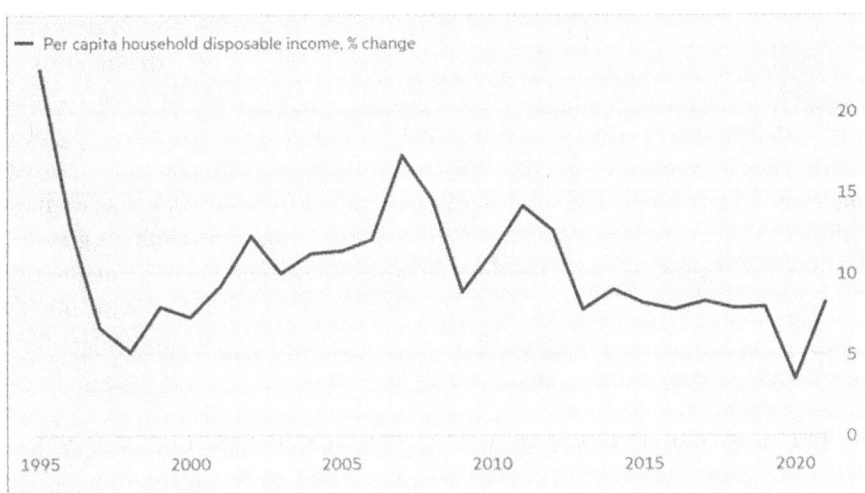

FIGURE 3.6  Uncommon prosperity: after booming, China's urban household income is slowing
PUBLISHED IN THE UK *FINANCIAL TIMES* AND REPRODUCED AT ADAM TOOZE, "CHARTBOOK-UNHEDGED EXCHANGE: CHINA UNDER PRESSURE, A DEBATE", *SUBSTACK*, 24 MARCH 2022, ACCESSED 29 SEPTEMBER 2023, HTTPS://ADAMTOOZE.SUBSTACK.COM/P/CHARTBOOK-UNHEDGED-EXCHANGE-CHINA?S=R. DATA FROM CHINA NATIONAL BUREAU OF STATISTICS AND BLOOMBERG.

a revolution in consumption and social expectations following Western patterns. Consequently, there have been overly optimistic, if not unbelievable, estimates provided by the media and research organisations. These estimates often characterise the middle class as nothing more than a statistical segment within the income scale, or, more precisely, as the statistically potential or actual middle segment.

This viewpoint can be either at odds or in alignment with the issue of poverty in emerging nations. Regarding this matter, it is noteworthy that, over the past three successful decades, China's contributions accounted for 75% of the world's decline in poverty, as reported by the World Bank.[177] China's political leadership is acutely aware that when they refer to the 'middle class', they are referring to an overall increase in incomes, beginning with the urban 'ordinary'

---

177  Haishan Fun and Nada Hamadeh, "New Results from the International Comparison Program Shed Light on the Size of the Global Economy", World Bank blog, 19 May 2021, accessed 29 September 2023, https://blogs.worldbank.org/opendata/new-results-international-comparison-program-shed-light-size-global-economy.

population. This income increase has reshaped the distribution of domestic wealth from a pyramid shape to a more compressed form, with the majority of the population now situated in the middle. However, this middle class in China still cannot compete with the Western-style middle class according to global standards of income and consumption.[178] In other words, economic growth has taken precedence over wealth redistribution thus far. However, as we have observed from various perspectives, redistribution is also becoming a growing priority, motivated by reasons of social stability and the need for qualitative changes in the growth pattern itself. The 'discourse' on China's growing middle class—the middle-income group (*zhongdeng shouru qunti*) appropriate for a moderately prosperous society (*xiaokang*)—revolves around this political issue.[179]

It is beyond the scope of this discussion to delve deeply into the question of the role and political prospects of Chinese middle classes in materialistic terms. This would entail analysing their differentiated positions and functions in production relationships, which do not always align with income levels or types of employment. Nonetheless, Chinese scholars have produced analyses on this subject, which began to emerge in the 2010s, with an initial emphasis on social stratification that extends beyond mere statistical definitions.[180] From these studies, two interrelated aspects emerge with potential political relevance.

First and foremost, the 'middle class' is no longer perceived as a homogeneous, ascendant, or aspirational social group. Its heterogeneity is acknowledged, albeit within a theoretical framework that still lacks clarity, primarily employing sociological terms to differentiate between various production positions.[181] This distinction categorises the middle class into three subgroups:
1. The 'old middle class': comprises small business owners, akin to the classic petit bourgeoisie, and self-employed workers running private services.

---

178   Branko Milanović, *Global Inequality: A New Approach for the Age of Globalization* (Cambridge, MA: Belknap Press of Harvard University Press, 2016).
179   David S. G. Goodman, "Middle Class China: Dreams and Aspirations", *Journal of Chinese Political Science* 19 (2014): 49–64.
180   Cheng Li, "Chinese Scholarship on the Middle Class: From Social Stratification to Political Potential", in *China's Emerging Middle Class: Beyond Economic Transformation* (Washington, DC: Brookings Institution Press, 2010), 55–83.
181   Cheng Li, "Characterizing China's Middle Class: Heterogeneous Composition and Multiple Identities", in ibid., 135–56; Céline Bonnefond, Matthieu Clément, and François Combarnous, "In Search of the Elusive Chinese Urban Middle Class: An Exploratory Analysis", *Post-Communist Economies* 27 (2015): 41–59, https://doi.org/10.1080/14631377.2015.992223.

Often hailing from rural backgrounds, they find themselves teetering on the borderline between lower-status jobs and social advancement.
2. The 'new middle class': composed of qualified employees, such as managers, technicians, and professionals with medium-to-high levels of training and education. They typically hold roles involving the control and supervision of work processes, which are increasingly industrialised. These individuals can be found in both the public service sector and large state or private enterprises.
3. The 'lower middle class': includes white-collar workers and skilled labourers with medium incomes.

While the position of small industrial enterprises with a low number of salaried employees remains somewhat uncertain, these analyses provide clarity regarding capitalist enterprises, particularly private ones, which are characterised by well-defined ownership of the means of production. This distinction surpasses the vagueness of the typology mentioned earlier.

Second, these studies emphasise a crucial feature of the emerging class structure, which is the predominance of wage incomes over self-employment or small business ownership among a substantial portion of the middle classes. This shift indicates the existence of a growing stratum of wage earners, interconnected—albeit with variations between civil servants, employees of state-owned enterprises, and private sector workers—with the Chinese economy's ongoing technological upgrade that we have explored in previous sections. This stratum continues to expand annually as new graduates, particularly those entering state-owned enterprises, join its ranks. This underlines the significant role played by the party-state in reshaping the class structure of Chinese society[182] and its renewed appeal to a segment of the youth population that views a reform of the Dengist reforms favourably. Moreover, it is important to note that a portion of the CCP's membership originates from these social strata, contributing significantly to the internal political dynamics and balances within the party.

The growth of a wage-earning middle class and the continued presence of significant intermediate layers between the proletariat and capital mark the shift from an extensive pattern of capitalist development, which was asymmetric and imbalanced concerning the Western imperialist powers, to a more intensive development model aimed at positioning China as a relative equal

---

182 The party-state still maintains significant control over the sector of intellectual professions that have already undergone industrialisation and are integrated into the information-media circuit (a sector that has, in comparison, achieved relative autonomy in the West).

among global competitors. However, this restructuring process is far from smooth and presents challenges to internal class dynamics. In this context, what kinds of political demands will be made by various segments of the middle class? How will these demands relate to state policies and the aspirations of the proletarian class?

The transition towards a more democratic society appears plausible, considering China's historical trajectory in the context of global capitalism and the characteristics of the present phase. As middle-class segments become more aware and achieve greater economic well-being, they may press for democratic reforms and increased individual autonomy. These democratic[183] claims will play a significant role in the future, as part of the gradual democratisation of state institutions and the maintenance of social stability. In the abstract, the growth of China's domestic market and its expanding global economic presence should be sufficient to serve national interests without the need for rigid centralised state leadership. However, the critical variable remains China's complex relationship with the United States and Western markets, which will influence the course of these developments.

So, a dividing line will probably arise—although it is difficult to predict how clear-cut this division will be—within the dynamics of the Chinese middle classes. On one hand, a portion of the technical and professional middle classes who are wage earners may be more inclined to support a robust role for the party-state as China continues to rise, and they might not be hostile to moderate working class demands. On the other hand, the remaining intermediate strata, closely tied to the fluctuations of small and self-employed enterprises, may seek to benefit from the removal of further market constraints. Within these sectors, private entrepreneurs from coastal areas with ties to exports could potentially exercise economic, political, and cultural hegemony. These entrepreneurs are already concerned about the evolving relations with the West, potential consequences of state-led rebalancing between coastal provinces and the country's interior, and wage dynamics influenced by proletarian struggles.

While the private bourgeoisie currently relies on central state support to compete in the global market, it is increasingly inclined to demand more freedom for its business operations and to oppose alternative policies. The degree to which the private bourgeoisie can influence and mobilise the intermediate sectors remains uncertain, as does its role within the CCP. Importantly, there is

---

183   The term is fraught with ambiguity. In this context, we are referring to political and social demands made by intermediate social strata situated between capital and the proletariat. These demands are not inherently anti-capitalist in nature.

a possibility that the spontaneous dynamics of accumulation, at the expense of state intervention, will drive a more pronounced separation of the more developed provinces from the rest of the country and the political centre. This is what the West fervently hopes for—that the, as it sees it, centralist and nationalist Chinese state will transform into a liberal and democratic state, relinquishing top-down interventionism and granting unfettered freedom to private capital and the unrestrained middle classes. Such a scenario would resemble the Hong Kong pattern that emerged from the mobilisations of the failed 2019 so called coloured revolution.

However, this shift cannot occur without a significant disruption of the current political trajectory in Beijing, potentially even leading to a regime change. It runs counter to the emerging prospect of a more centralised domestic market focused on national capital and a labour force that is increasingly aware of its own strength and rights. Presently, the Chinese state enjoys broad inter-class support, based on the promise of economic development and shared prosperity across all classes. This social compact, however, remains stable only as long as the overall trajectory of improvement for Chinese society remains uninterrupted. The delicate balance on this ridge becomes even more precarious in the future. A segment of the middle classes, particularly educated youth often referred to as the 'aspiring middle class', may be enticed by the idea of direct access to the global market without state intermediation. This could occur if they fail to find employment that matches their qualifications and expectations based on their acquired knowledge. Conversely, another part of the middle classes, influenced by the global geopolitical climate, is growing increasingly wary of the West and its proposed solutions. Instead, they may favour state policies focused on widespread social protection and gravitate towards social and national self-awareness. Consequently, some of the wage-earning middle classes, or at least a portion of them, could incline towards an 'anti-American' nationalism, in opposition to the uncertainty and chaos that a shift away from the new Chinese course would entail. The intersection of this nationalism with, or its separation from, the positioning of the proletarian and peasant strata is a critical aspect that could come to the forefront, especially in the context of deepening confrontation with the United States.

As globalisation approaches its crisis phase, which marks the culmination of its upward trajectory characterised by the unchallenged dominance of dollar imperialism, all social strata, not just the proletariat, will be compelled into action. China is no exception in this regard. Amid these transformations, there exists a dynamic interplay between the middle classes and the proletariat ... with no Great Wall between them.

### 5.6 Provisional Conclusions

We have limited ourselves to exploring the critical challenges and potential roadblocks facing the transition of Chinese capitalism (or 'market socialism'). The Chinese leadership recognises these challenges and is well aware of the need to shift from an economy driven by infrastructure and real estate to one that focuses on high-tech sectors and increased social spending. Failure to make this transition could lead China down a path of stagnation similar to Japan's experience, without ever achieving the same income levels.

What, then, is the overall emerging picture? Does China intend to pursue a symmetrical decoupling from global markets? Not exactly. Why not? There are several factors. First, the broader context of global capitalism, despite some signs of slowing globalisation, a post-pandemic recovery marked by inflation, and ongoing trade tensions, does not seem to be unambiguously heading towards complete deglobalisation. Second, the decoupling strategy employed by the United States is currently selective. While there are intensifying signs of economic disengagement, it has not yet aimed at a complete severance of economic ties with China. Total decoupling may only become a reality in the event of a severe breakdown, which is not entirely unlikely in the aftermath of the Ukrainian conflict. Most importantly, China's intentions are not aligned with pursuing full economic isolation. Beijing aims to balance its push for greater economic autonomy with the undeniable need for increased integration into global markets, albeit on its own terms.

This pursuit of greater economic autonomy entails both internal and external reinforcement of China's economic structure. Autonomy, in the context of today's globalised capitalism, does not imply a return to isolation or autarky for Beijing. Instead, it signifies the capacity to compete on equal terms with the Western world on the global stage.[184] This ambition extends beyond merely exporting Chinese goods, especially those with medium-low technological content, and encompasses a multifaceted approach:

1. Commercial expansion: China seeks to establish a strong presence in international trade through regional free trade agreements, notably in East Asia.
2. Infrastructural development: Initiatives like the 'New Silk Roads' aim to enhance China's global influence by developing vital infrastructure and connectivity projects.

---

184  State Council Information Office of China, "China's International Development Cooperation in the New Era" (white paper, 10 January 2021), posted in English at the Xinhua News Agency website, accessed 29 September 2023, https://english.www.gov.cn/archive/whitepaper/202101/10/content_WS5ffa6bbbc6d0f72576943922.html.

3. Technological advancement: China is actively involved in building 5G networks and promoting the 'Digital Silk Road', enhancing its technological capabilities on the global stage.
4. Financial and monetary integration: Efforts to internationalise the renminbi yuan, digital currency adoption, and involvement in commodity futures markets play a significant role in China's external economic strategy.
5. Political and military networks: China is also expanding its geopolitical reach, responding to containment strategies by the United States and strengthening political and military partnerships.

The primary challenge for Beijing lies in changing its development pattern without undermining globalisation, which has historically been advantageous and continues to benefit China. Achieving modernisation and greater international engagement necessitates China's active participation on the global geopolitical stage. In the context of China's relationship with the European Union, particularly Germany, there is a recognition that further advancement of Chinese capitalism may reduce complementarity with advanced machinery-producing countries and increase competition. This is especially relevant in terms of economic engagements with emerging and impoverished nations, which might view Beijing as a more beneficial partner to counter the exploitative practices of Western capital.[185]

As the trajectory of world capitalism becomes increasingly turbulent and shows signs of a downward spiral, inter-capitalist conflicts will intensify. This sharpening of rivalries will leave China with fewer opportunities for its non-confrontational integration into the tightly interwoven fabric of global capitalism. Although the possibility of a Chinese-style decoupling cannot be ruled out in the future, it would signify a significant escalation in the clash with the United States. However, Beijing is not in a position to halt its strategic efforts, as renouncing this strategy would jeopardise the significant progress it has made thus far.

These underlying issues should be considered within the broader economic context. By the end of 2022, China's economic landscape is not particularly favourable. Following the post-pandemic rebound, China's economic growth has begun to decelerate, accompanied by diminishing demand in Western

---

185 Chinese machinery exports exceeded (albeit slightly) German exports for the first time in 2020. However, it should be noted that the quantitative figure does not tell the whole story. See "Die Ängste des 'Exportweltmeisters'", German-Foreign-Policy.com, 9 August 2021, accessed 29 September 2023, https://www.german-foreign-policy.com/news/detail/8682/.

export markets. Furthermore, the Ukrainian crisis has added another layer of uncertainty and tension to Western–Russian relations, which also has adverse implications for Beijing on the geopolitical front.[186] This crisis has driven energy and commodity prices higher and expanded the scope of US financial sanctions. Simultaneously, the US Federal Reserve has initiated a monetary policy tightening phase.

It is important to note that the global landscape is continually evolving. However, one thing remains clear: the comprehensive reform initiated by Beijing is not only a significant test for Chinese leadership but also a factor that could make China the potentially vulnerable link in the global capitalist chain. This vulnerability arises from the concurrent restructuring of the development model amid an intense rivalry with the United States, previously considered irreversible, and from the fact that internal class relationships are being strained and reconfigured. The outcomes of these developments remain uncertain and will have implications for both China and the global system. In many ways, China stands at a critical crossroads.

## 6     Globalisation, the Chinese Way

Certainly, the new direction of Chinese politics towards greater economic autonomy necessitates a more pronounced external projection. This is not solely about gaining access to foreign capital and advanced technologies, which are becoming increasingly difficult due to Western states' regulatory measures. It also involves creating markets and spheres of influence for Chinese products and, by doing so, reaching a critical threshold that could potentially reduce China's dependence on the US dollar as the dominant international currency.

### 6.1    *The 'New Silk Roads'*

In the aftermath of the global financial crisis, Beijing significantly ramped up its investments and trade relationships with several regions. These efforts included closer ties with former Soviet Central Asia, marked by the inauguration of an oil pipeline from Kazakhstan and a gas pipeline from Turkmenistan between 2009 and 2010. China also deepened its engagement with Russia through the Shanghai Cooperation Organisation's regional security treaty.

---

186   Hu Wei, "Possible Outcomes of the Russo-Ukrainian War and China's Choice", translated by Jiaqi Liu, *U.S. China Perception Monitor* (published by the Carter Center), 12 March 2022, accessed 29 September 2023, https://uscnpm.org/2022/03/12/hu-wei-russia-ukraine-war-china-choice/.

Additionally, China became the leading importer of oil from Saudi Arabia and Iran since 2010. The nation also ventured into investment activities in countries like Algeria and Libya (before Western military interventions in 2011) and established stronger trade and investment links with many African and Latin American countries, even within the United States' traditional sphere of influence, its 'backyard'. These endeavours aimed to diversify energy and food supplies, as well as export and investment markets. Notably, China forged closer ties with East Asian economies, exemplified by the enactment of the first free trade agreement, the ASEAN–China Free Trade Area (ACFTA), in 2010 between China and South-East Asian nations. Concurrently, China continued to build maritime infrastructure along the Indian Ocean, creating what is known in the West as the 'Chinese pearl necklace'. This strategic development included projects like the Pakistani port of Gwadar, connected to China via the Sino-Pakistani Corridor and Karakoram Highway. Of particular importance is the proposed Iran–Pakistan oil pipeline, currently hindered by US sanctions. Once realised, this pipeline would facilitate the transport of Iranian oil, bypassing the Washington-controlled bottlenecks of the Straits of Hormuz and Malacca, and strengthening the economic and political ties between Iran and China.[187]

Under President Xi Jinping's leadership, there has been a noticeable acceleration of China's economic geostrategy, primarily along three significant lines:

1. The Silk Road Economic Belt:[188] This project was officially launched in November 2013, setting the stage for extensive economic collaboration and infrastructure development along ancient Silk Road trade routes.
2. Trade agreements with Moscow: Starting in May 2014, China initiated trade agreements with Moscow, bolstering economic cooperation and fostering stronger ties between the two nations.
3. Establishment of international financial institutions: China played a pivotal role in the creation of the New Development Bank, designed to provide financial support to BRICS countries[189] as an alternative to relying on institutions like the IMF. Additionally, the Asian Infrastructure

---

187 Such a scenario could represent the so-called Confucian–Islamic connection feared by Samuel Huntington, author of the infamous *The Clash of Civilizations and the Remaking of World Order* (New York: Simon & Schuster, 1996).
188 For a historical perspective, see Peter Frankopan, *The Silk Roads: A New History of the World* (London: Bloomsbury, 2015).
189 The BRICS countries are Brazil, Russia, India, China, and South Africa. On links with Turkey, see Burak Gürel and Mina Kozluca, "Chinese Investment in Turkey: The Belt and Road Initiative, Rising Expectations, Ground Realities", *European Review* 30, no. 6 (2022): 806–34, https://doi.org/10.1017/S1062798721000296.

Investment Bank (AIIB) was founded to facilitate foreign investments and enhance the international circulation of the Chinese currency.

The 'New Silk Roads' now form the backbone of the endeavour popularly known since 2015 as the Belt and Road Initiative (BRI), having evolved from the earlier name 'One Belt, One Road' (see Map 3.1). The BRI represents one of the most ambitious projects since China's embrace of economic globalisation. It serves as a comprehensive and strategic economic roadmap, designed to span a three-decade period. This initiative has garnered such significance that it was formally included in the Chinese Constitution in 2017 and subsequently reaffirmed in a white paper issued in January 2021.

The BRI has evolved into the linchpin of China's unique brand of globalisation. This strategic vision encompasses a vast network of infrastructural interconnectivity, fostering multilateral and bilateral regional cooperation with the aim of achieving integration across various dimensions—commercial, financial, monetary, and digital—among the participating nations. This multifaceted initiative encompasses three continental routes, each delineated

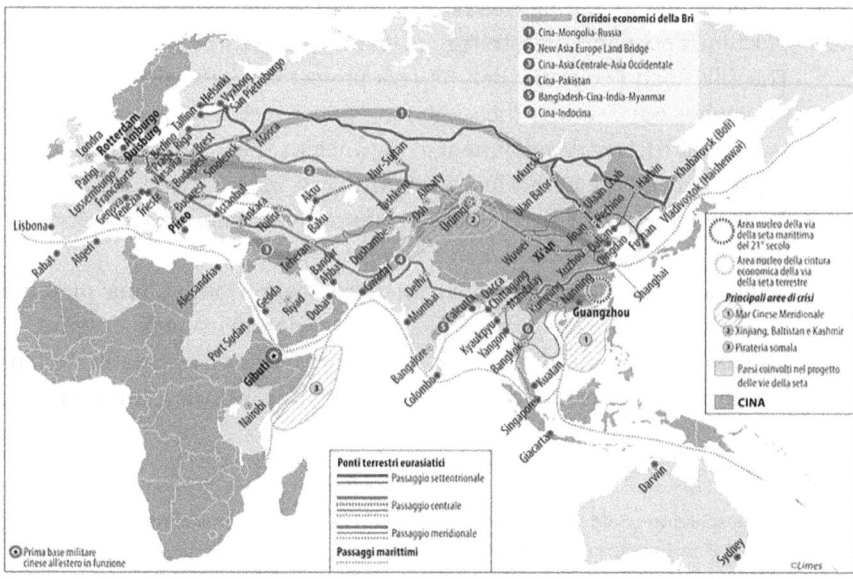

MAP 3.1    One Belt, One Road
REPRODUCED FROM "NUOVE VIE DELLA SETA CORRETTA", *LIMES: RIVISTA ITALIANA DI GEOPOLITICA*, HTTPS://WWW.LIMESONLINE.COM/CARTA CEO/IL-TRENO-SINO-RUSSO-CORRE-LENTO-SULLE-NUOVE-VIE-DELLA-SETA /MONDO-PIATTO-LARGO-46. DATA FROM SINOMAPS PRESS, 2018 AND LIMES' AUTHORS.

by six corridors: (1) the route heading towards Central Asia and Europe, (2) the route leading to the Persian Gulf and, subsequently, branching into the Mediterranean and East Africa, and (3) the route stretching towards South East Asia and the Pacific, extending its reach to Latin America. Additionally, there is a maritime route that navigates from the Indian Ocean, transiting through the Suez Canal, and culminating in the Mediterranean.[190] At its core, the BRI revolves around the seamless fusion of physical, logistical, and digital infrastructure between China and the Eurasian continent, stretching towards Western Europe on one axis and the East Asian region on the other.

On a commercial front, these regions are marked by intraregional import and export flows, with the East Asian region already exhibiting substantial integration with China, accentuating China's pivotal role. These areas also serve as the focal point for the majority of China's foreign investments, primarily stemming from state-owned banks that support the business activities of state-owned enterprises. It is noteworthy that the primary beneficiaries of these investments are typically developing or emerging countries, marked by a concentration of investment in a select few major infrastructure projects. The significance of these investments extends beyond the direct support of Chinese exports, notably in sectors such as heavy industries, which are approaching overcapacity. They also contribute to the increased integration of global supply chains within BRI participant countries, manifested by the rising share of Chinese-added value in both their imports and exports to third-party nations.[191]

Investments in the telecommunications sector, while still in their infancy, are showing a marked upward trajectory, accompanied by a surge in engagement from private Chinese enterprises. These endeavours have been framed within the broader 'Digital Silk Road' initiative,[192] which began its journey in 2015 and is intrinsically linked to the 'Made in China 2025' strategy. The 'Digital Silk Road' is steadily taking form in several dimensions (see Map 3.2). First,

---

190 Michele Ruta, Matias Herrera Dappe, Somik Lall, Chunlin Zhang, Cristina Constantinescu, Mathilde Lebrand, Alen Mulabdic et al., *Belt and Road Economics: Opportunities and Risks of Transport Corridors* (Washington, DC: World Bank and International Bank for Reconstruction and Development, 2019), accessed 29 September 2023, https://www.worldbank.org/en/topic/regional-integration/publication/belt-and-road-economics-opportunities-and-risks-of-transport-corridors.
191 Zhiheng Wu, Guisheng Hou, and Baogui Xin, "Has the Belt and Road Initiative Brought New Opportunities to Countries Along the Routes to Participate in Global Value Chains?", *SAGE Open* 10, no. 1 (2020), https://doi.org/10.1177/2158244020902088.
192 Tyson Barker, "Withstanding the Storm: The Digital Silk Road, COVID-19 and Europe's Options", in Amighini, *China after COVID-19*, 108–138.

there has been a substantial laying of submarine digital cables, with more than thirty projects already initiated, particularly in the South East Asian region. Second, and more generally, regional technological ecosystems centred on Chinese standards untethered from those of the West have been established. In geopolitical terms, one noteworthy development is the advanced laying of the PEACE (Pakistan East Africa Cable Express) fibre optic cable. This vital infrastructure will establish a high-speed communication link, uniting Pakistan and East Africa with China, thus seamlessly integrating these regions into the broader Eurasian network (see Figure 3.7).[193]

Further expanding China's digital frontier is the relentless expansion, uninterrupted by the pandemic crisis, of 5G internet network. Huawei, an industry leader, has played an instrumental role in deploying this high-speed internet infrastructure, particularly in the Gulf countries and the African continent. As part of the BRI, China is also setting the stage for the establishment of the Chinese Beidou satellite navigation system. This indigenous navigation system offers an alternative to the US Global Positioning System (GPS) and, in addition to its navigational utility, may also serve as a crucial enabler for the international proliferation of the digital yuan, underpinning the internationalisation of China's currency.[194]

### 6.2  *Potential, Fragility*

It is evident, even from the general overview presented here, that the BRI holds significant potential for expansion.[195] For China, external economic projection, as part of its 'get out' strategy,[196] is not merely a choice but a compelling necessity at its current stage of domestic development. This imperative arises from the increasingly stringent constraints imposed by the US-centric global economic system. To continue its path of harmonious development and

---

193  The Pakistan–China link was completed in February 2021.
194  An additional dimension of the BRI that merits attention is the 'vaccine diplomacy' of the so-called 'Health Silk Road'. Amid the challenges posed by the COVID-19 pandemic, China took a proactive role in promoting global health by offering vaccines and other essential health assistance. This initiative saw China providing access to vaccines at affordable prices, and in some cases, offering vaccine donations to countries in need.
195  Gisela Grieger, "China's Maritime Silk Road Initiative Increasingly Touches the EU", briefing paper, European Parliamentary Research Service, March 2018, accessed 29 September 2023, https://www.europarl.europa.eu/RegData/etudes/BRIE/2018/614767/EPRS_BRI(2018)614767_EN.pdf.
196  Yiping Huang, "Understanding China's Belt & Road Initiative: Motivation, Framework and Assessment", *China Economic Review* 40 (2016): 314–21, https://doi.org/10.1016/j.chieco.2016.07.007.

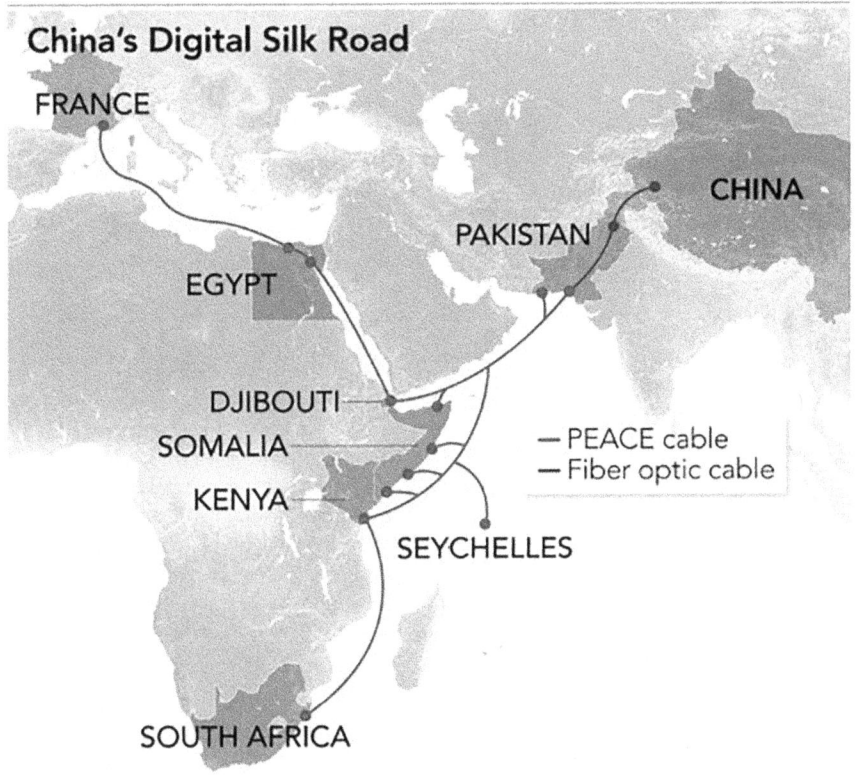

MAP 3.2    China's 'Digital Silk Road'
REPRODUCED FROM HTTPS://TRIBUNE.COM.PK/STORY/2282931/CHINA-BUI
LDS-DIGITAL-SILK-ROAD-TO-BYPASS-INDIA-FOR-PAKISTANI-INTERNET-TRAF
FIC, ACCESSED 23 SEPTEMBER 2023. PEACE CABLE INTERNATIONAL
NETWORK, PAKISTAN GOVERNMENT.

prevent the complete proletarianisation of its rural population, Beijing must reduce the excessive profits extracted by the West. However, this objective remains unattainable as long as Western markets maintain their dominance, wielding superior monetary, financial, technological, and industrial resources. The 'New Silk Roads' are conceived to address this challenge, encompassing its geopolitical dimension: counteracting imperialist encirclement from the east and south by projecting westward,[197] thereby establishing new markets. These

---

197   Wang Jisi, "'Marching Westwards': The Rebalancing of China's Geostrategy" (IISS Report No. 73, Peking University—Institute of International and Strategic Studies, 7 October 2012), accessed 29 January 2022, http://en.iiss.pku.edu.cn/research/bulletin/1604.html, later

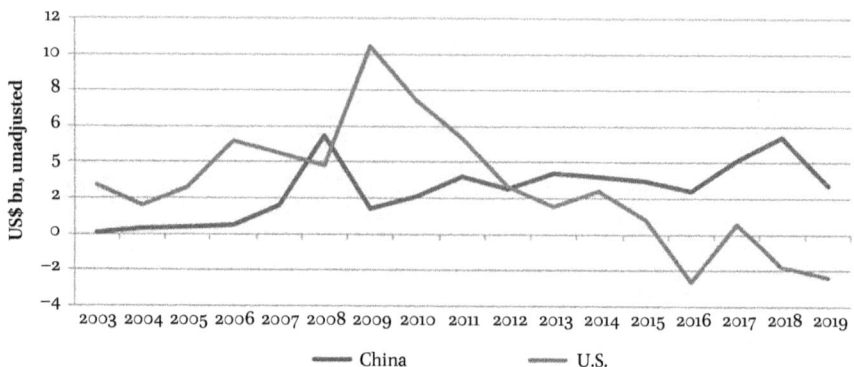

FIGURE 3.7   Flow of Chinese vs. US foreign direct investment to Africa
REPRODUCED FROM ERIC OLANDER, "FIVE REASONS WHY CHINESE PRIVATE INVESTMENT IS FLOWING INTO AFRICA", CHINA GLOBAL SOUTH PROJECT, 6 APRIL 2021, ACCESSED 29 SEPTEMBER 2023, HTTPS://CHINA GLOBALSOUTH.COM/2021/04/06/FIVE-REASONS-WHY-CHINESE-PRIV ATE-INVESTMENT-IS-FLOWING-INTO-AFRICA/. DATA (JANUARY 2021) FROM THE *STATISTICAL BULLETIN OF CHINA'S OUTWARD FOREIGN DIRECT INVESTMENT* (US BUREAU OF ECONOMIC ANALYSIS), THE CHINA AFRICA RESEARCH INITIATIVE, AND THE JOHN HOPKINS SCHOOL OF ADVANCED INTERNATIONAL STUDIES.

markets are intended to serve a dual purpose: absorbing a growing share of goods that were previously destined for Western export markets and providing opportunities for greater financial (through investment strategies), monetary (via the internationalisation of the yuan), and technological autonomy.[198] In parallel, this initiative complements the promotion of China's inland regions, helping to partially bridge the regional disparities between coastal and inland areas while advancing the dual circulation strategy and expanding the domestic market.

In pursuit of these objectives, it is important to acknowledge that Beijing's actions are not driven by inherent benevolence, albeit they mark a significant departure from the practices of Western imperialism, which have historically involved predatory investments and political interference. Western powers

---

published in *The World in 2020 According to China: Chinese Foreign Policy Elites Discuss Emerging Trends in International Politics*, edited by Shao Binhong (Leiden: Brill, 2014), 129–36. At this point, a disruptive Ukrainian conflict was not anticipated.

198   Ana Lucia Abeliansky and Inmaculada Martínez-Zarzoso, "The Relationship Between the Chinese 'Going Out' Strategy and International Trade", *Economics* 13 (2019): 1–18, https://doi.org/10.5018/economics-ejournal.ja.2019-21.

often use foreign investments to impose political conditions, encourage so-called structural economic reforms, and set in motion a self-perpetuating cycle of debt dependency. Chinese investments, on the other hand, are designed to foster a more self-sustaining economic foundation. This approach seeks to stimulate both economic and social *development*, rather than merely financialised *growth*, with the aim of expanding domestic markets and enhancing their solvency. It is not coincidental that the BRI has garnered substantial interest, primarily from emerging and less affluent nations. These nations, particularly those not led by neoliberal elites or technocratic governments subjected to the dictates of the IMF and World Bank, see in Chinese investments an opportunity for development. Embracing these opportunities may, however, require resisting a wide range of Western pressures, including military ones,[199] which often portray Chinese investments as imperialistic.[200]

At this juncture in our discussion, it is crucial to understand that China's approach in this context is not attributed to the non-capitalist nature of its

---

199  For example, see Libya, Sudan, Syria, and Ethiopia.
200  Another criticism frequently levelled at Chinese infrastructure projects in Africa is that Chinese companies predominantly rely on their own workforce, rather than employing local labour. However, this assertion is contradicted by findings in a 2017 report from the McKinsey Institute, which found that approximately 90% of the workforce employed in these projects across Africa is comprised of local workers. See Irene Yuan Sun, Kartik Jayaram, and Omid Kassiri, *Dance of Lions and Dragons: How are Africa and China Engaging, and How Will the Partnership Evolve?* (New York: McKinsey Global Institute, 2017), accessed 29 September 2023, https://www.mckinsey.com/~/media/mckinsey/featured%20i nsights/middle%20east%20and%20africa/the%20closest%20look%20yet%20at%20 chinese%20economic%20engagement%20in%20africa/dance-of-the-lions-and-drag ons.ashx#:~:text=Chinese%20%E2%80%9Cdragons%E2%80%9D%E2%80%94%20fi rms%20of%20every%20size%20and%20sector%E2%80%94,economies%20are%20of ten%20referred%20to. The Atlantic Council has commented more generally that "A final myth is that African governments are passive in negotiating contracts with the Chinese and regularly coerced into accepting bad deals". See Aubrey Hruby, "Dispelling the Dominant Myths of China in Africa", Atlantic Council blog, 3 September 2018, accessed 29 September 2023, https://www.atlanticcouncil.org/blogs/new-atlanticist/dispelling-the -dominant-myths-of-china-in-africa/. Finally, the *Washington Post* admitted that most Chinese projects in Africa have had a positive impact on economic growth. See Deborah Bräutigam, "U.S. Politicians get China in Africa All Wrong", *Washington Post*, 12 April 2018, accessed 29 September 2023, https://www.washingtonpost.com/news/theworldpost/wp /2018/04/12/china-africa/ (subscription required). Be that as it may, the United States has a higher stock of foreign direct investment in Africa compared to China. However, China's growth rate in the realm of FDI in Africa has been increasing, particularly in recent pandemic years. See UNCTAD, *World Investment Report 2018—Investment and New Industrial Policies*, UNCTAD/WIR/2018, accessed 29 September 2023, https://unctad.org/system/files /official-document/wir2018_en.pdf.

socio-economic structure. Moreover, the absence of an overtly imperialist projection does not stem (only) from a lack of expansionist tradition and structure. Rather, it can be seen as a form of 'temporal lag' on China's part, which is unlikely to be completely rectified without significant upheaval for the entire global market.

Analysing China's outbound direct investments is revealing.[201] In terms of sheer numbers, China's outbound direct investments, reaching approximately $120 billion in 2019 (before the pandemic), represented about 9% of the world's total, securing Beijing's position as the fourth-largest source of outbound capital on a global scale.[202] However, when we delve into the qualitative aspects, a more nuanced picture emerges. The majority of China's foreign direct investments associated with the BRI are funnelled into low-income countries,[203] primarily for physical infrastructure projects. These investments are characterised by longer-term prospects for returns, as well as the potential for deeper integration into the Chinese domestic market. Still, in the short term, they cannot replace China's dependence on Western export markets.

Contrastingly, China's efforts to gain ownership or participate in technologically advanced Western companies have faced considerable obstacles since the mid-2010s.[204] This is due to the economic warfare initiated by Washington

---

201   Clemens Fuest, Felix Hugger, Samina Sultan, and Jing Xing, "Chinese Acquisitions Abroad: Are They Different?" (CESifo Working Paper No. 7585, Center for Economic Studies & Ifo Institute, Munich, April 2019), accessed 29 September 2023, https://www.econbiz.de/Record/chinese-acquisitions-abroad-are-they-different-fuest-clemens/1001 1992349; Stephen B. Kaplan, "The Rise of Patient Capital: The Political Economy of Chinese Global Finance" (working paper, IIEP-WP-2018-2, Institute for International Economic Policy, Elliott School of International Affairs, George Washington University, July 2018), accessed 29 September 2023 https://www2.gwu.edu/~iiep/assets/docs/papers/2018WP/KaplanIIEP2018-2.pdf.
202   UNCTAD, *World Investment Report 2020—International Production Beyond the Pandemic*, UNCTAD/WIR/2020 (16 June 2020).
203   Sebastian Horn, Carmen M. Reinhart, and Christoph Trebesch, "China's Overseas Lending" (NBER Working Paper 26050, National Bureau of Economic Research, Cambridge, MA, July 2019), accessed 29 September 2023, http://www.nber.org/papers/w26050.
204   Schmalz's analysis identifies three distinct stages in the trajectory of Chinese capital exports: the first stage, commencing in the late 1990s, involved investments in raw materials and infrastructure primarily in countries of the Global South; the second stage, emerging in the aftermath of the 2008 financial crisis, was characterised by China's ambitious attempts to acquire technologically advanced enterprises in Western nations; and the third stage, from 2017 onwards, witnessed a downturn in these acquisition attempts, with a general decline in this approach. See Stefan Schmalz, "The Three Stages of Chinese Capital Export", *Journal für Entwicklungspolitik* 35 (2019): 17–38, https://doi.org/10.20446/JEP-2414-3197-35-3-17.

# CHINA

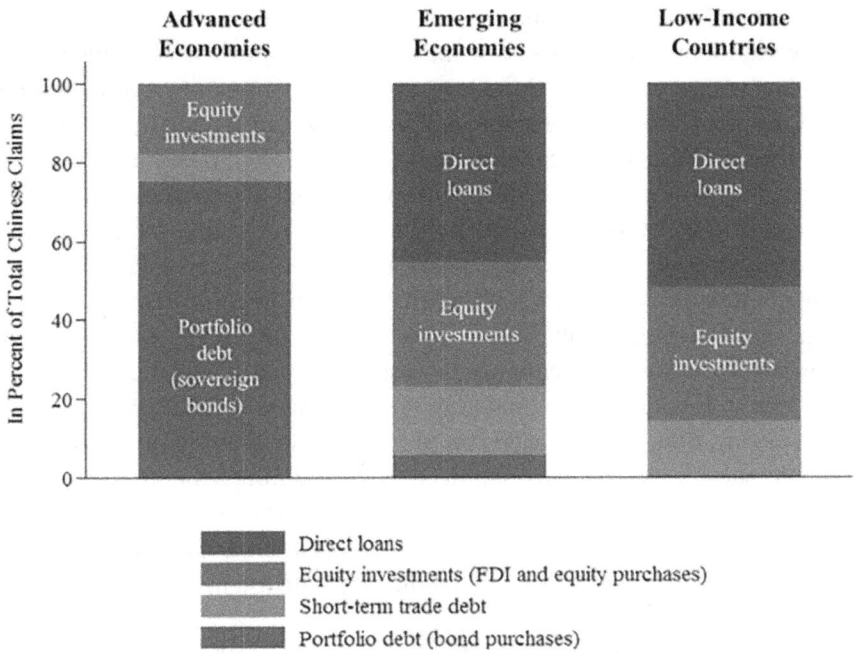

FIGURE 3.8   China's tailored approach of exporting capital (country groups)
REPRODUCED FROM HORN, REINHART, AND TREBESCH, "CHINA'S OVERSEAS LENDING", 38, FIG. 26. *NOTE*: COUNTRY CLASSIFICATION INTO INCOME GROUPS FOLLOWS THE IMF WORLD ECONOMIC OUTLOOK DATABASE. DATA ON CHINESE CLAIMS IS BASED ON NUMEROUS DATA SOURCES (SEE APPENDICES I AND II OF THE HORN ET AL. WORKING PAPER).

and the constraints imposed by the European Union. Therefore, while China has started to shift away from a traditional dependency on purchasing state bonds in dollars and euros (at least four times greater than direct loans), its capital exports to Western nations largely remain in the form of sovereign bond purchases and, to a lesser extent, portfolio investments. In essence, this shift underscores a distinctive pattern: Chinese investments in Western countries are primarily channelled into sovereign bond purchases and portfolio investments, while direct investments are concentrated in emerging and developing countries (see Figure 3.8). This signifies a shift from a classical dependency relationship but does not represent a fully-fledged entry into the exclusive club of imperialist nations.

In the realm of South–South relations, China achieved the status of being the world's largest creditor to low-income countries in 2020.[205] This comes with its own set of risks, as these investments predominantly revolve around fixed infrastructures. These assets are not easily transferable in the volatile landscape of Western speculative capital and are often denominated in US dollars. Furthermore, these investments are located in countries with uncertain political and financial stability.[206] It is noteworthy that the majority of these investments are sovereign loans, established from one state to another through state-owned banks such as the Chinese Export-Import Bank and China Development Bank. They typically carry low-interest rates, ranging between 2–3%. Similar to commercial loans, these loans are often secured by collateral in the form of raw materials[207] or the right to claim profits, should there be any, from the entities involved in the projects. Additionally, they are partially safeguarded against potential debt crises through the stipulation that Chinese companies will be assigned at least half of the project's total value. It is important to note that although private Chinese firms have played a more prominent role in recent years, they primarily function as contractors rather than direct investors.

In the years preceding the pandemic, Chinese foreign investments within the BRI framework experienced both a quantitative decline and a qualitative reorientation in terms of targets. This shift was accompanied by an increased participation of private commercial banks.[208] Several factors contributed to this transformation, including stricter domestic financial constraints, debt issues in recipient countries, and the relentless criticism from Western institutions and media.[209] Nonetheless, it is crucial to note that despite the

---

205  Horn, Reinhart, and Trebesch reported that the debt-to-GDP ratio in low-income countries that receive Chinese loans is roughly between 10–15%, while in emerging countries, it is closer to 6–7%. The regions most exposed to this phenomenon are Central and South East Asia. See Horn, Reinhart, and Trebesch, "China's Overseas Lending". According to the IMF, the portion of Chinese loans extended to the seventy-three highly indebted poor nations surged from 2% in 2006 to 18% by 2020. In parallel, private loans from China also saw an increase, rising from 3% to 11% during the same period. In contrast, the share of conventional lenders, including the IMF, World Bank, and Paris Club, saw a decline from 83% to 58%.

206  Brown, Gunter, and Zenglein, "Course Correction".

207  To be more precise: backed by the value of commodity sales at current spot market prices.

208  Matthew Mingey and Agatha Kratz, "China's Belt and Road: Down But Not Out", research note, Rhodium Group, 4 January 2021, accessed 29 September 2023, https://rhg.com/research/bri-down-out/.

209  The launch of initiatives explicitly challenging the BRI, such as the American 'Build Back Better World' (B3W) initiative by the Biden administration and the European 'Global

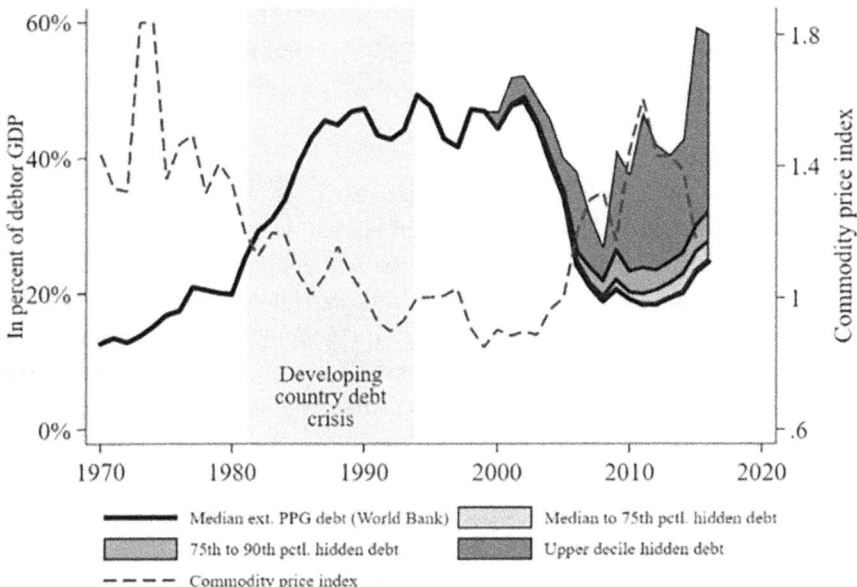

FIGURE 3.9 Long-run debt and commodity price trends in developing and emerging countries
Note: Data for ninety-five developing and emerging countries.
REPRODUCED FROM HORN, REINHART, AND TREBESCH, "CHINA'S OVERSEAS LENDING", 30, FIG. 17. DATA FROM THE HRT DATABASE, THE IMF, THE WORLD BANK, AND JAMES BOUGHTON, "COMMODITY AND MANUFACTURES PRICES IN THE LONG RUN" (IMF WORKING PAPER NO. 91/47, 1 MAY 1991).

challenges posed by the COVID-19 crisis, the BRI continued to advance, albeit with more precise and targeted objectives. Beijing must confront an increasingly uncertain landscape, where renegotiating debts with recipient countries facing crises is becoming a necessity. The outlook is uncertain and will be closely linked to developments in commodity prices and global interest rates (see Figure 3.9).[210]

Regarding the implications of the Ukrainian conflict, it is challenging to make definitive statements at this stage. Russia has been the primary recipient of Chinese state loans, accounting for 15% of BRI-related loans between 2013

---

Gateway' strategy by the European Union, currently appears to be primarily a matter of propaganda in tone.

210 Deborah Bräutigam and Kevin Gallagher, "Bartering Globalization: China's Commodity-Backed Finance in Africa and Latin America", *Global Policy* 5, no. 3 (2014): 346–52, https://doi.org/10.1111/1758-5899.12138.

and 2017, with a total of $125 billion since 2000.[211] However, these loans are predominantly associated with energy resources and are secured as advance payments for oil or gas sales, reflecting a robust geopolitical connection.[212]

### 6.3  Obstacles

In the pursuit of its Belt and Road Initiative, China faces a complex web of challenges. To ensure the cohesiveness of economic and social development within BRI participant countries while reaping economic benefits for itself, several critical factors come into play. Notably, the systemic variables hold immense significance. Equally pivotal are the geopolitical determinants that shape the 'New Silk Roads'. Beijing's aims are clear: circumventing the potential threat posed by a US maritime blockade, primarily epitomised by the Malacca Strait bottleneck—a conduit through which three-quarters of China's oil and a quarter of its gas traverse. The strategic priorities extend to establishing geostrategic stability and creating a direct connection to Europe, ultimately forging the groundwork for a more balanced relationship with the United States.

However, the omnipresent shadow of US pressure looms large, extending beyond mere allegations of Chinese debt-trap diplomacy[213] or economic sanctions. Washington's playbook encompasses stirring real conflicts within countries and regions vital to the development of the BRI. This pertains to tangible or potential military aggression, exemplified by scenarios involving Iran (following a tumultuous course of events in Libya and Syria) and political or diplomatic manoeuvres that impact nations such as Turkey, Pakistan,[214] and Myanmar. Further, the outcome of the long-standing turbulence Washington

---

211  Carmen Reinhart, Christoph Trebesch, and Sebastian Horn, "China's Overseas Lending and the War in Ukraine", *VoxEU*, 11 April 2022, accessed 29 September 2023, https://cepr.org/voxeu/columns/chinas-overseas-lending-and-war-ukraine.

212  A BRI investment report by Nedopil shows that while no new projects have been reported in Russia, Sri Lanka, and Egypt, the bulk of the investments, constituting more than half of the total, flowed into the Middle East, with a particular focus on Saudi Arabia. These investments were predominantly directed towards the energy sector. See Christoph Nedopil, *China Belt and Road Initiative (BRI) Investment Report H1 2022* (Shanghai: FISF Fudan University—Green Finance & Development Center, July 2022), accessed 29 September 2023, https://greenfdc.org/wp-content/uploads/2022/07/GFDC-2022_China-Belt-and-Road-Initiative-BRI-Investment-Report-H1-2022.pdf.

213  Ajit Singh, "The Myth of 'Debt-Trap Diplomacy' and Realities of Chinese Development Finance", *Third World Quarterly* 42, no. 2 (2020): 239–53, https://doi.org/10.1080/01436597.2020.1807318.

214  In April 2022, a 'minor coup' effectively removed Imran Khan, who had been supportive of strengthening economic ties with Beijing, from his position as the leader of the government.

has fostered in Ukraine, seen as a pivotal hub in the BRI network, remains unpredictable. To exacerbate the geopolitical tapestry, the United States has been steadily exerting diplomatic, economic, and military pressure on Latin American countries. This includes direct political and military pressure on nations like Venezuela and Bolivia. The manoeuvres extend to diplomatic nudges, such as Ecuador's exclusion of Huawei, and pressures on countries like Panama, aimed at thwarting Beijing-funded infrastructure projects. In parallel, the focus intensifies on Chile, where the exclusion of Chinese companies from a trans-Pacific submarine cable project has been pushed. Even Brazil has not been spared, facing opposition to Huawei's involvement (although readmitted in light of China's vaccine diplomacy).[215] Simultaneously, in East Asia, the recent Japanese government has made explicit commitments to collaborate with the United States in countering the BRI, particularly in the realm of infrastructure investments and the development of 5G networks.

Undoubtedly, the list of 'local' crises along the BRI's routes and beyond will continue to grow. Additionally, there seems to be a lack of receptiveness to Beijing's positive message by the European Union. Initially, many European countries, including the UK, showed interest in the 'New Silk Roads' financing bank, but their enthusiasm has waned as opposition from the United States has intensified. Germany, for instance, has been slowly warming up to the BRI over the past decade through rail and port terminals development, contributing to the advancement of Chinese technologies. However, it has also participated in actions like the destruction of Libya, attempts at regime change in Syria (weakening Iran), and pressure tactics against countries like Venezuela and Bolivia. These actions are not solely driven by submission to the United States but also aimed at safeguarding Germany's own imperialist interests. While there may be willingness to engage in trade relations with Beijing, such as Volkswagen's substantial car sales in China (it sells 40% of its cars there), it does not necessarily indicate an openness to altered terms of trade with the rest of the world, especially countries that produce raw materials (an apparent objective of the envisioned green transition). In the face of hesitations and vulnerabilities in other European countries and a growing anti-Chinese sentiment in Brussels (increasingly hostile to Beijing's direct investments[216]),

---

215  See Vijay Prashad, "US Doing Its Best to Lock China Out of Latin America", *Asia Times*, 4 November 2020, accessed 29 September 2023, https://asiatimes.com/2020/11/us-doing-its-best-to-lock-china-out-of-latin-america/.

216  Agatha Kratz, Max J. Zenglein, and Gregor Sebastian, *Chinese FDI in Europe: 2020 Update: Investment Falls to 10-Year Low in an Economically and Politically Challenging Year*, Berlin: MERICS and Rhodium Group, 16 June 2021, accessed 29 September 2023, https://merics.org/en/report/chinese-fdi-europe-2020-update.

Berlin attempted to push for a comprehensive Sino-European investment agreement, which was indeed signed at the end of 2020, largely due to the support of German industry. Nevertheless, it faced strong opposition from the Biden administration. Subsequently, it has remained stagnant, particularly after Angela Merkel's departure from the political scene. The crisis stemming from the war in Ukraine not only extinguished any independent European ambitions concerning Russia but also, as a by-product, paved the way for a more assertive stance towards Beijing. In the short to medium term, Germany appears to be unable to resist the external and internal pressure to align itself completely with the Atlanticist front.

In sum, every Chinese effort to ascend the value chains and diminish dollar constraints through non-disruptive means consistently encounters obstacles erected by US imperialism, and these challenges persistently escalate the level of conflict, either directly or indirectly, as seen in the Ukrainian situation.

**6.4   *The East Asian Region***

It is important to recognise the interplay between the BRI and the ongoing process of economic integration within East Asia. This integration holds immense significance for both China's economic strategy and its geopolitical outlook, particularly because the region has been encompassed within US military and alliance arrangements since the conclusion of World War II.[217] The critical question is whether the future of this region will be predominantly shaped by the geopolitical strategy of containing China or, conversely, by the burgeoning role of East Asia in the global economy, with China as a central pivot. In the former scenario, Washington would seek to deploy its alliances to obstruct its adversary's economic ascension. In the latter scenario, Beijing would be tasked with not only assuring regional states by sustaining economic growth but also with steering its own strategic reorientation to transform the area into an economic hub that can rival the United States and Europe. Outcomes on this front remain unpredictable, as disentangling the grip of dollar imperialism on Asian economies poses substantial challenges.

Clearly, Beijing holds certain advantages over the United States in exercising its economic influence in East Asia.[218] Without delving into exhaustive details, it is noteworthy that trade between China and the ASEAN countries continued to expand even during the height of the pandemic. It is worth mentioning that in the year 2000, trade between the ASEAN countries and the United States

---

217   Sciortino, *Oltre il bipolarismo*, sec. 3.1.
218   Hanania, "Inevitable Rise of China".

# CHINA

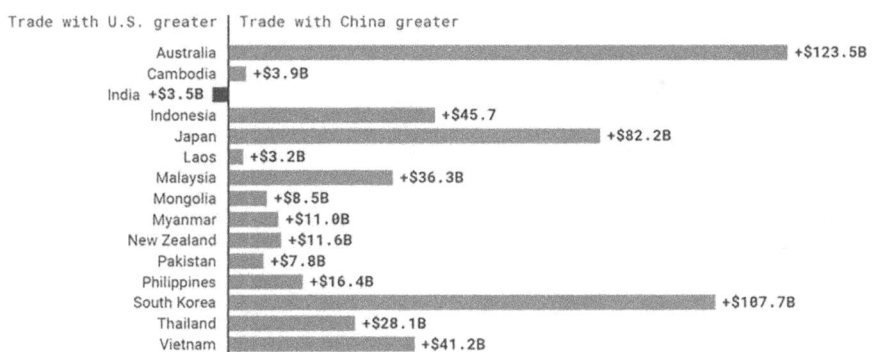

FIGURE 3.10 Net difference in total trade in goods with US vs. China in the Indo-Pacific, 2019 REPRODUCED FROM HANANIA, "INEVITABLE RISE OF CHINA". DATA (2019) FROM UNITED NATIONS COMTRADE.

surpassed that with China by a factor of three. However, by 2020, the trade volume with China had grown to be twice as large as that with the United States (see Figure 3.10).[219]

ASEAN countries have emerged as China's most significant trading partner, eclipsing even the European Union in terms of trade volume. Over recent years, there has also been a notable upswing in mutual direct investments. It is noteworthy that, as of 2020, almost fifty percent of each country's exports within the region were destined for other ASEAN nations. With a combined population of over 2.3 billion people, the region has experienced nearly uninterrupted economic growth for several decades. Its total GDP is now equivalent to 30% of the world's GDP (adjusted for purchasing power parity), placing it on par with the United States or Europe. Furthermore, the region has forged numerous bilateral trade agreements, covering more than 80% of individual countries' trade. A key driver of China's role in this context is the robust demand for various types of infrastructure development. This demand attracts medium- to long-term investments, for which Western capital is often unavailable due to a range of factors (see Map 3.3).

The RCEP agreement (Regional Comprehensive Economic Partnership),[220] signed by Australia, Brunei Darussalam, Cambodia, China, Japan, Laos, New

---

219 Kishore Mahbubani, "In Asia, China's Long Game Beats America's Short Game", *Foreign Policy Magazine*, 12 December 2021, accessed 29 September 2023, https://foreignpolicy.com/2021/12/12/china-us-asean-trade-geopolitics/ (subscription required).

220 ASEAN, "ASEAN Hits Historic Milestone with Signing of RCEP", news release, 15 November 2020, accessed 30 September 2023, https://asean.org/asean-hits-historic-milestone-with-signing-of-rcep/.

MAP 3.3    Chinese share of total trade in goods from Comprehensive and Progressive Agreement for Trans-Pacific Partnership (CPTPP) countries, 2020
REPRODUCED FROM ISPI, "GLOBAL WATCH: SPECIALE GEOECONOMIA N.72", 24 SEPTEMBER 2021, ACCESSED 29 SEPTEMBER 2023, HTTPS://WWW.ISP IONLINE.IT/IT/PUBBLICAZIONE/GLOBAL-WATCH-SPECIALE-GEOECONO MIA-N72-31775. COMPILED BY ISPI BASED ON IMF DIRECTION OF TRADE STATISTICS DATA.

Zealand, Singapore, Thailand, and Vietnam, enacted in 2020, and entered into force on 1 January 2022, is an integral part of this regional framework.[221] It can be viewed as a by-product of the global financial crisis of 2008–9, with initial negotiations commencing in 2012. In a broader historical context, it could be considered an outcome of the Asian crisis in 1998, which had previously resulted in the formation of the ASEAN + 3 agreement (comprising China, Japan, and South Korea). The RCEP represents a trade agreement with a primary focus on eliminating industrial tariffs. Conspicuously absent are provisions related to intellectual property, labour standards, and environmental regulations, which have long been stalking horses through which the West can impose its own conditions. One of the most pivotal aspects of this agreement is the establishment of rules aimed at fostering greater integration of manufacturing supply

---

221   India has not joined the RCEP.

chains. Specifically, the 'rules of origin' have been streamlined and relaxed, defining the nationality of products in a manner that facilitates their free circulation and use as intermediate inputs across member countries, ultimately contributing to the assembly of final goods. It will of course depend on how implementation is agreed, but one can expect the outcome to be a strengthening of regional value chains.

The geo-economic and geopolitical significance of this agreement is unmistakable. It is poised to partially counterbalance the effects of selective decoupling initiated by the United States,[222] while also paving the way for more extensive regionalism and trade standards more aligned with China's interests in the context of BRI projects.[223] Of course, the member states' geopolitical heterogeneity could potentially constrain China's strategic latitude. Furthermore, Japan, still a leading investor in the region, is set to play a substantial role, serving as a counterweight to Beijing (the more so in light of India's self-exclusion). This is particularly significant as Japan currently outpaces China in terms of investments in the region.[224] Beijing must also take into account the need to avoid exacerbating existing tensions concerning the South China Sea, especially with nations such as Vietnam, the Philippines, Malaysia, Brunei, and Indonesia.[225]

The CPTPP (Comprehensive and Progressive Trans-Pacific Partnership) agreement, which emerged in 2018 as a successor to the defunct TTP (Trans-Pacific Partnership) after the US withdrawal under the Trump administration, highlights the challenging economic landscape facing Beijing. The CPTPP includes Japan, Australia, New Zealand, Canada, Mexico, Brunei, Chile, Malaysia, Peru, Singapore, and Vietnam. Notably, it can be seen as a counterpart

---

222　Peter A. Petri and Michael G. Plummer, "East Asia Decouples from the United States: Trade War, COVID-19, and East Asia's New Trade Blocs" (Working Paper 20–9, PIIE, Washington, DC, June 2020), accessed 30 September 2023, https://www.piie.com/publications/working-papers/east-asia-decouples-united-states-trade-war-covid-19-and-east-asias-new; Uri Dadush, "The Impact of the New Asian Trade Mega-Deal on the European Union", Bruegel blog, 19 November 2020, accessed 30 September 2023, https://www.bruegel.org/blog-post/impact-new-asian-trade-mega-deal-european-union.

223　Mark Beeson, "Geoeconomics with Chinese Characteristics: The BIS and China's Evolving Grand Strategy", *Economic and Political Studies* 6, no. 3 (2018): 240–56, https://doi.org/10.1080/20954816.2018.1498988.

224　Michelle Jamrisko, "China No Match for Japan in Southeast Asia Infrastructure Race", *BQ Prime* (Bloomberg), 25 June 2019, accessed 23 November 2021, https://www.bloombergquint.com/china/china-no-match-for-japan-in-southeast-asia-infrastructure-race.

225　Michiel Haasbroek, "A Glimpse into China's Changed Financial Sector", MERICS, 15 July 2020, accessed 30 September 2023, https://merics.org/en/comment/glimpse-chinas-changed-financial-sector.

to the RCEP, and it imposes more stringent trade rules. Its underlying objective is to thwart Beijing's efforts to establish trade standards in the Indo-Pacific region. However, it must be said that Washington maintains a foreign direct investment stock in the region nearly three times that of China.

However, the heart of the matter lies in the structural transformations occurring within China's production and trade patterns. In recent years, Chinese private enterprises have surpassed foreign companies in the overall exportation of products assembled in China. Nonetheless, many of these exports still depend on foreign research and design, as well as the importation of higher value-added intermediate goods used as inputs. The overarching goal is to reduce reliance on these specific imports. Through advancements in the value chain, China has begun exporting intermediate goods and medium- to high-tech services, becoming a hub for numerous Asian nations. Simultaneously, it has started relocating low value-added production to countries in the region with lower labour costs. For this transformation to solidify, it necessitates an increase in domestic generation of relative surplus value, as well as a conducive external trade, financial, and monetary environment.

The establishment of an integrated economic area in the East Asian region could facilitate this transition by altering the composition of China's value-added contributions. In principle, China, Japan, and South Korea, now connected by a formal trade agreement for the first time, are already complementary economies with a significant volume of mutual trade. The East Asian market surrounding these economies holds immense potential for intra-regional growth, even without the stringent institutionalisation seen in the European model. It also promises greater autonomy from Western economic dynamics. However, it is important to note that, until now, a substantial portion of the higher value-added intermediate components used in Chinese factories have been sourced from the Asian region.

Should China's structural position in the regional and global production network undergo transformation, the role of Japanese, and to a lesser extent, South Korean and Taiwanese multinationals, will inevitably diminish. This change will not occur automatically or without potential interference, particularly from Washington, which can be expected to exert influence due to its strong hold on Tokyo and Seoul. Furthermore, China's emergence as the regional focal point demands both quantitative and qualitative expansion of its domestic market. This is essential for attracting and absorbing a growing share of the region's production. Additionally, the internationalisation of China's currency is a pivotal aspect of this development. These dynamics present significant challenges and opportunities on the economic front for China, with far-reaching consequences for both regional and global trade and finance.

## 6.5 Western Asia

In examining China's relationships with Iran and the Gulf countries in the context of the 'Middle East' region, it is crucial to understand their enormous importance to Beijing. There are two primary reasons for this significance: first, the region serves as a major supplier of oil and is a strategically vital energy hub, and second, it plays a critical role as a transit point for the southern routes of the BRI.

Within this context, Iran holds a central position in the geopolitical tension between the United States and the Eurasian region. It also serves as a pivotal juncture for the BRI. Chinese access to the Middle East and Europe would be severely compromised without Iran's cooperation, and it would significantly hamper the entire BRI project. This situation has been exacerbated by the fact that Iran has been the target of the harshest US sanctions for several years. These sanctions were only partially lifted by the Obama administration following the 2015 agreement on the Iranian nuclear programme (the Joint Comprehensive Plan of Action or JCPOA). However, this agreement was unilaterally terminated by the Trump administration in 2018, further escalating tensions, especially after the US airstrike that killed Iranian Revolutionary Guards chief Suleimani in January 2020. In response to these challenges, Iran has taken steps to promote economic development with the aim of reducing its dependence on oil. In this endeavour, Chinese support has become indispensable, particularly due to Iran's isolation from the West and the significant impact of the pandemic. However, this aid has not come without conditions, and China has exerted pressure on Iran to adopt a more conciliatory stance towards Saudi Arabia. For China's BRI development and secure access to oil supplies, it is imperative to have a region free from excessive tensions. As a result, Tehran has discreetly initiated efforts to ease tensions with its Arab neighbours,[226] while Beijing has increased its imports of Iranian oil by circumventing US secondary sanctions.

This complex scenario, which is only briefly outlined here, culminated in a significant twenty-five-year cooperation agreement signed in Tehran in March 2021 between China and Iran, often referred to as 'strategic partners'. This landmark agreement involves Chinese investments totalling $400 billion in five key sectors, with a particular emphasis on infrastructure development, including the expansion of the Jask port to circumvent the bottleneck of the Strait of Hormuz and serve as a terminal for oil shipments to East Asia.

---

226 It is reasonable to surmise that the assassination of General Suleimani in January 2020 was likely an attempt to disrupt the diplomatic channels that had been established between Tehran and Riyadh.

The digital sector is another focal point of collaboration. In return for these investments, China secures a stable supply of crude oil from Iran at favourable prices. Beyond the economic aspects, this agreement also carries significant military implications, including joint manoeuvres, arms production, and the possibility of granting China access to Iranian airspace. Additionally, the deal holds strategic importance for the development of the BRI. In early 2022, Syria, a long-standing ally of Iran, also expressed its intention to join this initiative. Moreover, the cooperation paves the way for transitioning to payments for Iranian oil in Chinese currency, as the yuan is already the primary reserve currency held by Iran's central bank. This development contributes to the emergence of 'emerging globalisation' in Asia, which partly serves as an alternative to Western globalisation, spearheaded by countries like China, Russia, and Iran. This trend may gain further momentum with the potential for a normalised situation in Afghanistan following the US military withdrawal.

China has been increasingly strengthening its ties with Gulf countries and became their leading trading partner in 2020. These countries, including Bahrain, Saudi Arabia, Kuwait, Oman, and Qatar, play critical roles as China's key suppliers of Middle Eastern oil and gas (see Map 3.4). The Gulf monarchies are exploring economic diversification projects, which include high-tech sectors and digital infrastructure, aligning with China's expertise in these areas. A free trade agreement with Beijing would be part of these diversification efforts. Projects in the direction of high-tech sectors and digital infrastructure, which China can offer. Saudi Arabia's 'Vision 2030' project, for example, can synergise well with the BRI, where Saudi Arabia ranks second in terms of project value.[227] Additionally, China is well-positioned to fill any potential void created by the shifting focus of US geopolitical activities towards the Indo-Pacific, especially in the Gulf region.

China is playing a mediating role between the Gulf countries and the potential resumption of the Iranian nuclear agreement, contributing to regional stability. Furthermore, it is deepening its military collaboration with Saudi Arabia by not only selling weapons but also supporting local production of ballistic missiles.[228] Meanwhile, in the United Arab Emirates, where the decisions to choose Huawei's 5G network and cancel the purchase of US F-35 fighter jets

---

227   Dario Di Conzo, "The AIIB in the Post-Pandemic World", T.Note No. 85, Turin World Affair Institute, 16 July 2020, accessed 30 September 2023, https://www.twai.it/journal/tnote-85/.

228   Edna Mohamed, "New Evidence Shows Saudi Arabia Building Ballistic Missiles with China's Help", *Middle East Eye*, 23 December 2021, accessed 30 September 2023, https://www.middleeasteye.net/news/saudi-arabia-china-building-ballistic-missiles-images.

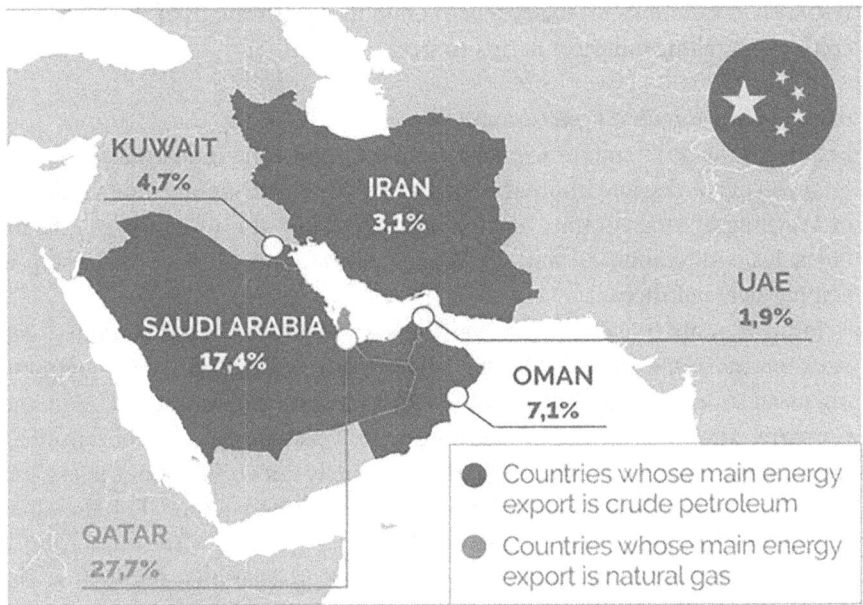

MAP 3.4   Gulf countries' share in China energy imports, by percentage, 2019
REPRODUCED FROM ISPI, "THE GULF AND CHINA: A BROADENING PARTNERSHIP?", ISPI MED THIS WEEK, 14 JANUARY 2022, ACCESSED 30 SEPTEMBER 2023, HTTPS://WWW.ISPIONLINE.IT/EN/PUBLICATION/GULF-AND-CHINA-BROADENING-PARTNERSHIP-32872. ORIGINAL DATA FROM THE OBSERVATORY OF ECONOMIC COMPLEXITY.

have already drawn scrutiny, Washington has voiced concerns and sought to blame Beijing for the construction of a port in the region with possible military applications. Washington's response to China's expanding economic influence has been evident, extending even to its ally, Israel, with repeated warnings against cooperation agreements with Beijing.

The crux of the matter lies in Washington's insistence that Saudi Arabia and the other Gulf nations continue to rely on oil priced in US dollars, and they should resist Chinese demands to use yuan for payment. The Pentagon, with input from Israeli intelligence services, has long had plans prepared for the fragmentation of the Saudi state and the entire region. These plans could be set in motion if Riyadh shows signs of pursuing a more independent role, such as deepening its engagement with the 'New Silk Roads', securing the supply of Chinese missiles, reaching a stable agreement with Russia on oil production quotas (known as OPEC+), or establishing a modus vivendi with Tehran. The Gulf nations' refusal to comply with US pressure to increase oil production in response to sanctions on Russian extraction in the aftermath of the Ukrainian conflict is a telling indicator in this context.

### 6.6  Drawing First Conclusions

Beijing's strategy therefore revolves around establishing industrial platforms, financial networks, and international partnerships that operate independently of Washington's constraints and pressures. Despite the progress, significant obstacles, vulnerabilities, and challenges persist, and Chinese leadership is acutely aware of them.

From a geopolitical perspective, the BRI highlights the substantial gap between maritime and continental routes, with the United States maintaining naval superiority. Meanwhile, the willingness of the European Union and Germany, pivotal in the Euro-Asian continental exchange, to collaborate effectively on the project's success appears increasingly uncertain. Nonetheless, BRI presents a significant challenge by offering an alternative model of globalisation distinct from the Western paradigm.

Regarding East Asia, the trend towards regionalisation—marked by the development of a more self-sufficient economic area in terms of trade and industry, less reliant on international US finance and currency—is a tangible reality. This trend raises alarm bells for the United States and European Union. However, challenges persist, including tense Sino-Japanese relations, the region's continued dependence on Western markets and the dollar, the crucial role of US geopolitics, and the lack of a dominant economic centre to replace the United States in the region. In replacing the United States, such a centre would need to serve as an essential outlet market for goods and a critical hub for capital flows denominated in a universally accepted currency, such as the dollar, which still functions as a reserve of value and a universally accepted means of payment for all global economic actors. In the absence of an alternative economic centre, even with ongoing regionalisation, any regionalism remains incomplete. While regionalisation signifies shifting global balances, it lacks the strength to overturn the existing global order entirely, especially without China's ability to assume the role of a dominant centre in East Asia.

## 7  The Internationalisation of the Renminbi Yuan

The strategies of dual circulation and external projection, the transformation of China's development model, and the reconfiguration of globalisation to better align with Chinese interests inevitably impact the role of its currency. China's engagement with the global economy has historically been under the shadow of the dominant dollar imperialism. While this engagement facilitated China's economic ascent, it has also become a constraint and potential barrier to further progress. In this context, the internationalisation of the renminbi yuan becomes a pivotal concern. The questions that arise are multifaceted. How can China enhance the global presence of the renminbi yuan? What strategies should it employ to increase its adoption and usage on the international stage? What are the current vulnerabilities of the renminbi yuan concerning its internationalisation, and how can these be mitigated or rectified? Equally, what intrinsic strengths can be harnessed to expedite its global acceptance? Finally, in the face of Washington's strategic utilisation of the dollar, particularly as exemplified during the Ukraine crisis, what are the potential pathways for China to maintain and enhance the international standing of the renminbi yuan? This chapter aims to provide some answers to these questions.

## 7.1   *The State of Affairs*

China now boasts a substantial one-sixth share of the global gross product, but its currency, the renminbi yuan (hereinafter referred to as 'yuan', adhering to common, albeit incorrect, practice), makes up a mere 2% of the world's reserves.[229] This pales in comparison to the dollar, accounting for around 60%, and the euro at 20%. Moreover, regarding international SWIFT payments, the yuan falls far short, representing just over 40% of those settled in the US currency and 35% in the euro.[230] Furthermore, despite China's pivotal role in world trade, the yuan is utilised in only about 20% of transactions to and from the country. In the realm of international finance, yuan-denominated bonds held overseas constitute a mere 3% of the global total in 2021, while dollar-denominated bonds make up a substantial 30%. This is despite there being a substantial 16 trillion yuan in bonds issued within China.

Interestingly, the dominance of the US dollar is not entirely proportional to the United States' share of the world's GDP (see Figure 3.11). Even with an overall negative international financial position of over $18 trillion by the end

---

[229] Sharnie Wong and Francis Chan, "Yuan Could Globalize on Digital Currency, De-dollarization Steps", Bloomberg, 4 February 2021, accessed 30 September 2023, https://www.bloomberg.com/professional/blog/yuan-could-globalize-on-digital-currency-de-dollarization-steps/.

[230] Swift, *RMB Tracker: Monthly Reporting and Statistics on Renminbi (RMB) Progress Towards Becoming an International Currency*, La Hulpe, Belgium, updated November 2021, accessed 30 November 2021, https://www.swift.com/swift-resource/251736/download; Mrugank Bhusari and Maia Nikoladze, "Russia and China: Partners in Dedollarization", Atlantic Council blog, 18 February 2022, accessed 30 September 2023, https://www.atlanticcouncil.org/blogs/econographics/russia-and-china-partners-in-dedollarization/.

of 2021 (up from $14 trillion at the end of 2020), driven by foreign liabilities for direct investments and portfolio investments, and a trade deficit touching $800 billion in 2021, the US can finance itself from abroad with ease to pay for its domestic budget and balance of payments deficits.[231] This privilege is granted by the near-monopoly status of the dollar as the international currency, which remains the monetary and geopolitical linchpin for two-thirds of the world's GDP. Notably, the yuan was pegged closely to the dollar until 2005, and it has only experienced limited fluctuation since 2015, within a 2% band. As a result, any notion of American decline should be approached with great caution, considering the enduring strength of the dollar.[232]

It is essential to recall that all these dynamics are intertwined with the intricate structure of contemporary imperialism, the basis of so-called globalisation. This foundation has underpinned the asymmetrical yet mutually vital economic and geopolitical relationship between the United States and China for the past three decades. Presently, the imperative requirements of China's capitalist development and the strategic direction set by the party-state over the past ten years have initiated a shift towards reducing their reliance on American finance.

More recently, the deteriorating relations with Washington, coupled with the weaponisation of currencies in the Ukrainian conflict, have convinced Chinese leadership that continued exposure to the dollar-dominated system entails growing risks that are no longer balanced by the benefits of access to Western export markets. In short, China can no longer adhere to the rules dictated by the Federal Reserve, regardless of the circumstances. This is where another pivotal element comes into play—the strategy commonly referred to as the internationalisation of the Chinese currency. According to Beijing's intent, this strategy should be cautious and well-regulated, but simultaneously viewed as an imperative choice.

The first significant push in this direction came as a response to the global crisis of 2008–09. Despite amassing considerable dollar reserves from trade surpluses, China recognised that it had become overexposed to the volatility of the dollar-centric financial system and the loose monetary policies of the

---

231  US Department of Commerce—Bureau of Economic Analysis, "U.S. International Investment Position, Fourth Quarter and Year 2021", news release, BE 22–12, 29 March 2022, accessed 30 September 2023, https://www.bea.gov/news/2022/us-international-investment-position-fourth-quarter-and-year-2021.

232  The global prevalence of a currency depends not only on the reserves held by other nations but also on its role as a medium of exchange, the currency in which bonds and debts are denominated, exchange controls, and various other factors.

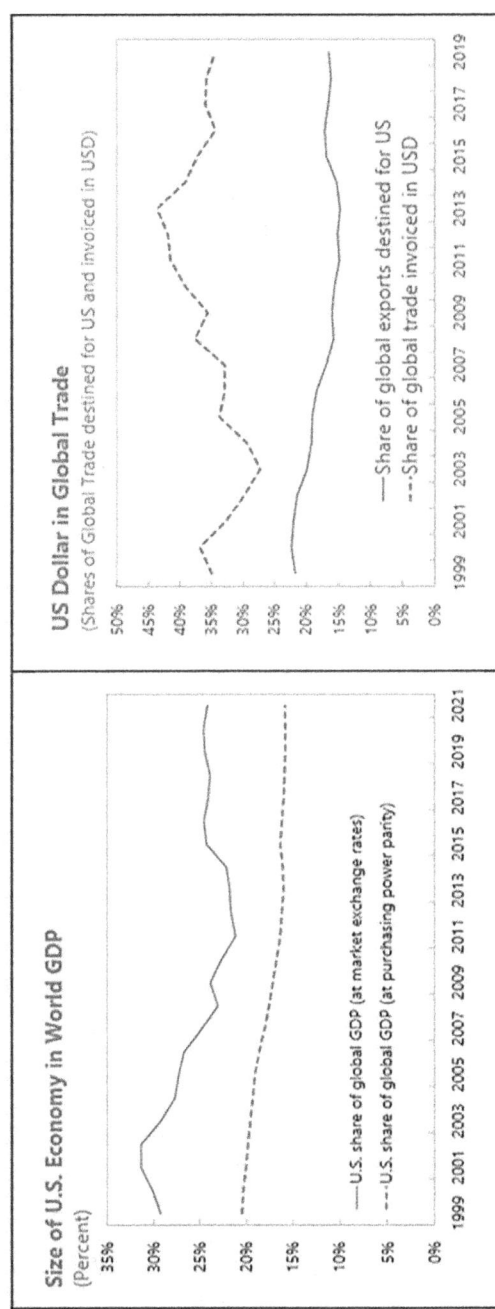

FIGURE 3.11  Standard determinants of US dollar share of reserves
Left: Size of US economy in world GDP (percent); right: US dollar in global trade (shares of global trade destined for the US and invoiced in US dollars).
REPRODUCED FROM SERKAN ARSLANALP, BARRY J. EICHENGREEN, AND CHINA SIMPSON-BELL, "THE STEALTH EROSION OF DOLLAR DOMINANCE: ACTIVE DIVERSIFIERS AND THE RISE OF NONTRADITIONAL RESERVE CURRENCIES" (IMF WORKING PAPER NO. WP/2022/058, WASHINGTON, DC, 24 MARCH 2022), ACCESSED 30 SEPTEMBER 2023, HTTPS://WWW.IMF.ORG /EN/PUBLICATIONS/WP/ISSUES/2022/03/24/THE-STEALTH-EROSION-OF-DOLLAR-DOMINANCE-ACTIVE-DIVERSIFIERS-AND -THE-RISE-OF-NONTRADITIONAL-515150, FIG. 2. DATA FROM IMF INTERNATIONAL FINANCIAL STATISTICS, IMF WORLD ECONOMIC OUTLOOK, AND BOZ ET AL., "PATTERNS IN INVOICING CURRENCY IN GLOBAL TRADE" (IMF WORKING PAPER NO. 20/126, WASHINGTON, DC, JULY 2020).

Federal Reserve.²³³ This vulnerability was further exacerbated first by the massive issuance of currency by Washington in reaction to the pandemic crisis, which contributed to global inflationary pressures. Subsequently, the monetary tightening initiated in 2022, while its effectiveness in combating inflation remains debatable, had the effect of strengthening the dollar and attracting capital back to the United States from the rest of the world through a well-established 'accordion' mechanism we analysed in chapter 2.²³⁴

Given this backdrop, Beijing has taken several significant steps over the past decade, which were deemed essential prerequisites for a more assertive internationalisation of its currency. China's increased involvement in international trade, not limited to exports, and its investments in the BRI have given rise to a multitude of trade and banking transactions conducted in yuan on foreign soil. Simultaneously, since 2015, Beijing established its own international interbank payment system called the Cross-Border Inter-Bank Payments System or CIPS, notably for oil trade, which operates independently of SWIFT. SWIFT, as evidenced during the recent Ukrainian crisis, is effectively controlled by US financial institutions and the US government. In 2016, the yuan was included in the IMF's basket of currencies that determine the value of Special Drawing Rights or SDRs. Subsequently, the rules governing the foreign purchase of Chinese currency bonds were relaxed.²³⁵

---

233   William Overholt, "Renminbi Internationalisation Deferred", Official Monetary and Financial Institutions Forum, 15 May 2020, accessed 30 September 2023, https://www.omfif.org/2020/05/renminbis-limited-internationalisation/.

234   Data from the early part of 2022 revealed a significant reduction in foreign investors' participation in Chinese equities and bonds. This withdrawal bore some resemblance to the situation in 2015–16, which had necessitated robust interventions in currency and capital markets to stabilise the situation. In contrast, leading up to 2021, China had experienced substantial inflows of foreign direct investment, totalling $173 billion. A potential consequence of any further depreciation of the yuan could be an increase in the cost of importing technology and raw materials. See Amanda Lee, "China's Forex Reserves Fall by US$26 Billion Amid Ongoing Capital Outflows Following Russian Invasion of Ukraine", *South China Morning Post*, 7 April 2022, accessed 30 September 2023, https://www.scmp.com/economy/economic-indicators/article/3173454/chinas-forex-reserves-fall-us25-billion-amid-ongoing; Tyler Durden (pseudonym), "Whispers of Yuan Devaluation After Biggest Weekly Plunge Since 2015", ZeroHedge, 22 April 2022, accessed 29 May 2022, https://www.zerohedge.com/markets/whispers-yuan-devaluation-after-biggest-weekly-plunge-2015.

235   Andrew Galbraith, "Explainer: Foreign Access to China's $16 Trillion Bond Market", Reuters, 23 September 2020, accessed 30 September 2023, https://www.reuters.com/article/china-bonds-market/explainer-foreign-access-to-chinas-16-trillion-bond-market-idUSKCN26E0UE. On the (thus far timid) liberalisation of the Chinese financial market, see Michel Aglietta, Guo Bai, and Camille Macaire, *La course à la suprématie monétaire mondiale* (Paris: Odile Jacob, 2022), 86ff.

Additionally, Beijing has planned the launch of a digital currency under the central bank's control, which is anticipated to further facilitate the global dissemination of the yuan, particularly within the BRI and the East Asian region. This digital currency also offers centralised access to vast amounts of data related to monetary transactions, currently predominantly monopolised by Washington. Furthermore, China's decisions to slow down the purchase of US Treasury bonds and to amass commodities, including substantial amounts of gold, should be interpreted within this context. These actions serve as protection against the volatility of foreign exchange markets and as a response to the Federal Reserve's quantitative easing policy.

These initial measures, while commendable, are not yet sufficient to achieve complete autonomy from the dollar and the US debt-focused financial system. However, they do represent important steps in addressing critical issues that are vital for China's ongoing development. Two of these issues stand out as particularly significant. First, there is the challenge of breaking the self-perpetuating cycle where excessive dependence on exports, at the expense of the domestic market, leads to the accumulation of reserves in a currency that remains susceptible to devaluation due to US monetary policies. These reserves can be viewed as a sort of obligatory loan, which, in reality, cannot be collected.[236] The second critical issue pertains to the no longer arbitrary threat from Washington of imposing sanctions, potentially blocking the use of accumulated dollars and access to the SWIFT international payment system.[237] In this context, China is not merely at a midpoint but is, as mentioned earlier, taking its initial steps towards addressing these challenges. Regardless of the current position, these steps could mark an irreversible trajectory in a complex interplay of actions and reactions involving the United States, with profound implications for the global economic landscape. Let us delve into the primary implications in more detail.

---

236  As of mid-2022, China's foreign exchange reserves stood at approximately $3.2 trillion, a notable decrease from the roughly $4 trillion recorded in 2015.

237  During an emergency meeting held in late April 2022, attended by government officials and major Chinese banks to address the risk of potential US sanctions similar to those imposed on Russia, no viable solutions appeared to emerge due to the high level of dependency of the Chinese economy on the existing financial system. See Sun Yu, "China Meets Banks to Discuss Protecting Assets from US Sanctions", *Financial Times*, 30 April 2022, accessed 23 May 2022, https://www.ft.com/content/45d5fcac-3e6d-420a-ac78-4b439e24b5de (subscription required).

### 7.2   Vectors of Yuan

A crucial driver of the initial internationalisation of the Chinese currency is undeniably the BRI. This is due to the fact that foreign investments and trade generate a growing demand for the yuan within member countries. The financial backing for the BRI consists of several components: direct Chinese bank loans (with approximately three-quarters of them denominated in yuan), equity financing for the involved companies, and yuan securities issued by foreign BRI member companies and countries on the Chinese market (commonly referred to as panda bonds). Moreover, there are over forty bilateral agreements enabling the direct exchange of currencies between central banks (commonly known as currency swaps).[238] These swaps serve as a safeguard against the fluctuating exchange rate of the dollar and the associated risks of its availability.

All these measures have naturally led to an increased use of the yuan in foreign economies along the Belt and Road routes. This is evident in the expansion of bank deposits in yuan across the regions encompassed by the 'New Silk Roads', including countries such as Pakistan, Mongolia, South Korea, and, most notably, Russia. In 2020, for the first time, dollar exchanges in Russia fell below 50%, and Moscow has been consistently increasing its yuan reserves, which now represent a quarter of the world's total yuan reserves. Additionally, Latin American countries, such as Argentina and Brazil, have also become involved in the yuan's global circulation.

Indeed, the increasing volume of foreign trade, especially the rising share of imports, is currently a significant driver for the broader international adoption of the Chinese currency. This trend extends beyond the BRI and the specific case of Russia, impacting other nations as well. The BRICS countries have felt the influence, but it is most notable in East Asia. In this region, roughly 30% of intraregional trade with China is conducted in yuan, while 70% still hinges on the dollar. Europe, another substantial market for Beijing, accounting for 18% of its imports before the pandemic, has also embraced the use of the yuan (representing 10% of the total). Surprisingly, London remains the epicentre for clearing transactions, despite post-Brexit expectations of Frankfurt taking the lead. Nevertheless, European aspirations for closer ties with Beijing have been shelved in recent years due to the European Union's increasing mistrust and, more recently, China's involvement in the Ukraine crisis.

---

238   Sebastian Horn, Carmen M. Reinhart, and Christoph Trebesch, "How Much Money Does the World Owe China?", *Harvard Business Review*, 26 February 2020, accessed 30 September 2023, https://hbr.org/2020/02/how-much-money-does-the-world-owe-china.

Primarily, it is the countries that supply China with agricultural and mineral raw materials that are progressively adopting the yuan. Beijing, which has held the title of the world's leading oil importer since 2017, is actively establishing its own system of commodity exchanges and an independent futures market. This strategy aims to reduce its dependence on the Anglo-Saxon monopoly, which currently prevails with Chicago (CBOT) for agricultural commodities, London (LME) for metals, and New York (NYMEX) for oil, among others. While China's influence on price determination remains limited for now, the debut of the first oil futures contract in yuan in 2018 on the Shanghai marketplace was a significant milestone. It may pave the way, in the near future, for the direct sale of Middle Eastern crude oil, particularly from Saudi Arabia (after Russia, Iran, and Venezuela), alongside other commodities (such as copper since November 2020), all transacted in yuan backed by gold, rather than in dollars.[239]

For Beijing, the promotion of the yuan in trade transactions serves a dual purpose: not only to encourage the yuan's use in commerce but also to insulate itself as much as possible from the potential impact of further US sanctions, similar to the ones imposed on Russia. Nevertheless, it would be premature to describe this as a fully established alternative payment system to the dollar. While it is true that 25% of commercial transactions with countries involved in the BRI are conducted in renminbi (compared to less than 1% in 2009), this still represents less than 2% of international payments overall. Furthermore, the issuance of Chinese bonds on the global financial markets, which is another means to enhance the international presence of the yuan, remains relatively small when compared to the volume of domestic bonds. Although companies in China, often referred to as 'Dragon companies', looking to raise funds in international capital markets can open accounts in Chinese currency, and foreign investors can participate through the issuance of bonds known as 'dim sum bonds' on the Hong Kong offshore market, these efforts are just part of the broader strategy. There has also been authorisation for daily trading of the convertible currency, known as CNH, on the foreign exchange market, in contrast to the onshore inconvertible yuan, CNY.[240]

---

239 M. K. Bhadrakumar, "US' Coercive Diplomacy with Saudi Arabia", *Indian Punchline* (author's blog), 6 May 2022, accessed 30 September 2023, https://www.indianpunchline.com/us-coercive-diplomacy-with-saudi-arabia/.

240 Due to the absence of a fully convertible yuan, Hong Kong still retains a significant, though not as pivotal as in the past, role as an intermediary for financial transactions with foreign countries. A substantial portion of Chinese direct investment, including from state-owned enterprises, continues to flow through Hong Kong, highlighting its ongoing importance in facilitating China's international financial dealings. However, it is worth noting that Hong Kong's contribution to China's GDP has diminished over the years. In 1997, it

In essence, China is gradually moving towards making the yuan more convertible while maintaining centralised control over liquidity to a limited extent. To be more precise, Beijing is actively encouraging the international use of the yuan, primarily through foreign trade and closely related investments.[241] However, it is not yet fully embracing internationalisation, which would necessitate complete convertibility and the opening of the capital account.[242] This approach reflects the delicate balance China is trying to maintain between various, sometimes conflicting, goals: maintaining a stable exchange rate without triggering internal inflation, controlling capital flows to prevent speculative activities, and yet gradually allowing greater external use of the yuan. Achieving this balance is not a straightforward task. This complexity is further mirrored in the internal dynamics within China, where different factions advocate for varying degrees of currency liberalisation, with some pushing for full convertibility while others express concerns about potential overvaluation and vulnerability to international financial speculation, as was witnessed during the stock market and currency crisis of 2015–16. Nonetheless, China is preparing for the next phase of this process.

### 7.3 Digital Yuan

As mentioned earlier, the introduction of a digital currency controlled by the central bank is poised to significantly aid the global expansion of the yuan. Thus far, it has primarily comprised a series of domestic experiments with two primary objectives. First, these experiments sought to encourage electronic payments, a practice that has already gained extensive popularity among the Chinese population, especially following the COVID-19 pandemic. China has notably become a global leader in cashless mobile payments, accounting for 16% of its GDP, which is nearly half of the global average. The country's advanced electronic payment systems process a significantly higher number of transactions annually compared to the United States or Europe. Second, these experiments aimed to replace traditional currency with a state-backed virtual

---

accounted for a substantial 16% of China's GDP, whereas by the present day, its share has shrunk to just over 3%. Differing opinions regarding Hong Kong's current role are evident. For an exemplary contrast of viewpoints, see Tianlei Huang, "Why China Still Needs Hong Kong", PIIE blog, 15 July 2019, accessed 30 September 2023, https://www.piie.com/blogs/china-economic-watch/why-china-still-needs-hong-kong; Eswar S. Prasad, "Why China No Longer Needs Hong Kong", *New York Times*, 3 July 2019, accessed 30 September 2023, https://www.nytimes.com/2019/07/03/opinion/hong-kong-protest.html.

241  Abeliansky and Martínez-Zarzoso, "Chinese 'Going Out' Strategy and International Trade".
242  Eswar Prasad, *Gaining Currency: The Rise of the Renminbi* (Oxford: Oxford University Press, 2017).

currency. This digital money is directly deposited into digital wallets held by the central bank, bypassing commercial banks, and is removed from the purview of private sector credit cards and online trading platforms.

The concept of the digital yuan traces back to at least 2014–16, with initial experimentation involving collaboration between the central bank and select commercial banks beginning in 2017. Pilot tests took place from 2019–20 in numerous cities, culminating in the official use of the digital yuan during the Beijing Winter Olympics in the winter of 2022. In the interim, the number of e-wallets has surged to over 120 million, making digital state currency a reality, although it has not yet become ubiquitous. The architectural framework tested during these experiments is expected to be the one fully implemented. It operates on a two-tier system, with the central bank and commercial banks serving as intermediaries. The digital yuan is designed as a monetary base, not an interest-bearing deposit, to mitigate risks of instability within the banking system, which could result from money creation outside central control.

The introduction of the digital yuan serves a multitude of objectives, addressing both internal and external concerns. On the domestic front, it is designed to provide direct access to over 200 million citizens, primarily in rural areas, who currently lack bank accounts. This expansion aims to foster domestic market growth and integrate segments of the population that have been less involved with formal financial services. Additionally, the digital yuan initiative seeks to curb the influence of private digital giants who have developed extensive electronic payment and microcredit systems. This move aims to regulate platforms like Alibaba's Alipay and Tencent's WeChat Pay, which have grown considerably in recent years and are now subject to more stringent state oversight. Simultaneously, the implementation of the digital yuan will significantly enhance the real-time collection of transaction data. This capability will prove instrumental in combating illegal activities and reducing tax evasion, given the need for a more efficient tax collection system. It will also provide broader control over capital flows, facilitating improved financial oversight and regulation. The decision to ban all cryptocurrencies in September 2021 should also be considered within this context. China had previously attracted numerous bitcoin 'miners', but cryptocurrencies, in the Chinese perspective, presented challenges in terms of control and were perceived as vehicles for financial speculation often originating from the United States.[243]

---

243  Erik Townsend, *Beyond Blockchain: the Death of the Dollar and the Rise of Digital Currency* (independently published, 2018).

At present, the majority of the world's currency transaction data is under the dominance of Washington, chiefly through the SWIFT system and associated mechanisms. The central bank's digital yuan initiative serves the purpose of enabling Chinese authorities to effectively monitor not only the domestic market but also the flow of balance of payments. It also facilitates the direction of cross-border trade payments, spanning from the BRI to the RCEP and beyond, in a form that circumvents dollar intermediation. This, in turn, helps evade US controls and the potential risk of being excluded from the SWIFT payments system. Over time, the central digital currency is poised to become the linchpin in establishing an international payments infrastructure with its own technology and standards. This infrastructure promises to be more cost-effective and streamlined compared to the existing system. It offers a solution to a range of economic players who engage in trade relations with China. An initial experiment in this direction is the cross-border digital currency exchange platform initiated by China, Thailand, the United Arab Emirates, and Hong Kong, launched in early 2021 (the multiple central bank digital currency bridge, aka MBridge or M-CBDC Bridge). This platform serves as a prototype for a potential future hub on a larger scale. Looking ahead, a critical element that will shape the future is the ever-closer integration of monetary technological innovation with the development of a logistics network grounded in big data and artificial intelligence. This development means that the organisation of zero stock and just-in-time payments will form a network of supply chains that allows exporters and importers to monitor the movement of goods in real time. Moreover, it enables them to bypass, rather than immediately replace, the dollar typically used for international payments and kept in offshore deposits. As a result, there will be no longer the need to commit to contracts in a volatile foreign currency in advance to secure transactions with costly insurances, which are predominantly denominated in dollars, or to rely on international banks for financing at associated expenses.[244] The significance of the 'Digital Silk Roads' comes to the forefront here, even though its reach is largely confined to developing countries for the time being.

In summary, the introduction of the central bank's digital yuan constitutes another integral component in China's comprehensive strategy aimed at solidifying its position in finance, international trade, foreign investment, and technology. The ultimate outcome and whether it will culminate in a digital yuan–dominated sphere or potentially create a divergence within the global

---

244   David P. Goldman, "China's Digital Yuan Displaces the Dollar", *Asia Times*, 21 April 2021, accessed 30 September 2023, https://asiatimes.com/2021/04/chinas-digital-yuan-displaces-the-dollar/.

internet network with varying technical and regulatory systems is challenging to predict. In practice, Beijing, despite being open to the idea of a more multilateral international monetary system, has not (yet) committed to full currency convertibility or embraced the responsibility of establishing the yuan as an international reserve currency. Simultaneously, it has adopted a measured approach, which includes providing access, rather than restricting, its domestic payment services in yuan to international industry giants (such as American Express, Visa, Mastercard). This approach is a precautionary measure to safeguard against further measures of US decoupling. Consequently, the initiatives outlined appear to be predominantly defensive in nature, though the ramifications, as often is the case, could extend far beyond initial intentions, particularly if this progress leads to pegging the digital currency, characterised by its potential, to central reserves that are explicitly tied to gold, rather than the dollar. This brings us to the question of what is commonly referred to as 'de-dollarisation'.

## 7.4  *De-dollarisation?*

The topic of de-dollarisation has recently gained prominence in public discussions, particularly in the aftermath of the Ukraine crisis and the sanctions imposed by Western nations on Russia. These sanctions have had a sweeping impact on the Russian economy, leading to its disconnection from the SWIFT payment system, the seizure of private assets belonging to Russian so-called oligarchs, and the indefinite freezing of the Russian central bank's dollar and euro reserves. Furthermore, sales of energy raw materials have been progressively subjected to something resembling an embargo, and access to advanced technologies has been severely restricted. Historian Adam Tooze, who is not typically associated with anti-American sentiments, characterised these measures as a pivotal moment for the entire international monetary system, extending well beyond the Western–Russian relationship.[245] In addition, the IMF released a report at the outset of the Ukrainian crisis, highlighting the "erosion of the dollar's dominance".[246] To navigate this intricate issue, we must distinguish between the strategies of key stakeholders, ongoing processes, observable effects, and potential implications. Our primary focus is on how this issue directly relates to China and its overarching strategy.

---

245  Adam Tooze, "The World is at Financial War", *New Statesman*, 2 March 2022, accessed 30 September 2023, https://www.newstatesman.com/ideas/2022/03/ukraine-the-world-is-at-financial-war.
246  Arslanalp, Eichengreen, and Simpson-Bell, "Stealth Erosion of Dollar Dominance".

De-dollarisation, strictly speaking, refers to the process of diminishing the dominance of the US dollar as the world's primary reserve currency and the key international payment method. This dominance was the linchpin of financial imperialism that allowed the United States to navigate its way out of the capitalist crisis of the 1970s, ultimately preserving and even reinforcing its global hegemony during the era of globalisation. As evident from the data presented at the beginning of this chapter, it is clear that we are not currently witnessing the advanced erosion of the US dollar's supremacy. However, this does not negate the fact that the question of de-dollarisation is now emerging in the strategic considerations of Washington and in the strategic plans of other powerful global actors, especially Russia and China. Russia is in this discussion because uncoupling from the dollar has evolved from a strategic objective to an established reality. China, on the other hand, is involved due to the intricate factors outlined in this book. Moreover, it is important to acknowledge that, irrespective of the different strategic goals of the involved players, there is indeed a global process of diversification away from overreliance on the US dollar. Under certain circumstances, this diversification could genuinely erode the dollar's worldwide dominance. In this context, it is entirely valid to view de-dollarisation as one of the pivotal battlefields that will shape the future of global capitalism and potentially influence a broader crisis within the system. Consequently, it plays a significant role in the ongoing competition between the United States and China.

Currently, Moscow stands as the most proactive participant in challenging Washington's financial dominance. Its actions are driven both by choice and necessity. In contrast, nations like Iran and Venezuela, compelled by American imperialism, have been drawn into this arena. While their efforts alone might not significantly concern Washington, they have garnered support from Beijing. Meanwhile, countries such as Pakistan, India, Turkey, and most recently Saudi Arabia are in a holding pattern, cautiously weighing their potential alternatives. They closely observe the endeavours to reshape the international monetary system with great interest.[247] However, only China could, under certain conditions, make a real difference in this arena.

Moscow initiated a comprehensive de-dollarisation strategy in 2014, formalising it in 2018 in response to Western sanctions related to the Crimea reunification process.[248] As part of this strategy, Russia divested itself of almost all

---

247    Anne Korin and Gal Luft, *De-dollarization: The Revolt Against the Dollar and the Rise of a New Financial World Order* (independently published, 2019).
248    Putin's economic adviser Sergei Glazyev, who previously held a ministerial position during the Yeltsin era, is widely recognised as the mastermind behind this strategy.

US Treasury bonds in favour of gold acquisitions. It diversified its reserves and trade transactions to include the euro and the yuan, with the Russian central bank holding a significant share of yuan reserves held by foreign central banks. Additionally, it aimed to promote the use of the Russian rouble in international trade, although with less success. The euro was adopted for much of the energy trade with the European Union, and economic ties with Germany, including the Nord Stream 2 gas pipeline (subsequently blocked; see chap. 2.1.10), were reinforced. The efficacy of this strategy in light of the Ukraine intervention, US responses, and EU relations remains to be seen. It is uncertain whether it will lead to a broader diversification away from the dollar among non-Western countries, given the current geopolitical developments. Russia's counteractions, such as requiring payment in roubles for energy purchases from 'hostile countries', and agreements with India, could act as a catalyst for more widespread de-dollarisation. This process might manifest at the organisational level, such as the Shanghai Cooperation Organisation discussing increased trade transactions in national currencies among members. The BRICS countries also explored the R5 initiative in 2018, aiming to create a common currency based on their national currencies for payment and mutual compensation, although this goal appears distant for now. In either case, China's role would be pivotal in driving these efforts forward.

Iran is another country actively engaged in the de-dollarisation process, which has been exacerbated by prolonged and severe US sanctions (perhaps second only to Russia). Iran's experience with sanctions, spanning decades, has compelled it to move away from the dollar in its international transactions, particularly in the energy sector. Iran has become adept at evading sanctions, sometimes resorting to barter arrangements to maintain its global trade. One notable shift has been the adoption of the Chinese yuan as the primary currency for Iranian oil payments, significantly contributing to the yuan's status as the main reserve currency held by Iran's central bank. Tehran has also expanded its use of its currency in trade with several countries, including Lebanon, Syria, Iraq, and India, in the last case, exporting oil and gas in exchange for rupees as part of a November 2018 agreement. It is presently pursuing similar arrangements with Turkey. However, efforts to maintain trade ties with Iran in euros through a special currency clearing channel called INSTEX, initiated by Europe, have failed due to pressure from the US and concerns of European business interests. While de-dollarisation is crucial for Iran's survival under the weight of US sanctions, it carries significantly less global weight than Russia.

Two countries that have embarked on a path of voluntary, selective, and partial de-dollarisation are Turkey and Saudi Arabia. These nations have taken steps to diversify their international trade transactions away from the

US dollar. Turkey, in the face of sustained pressure on the Turkish lira from US financial markets,[249] has pursued trade agreements with various countries using their respective national currencies. Notable partners include Qatar, the United Arab Emirates, Russia, China, and South Korea. Saudi Arabia, as previously mentioned, has been exploring the possibility of selling oil to China in exchange for the yuan, which would have notable implications for the petrodollar system.[250] In addition to Turkey and Saudi Arabia, India has also demonstrated a willingness to engage in de-dollarisation, particularly in its dealings with Moscow and Tehran. While these steps primarily represent diversification rather than a direct challenge to the US dollar's global hegemony, they are meaningful in the context of the currency's gradual erosion. These actions do not, however, guarantee a swift transition away from the dollar but indicate a willingness to explore alternative arrangements and gradual shifts in the international monetary landscape.

The fact is, as previously mentioned, that only China has the potential to truly influence the de-dollarisation process. It is crucial to examine the interplay between China's strategy of cautious and regulated yuan internationalisation and the broader issue of de-dollarisation in its multifaceted dimensions. There is indeed a growing awareness of this issue among China's ruling elite and in public discourse, especially in light of various challenges, such as the trade war, penalties imposed on companies like ZTE, attacks on Huawei, and the looming threat of decoupling from the US-based international payment system, a risk that has been starkly emphasised by the Ukraine crisis.

China has enacted legislation to counter the US sanctions regime, but Chinese firms remain exceedingly cautious about the possibility of being targeted under secondary sanctions, leading to their inclusion on the US Department of Commerce's Entity List.[251] However, the Chinese government, with a pragmatic assessment of the global power balance, is not pursuing a symmetrical response to the United States, resembling a Chinese-style decoupling. Instead, it aims to secure greater manoeuvrability across various fronts, as long as it aligns with its overarching strategies of technological advancement and

---

249  Raffaele Sciortino, *I dieci anni che sconvolsero il mondo. Crisi globale e geopolitica dei neo-populismi* [The ten years that shocked the world: Global crisis and the geopolitics of neo-populisms] (Trieste: Asterios, 2019), available via https://www.researchgate.net/publication/352212013_I_DIECI_ANNI_CHE_SCONVOLSERO_IL_MONDO_Crisi_globale_e_geopolitica_dei_neopopulismi, 115–19.

250  MEE staff, "Saudi Arabia Considers Accepting Yuan Instead of Dollars for Oil Sales, Report Says", *Middle East Eye*, 15 March 2022, accessed 30 September 2023, https://www.middleeasteye.net/news/saudi-arabia-considers-accepting-yuan-instead-dollars-oil-sales.

251  Huang and Lardy, "China is Too Tied".

dual circulation. Dual circulation hinges on maintaining integration with the world market, and therefore, complete decoupling is not the current objective.

For these reasons, China's efforts to internationalise the yuan have not yet progressed beyond the promotion of its international usage without achieving full convertibility. Consequently, the yuan has not attained a robust international position among reserve currencies. However, its role as a means of payment continues to expand and will likely grow further, especially with the introduction of the central digital currency. Nevertheless, these developments primarily pertain to bilateral trade relationships, predominantly with developing and emerging nations, rather than constituting a comprehensive challenge to the US dollar's dominant status in the global financial system.

The case of China's relations with Russia, aside from its crucial geopolitical implications, is emblematic. In the wake of the initial Ukrainian crisis in 2014, the two nations struck a momentous deal for the supply of Russian natural gas to China via a Siberian corridor, a thirty-year agreement at an exceptionally competitive price. This move significantly impacted the market for liquefied gas supplies in the Pacific region, which had been a cornerstone for large producers from the United States, Canada, and Australia. Subsequent to this gas deal, there have been further agreements to continue the supply of Siberian gas to China, and both countries have actively worked to minimise their reliance on the US dollar for trade transactions, especially since 2018.[252] These agreements are complemented by the establishment of an alternative mutual payments system, substantial Chinese investments in the Russian economy via the BRI, with Moscow being the foremost beneficiary of BRI investments. Moreover, the two countries have engaged in currency swaps facilitated by their respective central banks. As a result, the bilateral trade relationship between China and Russia reached a value of $150 billion in 2021, and there are intentions to elevate this to $200 billion by 2024. This aspiration appears entirely feasible, particularly in the context of the current geopolitical situation, where Russian-European trade, which has historically outweighed Russian-Chinese trade (comprising 15% of Russian exports and 25% of imports), is inevitably on course for a significant reduction.

The significance of the China–Russia interchange is not merely its potential to challenge the dominant role of the US dollar; rather, and more interestingly, it has initiated a profound shift towards de-dollarisation in the energy trade sector. By 2020, only around 20% of Russia's exports to China, primarily

---

252 Dimitri Simes, "China and Russia Ditch Dollar in Move Toward 'Financial Alliance'", *Nikkei Asia*, 6 August 2020, accessed 30 September 2023, https://asia.nikkei.com/Politics/International-relations/China-and-Russia-ditch-dollar-in-move-toward-financial-alliance.

in the form of energy products, were denominated in dollars. Today, Chinese purchases from Russia are almost exclusively settled in yuan, and the projected demand for Russian energy products, including coal, is anticipated to surge in the coming years.[253] This transformation reflects a more extensive process spearheaded by Beijing, especially within the critical energy import sector, constituting almost 20% of its total imports. This process is not limited to the Eurasian region but, as we have observed, is gradually extending into the Middle East as well. Central to this restructuring is the role of oil, which stands as the most widely traded commodity in the global commodities market, an arena valued at $5 trillion annually, with three trillion of it dedicated to energy and minerals. Importantly, these markets are predominantly controlled by governments.

The significance of oil as a pillar in defending the international status of the dollar dates back to the 1970s, particularly due to the agreements established between the Nixon administration and Saudi Arabia following the decoupling of the dollar from gold. Subsequently, most transactions, not involving the United States, were conducted in dollars. A substantial portion of the oil revenues from the Middle East, where one-quarter of global oil exports emanate from the Gulf Cooperation Council countries, flows into US financial markets in exchange for the military guarantees offered by Washington. This system fundamentally underpins the United States' capacity to sustain both its dual debt, encompassing domestic and foreign obligations, while simultaneously escalating its military expenditures. Should the petrodollar fall, the damage to US global hegemony would be considerable.

Still, for now, this is only a hypothesis, with little concrete evidence. There is the indication of Saudi Arabia's willingness to consider yuan-based oil sales due to Chinese investments associated with the BRI. Furthermore, the OPEC countries have displayed a somewhat more autonomous stance, particularly as their relations with Russia have improved following the 2014 price war and a temporary resolution of the Syrian crisis. This is evident in their rejection of pressures from the United States and Europe to boost production amid the Ukrainian crisis. Additionally, there is Iraq's endeavour to regain stability, while nations like Iran, Libya, Venezuela, and Russia are poised to remain outside the Western sphere for an extended period, if not indefinitely. On the other side of this equation, we witness the initial strides in the petroyuan, which could

---

253 Chen Aizhu, "Russia, China Agree 30-Year Gas Deal via New Pipeline, to Settle in Euros", Reuters, 4 February 2022, accessed 30 September 2023, https://www.reuters.com/world/asia-pacific/exclusive-russia-china-agree-30-year-gas-deal-using-new-pipeline-source-2022-02-04/.

potentially set the stage for a comprehensive restructuring of the entire Asian energy market. Currently, this market is influenced by an externally controlled price regime that results in prices lagging behind Western benchmarks by one to two dollars per barrel. The extent to which yuan-based oil trading will succeed in establishing itself beyond the Chinese market, particularly in East Asia and the Middle East—where the petrodollar still maintains dominance—remains an open question. Naturally, as this situation approaches a tipping point, the process will undoubtedly shift to the geopolitical stage, potentially triggering various crises, including military conflicts, which may be 'spontaneously induced' by the United States. The Ukrainian conflict could just be a precursor to these developments.

Another critical factor shaping the prospects for further de-dollarisation pertains to gold. Given the previous dollar–gold decoupling and the inherent volatility (depending on American power centres) of the greenback, nations interested in reducing their dependence on US financial mechanisms could conceivably counterbalance a less centralised international monetary system through the reintroduction of national currencies partially backed by gold reserves. It is worth noting that for several years, China, following in Russia's footsteps, has been actively accumulating significant quantities of gold on international markets. This strategic move is not surprising, considering that China is one of the world's largest gold producers. Nonetheless, it seems more plausible that these actions represent a defensive approach on Beijing's part, particularly in the short to medium term. The primary aim appears to be diversifying its holdings to mitigate risks associated with an inflated dollar that could deplete its currency reserves, rather than a comprehensive de-dollarisation strategy. This accumulation of gold may serve as a safeguard in the event of a new global financial crisis, while simultaneously strengthening the international credibility of the digital yuan in the medium term.

## 7.5   *A New Bretton Woods?*

So, can we safely conclude that those who believe we might be heading towards a new international monetary system in the short or medium term, emerging from the decline of dollar dominance, are correct in their assessment? This hypothesis must be approached with utmost caution, whether we envision it as a potential multilateral institutionalisation of new monetary arrangements to replace the so-called Bretton Woods II system, which transitioned from the dollar–gold standard to the dollar–dollar standard,[254] or whether we see it as

---

254   Michael P. Dooley, David Folkerts-Landau, and Peter Garber, "An Essay on the Revived Bretton Woods System" (NBER Working Paper 9971, National Bureau of Economic

the de facto formation of two monetary blocs. These two blocs might mirror an irreversible division in the world market, commencing with the division of the commodities market. In this scenario, one bloc would revolve around the Russian-Chinese (and potentially Indian) axis, positioning commodities as a stable foundation, effectively replacing the dollar, underpinning non-inflationary currencies, and possibly elevating the yuan to a new role as a reserve and exchange currency. The other bloc would be Western, still adhering to fiat-money creation without a direct link to a tangible commodity base, which could render it prone to devaluation and inflation. However, any concrete predictions about the shape of the future international monetary system should be treated with caution.

From the comprehensive analysis presented in this book, it becomes evident that the notion of separate economic blocs is currently unrealistic in the short to medium term, barring a sudden and dramatic collapse of global capitalist accumulation and geopolitical arrangements. This lack of realism stems from several factors. First, in terms of capital's ongoing processes of internationalisation, a complete disintegration or sharp reversal is not on the immediate horizon. While there may be challenges and adjustments, the global capitalist system remains interconnected. Second, the existing power dynamics between American imperialism and China do not support the emergence of separate blocs. China's ascent, while substantial, is not of a magnitude that it poses a direct challenge to the United States' hegemony, let alone the establishment of a distinct economic bloc. China's continued rise necessitates further integration into the global market, as well as the opening of the global market, in its entirety, to China. As a result, Beijing's strategic approach is geared towards securing a more autonomous role within global capitalism, without risking isolation due to aggressive US strategies. Therefore, on the monetary front, Beijing is not yet prepared to confront the global dominance of the US dollar. Nevertheless, China is keen to gradually expand the international use of its currency, which holds several advantages, particularly for raw material producers with a surplus in trade with China. This move also serves to mitigate risks associated with dependence on the dollar, even though it is unlikely to replace the dollar entirely. The challenge for China lies in striking a balance between asserting itself as an international economic player and avoiding a direct showdown with the existing global financial order.

---

Research, Cambridge, MA, September 2003), accessed 23 September 2023, https://www.nber.org/papers/w9971.pdf.

Leaving aside the fact that the majority of the world's producers, with few exceptions, do not view the prospect of global bifurcation favourably, the United States is not currently pursuing a return to bipolarism based on blocs, akin to the Cold War era. There are several reasons why. First, reverting to such a bipolar structure would constitute a self-inflicted retreat from the position of global hegemony that the United States currently occupies in terms of geopolitical power distribution. Moreover, and perhaps more crucially, the system of accumulation—of which both the United States and China are integral components—relies on a worldwide scope. In other words, this system requires continuous reinforcement through finance, the US dollar, high-tech industries, and military capabilities to support the value generated and circulating globally.

China's role within this global system is essential, and the US aims to control and maintain its subordinate position while avoiding granting China excessive autonomy. The Ukrainian crisis exemplifies this strategy: the long-prepared trap set against Moscow serves the US intention of weakening Russia. By doing so, the US seeks to expose a critical geopolitical and geo-economic flank of Chinese strategy. If this endeavour is successful, it could not only hinder attempts at de-dollarisation for a considerable duration but also potentially disrupt the BRI and the gradual internationalisation of the yuan that has been discussed earlier.

When considering the institutionalisation of a multilateral monetary system aimed at diminishing the dominance of the dollar, an excessively volatile and increasingly predatory currency, there are several key factors to bear in mind. One crucial aspect is that any such transformation would require the cooperation of Washington, as the United States remains pivotal in the global financial landscape. However, it is highly unlikely that the United States would willingly support such an initiative due to its vested interests, as was evident when it opposed Keynes' proposals at the Bretton Woods conference after World War II. We should acknowledge that the mere creation of a basket of major currencies, with a more prominent role for the yuan today, might not be sufficient to ensure a more stable international trade system without the consent and cooperation of the dominant global power. The current global financial system remains highly dependent on the dollar, and any major changes would require a fundamental transformation of the existing system, possibly only occurring in the event of a drastic decline of the United States' power and influence, which may lead to the disconnection of the entire international system.

The central challenge to any counter-proposal or alternative perspective is that no entity other than the United States possesses the critical mass of financial capital and liquidity necessary to facilitate and lubricate the global value circuit. The dollar, in its role as a world reserve currency, continues to be the linchpin in this process, despite its increasing volatility and predatory behaviour. This contradiction lies at the core of the current international monetary system, which is progressively favouring a shrinking number of participants. As we have already discussed, China is not in a position to unseat the United States in this global function. Achieving such a role would necessitate full convertibility of the yuan, which would potentially compromise control over capital flows and domestic inflation. Furthermore, it would entail the establishment of a substantial financial market with securities denominated in Chinese currency to rival the well-established dollar-dominated financial market. Ultimately, this would require the capability to issue reserve assets for the benefit of the global capital market, a capacity that remains beyond China's reach, primarily due to its persistent trade surpluses, which have only recently started to diminish and primarily in the commodity markets of less developed countries. Any attempt to challenge the dollar's dominance on the international stage would require a profound transformation of the global financial system, immense trade and budget deficits, and significant liquidity provisions, factors that are challenging to realise under the existing global capitalist framework.

In the context of finance capital's domination, it is important to recognise that China is, to some extent, part of the problem rather than the solution. Given its current stage of capitalist development, China would paradoxically suffer from a narrowing of the monetary and credit base of world accumulation that could result from a downgrading of the dollar or a hypothetical return to something akin to the gold standard. This underscores that China increasingly stands to lose from the dollar mechanism, even though its role in global finance continues to expand. This is another important facet of the systemic contradictions at play here.

However, let us be clear, this does not preclude the possibility of unpredictable effects stemming from an increasingly precarious global situation, particularly from a monetary perspective. On the US side, such effects could manifest as a progressive loss of control over the commodities market, leading to a reduction in global demand for dollars, or a new recession and financial crisis. Similarly, on the Chinese side, there may come a point where pragmatic realism, which has long characterised Chinese policy, could give way to a more hardened political stance amid economic and social transition and growing external pressures, especially from the United States. The ongoing Ukrainian crisis provides a glimpse of this emerging shift. Any effective de-dollarisation is contingent on reaching a critical juncture in international power relations and the US–China rivalry. This scenario would likely coincide with a profound internal crisis within US society. Such a transformation, if and when it occurs, will not signify an ongoing change of hegemony, nor will it necessarily usher in a new and fairer 'international order'. Rather, it will signal the disconnection of the existing world system.

## 8  China's Geopolitics

The geopolitical dimension of China's strategy has become increasingly prominent as its economic rise unfolds. This shift was already implicitly evident in its efforts to ascend the international value chain, expand its influence through the BRI, and promote the internationalisation and digitalisation of the yuan. Starting around 2008, even before Xi Jinping's presidency, which itself reflects evolving domestic and international dynamics,[255] Beijing began to adopt a more assertive stance in response to new US containment strategies. This transformation aligns with China's shifting perceptions, which have grown more pessimistic about the international system's trajectory. In response to these challenges, China has adopted a more multipolar approach, marked by shades of Asiatism, as a counterbalance to Washington's unilateralism and decoupling strategies. Consequently, Beijing faces the challenging task of striking a delicate balance between demonstrating increased assertiveness while avoiding escalation with Washington. Simultaneously, it must work diligently to maintain its position in the upper echelons of the world market and counter Washington's economic and geopolitical manoeuvres in East Asia. All of this occurs while China is well aware of its clear military inferiority.

### 8.1  *Changed Perceptions*

Over the past decade, a significant shift has occurred in Chinese perceptions of the international system. Benevolent illusions about the United States have been completely abandoned,[256] and there is a growing sense of pessimism, if not outright realism, regarding the global economic landscape. Chinese President Xi Jinping's words in March 2022 reflect these evolving views, serving as an indicator of the complex internal debate within China. He remarked that, while the tensions among the great powers having become more intense,

---

255  Harold Hance Sprout and Margaret Sprout, *Man-Milieu Relationship Hypotheses in the Context of International Politics* (Princeton, NJ: Center of International Studies, 1956).

256  Eyck Freymann and Brian Y. S. Wong, "Young People in China Are Losing Faith in the West", *Foreign Policy Magazine*, 22 March 2021, accessed 30 September 2023, https://foreignpolicy.com/2021/03/22/racist-attack-asian-americans-china-lost-faith-west/ (subscription required).

the world has entered a phase of turbulence.[257] As early as 2014, Xi Jinping recognised the need for a comprehensive national security perspective, acknowledging that China would face "the most complicated internal and external situation in its history".[258] This realisation has been thoroughly discussed and digested within Chinese leadership circles.[259]

Today, most Chinese experts view 'strategic competition' with the United States as an inevitable prospect, if it has not already materialised. However, this does not imply an inevitable military confrontation, which is not something Beijing currently desires. It also does not negate China's awareness of US superiority across various domains. Instead, it underscores the adversarial nature, across all levels, of the ongoing trend—although the Chinese do not consider it a fait accompli—towards closing the 'great divergence' between the West and Asia.[260] This turning point in Sino-American relations is widely seen as having occurred in the wake of the 2008 financial crisis. The resurgence of unilateralism and, in particular, the measures undertaken by both Trump and Biden administrations to economically decouple from China and disrupt its supply chains have firmly established that this is not a matter of transient choices linked to a particular US administration or specific circumstances like the pandemic. Rather, it represents a lasting strategic shift. Chinese scholars and politicians, however, do not generally subscribe to the idea of a hegemonic, as opposed to relative, decline of the United States. While they acknowledge the United States' weakening, particularly in economic terms, and recognise signs of internal legitimacy crises,[261] the Chinese political and intellectual elite still begins with the premise that China, despite four decades of uninterrupted ascent, is a nation in the process of 'catching up' with the West. They believe that any missteps or hegemonic ambitions could come at a significant cost to China.[262]

---

257   Statement reported by *Chinanews*, 8 March 2022.
258   Jude Blanchette, "Xi's Gamble: The Race to Consolidate Power and Stave Off Disaster", *Foreign Affairs*, 22 July 2021, accessed 30 September 2023, https://www.foreignaffairs.com/articles/china/2021-06-22/xis-gamble (subscription required).
259   Minghao Zhao, "Is a New Cold War Inevitable? Chinese Perspectives on US–China Strategic Competition", *Chinese Journal of International Politics* 12, no. 3 (2019): 371–94, https://doi.org/10.1093/cjip/poz010.
260   Kenneth Pomeranz, *The Great Divergence: China, Europe, and the Making of the Modern World Economy* (Princeton, NJ: Princeton University Press, 2000).
261   Rush Doshi, *The Long Game: China's Grand Strategy to Displace American Order* (New York: Oxford University Press, 2021).
262   Hou Aijun, "Le dieci lezioni che la cina ha appreso dal crollo dell'URSS", *Limes*, 13 December 2021, accessed 30 September 2023, https://www.limesonline.com/cartaceo/le-dieci-lezioni-che-la-cina-ha-appreso-dal-crollo-dellurss.

## 8.2  Change of Pace

The fundamental argument presented in this book firmly rules out the possibility of Chinese global hegemony due to objective reasons. Moreover, it argues that such a strategy has not been consciously pursued by China to date. However, Beijing finds itself compelled to work towards changing the current international order, aiming for a reduction in the prevailing asymmetry with the United States. This change is envisioned as being 'orderly' and gradual, potentially achieved through agreements with other global actors, but pursued with determination. The objective is to align China's international standing with the realities of the new global economic balances. This alignment does not necessitate a comprehensive overhaul of the international order but rather a reform of certain key aspects and the acknowledgement of China's status as a major power, especially within the Asian regional context. The overarching goal is to establish a multipolar order characterised by sovereign states and multilateral forms of governance. Such a transformation would inherently diminish the US role in Asia and, consequently, on the global stage.[263]

This geopolitical perspective is now regarded in Beijing as an indispensable precondition, no longer subject to delay, in order to effectively pursue the previously discussed economic strategy. It represents a significant departure from the earlier Dengist foreign policy doctrine of acting but 'keeping a low profile' (*tao guang yang hui*). It also marks a noticeable shift from the peaceful rise approach adopted in the early 2000s, particularly during Hu Jintao's presidency.[264] During the Obama administration, President Xi Jinping had presented a proposal to reconfigure the Sino-American relationship, aiming for a new type of great-power relationship characterised by greater equality. This envisioned partnership had the potential to rewrite the global rules of engagement in accordance with the evolving international landscape, eventually

---

263   Particularly noteworthy here is the Global Security Initiative launched by Xi Jinping in 2022. See Kathrin Hille, "China Builds Coalition to Counter America's 'Barbaric and Bloody' Leadership", *Financial Times*, 22 May 2022, accessed 30 September 2023, https://www.ft.com/content/377cdb02-8a45-4ba2-b6ee-88620eb48f0b (subscription required); Feng Weijiang, "The Theoretical Foundations of the Global Security Initiative: The Holistic View of National Security", *Interpret: China*, originally published 16 June 2022 at Chinese Academy of Social Sciences, accessed 30 September 2023, https://interpret.csis.org/translations/the-theoretical-foundation-of-the-global-security-initiative-the-holistic-view-of-national-security/.

264   Zheng Bijian, "China's 'Peaceful Rise' to Great-Power Status", *Foreign Affairs*, 1 September 2005, accessed 30 September 2023, https://www.researchgate.net/publication/272587685_China's_Peaceful_Rise_to_Great-Power_Status; Mark Leonard, *What Does China Think?* (New York: PublicAffairs, 2008).

leading to a rebalancing in a multipolar, if not bipolar, direction.[265] In practice, various factors, including the BRI along the Eurasian route, the 'Made in China 2025' strategy, the emphasis on autonomous technological innovation, the shift towards the domestic market with reduced dependence on exports, the diversification of energy sources, the increased use of the yuan in international trade, and the strategic realignment with Moscow, effectively ending the strategic triangle that had evolved since the Sino-American rapprochement in 1972, all served to underscore a pronounced geopolitical dimension. This dimension became particularly apparent during the Trump administration.[266]

### 8.3 Encircled and Isolated in East Asia?

The primary battleground for the geopolitical struggle between the United States and China is situated in East Asia. In this vast region, which stretches from the East China Sea to the South China Sea with Taiwan in the middle, Washington has adopted a strategy of encirclement against its Chinese adversary. On one hand, this strategy involves deploying a formidable military presence, while on the other, it relies on a well-established network of alliances dating back to the post–World War II era.[267] Although these alliances are undergoing a process of reconfiguration, the critical concern for Beijing is the potential chokepoint in the South China Sea. This area is not only rich in energy resources but also vital for global commerce, accounting for one-third of the world's maritime trade, two-thirds of China's international trade, and one-third of China's crude oil imports. In addition to fostering a more integrated East Asian market through initiatives like ASEAN + 3 and the recent RCEP, as discussed earlier, Beijing is gradually working towards the establishment of an overarching 'Asian security' framework. This vision aims to create a region that is more self-reliant and less influenced by US intervention. Nevertheless, many countries in the region find it convenient to maintain a balancing act between expanding economic ties with China and retaining the security assurances provided by Washington.

---

265 Information Office of the State Council, The People's Republic of China, *China's National Defence in 2010*, Beijing, March 2011, accessed 30 September 2023, https://www.fmprc.gov.cn/mfa_eng/wjb_663304/zzjg_663340/jks_665232/kjfywj_665252/201104/t20110402_599668.html.

266 Atlantic Council, *The Longer Telegram: Toward a New American China Strategy*, 2021, accessed 2 October 2023, https://www.atlanticcouncil.org/content-series/atlantic-council-strategy-paper-series/the-longer-telegram/.

267 James Stavridis, "If the US Went to War with China, Who Would Win?", *Asia Nikkei*, 30 May 2021, accessed 30 September 2023, https://asia.nikkei.com/Opinion/If-the-US-went-to-war-with-China-who-would-win.

China, which finds itself in a somewhat isolated position, has been diligently developing and bolstering its military capabilities in the waters surrounding its mainland territory. This includes the creation of artificial islands in the South China Sea, such as the Paracelsus and Spratly Islands, which are now being used as military installations. The immediate objective of these efforts is to push its defensive perimeter as far from its coastline as possible. In the long run, China hopes to break free from the encirclement created by the first chain of islands.[268] However, achieving this goal is an extremely challenging task, particularly when considering that China has only three aircraft carriers, compared to the eleven US carriers deployed in the same waters. Nevertheless, the United States does face the drawback of operating from a considerable distance away from its home bases.

China's expansion into the southern waters has triggered protests and discontent from other coastal nations in the region, including Vietnam, Brunei, Malaysia, the Philippines, and Indonesia. This situation aligns with the US strategy of isolating China. Furthermore, there has been a noticeable increase in tensions with Tokyo. Japan is in the process of rebuilding its naval capabilities, with potential ambitions to acquire military nuclear power in the near future. This move is part of a more overt offensive projection by the so-called Japanese Self-Defence Forces. The dispute over control of the Diaoyu-Senkaku Islands, which are contested with Beijing, is just one facet of this issue. There is also direct concern regarding Taiwan and the surrounding waters.

In the spring of 2022, Beijing tried to establish an agreement with several South Pacific island nations for economic and security cooperation. This move was partly in response to the Indo-Pacific Economic Framework (IPEF). However, the United States and its regional ally Australia reacted swiftly and strongly. They particularly voiced their opposition to Beijing's first bilateral security agreement with the Solomon Islands.[269] As a result, the counteroffensive by the United States and Australia has been largely successful. The other island nations have chosen to delay discussions with Beijing about potential security agreements.

Meanwhile, Fiji decided to join IPEF, and the government of New Zealand, traditionally more neutral in its stance, seems to be increasingly inclined to

---

268  US Department of State, "U.S. Position on Maritime Claims in the South China Sea", news release, 13 July 2020, accessed 30 September 2023, https://2017-2021.state.gov/u-s-position-on-maritime-claims-in-the-south-china-sea/.

269  Charles Edel, "A Fault Line in the Pacific: The Danger of China's Growing Sway Over Island Nations", *Foreign Affairs*, 3 June 2022, accessed 30 September 2023, https://www.foreignaffairs.com/articles/china/2022-06-03/fault-line-pacific (subscription required).

align with the geopolitical offensive led by the Biden administration in the region. This demonstrates a recurring pattern where Beijing, in its efforts to blend economic and geopolitical influence to break free from isolation and introduce an alternative regional security structure, encounters an immediate roadblock created by Washington.

### 8.4 Is Taiwan like Ukraine?

Taiwan stands as the epicentre of the ongoing geopolitical struggle between the United States and China. It serves as a clear red line for Washington, the crossing of which would lead to a strengthening of its adversary and a potential domino effect in the regional balance of power. Furthermore, Taiwan holds immense significance for Beijing due to its political and geopolitical value. The reunification with Taiwan would grant China unobstructed access to the Pacific, turning the island into an invaluable 'aircraft carrier' of immense military importance. Without Taiwan, China would remain under pressure from Washington along its shores, devoid of open-sea access, and thus lacking full maritime power.

China's goal of reunification with Taiwan remains a vital objective, but a military conquest is not a realistic option at this time.[270] Beijing's 'rhetoric' conveys the seriousness of its long-term intent, yet it has not led to an impractical approach to the current situation. Nevertheless, the strategy of peaceful reunification, which has been in place since the 1972 Sino-American rapprochement, is becoming increasingly challenging. Despite China's extensive economic connections with Taiwan, the United States' targeted decoupling efforts are having an impact. This is especially evident in the disruption of the supply of advanced microprocessors from companies like TSMC to the Chinese industry, as we have previously highlighted. Furthermore, beyond US pressures, separatist sentiments on the island have gained strength over the past two decades, partly due to the actions of Taiwan's Democratic Progressive Party. It has pursued a twofold approach by deepening political and military ties with Washington and Tokyo, while also emphasising a distinct 'Taiwanese identity'.

In Taipei, discussions continue, often influenced by US advice, regarding the most suitable military strategy vis-a-vis Beijing. Presently, the prevailing approach is a defensive one, characterised by a porcupine-like defence, aiming

---

270 Brendan Rittenhouse Green and Caitlin Talmadge, "The Consequences of Conquest: Why Indo-Pacific Power Hinges on Taiwan", *Foreign Affairs*, 16 June 2022, accessed 30 September 2023, https://www.foreignaffairs.com/articles/china/2022-06-16/consequences-conquest-taiwan-indo-pacific (subscription required).

to create conditions for asymmetrical warfare that would make the cost of a Chinese invasion prohibitively high. However, there is also consideration of a more offensive strategy, centred on long-range missiles capable of targeting the Chinese mainland, with the backing of Washington. Domestic factors play a crucial role in shaping Taiwan's strategy. One key element is the development of a social and political coalition that could potentially support a declaration of independence. This coalition, primarily composed of a burgeoning middle class, both in a socio-economic and political sense, increasingly views the Western model as a preferable alternative, especially after experiencing significant economic growth in past decades. This demographic is often reluctant to acknowledge the contribution made by the opening of the Chinese market and, as a result, identifies less and less with their 'Chinese' identity. This shift in sentiment is reflected in the declining influence of the Kuomintang, which faltered in the 2010s due to widespread social and political opposition to rapprochement with Beijing. Despite these shifts, Taiwan has not (yet) exhibited a 'Ukrainian' trajectory. The majority of the population remains of Han ethnicity, communicates in Mandarin, and, most importantly, prefers the current political status quo with mainland China, with which it maintains substantial trade relations, over any prospect of military conflict or escalation.

On Beijing's part, any military intervention in Taiwan would be a complex and risky endeavour.[271] It would not only encounter resistance from a significant portion of Taiwan's population but also jeopardise China's soft power and regional influence—a situation that aligns with Washington's objectives. Consequently, China is inclined to maintain its strategy of *strategic patience* and avoid hasty actions regarding the reunification deadline. However, the United States could, in the not-too-distant future, take actions that cross China's red lines, possibly by supporting Taiwanese independence, which would force Beijing to respond, potentially leading to conflict. The Chinese leadership is convinced that the US approach to the Ukrainian conflict is a precursor to the strategic dilemma that Beijing will eventually face, both militarily and economically, as part of the so-called Indo-Pacific Strategy. The Chinese debate on this issue is quite clear: Ukraine serves as a harbinger of the strategic challenges Beijing will encounter at the hands of the United States, both

---

271  Such a scenario would likely involve a costly and challenging amphibious landing by Beijing. To capture Taiwan, China would need to adopt an offensive military strategy, navigating the formidable hybrid anti-access warfare defences that Taiwan has put in place—a strategy similar to the one China has employed towards deterring Washington in the region.

militarily and economically.[272] Furthermore, explicit US statements have indicated such a direction.[273] What exacerbates this situation is that Taiwan holds a more substantial role in US strategic interests than Ukraine, much like how China, not Russia, is viewed as its primary strategic rival and, consequently, its foremost adversary. It is perhaps worth recalling here one of the main theses of this study: the transition from globalisation (in crisis) to a more decisive course of deglobalisation will not occur without a major geopolitical crisis directly involving China and the United States.

### 8.5    China and Russia

China has understandably adopted a somewhat cautious stance on the Ukrainian crisis due to its evolving strategic alignment with Russia and concerns about potential secondary sanctions from the United States on its businesses and banks. Nevertheless, China *has* been providing substantial political support to Moscow. In various diplomatic forums, Beijing has firmly placed the blame for the conflict on the North Atlantic Treaty Organization's (NATO) expansionist policies. Moreover, given the strong rapport between Beijing and Moscow, it is unlikely that China remained uninformed about Russia's planned military action. Russia's decision to reduce gas supplies to European nations in mid-June 2022 coincided with increased purchases of Russian gas and crude oil by China, as well as India. There is even speculation that China might have discreetly assisted Russia in safeguarding part of its dollar reserves that were inaccessible due to Western sanctions.[274] Furthermore, China has consistently opposed anti-Russian sanctions and has been actively involved in global diplomacy efforts to challenge the Western narrative regarding the crisis in regions across the Global South.

---

272   See the interview with Zheng Yongnian in the *Global Times*: Li Aixin and Bai Yunyi, "Russia-Ukraine Conflict Can Be Regarded as a 'Preview' of US' Possible Acts in Asia: Zheng Yongnian", *Global Times*, 17 March 2022, accessed 30 September 2023, https://www.globaltimes.cn/page/202203/1255162.shtml.

273   US Department of State, "The Administration's Approach to the People's Republic of China" (speech by Antony J. Blinken, 26 May 2022), accessed 30 September 2023, https://state.gov/the-administrations-approach-to-the-peoples-republic-of-china/.

274   Benn Steil and Benjamin Della Rocca, "Is China Helping Russia Hide Money? The Kremlin May Have Stashed Billions in Offshore Accounts", *Foreign Affairs*, 21 March 2022, accessed 30 September 2023, https://www.foreignaffairs.com/articles/ukraine/2022-03-21/china-helping-russia-hide-money (subscription required).

While Washington's explicit aim in the Ukrainian crisis is to exhaust Russia,[275] Beijing is wary of the consequences of a Russian collapse, which would disrupt its overarching strategy. Aligning with the United States in this crisis would not serve China's interests, as it would not loosen Washington's grip on the Indo-Pacific or significantly reduce the threat of decoupling, including potential financial measures like SWIFT restrictions.[276] In fact, there is a possibility that NATO's next line of defence could shift to the South China Sea, as discussed at the Madrid alliance summit in June 2022. Therefore, Ukraine cannot be considered a mere distraction for Washington, unlike the previous 'war on terror', given the current geopolitical landscape.

This situation underscores the ongoing geopolitical rapprochement between China and Russia, which has deepened since 2014, particularly in the aftermath of the earlier Ukrainian crisis. Although it was not initially planned, it was largely induced by US policy. While it has not evolved into a formal military alliance, it has served as a counterbalance to US influence and has become a significant reference point for an alternative international network outside the Western sphere. The Sino-Russian relationship is founded on robust factors emanating from the current international order that are likely to further consolidate unless there are significant political changes in either country. These factors encompass various dimensions. In terms of economic exchange, China and Russia have developed increasingly strong ties, with both nations becoming more reliant on each other. On the monetary level, despite the limitations we discussed earlier, there is a concerted effort to reduce reliance on the US dollar, reflecting the determination to circumvent dollar-based transactions. The energy sector, crucial for both countries, serves as a focal point for cooperation. The Siberian Power pipeline, operational since 2019, is set to be complemented by a new pipeline from East Siberia.[277] Military collaboration is another facet of this relationship. China's acquisition of some of Russia's most advanced weapon systems, such as the S-400 missiles and Su-35 fighter

---

275 Julian Borger, "Pentagon Chief's Russia Remarks Show Shift in US's Declared Aims in Ukraine", *Guardian*, 25 April 2022, accessed 30 September 2023, https://www.theguardian.com/world/2022/apr/25/russia-weakedend-lloyd-austin-ukraine.

276 Yan Xuetong, "China's Ukraine Conundrum: Why the War Necessitates a Balancing Act", *Foreign Affairs*, 2 May 2022, accessed 30 September 2023, https://www.foreignaffairs.com/articles/china/2022-05-02/chinas-ukraine-conundrum; Wei, "Possible Outcomes".

277 Since the outbreak of the conflict in Ukraine, Russia has ascended to the position of China's primary oil supplier, surpassing Saudi Arabia. See "China Oil Imports from Russia Surge amid Ukraine War Sanctions", *Al Jazeera*, 20 June 2022, accessed 30 September 2023, https://www.aljazeera.com/economy/2022/6/20/china-oil-imports-from-sanctioned-russia-skyrocket-surpass-saudi.

jets, demonstrates the growing military cooperation. Moreover, there is an increasing exchange of electronic components and a rising number of joint land, naval, and air exercises, including joint patrols in East Asia since 2018. Lastly, a comprehensive space cooperation programme is in place, featuring joint lunar projects and, most notably, efforts to ensure the interoperability of their respective satellite systems.[278]

In summary, the partnership between Beijing and Moscow has evolved from a pragmatic arrangement to something approaching a quasi-alliance, although both sides avoid formalising it as such. They steer clear of the term 'alliance' because they reject the notion of forming military blocs, and recognising a formal alliance would signify a point of open military rupture with Washington.[279]

This evolution was underlined by the Joint Statement issued on 4 February 2022, during a meeting between Putin and Xi Jinping, which took place on the eve of the Russian military operation in Ukraine.[280] The statement outlined a comprehensive vision for the current international landscape, emphasising the promotion of "a new type of international relations" and the emergence of a multipolar world characterised by "a new era of rapid development and profound transformation", which entails a reconfiguration of global power dynamics. Beijing and Moscow affirm that the "friendship between the two States has no limits, there are no 'forbidden' areas of cooperation", hinting at potential expansion into the military domain. Notably, both parties expressed criticism of Western actions in Eastern Europe and the United States' provocative stance on issues such as Taiwan and the Indo-Pacific.

Despite the strategic importance of their economic complementarity, China cannot replace its integration into the world market with Russia. Furthermore, a strictly military alliance is currently deemed undesirable, as it would disrupt the intricately woven fabric of their alternative approach to global engagement. Consequently, alternative responses are being explored to address this complex geopolitical landscape.

---

278  Vasily Kašin, "La russia cosmica non rinuncia alla cina" [Cosmic Russia will not give up on China], *Limes* 12 (December 2021), accessed 14 April 2022, https://www.limesonline.com/cartaceo/la-russia-cosmica-non-rinuncia-alla-cina (subscription required).
279  Alexander Lukin, *China and Russia: The New Rapprochement* (Cambridge: Polity Press, 2018).
280  President of the Russian Federation, "Joint Statement of the Russian Federation and the People's Republic of China on the International Relations Entering a New Era and the Global Sustainable Development", 4 February 2022, accessed 28 February 2023, http://en.kremlin.ru/supplement/5770.

## 8.6  Hard Power

Beijing's military strategy is built upon a candid acknowledgement of its quantitative and technological inferiority relative to the United States. It hinges on the premise that continued economic development is a prerequisite for the qualitative modernisation of its armed forces. The overarching goal is to avoid a military confrontation with the United States while steadfastly defending its core national interests. To accomplish this, China is concentrating on the short to medium-term development of so-called 'asymmetrical capabilities'.[281] These capabilities serve the dual purpose of deterring the adversary's freedom of action and buying time to enhance its conventional and nuclear military strengths. The comprehensive modernisation programme, spanning various military capabilities, is currently scheduled for completion by 2035, although this timeline might be somewhat optimistic. Be that as it may, a change of pace[282] is also evident from the Dengist strategy, which achieved the transition from the *Maoist people's war* to the *modern people's war* and *local warfare*. It signifies a move away from a low-profile, minimalistic, and strictly defensive nuclear doctrine. Nevertheless, the fundamental tenet of the People's Liberation Army remains staunchly rooted in deterrence, devoid of any offensive inclinations. The objective is to mitigate tensions with Washington, confining conflicts primarily to the economic arena and diplomatic channels while adhering to the steadfast refusal to embrace hegemonism or military alliances.

Three aspects emerge. The first is military expenditures and technology. China's military expenditures have experienced a notable increase, primarily directed towards advanced technological fields such as aerospace, ballistics, and electronics. However, these expenditures remain relatively modest, hovering around 2% of the country's GDP. This level of military investment, while marked by growth, does not indicate signs of overextension or a full-blown arms race, especially when compared to the United States, which allocates 3–4% of its significantly higher GDP to defence.[283] Nonetheless,

---

281  Or a 'war without limits', to use the terminology employed in the famous 1999 publication by Qiao Liang and Wang Xiangsui, originally published in Chinese by the People's Liberation Army Literature and Arts Publishing House and made available in English translation in the same year by the Foreign Broadcast Information Service. The book is usually translated in English as *Unrestricted Warfare*.

282  As was witnessed by the national defence and armed forces reform approved in late 2015 and updated in the 2019 *Defence White Paper*.

283  In 2021, China's military expenditure per capita was only 1/22 of the United States and still just 1/5 that of Japan. See Alberto Bradanini, *Cina: l'irresistibile ascesa* (Rome: Sandro Teti, 2022), 119.

it underscores a persistent and challenging-to-close military gap with Washington.[284]

The second aspect is maritime control strategy. A core emphasis in China's technological and strategic investments is directed towards asserting control over the waters encircling mainland China. This objective aligns with a broader anti-access strategy that seeks to restrict the United States' capacity for power projection within the first island chain. The strategic aim is to compel enemy military assets to operate at increased distances, incurring substantial costs. Achieving comprehensive territorial waters control would potentially facilitate more extensive naval projection into the Pacific, though it remains more of a long-term vision than an immediate reality. The transition from a continental to a naval power is a complex and intricate process that cannot be hastily accomplished, if feasible at all.

The final aspect worth noting is nuclear deterrence doctrine. China adheres to a doctrine of prudent deterrence concerning its nuclear military programme. This doctrine strictly prohibits the first use of strategic nuclear weapons, often referred to as a 'no first use' doctrine. China maintains a relatively limited nuclear arsenal, encompassing approximately 300 devices, which is comparable in size to those of France and the United Kingdom. This arsenal is characterised by the presence of few land-based launchers and nuclear-capable bombers, with no tactical nuclear devices. Conversely, the United States, since 2002,[285] has not ruled out the prospect of engaging in a nuclear conflict with China even in response to 'intolerable damage' inflicted by conventional weapons. However, this scenario seems largely speculative, particularly given the geographical isolation of the United States. The US position was confirmed in 2018.[286] This American stance has had more immediate implications in the East Asian region. Specifically, during the Trump administration, the United States withdrew from the Intermediate-Range Nuclear Forces (INF) Treaty, signed with Moscow in 1987. This withdrawal signalled an intention

---

284  Andrea Gilli and Mauro Gilli, "Why China Has Not Caught Up Yet: Military-Technological Superiority and the Limits of Imitation, Reverse Engineering, and Cyber Espionage", *International Security* 43, no. 3 (2019): 141–89, https://doi.org/10.1162/isec_a_00337.
285  On 13 June 2022, the United States withdrew from 1972 Anti-Ballistic Missile Treaty.
286  Philipp C. Bleek, "Nuclear Posture Review Leaks; Outlines Targets, Contingencies", news release, Arms Control Association, April 2002, accessed 30 September 2023, https://www.armscontrol.org/act/2002-04/press-releases/nuclear-posture-review-leaks-outlines-targets-contingencies; US Department of Defense (under the Trump administration), *Nuclear Posture Review*, February 2018, accessed 30 September 2023, https://media.defense.gov/2018/Feb/02/2001872886/-1/-1/1/2018-NUCLEAR-POSTURE-REVIEW-FINAL-REPORT.PDF.

to potentially deploy intermediate-range missiles with minimal restrictions around the South China Sea.[287] In response to these developments, China embarked on a modernisation effort for its intercontinental and intermediate-range nuclear arsenal, which included the development of hypersonic missiles. Additionally, China has been working towards achieving a fully-fledged nuclear trident, enabling it to launch nuclear weapons not only from land but also from air and sea platforms.[288]

The extent to which China's investments in the cyber and space domains will yield progress remains uncertain.[289] China, alongside the United States, is one of the few countries with the economic resources necessary for the ongoing technological leaps in these fields. Recent advancements, such as the successful landing of the Chang'e-4 probe on the hidden side of the moon, the establishment of the Tiangong space station, and the completion of the BeiDou global satellite system network, demonstrate China's commitment to advancing in these sectors. However, these developments have not yet propelled China into a position of hegemonic challenge. While China has made notable strides, it has not reached a level of technological superiority capable of challenging the global status quo.

## 8.7  *Global South*

Beijing's focus on the Global South is a critical aspect of its diplomatic efforts, particularly in countering or mitigating a significant element of US containment—its network of international alliances. China's approach predominantly centres on economic relationships, where it still holds an advantage over Western powers. It can negotiate agreements that are relatively favourable to all parties involved and free from political conditionalities. This advantage stems from China's stance as a non-imperialist nation, allowing it to invoke the 'spirit of Bandung' and apply it to contemporary development

---

287   Nathan Levine, "Why America Leaving the INF Treaty is China's New Nightmare", *National Interest*, 22 October 2018, accessed 30 September 2023, https://nationalinterest.org/blog/buzz/why-america-leaving-inf-treaty-chinas-new-nightmare-34087; Lolita C. Baldor, "Esper: US to Soon Put Intermediate Range Missile in Asia", *Military Times*, 4 August 2019, accessed 30 September 2023, https://www.militarytimes.com/news/pentagon-congress/2019/08/04/esper-us-to-soon-put-intermediate-range-missile-in-asia/.
288   Fiona S. Cunningham, "Cooperation under Asymmetry? The Future of US-China Nuclear Relations", *Washington Quarterly* 44, no. 2 (2021): 159–80, https://doi.org/10.1080/0163660X.2021.1934253.
289   George Friedman, "Lo Spazio serve a farci la guerra", *Limes*, 30 December 2021, accessed 30 September 2023, https://www.limesonline.com/cartaceo/lo-spazio-serve-a-preparare-le-guerre-di-domani (subscription only).

issues as a prerequisite for a more equitable international order. China's endeavours to strengthen and formalise its relations with Global South countries align with this strategy. For example, the regular summits among BRICS countries, initiated in 2009 and culminating in the fourteenth summit in June 2022, place China at the centre of a network seeking to enhance coordination and cooperation with Russia, India, Brazil, and South Africa. Together, these nations envision international alignments that move away from Western dominance and potentially promote wider use of their national currencies in mutual trade. Additionally, they are exploring the establishment of a BRICS-specific payments system.[290]

China is also leveraging soft power, as seen during the COVID-19 pandemic. Beijing extended cooperation to numerous developing countries in their fight against the virus. In this context, China conveyed a universalist message, a departure from the traditional Western narrative, which often focuses on human rights. Instead, China emphasised the necessity of taking decisive global action and fostering cooperation to address pandemic-related challenges and broader economic and social development issues.

Once again, this approach does not indicate a revisionist stance towards the international order. Instead, it embodies a reformist outlook, distinctly distant from the anti-imperialist rhetoric of the past. Beijing frames its alignment with Moscow within these parameters. However, some critical aspects of China's diplomatic strategies are evident, particularly in its relationship with India, which is a vital player among the Global South nations.[291] In essence, President Xi's message has increasingly been oriented towards positioning Beijing as a leader in initiatives to establish an economic order alternative to US global dominance and promote a more cooperative international order in response to the chaos stemming from US unilateralism. Nevertheless, China's engagement with former Third World countries cannot serve as a complete economic replacement for Western markets, given the various complexities associated with this dependence. This includes the potential political instability of these governments, which, while turning to Beijing to escape the nooses of Western finance, may find themselves targeted by Washington-induced destabilisation efforts.

---

290  The objective is to broaden participation by including Argentina and, looking ahead, potentially expanding to encompass Indonesia, Senegal, Nigeria, Egypt, Saudi Arabia, Thailand, Kazakhstan, and the United Arab Emirates.

291  Consider the border clashes that occurred along the Himalayan frontier in the summer of 2021. While it remains uncertain, there is a possibility that China's growing alignment with Moscow could potentially help alleviate these tensions.

In conclusion, both structural and situational factors are converging to exacerbate Sino-US relations. The diplomatic stabilisers are diminishing, and there is growing room for mutual unfavourable perceptions. This is not a Chinese hegemonic challenge; structural constraints would not permit it, and China's leadership does not suffer from self-satisfied grandiosity. Rather, the basic premise of the ongoing trend is China's strategic aspiration for a multipolar order set within the context of an inevitable period of conflict to be managed through all necessary means, combined with tactical prudence to prevent exclusion from the world market.

## 9  Imperialism and China: Concluding Remarks

Without a doubt, a significant challenge has emerged, with the outcome having profound implications for the continued dominance of the United States within the global capitalist system. The fundamental question revolves around the character of this challenge, which not only influences its potential development and ultimate resolution but also charts the course of world capitalism and, consequently, the destiny of globalisation. The central thesis of this book is as follows: this challenge, from the Chinese perspective, falls somewhat short of a full-scale bid for hegemony, yet from a systemic viewpoint, it also transcends the U.S.-China clash. This opens the door to several hypotheses about the future dynamics of the imperialistic world system.

### 9.1  *Dollars but Not Only*

As we have explored, China's strategic aspirations are rooted in the pursuit of a multipolar world order. This ambition does not envision an (impossible) return to isolation or autarky. Rather, Beijing's quest for wider autonomy, with a reformulated social pact based on access to widespread wealth, is the outcome of China's historical socio-economic development and its internal class dynamics. Over time, China has made considerable sacrifices and progressed through various stages to emerge from 'underdevelopment', seeking to attain the capacity to compete with the West across all spheres. The goal is not necessarily parity but rather to dismantle the long-standing structural asymmetry, which, if left unaddressed, could compel China to retreat from its hard-earned positions.

This asymmetry extends beyond the mere geopolitical dimension and is closely linked to the dominance of the dollar system, a fundamental instrument of US hegemony. The Chinese party-state elite is acutely aware of this fact. For instance, the works of Qiao Liang, which resonate with the strategic perspective of some top military and political figures, assert that China's primary challenge lies in confronting financial hegemony. The United States has been crafting a dollar-centric economic cycle for almost four decades, enabling it to regulate and grasp global wealth, intermittently controlling the flow of monetary liquidity, often by engineering geopolitical crises to direct capital flows as needed.[292]

Additionally, the speeches delivered at the 2022 annual gathering of the Chinese Central Bank's School of Finance highlighted the contradiction between Washington's growing national deficit and the global role of the dollar as a reserve and international exchange currency. The stability of the dollar in this role hinges on the continued growth of the global economy, which perpetuates the demand for an international currency. Should this demand wane, the dollar may face devaluation, to the detriment of its creditors whose reserves essentially constitute low-interest-rate loans to Washington. Furthermore, there is the looming risk of these reserves being frozen through US sanctions, a scenario witnessed with Russia.[293]

China's path towards challenging the financial hegemony of the dollar is not without challenges and potential setbacks. In the future, China may face capital losses and imported inflation due to its strategic moves. The control it exercises over capital flows and the limited convertibility of the yuan serve as a relative defence against external financial upheavals. However, they also act as constraints on the international circulation of its currency and its capacity to issue liquidity. These constraints are essential for escaping the dominance of the dollar and for funding economic restructuring, both domestically and abroad.

The link between the yuan and the dollar has become something of a double-edged sword for Beijing. On one hand, the dollar is a crucial gateway for accessing Western markets and the latest technologies. However, it is increasingly

---

292  Qiao Liang, *Empire Arc: America and China at the Ends of Parabola* [in Chinese] (Hong Kong: Changjiang Literature Press, 2016). See also Zhang Yugui, "US Wages Economic War to Maintain Global Supremacy", *China Daily*, 1 April 2022, accessed 28 April 2022, http://www.chinadaily.com.cn/a/202204/01/WS6246c83da310fd2b29e54bb2.html.

293  Yu Yongding, "Abbiamo preso obbligazioni statunitensi costose e senza rendimento, cosa fare dopo?", translated by Alessandro Visalli, *Sinistrainrete*, 28 May 2022, accessed 1 June 2022, https://www.sinistrainrete.info/estero/23120-alessandro-visalli-yu-yongding-cosa-fare-con-le-obbligazioni-usa-aggiustamenti-nella-doppia-circolazione-cinese.html, originally published as "余永定: 我们用高成本借来了没收益的美国债，接下来怎么办" [We borrowed US debt with no returns at a high cost. What to do next?], *Guancha*, 20 May 2022.

becoming a trap, constraining China's financial autonomy.[294] Beijing is actively attempting to reduce its exposure, as evidenced by its decreased purchases of US Treasury bonds, declining from a record high of $1,316 billion in November 2013 to $1,072 billion in December 2020, with a slight uptick in 2022.

Nevertheless, the core issue remains that China's dependence on the dollar is deeply rooted in the international division of labour within the realm of imperialism. This is particularly evident in the manufacturing sector, where Chinese exports, even those not under the control of Western multinationals, still rely in part on foreign research and design, as well as imports of higher value-added inputs. China is deeply enmeshed in global value chains, yet it does not hold a dominant position in crucial sectors or segments, despite the development of some domestic industry leaders.

Interdependence plays a dual role in this context. On the one hand, China's contribution to global production is now indispensable, accounting for a substantial 35% of worldwide manufacturing output.[295] On the other hand, there persists an asymmetrical relationship in the distribution of value-added with respect to imperialist powers. As a result, China aims to move up the supply chains while shifting its focus towards extracting relative surplus value, a strategy that will inevitably escalate tensions with the United States.

This also holds true for international capital flows. While China's share in these flows has become quantitatively significant—representing nearly one-fifth of global direct investment by the end of 2021[296]— Chinese investments abroad, especially since the onset of the 'trade war' with Washington, have predominantly targeted countries in the Global South, emerging economies, and economically challenged nations participating in the 'New Silk Roads' initiative. In Western countries, Chinese investments have primarily been directed towards sovereign bonds and equities, contributing to a significant drop in direct investments, which have been halved since 2016.

Taking China's dollar reserves into account, this situation implies that Chinese foreign investments in Western nations are characterised by a more passive nature rather than being proactive. In contrast, investments in the

---

294 Eswar Prasad, *The Dollar Trap: How the U.S. Dollar Tightened its Grip on Global Finance* (Princeton, NJ: Princeton University Press, 2014).
295 Jonathan Woetzel, Jeongmin Seong, Nick Leung, Joe Ngai, James Manyika, Anu Madgavkar, Susan Lund, and Andrey Mironenko, *China and the World: Inside the Dynamics of a Changing Relationship* (New York: McKinsey Global Institute, 2019), accessed 30 September 2023, https://www.mckinsey.com/featured-insights/china/china-and-the-world-inside-the-dynamics-of-a-changing-relationship.
296 Huang and Lardy, "China is Too Tied".

rest of the world, particularly the East Asian region, are growing in importance. However, they do not yet reach a level where they can overturn existing imperialist hierarchies. Therefore, despite the narrowing gap between inward and outward financial flows, a substantial qualitative difference remains. Furthermore, the gap between China and the United States in terms of foreign investments, both in terms of stock and the direction of capital flows (inbound and outbound), is still considerable.[297]

### 9.2   An Existential Challenge

China is thus confronted with a situation that goes beyond mere economic underdevelopment, which could potentially be addressed through sustained economic growth, similar to the trajectory set by Deng Xiaoping, eventually leading to its inclusion among the 'handful of imperialist powers', as Lenin described. It is not solely a matter of unfavourable geopolitical power dynamics that could potentially be overturned at a later point in time.

The fundamental issue at hand is qualitative and revolves around the structural framework shaped by the dynamics of global capitalism, which we can still describe as imperialism,[298] albeit with unique historical features. On the international stage, what we observe is a form of 'super imperialism' (not in the Kautskian sense!) where West European and Japanese imperialisms, despite diminished sovereignty, find themselves economically and geopolitically interconnected and subordinated to the United States. This occurred after British world hegemony transitioned to the United States through two anti-German imperialist conflicts, which also marked the demise of the old colonial order.[299]

---

297   Prasad, *Gaining Currency*.
298   By imperialism I mean an irreversible stage in the development of the capitalist mode of production. It is marked by the extreme centralisation of capital and the growingly impersonal control over socialised means of production. These productive forces continue to expand, though often in increasingly catastrophic ways due to the inherent tendency of capital towards crisis. Imperialism does not suggest a linear path of decline; rather, it maintains the potential for relative rejuvenation through the reconfiguration of class relations and the international division of labour. This process, however, is not without the tumultuous episodes of chaos, wars, and potential revolutions. Imperialism embodies a world system characterised by the uneven and combined development of multiple capitals, in which a fundamental class divide is compounded by geo-economic disparities. This system inherently carries the tendency towards armed conflicts among competing capitalist entities. Imperialism is a global phenomenon but not a monolithic or uniform one in its various components. The theoretical underpinning for this perspective draws significantly from the post–World War II studies of left communist thinker Amadeo Bordiga.
299   I am alluding to the Marxist debates that unfolded on the cusp of and in the immediate aftermath of the international monetary system crisis in 1971. These debates,

Within this complex dynamic, we have two ascending socio-economic formations, China and Russia, competing with the Western powers but not as anti-systemic entities. Alongside them, we find vast 'dependent' (semi-)peripheral regions that are integrated into Western dominance through production and financial mechanisms or aspire to regional autonomy. This intricate, asymmetrical assemblage has been underpinned, particularly in recent decades, by the pivotal combination of global economic and financial integration on one side, and China's opening to the world market on the other. As a result, the United States, whose hegemonic position was shaken but far from shattered during the 1970s crisis, managed to reconfigure itself as the global epicentre of capital accumulation. This transformation was facilitated by commanding global financial flows through the dollar, supported by the supremacy of multinational corporations in high technologies and an unparalleled military establishment.

The United States has thus become the sole, and thus (to date) irreplaceable, hub of capital accumulation, boasting a concentration of capital assets denominated in a universally accepted world currency that keeps the circuits of global value in perpetual motion. It serves as the guarantor and, at the same time, the chief extortionist of the world's system of reproduction. In its custodial role, the United States ensures the smooth functioning of the world's value

particularly in Germany and France, revolved around crucial aspects, including the law of value in the world market, and the intricate relationship between the state, money, and capital. These discussions engendered intense disagreements regarding the nature of inter-imperialist relationships within the Western world and the specific role of the United States therein. For more on these debates and context, see Nicos Poulantzas, "L'internationalisation des rapports capitalistes et l'Etat-nation", *Les Temps Modernes* 319 (February 1973): 1456–1500, who discusses the 'internal' bourgeoisie of Europe (that is, internal to US imperialism). Seel also Suzanne de Brunhoff, *État et capital : recherches sur la politique économique* (Grenoble: Presses universitaires de Grenoble, 1976); Ernest Mandel, *Europe vs. America: Contradictions of Imperialism* (New York: Monthly Review Press, 1970); Martin Nicolaus, "The Universal Contradiction", *New Left Review* 59 (Jan/Feb 1970): 3–18, https://newleftreview.org/issues/i59/articles/martin-nicolaus-the-universal-contradiction (subscription only); Christel Neusüss, *Imperialismus und Weltmarktbewegung des Kapitals* (Erlangen: Politladen, 1972); Claudia von Braunmühl, "Weltmarktbewegung des Kapitals, Imperialismus und Staat", in *Probleme einer materialistischen Staatstheorie*, edited by Claudia von Braunmühl, Klaus Funken, Mario Cogoy, and Joachim Hirsch (Frankfurt: Argument Verlag, 1973); Robert E. Rowthorn, "Imperialism in the Seventies: Unity or Rivalry?", *New Left Review* 69 (1971): 59–83, https://newleftreview.org/issues/i69/articles/bob-rowthorn-imperialism-in-the-seventies-unity-or-rivalry (subscription only); Christel Neusüss, Bernhard Blanke, and Elmar Altvater, "Kapitalistischer Weltmarkt und Weltwährungskrise", PROKLA. *Zeitschrift für kritische Sozialwissenschaft* 1, no. 1 (1971): 5–116, https://doi.org/10.32387/prokla.v1i1.1223.

circuits by harmonising the inflow and outflow of capital across the globe, a role that no other nation has managed to match. Its unparalleled ability to import and export capital places it at a level of influence that goes unrivalled by any other player on the international stage. The United States is not the global hegemon because it solely wields dominance or control over global capitalism from an unassailable position of strength. It has simply ascended to its status as the most pivotal player in the intricate and interconnected world of capitalism. Over the course of history, it has evolved into the most apt and powerful entity, responding to the needs of capitalism as it has developed into an internationalised and highly integrated system of imperialist division of labour.

On the flip side, we find China, a nation with a unique trajectory into capitalism. Its journey began with an anti-imperialist peasant revolution, leading to the transformation of hundreds of millions of peasants into proletarians who now engage directly in global market production. While historical circumstances prevented China from gaining entry into the imperialist club due to its historical backwardness, it simultaneously gave rise to an exceptional scenario that distinguishes it from typical neo-colonial dependencies. China's distinguishing factor lies in the existence of a sizeable and disciplined proletariat, intricately intertwined in a dialectical relationship with a centralised party-state. This intricate relationship has fostered a virtuous cycle, fostering organic links between grassroots social dynamics and capitalist development. In this context, even though a substantial portion of the extracted surplus value has flowed to Western metropolises for many years, China's state has been able to centralise residual profits. This was not achieved by acting as a mere subordinate committee to imperialist powers but rather by pursuing a development project geared towards fostering a notably 'national' form of capitalism. The remarkable achievements up to this point, which were undeniably not bestowed upon China through Western benevolence, now face increasing risks, as elucidated in this study. Consequently, it becomes imperative for China to undertake a restructuring of its economic model, aimed at capturing a larger share of the global surplus value by advancing up the value chain. The ultimate goal is not to overthrow the world market but rather to enhance China's own position within it. This endeavour is essential for safeguarding social stability and reinforcing the resilience of the unitary state.

The crux of the matter lies in the fact that these endeavours invariably escalate the conflict with US imperialism due to their erosion of the material foundation underpinning US dominance over global value. A striking example is the peril Washington faces if it can no longer effortlessly secure cheap credit from the rest of the world to finance itself. This is particularly pertinent in the current historical phase, initiated by the global financial crisis, in which an ongoing capitalist crisis exacerbates the struggle for a piece of the shrinking economic pie. The transition in question is a pivotal one, and it leaves neither room for China to isolate itself, as it did during the Maoist era, nor to restrict its influence solely to the East Asian regional arena. The latter scenario would be unacceptable to Washington, considering the global reach of its capital. Even if it were to occur, it would merely serve as a steppingstone towards broader global competition. Hence, China finds itself at a crossroads: it must either take a momentous developmental leap forward or risk succumbing to the intense pressure exerted by imperialist forces. This challenge is not just consequential but *existential* in nature. It pertains to the endurance of China's economic development, the stability of its social class compromise, and the cohesion of its unitary state.

## 9.3    A Systemic Impasse

As we have noted, China's challenge to the international order is *not* hegemonic, despite widespread Western misconceptions. Beijing lacks the fundamental requisites to supplant the distinctive global role fulfilled by the United States or to completely reconfigure the entire world capitalist system, becoming its new linchpin. To think of these capacities as simply achievable over time is, in a Hegelian sense, to think abstractly of a cumulative and gradualist process, an ugly infinite, outside and beyond the objective contradictions inherent in the historical epoch that is unfolding.

This leads us to a pivotal aspect of the prevailing global power dynamics and the very trajectory of capitalism in the future. As the 'independent variable', represented by a global economic accumulation marked by a historical crisis of profitability, evolves within the established contours of imperialist hierarchies,[300] a critical juncture emerges. In this context, China signifies something that extends beyond any hegemonic challenge. More accurately, the inevitable global clash between China and the United States reflects what could be characterised as a *systemic impasse* within the capitalist system as a whole. Imperialism inherently possesses the capacity for (albeit disruptive) self-renewal through complementary (though not necessarily simultaneous) restructuring of the international division of labour and class relationships

---

300  In other words, this shift takes us from the broad concept of capital in general to the specific and tangible dynamics of many individual capitals. It also marks a transition from the traditional closed two-class system to a more complex and open framework that encompasses several distinct classes, international division of labour, and the dynamics of competition among different capitalist entities.

at various levels. To date, the former mechanism seems to be indefinitely obstructed, while the latter is temporarily frozen, contributing to severe systemic disorder effects.

In fact, regarding the first aspect, the succession of dominant powers within the capitalist mode of production—a historical process that has consistently expanded the limits of how much capital centralisation can be achieved while maintaining a competitive landscape among multiple capitals and nations—appears to have reached an historical limit with the United States.[301] This is not solely due to the sheer accumulation of various power indices, some of which may be in decline. Instead, it is rooted in the fundamental contradiction between, on one hand, the increasing burden of redistributing global value that damages the most dynamic centres of accumulation (such as Asia) and the satellites of US influence (Europe and Japan), and on the other hand, the ordering function that the United States fulfils as the world's lender and the consumer of last resort, responsible for maintaining the stability of the entire global system.

This indispensable function of the United States as an ordering force in the global economy cannot be readily replaced in the short to medium term, as there is a looming risk that a crisis within the US 'super imperialism' could potentially trigger systemic upheavals that no bourgeoisie could effectively manage. Simultaneously, other major players like China and Russia are actively striving for greater autonomy, primarily in response to the mounting financial burdens of their subordinate roles. Looking ahead, there is the looming prospect of a potential rupture in the trajectory of globalisation. Such a rupture may become probable if the United States and China continue their collision course amid a deepening global economic crisis or inevitable if a direct geopolitical confrontation, even of a military nature (though not an immediate one), emerges on the horizon.

This is not a contradiction confined solely to the United States, which is itself suffering the negative repercussions of the debt economy that its ordering function entails. Rather, it is a contradiction embedded within the broader context of the contemporary world capitalist system. Capitalism is not merely an economic system of production but has evolved into a comprehensive system of global reproduction. Money, credit, and fictitious capital are integral components of this system, serving as the (albeit increasingly unstable) mechanisms that balance capital's imperative for self-expansion with the internationalised production circuits that provide it with the essential resources

---

301　This is the anomaly highlighted by Giovanni Arrighi.

for growth. In this intricate web of balancing mechanisms, the United States, whether one likes it or not, plays a pivotal role. US finance does not just extract an ever-increasing portion of real value production; it is becoming increasingly entangled with productive capital, particularly the most highly concentrated sectors, by virtue of its capacity to facilitate the circulation and capture of value across the global landscape. However, this intertwining is less and less advantageous to any single player within the system.

The deadlock is even more pronounced on the second front: the restructuring of surplus value extraction and capitalist class relationships. In the face of a deepening crisis of profitability within the global system, which has been temporarily mitigated in the West through significant injections of liquidity, any comprehensive productive restructuring would *ideally* begin with the United States. Paradoxically, it is precisely there that the crisis has been largely postponed—constituting the second impasse factor in the present scenario. The situation is characterised by minimal or no change in the liquidity-to-manufacturing ratio, the inability to implement reshoring initiatives, challenges in decoupling from China and withstanding China's responses, and only partial progress in automating production and social reproduction processes. These factors collectively contribute to the preservation of profit-making methods that have been the status quo for several decades. Meanwhile, there is no visible emergence of a new social bloc capable of facilitating disruptive restructuring, despite some initial domestic shifts brought about by Trumpism.

Thus, while China is making arduous efforts to ascend the value chain, constrained domestically by historical legacies and hampered externally by imperialist pressures, the United States remains hesitant to initiate a process that would entail a significant devaluation of financial and productive capital and the potential rupture of international value circuits. Such a transformation, which involves considerable social repercussions and an exacerbation of geopolitical tensions, is not yet within the US elites' capacity to manage. As a result, the formulation of a Grand Strategy, as we discussed earlier, is challenging. A productive and financial restructuring, absent a full-scale offensive on China or preceding it, does not appear to be a realistic scenario, especially given the concern that Beijing might exploit such a situation. However, combining these two aspects is undoubtedly complex and infeasible without substantial upheavals across all dimensions. Consequently, Washington is likely to continue contributing to global chaos without offering comprehensive solutions.

### 9.4 *Hegel in Beijing*

The systemic impasse also becomes evident when considering the dialectical relationship inherent in capitalism between renewal and preservation.

Throughout the historical successions of hegemonic powers, the waning dominant force always represented the phase of conserving established forms of labour organisation and exploitation, and class and inter-capitalist relationships. In contrast, the rising power embodied the spirit of innovation, leading to more concentrated structures of domination aligned with greater socialisation of labour.

Applying this framework to the contemporary context, China is undeniably shaking up the established order. It represents a relatively young form of capitalism, albeit fused with a profoundly ancient civilisation, demonstrating a capacity for renewal and innovation in the realm of extracting surplus value. It symbolises the global aspiration of emerging 'many capitals' seeking to rejuvenate world capitalism. However, alongside this dynamism, China grapples with several distinct factors that prevent it from becoming the vanguard of advanced capitalism or an ideal platform capable of rejuvenating global capital circulation through massive inflows of debt.

To elaborate on these challenges, China's economy is marked by robust state regulation that does not always favour business competition, a delicate balance between old forms of class struggle and potentially social-democratic labour regulations, a 'solved' agrarian issue that inherently restricts high productivity levels, modest levels of domestic consumption, an inability to attract foreign immigrant labour, a continuing need for market protection through capital control, and a nascent stage of financial internationalisation,[302] among other factors. These facets collectively place China somewhat behind in the journey to unleash capital from all constraints and limitations, a feat that the United States has managed to accomplish thus far.

In this context, Beijing is unlikely to become the driving force of global capitalism in the short to medium term. While it significantly contributes to the resilience of the global economic system, it still lags behind in terms of breaking free from all constraints and ushering in an era of unrestricted capital movement. Beijing thus appears to align more with a Hegelian perspective that anticipates a 'regulationist ethical state' and a civil society whose dialectics revolve around the mutual recognition of social classes. This stands in contrast to Adam Smith's concept of the invisible hand or Marx's vision of class struggle. It is a Hegelian framework that may be embraced by the Chinese elite, rooted in the classical teachings of Confucianism. However, this perspective, while appealing, presents a precarious situation both domestically and on the global stage.

---

302  Howell, *Capital Wars*, chap. 9.

## 9.5  Scenarios

In light of potential misconceptions regarding the implications of this systemic impasse, it is important to clarify that this stalemate is temporary. The world market plays a crucial role in China's efforts to ascend the hierarchies of the international division of labour. However, in its current configuration dominated by Washington and with a looming general crisis, the price to be paid will progressively rise, posing challenges to domestic social stability. On the other hand, the United States is facing increasing difficulties in fulfilling its systemic role and will confront even more significant issues in the upcoming phase. In the midst of economic downturns, financial crises, geopolitical tensions, and social unrest, the US will, as always, seek to shift the costs onto other players. A clash becomes inevitable as Beijing and Washington both grapple with a systemic crisis that offers no simple way out.

There are three broadly conceivable scenarios, and their developmental trajectories will coexist for a significant period, sometimes aligning and at other times conflicting. Within these scenarios, a deepening crisis of globalisation will serve as the backdrop for the interplay between deteriorating international relations and the resurfacing of social class conflicts, albeit in a disorderly fashion.

First, the imperative need for international reordering based on multipolarism is poised to grow, driven by China's necessity to avoid insularity and supported by other relevant players like Russia and other BRICS countries. Such a rebalancing of imperialist relations would offer China the opportunity to continue its trajectory of constructing a vast domestic and external market that can uphold national interests. Simultaneously, it would provide room for creating a more robust social contract with urban and rural working classes, as well as salaried middle classes. This approach could also serve as a means to manage any potentially centrifugal tendencies within private enterprises and independent middle classes. Within this framework, China could progress beyond extensive development in the midst of an anti-American nationalist wave and, in turn, accommodate the requirements and forces stemming from the class struggle of the proletariat, which might lean towards a social-democratic stance.

The ongoing process carries its share of significant challenges. It is important to distinguish between the ongoing process and the likely outcomes. While the process is actively unfolding and will play a pivotal role in unlocking the global situation, achieving a multipolar outcome is an entirely different and highly challenging endeavour. Foremost, this multipolar path is hindered by the expected response from the United States. Although the US has predominantly expressed its concerns towards Beijing on the economic front thus far, these concerns are still in their early stages, and they will be addressed with every available means. On the other hand, forming a multipolar international configuration would necessitate a concerted effort with an equal and opposing thrust. However, creating an anti-American geopolitical bloc or even just a network of nations seeking greater autonomy from the dollar faces obstacles due to the disparities among potential participants and their divergent national interests. Their substantial dependence on the world market further compounds these challenges, especially given the extreme difficulty of achieving effective globalisation that is not conditioned by the US dominance. In the current stage of imperialist development, even deeper economic regionalisation cannot be considered as an alternative, let alone a substitute for the world market; it primarily serves as a platform for competing within that global arena. Therefore, even when viewed as an ongoing process, multipolarism can only be regarded as a transitional phase, historically consistent with capitalism, signalling the advent of intense inter-capitalist competition and potentially even war.

Hence, it is evident that a relatively stable multipolar order lacks structural support in the present stage of imperialism. Nonetheless, it is essential to recognise that China's resistance, along with other nations, serves as a significant check on the United States, particularly by instigating class contradictions that could emerge in Western nations and subsequently reverberate worldwide. In the current global geopolitical landscape, multipolarism, as a conflict-ridden process, can be viewed as a somewhat 'reformist' option. As such, it is inherently compromised and ultimately unattainable. Yet, it undeniably represents a genuine contradiction within the global capitalist system. Nevertheless, it is crucial to emphasise that, at best, this may lead to a chaotic and transitional international situation, which is destined to evolve into one of the two other conceivable scenarios.

Another conceivable scenario involves China succumbing to mounting pressure from an increasingly aggressive US offensive, coupled with a severe forthcoming economic crisis. If this were to occur, it would critically undermine the resilience of global networks and, subsequently, China's economic growth. The achievements of China's ascent so far would be at risk, potentially leading to the breakdown of the internal social pact and domestic stability. Such a situation might create a disconnection between the working classes and the party-state. Consequently, there could be a resurgence of social conflicts and increasing turmoil, particularly fuelled by segments of the middle classes and the younger generation advocating for more personal freedoms. This could challenge the control exercised by the party-state over the economy, potentially pushing towards political and economic liberalisation. In this scenario, the result might be a prolonged period of Western imperialist dominance, extending over several decades.

This is arguably the least desirable option for anyone not enamoured with US dominance or those who do not adhere to a radical Left perspective that regards the struggle for democratic rights and identity politics as the ultimate goals of history. Regardless, even this scenario would not prevent a phase of intense confrontation and, more or less forced, deglobalisation, potentially leading to heightened global chaos.

Thus opens up a third possible scenario: a protracted process of systemic disintegration that could result in one of two outcomes. First, it might lead to a state of chaos and 'barbarism', the exact contours of which are challenging to envision at this stage. Alternatively, it could lay the groundwork for a transitional phase towards a non-capitalist social organisation. Amid this tumultuous journey, marked by crises, conflicts, wars, and revolutions, fundamental alternatives would be at play, heralding a pivotal moment in history. This pivotal moment would not only be significant for individual nations but for the entire global human community. A prerequisite for this trajectory is a crisis of capitalist systemic reproduction that defies conventional solutions. In such a scenario, the vital challenges related to the reproduction of the working classes and humanity as a whole would become so acute that action would be necessitated, even before it is fully comprehended. Several factors could contribute to this catastrophic path, including the resistance of capitalist China and other nations and states to Western imperialism, profound domestic conflicts in the United States struggling with both a radical economic restructuring and the setbacks of an ailing international strategy. The increasing disarray in the rest of the world, which could encompass the unravelling of the Atlanticist bloc and the disintegration of the European Union, may further hasten this scenario. As the conflicting national ruling classes become increasingly incapable of offering effective solutions to a growing web of intricate and pressing issues, the world's population would find itself caught in an era of escalating problems.

This transformation will undoubtedly be accompanied by resurgent social and national conflicts. The unlocking of this complex global situation will coincide with the re-emergence of class struggles on a worldwide scale. However, we should understand that these struggles will not manifest uniformly across different regions, nor will they adhere to the familiar patterns of the past. The transition to the real subsumption of labour under capital, marked by significant disparities across various regions, has not fully reached its conclusion, even in areas characterised by advanced capitalism. Nevertheless, this transformation has profoundly altered production and reproduction processes, as well as the composition of social classes. Consequently, the breakdown of globalisation will give rise to increasingly bewildering and contradictory circumstances, with early indicators of this complexity already observable.

The purpose of this study is to shed light on the necessary, yet not entirely sufficient, conditions for the current impasse, both objective and subjective, to begin to unravel. First and foremost, a decisive weakening of US dominance, regardless of its source or the manner in which it may manifest. The most favourable correlation of global forces for triggering a potential 'transition' is, in fact, a crisis of American power. In this context, the ability of China to withstand Washington's offensive, regardless of how we characterise its economic and social structure or political system, becomes one of the critical elements. The weaker player may not achieve victory but, by resisting, can contribute to the deepening of systemic contradictions (which is not Beijing's intention, to avoid any pro-Chinese misconceptions). Once again, both China and the United States will play fundamental roles: the former objectively serving as a bridge between the Global North and South, as well as between the proletariat and the peasant masses; the latter, being the most socialised form of capitalism, serving as the harbinger of the most severe and decisive antagonisms. In the epochal clash between the United States and China—unless we perceive it as another tragic chapter in the history of great powers[303] or a clash of civilisations—nothing less than the future course of the world is at stake.

An entirely valid objection underlies this crucial perspective: the profound crisis of opposing subjectivities today, both bourgeois and proletarian, reveals an incapacity for a decisive class clash, which is the only catalyst for the emergence of an anti-systemic alternative. This objection cannot be dismissed, and the spectre of the 'common ruin of struggling classes' (to the extent that they do not engage in their own struggle) looms ominously.

Clearly, the mere intensification of the global crisis, while undeniably inevitable, will fall short of effecting meaningful change. Specific conditions must be cultivated to make a systemic alternative not only conceivable but also desirable, fostering a convergence of structural imperatives with the will and strategies of collective forces. But which forces are in question, and for what alternative? The impasse facing potentially anti-capitalist subjectivities remains a challenge that necessitates extensive re-evaluation. Addressing this

---

303   John J. Mearsheimer, *The Tragedy of the Great Powers* (New York: Norton, 2001).

requires an examination of the historical trajectory of the labour movement's attempts to break free from the clutches of capital and liberate itself from the condition of being a part of capital.

Reconnecting the strands of history with the present moment may help clarify the stakes of the impending struggles, which may be closer than we realise.

# Epilogue

By adding this chapter to the condensed translation of the original edition of October 2022, we aim at giving a concise account of the main developments that have been taking place over the past year. It confirms, we believe, the tendency towards a US-China disconnect and the reconfiguration of the world market, but still a few steps behind those dramatic developments that could lead to its actual fragmentation through economic, social and geopolitical crises with no way back. Thus, globalisation is less and less a given framework for world accumulation, while becoming more and more a terrain of bitter competition that from the level of individual capitals raises to a conflict between nation states in the framework of the basic opposition between the imperialist West and China.

We will start with the main novelty: the change of pace impressed by Washington on the anti-Chinese decoupling strategy, on the background of the growing US and Western difficulties in the Ukrainian war scenario. We will trace its first apparent effects on the already well-delineated dynamic of a general slowdown in globalisation. We will conclude with some remarks on the Chinese response, which in the face of the escalating confrontation with the United States is showing continuity of strategic line, and on the prospects of a world economy marked by uncertainty but not (yet) in general recession. This contributes to what we have called a 'reformist' challenge to the international order hegemonised by Washington.

## 1 The Changing Pace of Decoupling

As we have seen, the transition from the Trump to the Biden administration has resulted in a refinement of the decoupling strategy. Over the past year, this has decisively turned towards more restrictive technological, trade and financial control measures against Beijing. In parallel an industrial policy (so-called Bidenomics), with huge investments aimed at strengthening the technological system of enterprises also on the domestic front, has been launched.[1] Let us look at the main steps.

---

1 John Bateman, "The Fevered Anti-China Attitude in Washington Is Going to Backfire", *Politico*, December 15, 2022, accessed 13 September 2023 https://www.politico.com/news/magazine/2022/12/15/china-tech-decoupling-sanctions-00071723.

In August 2022, the *Creating Helpful Incentives to Produce Semiconductors (Chips) and Science Act* was passed, which aims at strengthening US manufacturing supply chains in leading sectors by investing in science and technology research. A budget of 52.7 billion is planned for the semiconductor industry alone, in the form of tax credits for new investments in the foundry segment to cover the cost gap with Asian manufacturers.[2] In addition, these incentives are available only if recipient companies do not invest in countries which posit risks to national security (read: China).

Also, in August 2022 the *Inflation Reduction Act* (IRA) was issued, formally aimed at incentivising investments in domestic energy production and promoting clean energy on the basis of tax credits of up to 369 billion dollars. In substance, these are protectionist subsidies for US manufacturing and energy production, in particular for electric vehicles, solar panels and batteries—segments in which China has considerable cost advantages—capable of attracting industrial investment from the rest of the world (not surprisingly, it even raised complaints from Europe).

The most striking escalation took place in October 2022—on the initiative of the Bureau of Industry and Security (BIS), an arm of the US Department of Commerce—with the export ban on the most advanced semiconductors needed for supercomputers and AI, and the ban on selling semiconductor manufacturing equipment useful for the production of chips smaller than 14 nanometres to China. In addition, based on the Foreign Direct Product Rule launched by Trump against Huawei, the ban extends to all foreign companies using US technology.[3] The move is seen by many as a genuine declaration of economic war.[4]

Finally, an executive order by President Biden on 9 August 2023 strictly restricts US venture capital and private equity investments in China in the three sectors of semiconductors, quantum computers, and artificial intelligence.[5]

---

2　Semiconductor Industries Association, *2022 State of the U.S. Semiconductors Industry*, Washington 2023, accessed 13 September 2023 https://www.semiconductors.org/wp-content/uploads/2022/11/SIA_State-of-Industry-Report_2022.pdf.

3　Gregory C. Allen, "Choking off China's Access to the Future of AI", Center for Strategic and International Studies, 11 October 2022, accessed 13 September https://www.csis.org/analysis/choking-chinas-access-future-ai.

4　Alex Paalmer, *An Act of War: Inside America's Silicon Blockade Against China*, The New York Times Magazine, July 12, 2023, accessed 13 September 2023 https://www.nytimes.com/2023/07/12/magazine/semiconductor-chips-us-china.html.

5　The White House, Executive Order on Addressing United States Investments in Certain National Security Technologies and Products in Countries of Concern, 9 August 2023, accessed 14 September 2023 https://www.whitehouse.gov/briefing-room/presidential-actions/2023/08/09/executive-order-on-addressing-united-states-investments-in-certain-national-security-technologies-and-products-in-countries-of-concern/.

These last measures in particular, affecting the entire semiconductor industry, had to face resistance from the directly involved allied countries. It took months of pressure from Washington to convince the Netherlands, home of ASML, and Japan, home of Tokyo Electron—key producers in the upper segments of the semiconductor supply chain—to adhere to the anti-Chinese restrictions on the basis of a multilateral alliance formalised in May 2023.[6] South Korea—already negatively impacted by the Ira Act in the production of electric vehicles—is more reluctant, since it is difficult for Samsung and SK hynix to replace the Chinese market: the Biden administration has therefore granted a one-year prorogation, unlikely to be further extended.[7]

Ultimately, Biden's moves have endorsed the hawkish posture against the hesitation that part of the US business establishment still has about the negative consequences of an anti-Chinese technology war. The goal of restricting and possibly blocking Chinese innovation remains, but the tools used to reach it are getting tougher.[8] The rebranding of the strategy as 'de-risking', based on diversifying and deepening partnerships, sounds more like a rhetorical device than anything else, and cannot counter the growing consensus in US political circles on the priority that is now given to 'national security'.[9] The 'new

---

6   Rintaro Tobita, "US calls out Japan and Netherlands over China chip curbs", *Asia Nikkei*, 6 November 2022, accessed 13 January 2023 https://asia.nikkei.com/Business/Electronics/U.S.-calls-out-Japan-and-Netherlands-over-China-chip-curbs; Reuters, "Dutch to Restrict Semiconductor Tech Export to China", *CNN*, 8 March 2023, accessed 24 March 2023 https://edition.cnn.com/2023/03/08/tech/dutch-china-chips-ban-hnk-intl/index.html; Cagan Cok, "ASML Hit with New Dutsch Limits on Chip Gear Export to China", *Bloomberg*, 30 June 2023, accessed 6 August 2023 https://www.bloomberg.com/news/articles/2023-06-30/dutch-publish-new-limits-on-asml-s-chip-gear-exports-to-china.
7   Kim Jaewon and Cheng Ting-Fang, "Samsung and SK Hynix face China dilemma from U.S. export controls", *Nikkei Asia*, 25 October 2022, accessed 13 November 2023 https://asia.nikkei.com/Business/Tech/Semiconductors/Samsung-and-SK-Hynix-face-China-dilemma-from-U.S.-export-controls.
8   Grey Anderson, "Strategies of Denial", *New Left Review Sidecar*, 15 June 2023, accessed 12 August 2023 https://newleftreview.org/sidecar/posts/strategies-of-denial.
9   "We don't negotiate on matters of national security" said U.S. Commerce Secretary Gina Raimondo in her two days in Beijing, end August (Evelyn Cheng, "Here's what the U.S. Hopes China Will Do after Raimondo's Trip", *CNBC*, 30 August 2023, accessed 12 September 2023 https://www.cnbc.com/2023/08/30/heres-what-the-us-hopes-china-will-do-after-raimondos-trip.html. See also "Remarks by Secretary of the Treasury Janet L. Yellen on the U.S.-China Economic Relationship at Johns Hopkins School of Advanced International Studies", U.S. Department of Treasury, 20 April 2023, accessed 23 May 2023 https://home.treasury.gov/news/press-releases/jy1425.

Washington consensus' launched by National Security Advisor Sullivan does indeed envisage friendshoring—the attempt to transfer part of the supply chains away from China to 'friendly' countries—under the conditions dictated by an industrial policy of protection of the US technological primacy to be defended with the 'small yard and high fence'[10] policy, and by 'non-traditional' trade agreements that do not intend to further open up the domestic market.[11] Foreign policy for the middle class also takes its toll on the allies.

Finally, to mark the start of the 2024 presidential election campaign in which the China issue will be one of the central themes, a new narrative has been added by the Biden administration about the looming—if not already raging—economic crisis in China, which would represent 'a ticking time bomb' at the heart of the world economy and determining a situation in which, according to Biden, 'when bad folks have problems, they do bad things'.[12]

## 2  Global Fallout

As for the effects of the US change of pace, one can generally agree that a quick and decisive decoupling of the US economy from China is not yet to be seen.[13] Nevertheless, neither its cumulative impact, which will manifest itself over time, nor its political significance, should be underestimated.

U.S.-China trade data only partially let see the pronounced decoupling trend. After the strong growth figures of 2021, as we have seen, bilateral trade in

---

10    The White House, "Remarks by National Security Advisor Jake Sullivan on the Biden-Harris Administration's National Security Strategy", 12 October 2022, accessed 13 January 2023 https://www.whitehouse.gov/briefing-room/speeches-remarks/2022/10/13/remarks-by-national-security-advisor-jake-sullivan-on-the-biden-harris-administrations-national-security-strategy/.
11    "We will unapologetically pursue our industrial strategy at home—but we are unambiguously committed to not leaving our friends behind.": The White House, "Remarks by National Security Advisor Jake Sullivan on Renewing American Economic Leadership at the Brookings Institution", 27 April 2023, accessed 13 August 2023 https://www.whitehouse.gov/briefing-room/speeches-remarks/2023/04/27/remarks-by-national-security-advisor-jake-sullivan-on-renewing-american-economic-leadership-at-the-brookings-institution/.
12    Michael D. Shear, "Biden Describes China as a Time Bomb Over Economic Problems", New York Times, 11 August 2023, accessed 16 August 2023 https://www.nytimes.com/2023/08/11/us/politics/biden-china-criticism-economy.html.
13    Peter Engelke, Emily Weinsten, "Global Strategy 2023: Winning the tech race with China", Atlantic Council Strategy Paper Series, 27 June 2023, accessed 18 August 2023 https://www.atlanticcouncil.org/content-series/atlantic-council-strategy-paper-series/global-strategy-2023-winning-the-tech-race-with-china/.

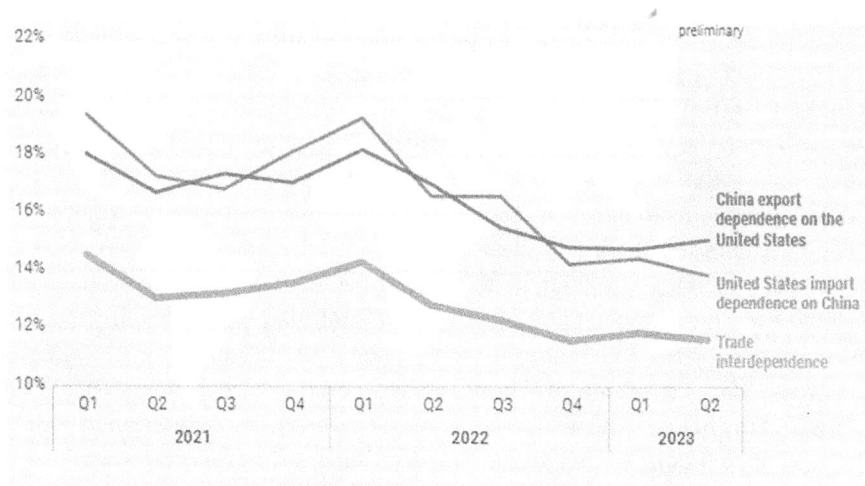

FIGURE E.1  Trade decoupling trade interdependence between China and the United States is declining
Note: China export dependence on the United States is calculated as China exports to the United States over total China exports. The United States import dependence on China is calculated as United States imports to China over total United States imports. The overall trade interdependence is calculated as bilateral trade (imports + exports) of United States and China over the sum of total trade of the two countries.
REPRODUCED FROM UNCTAD, GLOBAL TRADE UPDATE JUNE 2023, UNCTAD/ DITC/INF/2023/2, FEBRUARY 2023, ACCESSED 13 SEPTEMBER 2023 HTTPS:// UNCTAD.ORG/SYSTEM/FILES/OFFICIAL-DOCUMENT/DITCINF2023D2_EN.PDF. DATA FROM UNCTAD SECRETARIAT CALCULATIONS BASED ON NATIONAL DATA OF CHINA AND THE UNITED STATES.

2022 also grew for the third year in a row to an all-time high (reaching a record volume of $691 billion in goods), same as China's trade surplus ($382.9bn or 32,4% of total U.S. trade deficit). This was in line with the more general U.S. current-account deficit which continued to widen. In the first half of 2023, however, bilateral trade began to decline, although not dramatically, as did the two countries' trade interdependence (Figure E.1).[14]

Significant US dependence on Chinese supply chains still remains, particularly in sectors such as electronic components and consumer goods, batteries for electric vehicles and other 'green' devices, and to some extent on some

14  UNCTAD, *Global Trade Update June 2023.* UNCTAD/DITC/INF/2023/2, February 2023, accessed 15 April 2023 https://unctad.org/system/files/official-document/ditcinf2023d2_en.pdf.

critical minerals.[15] But signs of a redefinition of trade flows along geopolitical lines are multiplying, even if the pace does not yet appear to be sustained.

More significant is the figure for US foreign direct investment. Flows have been picking up from 2022 onwards, after the drop in the previous two years, both to and from the US. In this framework, Washington's focus on friendshoring investments, especially towards Mexico[16], Vietnam and South Asia, as well as Europe, to the detriment of China, is growing. But there are also increasing inward flows to the United States, especially from Europe, certainly linked to the new Federal subsidies and reshoring initiatives in the field of chip manufacturing and 'clean' technologies. Particularly significant are the announced greenfield investments for Taiwanese TSMC plants in Arizona and a Samsung plant in Texas. Consequently, mutual foreign investment between the US and China is decreasing (Figure E.2).

At the level of existing global value chains, however, the centrality of Chinese hubs remains, and cannot easily be easily circumvented in the short- to medium-term. This is true, for instance, for the ASEAN countries, one of the most dynamic areas in the world, where Sino-US competition has become fiercer—as we could see in the case of the intra-Asian RCEP trade agreement and the Indo-Pacific Initiative. Despite the Biden administration's anti-Chinese efforts, these countries have seen in recent years their economic relations with Beijing tighten as the main source of imports and exports for both final goods and intermediate components.[17] This is also partly true of microchip production itself. Not only is Washington still far from being able to cover the foundry segment, having only begun to allocate funds for plants and skilled labour; not only is it now impossible for any country to domestically cover the entire supply chain due to unsustainable costs; but by decoupling from the Chinese market, US companies in the high-end segment could even suffer significant losses that would jeopardise their global competitiveness and research funding. While Beijing is unlikely to be completely marginalised, it could, on the

---

15  Niccolò Conte, "Charted: America's Import Reliance of Critical Minerals", *Visual Capitalist*, 4 August 2023, accessed 23 August 2023 https://elements.visualcapitalist.com/americas-import-reliance-of-critical-minerals-charted/.

16  Alberto Guidi, "Poli manifatturieri: geo-rivoluzione in corso", *Ispi*, 21 April 2023, accessed 23 August 2023 https://www.ispionline.it/it/pubblicazione/poli-manifatturieri-geo-rivoluzione-in-corso-123781.

17  Abigal Dahlman and Mary E. Lovely, "US-led effort to diversify Indo-Pacific supply chains away from China runs counter to trends", PIIE, 6 September 2023, accessed 23 August 2023 https://www.piie.com/blogs/realtime-economics/us-led-effort-diversify-indo-pacific-supply-chains-away-china-runs-counter?utm_source=update-newsletter&utm_medium=email&utm_campaign=piie-insider&utm_term=yyyy-mm-dd.

FIGURE E.2  Insecurities and investments. United States and China, $bn
Note: only including deals worth over $1m; 2022: estimate.
REPRODUCED FROM "AMERICA'S PLAN TO VET INVESTMENTS INTO CHINA", THE ECONOMIST, 22 JUNE 2023, ACCESSED 25 JUNE 2023 HTTPS://WWW.ECONOMIST.COM/BUSINESS/2023/06/22/AMERICAS-PLAN-TO-VET-INVESTMENTS-INTO-CHINA. DATA FROM RHODIUM GROUP.

contrary, catch up, well beyond the slim chance of commercial retaliation.[18] All this is clearly shown, just to make two important examples, both by Apple's difficulties in parting from their Chinese suppliers and the Chinese market[19] and, after the harsh sanctions imposed by the Trump administration, by the

---

18  In May 2023, Beijing decided to ban the purchase of semiconductors produced by US-based Micron Technology in an attempt to create tensions between Washington and Seoul, whose companies could fill the gap: Jiyoung Sohn, Yang Jie, "China's New Chip Ban on Micron", *The Wall Street Journal*, 22 May 2023, accessed 23 August 2023 https://www.wsj.com/articles/chinas-new-chip-ban-on-micron-puts-south-korea-in-a-delicate-spot-21ce5259. In July, it restricted the export of gallium and germanium, important for the development of non-silicon-based semiconductors.

19  Patrick McGee, "How Apple tied its fortunes to China", *Financial Times*, 17 January 2023, accessed 24 August 2023 https://www.ft.com/content/d5a80891-b27d-4110-90c9-561b7836f11b.

recovery of Huawei, whose new smartphone contains an advanced chip that was both designed and manufactured entirely in China.[20]

Moreover, as mentioned before, all signs show that Washington will also increasingly push its allies towards a hard decoupling from China, but without in actuality being able to compensate their certain losses in the Chinese market with real incentives, all the more so in the face of growing US industrial protectionism. This, in perspective, makes the anti-Chinese front less solid and—unless there is clear economic coercion by Washington—should lead these countries to diversify rather than replace China altogether.[21]

All this becomes evident if we look at the overall picture of globalisation. Slowbalisation is continuing and even intensifying. We see this first of all at the level of world trade. After the rebound in 2021, the overall figures for 2022 showed a slowdown in growth (2.7 % year on year, but with a sharp drop in the last quarter) mainly due to the continuing anti-pandemic restrictions in China and geopolitical tensions between Washington and Beijing.[22] The slowdown has increased in the first three quarters of 2023, after a recovery at the beginning of the year due to the end of Chinese anti-pandemic measures. The forecasts of international institutions predict weak growth for the rest of 2023 and throughout 2024, even below the already low averages recorded after the global financial crisis. At the same time,–also as a result of the Biden administration's measures—the geographic proximity of international trade (nearshoring) has increased since the end of 2022 along with political proximity (friendshoring) as part of a general diversification of sources of supply—something that had not been the case between 2021 and much of the following year.[23]

---

20  Eva Dou, "New Phone Sparks Worry China Has Found a Way Around U.S. Tech Limits", *The Washington Post*, 2 September 2023, accessed 13 September 2023 https://www.washingtonpost.com/technology/2023/09/02/huawei-raimondo-phone-chip-sanctions/.
21  Gary C. Hufbauer and Megan Hogan, *CHIPS Act Will Spur US Production but Not Foreclose China*, PIIE, October 2022, accessed https://www.piie.com/sites/default/files/2022-10/pb22-13.pdf. See also interview with David Paul Goldman, an economic author for the *Asia Times*, at website CGTN, "U.S. Tech Restrictions", 28 August 2023, accessed 29 August 2023: https://news.cgtn.com/news/2023-08-28/U-S-tech-restrictions-impact-reasons-for-a-potential-tech-war-loss-1mCHAqKLOUo/index.html.
22  World Trade Organization, *Global Trade Outlook*, WTO, April 2023, accessed 24 August 2023 https://www.wto.org/english/res_e/booksp_e/trade_outlook23_e.pdf.
23  Olivia White, Jonathan Woetzel, Jeonmin Seong, and Tiago Devesa, *The complication of concentration in global trade*, Mckinsey, 12 January 2023, accessed 23 August 2023  https://www.mckinsey.com/mgi/Our-Research/The-complication-of-concentration-in-global-trade?cid=other-eml-nsl-mip-mck&hlkid=2d6128a7e7a546fa9da2b228eeb5752c&hctky=12874489&hdpid=d44b5f86-27cd-4c36-8ae9-dda34b3493a8.

At the level of FDI—a key qualitative component of the global capital stock—2022 saw a slowdown in absolute terms (-12%, to USD 1.3 trillion) after a strong recovery in 2021 (1.6 trillion, yet still below 2015 levels, that were the highest post-global financial crisis) even if greenfield investments grew compared to the massive M&As in the West the previous year.[24] Western multinational corporations accounted for two-thirds of total outflows, with a clear upturn in the US (almost three times that of Japan and China, second and third respectively) and a clear decline in European capital exports (with Germany at -13%). The year 2023 will, in all likelihood, be one of even weaker growth if the trend of the first quarter (-25% globally on the previous year) is confirmed, while investment restriction measures on the Western side continue to increase. Consequently, also in terms of foreign investments we see a starting trend towards flows that are increasingly concentrated among geopolitically aligned countries, particularly in strategic sectors. As the IMF suggests: "a shift in cross-border capital flows is about to take place".[25] This is especially hitting China, which remained the second largest global recipient behind the US in 2022, but with a number of projected new investments down from pre-pandemic levels, and with a decrease in inward investment of 18% (the lowest level since 2011). The trend is confirmed by the data available so far for 2023: an overall drop of 2.7% in inflows, back to the 2020 level at the height of the pandemic crisis and halved compared to 2019; Chinese takeovers of foreign companies decreased due to Western restrictions.[26] And this while the rest of Asia confirms its leading position in the volume of capital inflows.

On the one hand, this confirms the ongoing process of diversification and restructuring of global supply chains to the potential detriment of China. On the other hand, some time now China's centrality in global supply chains—and thus the flow of inward investment—has for no longer been based on low labour costs, but increasingly on production capacities and workforce qualification increased by continuous innovation, on a functional logistics network, and on the intertwining of differentiated manufacturing activities and

---

24  UNCTAD, *World Investment Report 2023: Investing in Sustainable Enegy for All*, 2023, accessed 26 August 2023 https://unctad.org/system/files/official-document/wir2023_en.pdf.

25  IMF, *World Economic Outlook 2023. A Rocky Recovery*, Washington, DC: IMF Publication Services, 2023, accessed 23 August 2023 https://www.imf.org/en/Publications/WEO/Issues/2023/04/11/world-economic-outlook-april-2023.

26  Glenn Barklie, *China's FDI decline: Why are foreign companies decreasing their dependency on Asian giant?*, February 16, 2023. See also: Bloomberg News, *China's Foreign Investment Gauge Declines to 25-Year Low*, August 7, 2023, accessed 27 August 2023 https://www.investmentmonitor.ai/insights/chinas-fdi-decline-foreign-companies-covid-geopolitics/.

services.[27] This is demonstrated, for example, by China's rise in the global production of electric vehicles,[28] but also by the fact that Beijing has acquired a dominant role in the export of intermediate goods—now half of total exports—in some important segments of the global market. And it has decisively increased domestic value added as opposed to foreign value added (still prevalent, however, in the semiconductor industry, as we have seen) as a share in global value chains.[29] In these, therefore, China's positioning is increasingly in the medium-high segments, downstream rather than upstream. For this reason, China continues to attract investment, albeit less than in the past, and increasingly in services and research and development. Not to mention that a non-negligible part of the investments to ASEAN countries involves Chinese capital, which in turn relocates also to circumvent US restrictions.

This has two important implications. Firstly, the fact that China is scaling up the value chains implies considerable costs for countries and multinational corporations that would have to radically diversify their production away from China, because of their dependence on Chinese intermediate goods and/or strong economic ties (as for Germany, Japan and South Korea).[30] Secondly, a certain reconfiguration of value chains is indeed taking place at the moment, but more in the form of a 'China + 1' strategy than as true decoupling. China, both as a supplier of components and as a sales market, is not being replaced altogether but becomes a part of the chain, in other ways diversified both regionally and globally. The chain thus tends to turn into a network, with what costs and consequences it is still too early to say.[31]

Against this backdrop, Washington's action is beginning to have visible effects on the reconfiguration of the world market. But rather than being able to block Beijing altogether, this reconfiguration seems to hold China at bay and gain time in order to strengthen U.S. world's technological primacy, domestic

---

27   Henry Wai-Chung Yeung, *Interconnected worlds: Global electronics and production networks in East Asia*, (Stanford: Stanford Business Books, 2022).

28   Felix Richter, "BYD and Tesla Dominate Global EV Sales", *Statista*, September 5, 2023, accessed 26 August 2023 https://www.statista.com/chart/30758/most-popular-plug-in-electric-car-brands/.

29   A reverse trend to the German one: Alicia Garcia Herrero, "Resilience of Global Supply Chain: Facts and Implications", ADBI Working Paper 1398, Tokyo: Asian Development Bank Institute, 2023, https://doi.org/10.56506/UKPK2510.

30   Laura Alfaro and David Chor, "Global Supply Chains: the Looming "Great Reallocation"", working paper 31661 National Bureau of Economic Research, Cambridge, MA, September 2023, accessed 27 September 2023 https://www.nber.org/system/files/working_papers/w31661/w31661.pdf.

31   Alicia Garcia Herrero, "Resilience of Global Supply Chain", 23: "It is clearly still too early to measure the degree to which supply chains are being reshuffled".

production structure and geopolitical hegemony. Anyhow, this is not the only level of the ongoing disconnect.

## 3 Geopolitical Disconnections

The growing difficulties of US imperialism in maintaining economic control over China must spill over onto the geopolitical level as a concentrated expression of the contradictions of world capitalist accumulation. There are currently two theatres of greatest tension: East Asia with Taiwan, where the conflict between the two states is almost direct and the Ukrainian conflict, in which China plays an indirect but important role.

In the first scenario, there are no resounding new developments. As for the Taiwanese issue, after the provocative trip to Taipei by Democratic Party leader Nancy Pelosi in August 2022, we can record Biden's decision, still within political provocations, to send weapons to the island on the basis of a programme envisaged only for military aid to sovereign states, and the idea expressed by some US Congressmen to blow up the island's semiconductor factories in the event of a Chinese attack.[32] Closely related to this is the planned increase of the US military presence in the area through an agreement with the Philippines and Papua New Guinea.[33]

Of greater significance in perspective was the Camp David summit in August 2023 between the US, Japan and South Korea, which underlined Washington's intention to move towards an anti-Chinese 'Asian NATO', which could pass through the accession of the two Asian countries, historically opposed to each other, to the AUKUS military bloc. Currently, a 'commitment to consult' one another when crises arise, a new intelligence-sharing pact, and a plan to hold annual military exercises have been agreed.[34] Added to this is a vague commitment to cooperation on supply chains: vague, because of the US opposition to any trade agreement that would further open up the domestic market. It

---

32  Jason Willick, "Blow Up the Microchips? What a Taiwan Spat Says About U.S. Strategy", *The Washington Post*, 12 May 2023, accessed 27 May 2023. https://www.washingtonpost.com/opinions/2023/05/12/microchips-us-taiwan-strategy/.

33  Chad De Guzman, "U.S. and Philippines Announce New Sites for Military Cooperation", *Time*, 4 April 2023, accessed 23 May 2023 https://time.com/6268379/philippines-us-military-bases-china/.

34  Alexandra Sharp, "U.S., South Korea, Japan Bolster Ties at Camp David Summit, Foreign Policy", 18 August 2023, accessed 23 August 2023 https://foreignpolicy.com/2023/08/18/camp-david-summit-us-japan-south-korea-china-commitment-consult-military-drills/?tpcc=recirc_latest062921.

should not be forgotten that South Korean exports to China, although declining due to Washington's coercive measures, remain crucial, and that the South Korean domestic political framework is very distrustful of Japan.

But it is the Ukrainian theatre that is currently of the greatest importance, not only for Moscow and Kiev, and for the United States, but also for China, to the extent that it will be affected by the evolution of the global power equation that will result from the outcome of the war. A year and a half after the outbreak of the conflict, the fumes of the hammering Western propaganda have begun to clear at least sufficiently to confirm some of the hypotheses already put forward in this volume.

First of all, as NATO Secretary Stoltenberg also recently stated, "the war didn't start in February last year. It started in 2014". And: "President Putin declared in the autumn of 2021, and actually sent a draft treaty that they wanted NATO to sign, to promise no more NATO enlargement. That was what he sent us. And was a pre-condition for not invade Ukraine. Of course we didn't sign that ... So he went to war to prevent NATO, more NATO, close to his borders."[35] Here we have confirmation, if any was still needed, of both NATO's aggressive posture towards enlargement and what we have called the 'Ukrainian trap'. Secondly, it is now public knowledge that in the aftermath of the conflict Kiev and Moscow were conducting negotiations on an agreed document, negotiations from which Zelensky had to withdraw due to Anglo-American pressure. Thirdly, since the outcome of the NATO summit in Vilnius in July 2023, which postponed Ukraine's membership of the Atlantic organisation until a later date to avoid direct armed confrontation with Moscow, it has become clear that, for Washington, Ukraine is and must remain a low-cost, high-benefit battleground, and that the Ukrainians are nothing more than cannon fodder. This is demonstrated by the Ukrainian counteroffensive that began in June 2023, which was bloody for Kiev and has so far failed to achieve its objectives.[36] Not only it was imposed by Washington for political reasons (in particular, the need to show some results on the battlefield to increasingly sceptical Western public opinion), but also carried out without the appropriate military conditions

---

35  NATO, Secretary General Jens Stoltenberg at the joint meeting of the Committee on Foreign Affairs (AFET) and the Subcommittee on Security and Defense (SEDE) of the European Parliament, 7 September 2023, accessed 9 September 2023 https://www.repor tdifesa.it/nato-secretary-general-jens-stoltenberg-at-the-joint-meeting-of-the-commit tee-on-foreign-affairs-afet-and-the-subcommittee-on-security-and-defense-sede-of-the -european-parliament/.

36  Daniel Davis, "The Hard Reality", *1945* blog, September 7, 2023, accessed 13 September 2023 https://www.19fortyfive.com/2023/08/the-hard-reality-ukraines-last-gasp-offens ive-has-failed/.

(number of fighters, artillery, air cover).³⁷ Kiev obviously had to accept on the principle that he who pays commands.

That said, where are we today?

In Washington, there is still the bipartisan view (Trump aside) that the Ukrainian 'investment' is paying off, since the war has greatly degraded Russia's military strength, tightened the ranks of the NATO alliance, and frightened China. All without American boots on the ground.³⁸ On a less superficial analysis, the reality of the facts appears somewhat different. Without denying the immediate advantages for Washington and the certain attrition to which Russia is subjected, all the elements of a possible backlash in the medium- to long-term indicated in this book are confirmed.

Firstly, the war has so far brought Russia to its knees neither militarily nor economically. On the contrary, it is straining NATO's military-industrial apparatus to such an extent that it is uncertain whether, under the given conditions, it will be possible to continue the current level of military support to Kiev for much longer. Moreover, the lack of a Ukrainian-US victory—as well as further distancing Ukrainian entry into NATO—is increasingly alienating a large part of the European population (but not the political leaderships) from the continuation of the conflict and the dispatch of Western weapons, all the more so as the economic situation on the European continent turns for the worse. Secondly, the weapon of anti-Russian sanctions has proved to be anything but successful. On the contrary, Moscow's economic ties with Asian and Global South countries have strengthened, from Iranian drones to microchip smuggling, to the energy markets of China and emerging countries. Not only that: also politically, Moscow has been all but isolated internationally, with most of the Southern countries reluctant to embrace the Western thesis on the war—as evidenced by the enlargement of the Brics (see below) and the G20 summit in September 2023. Finally, and most importantly, any hope of distancing Beijing from Moscow has turned out to be wishful thinking.³⁹

---

37 Aaron Mateè, "John Mearsheimer: Ukraine War Is a Long Term Danger", *The Grayzone* Blog, 30 July 2023, accessed 13 September 2023 https://thegrayzone.com/2023/07/30/john-mearsheimer-ukraine-war-is-a-long-term-danger/.

38 Ctpost, Sen. Blumenthal (opinion): 'Zelensky doesn't want or need our troops. But he deeply and desperately needs the tools to win', 29 August 2023, accessed 12 September 2023 https://www.ctpost.com/opinion/article/sen-blumenthal-opinion-ukraine-tip-spear-18335871.php.

39 Bonny Lin, "The China-Russia Axis Takes Shape", *Foreign Policy*, 11 September 2023, accessed 14 September 2023 https://foreignpolicy.com/2023/09/11/china-russia-alliance-cooperation-brics-sco-economy-military-war-ukraine-putin-xi/?utm_source=Sailthru&utm_medium=email&utm_campaign=Editors%20Picks%20-%2009122023&utm_term=editors_picks#cookie_message_anchor.

Where do we (presumably) go from here?

The war could last much longer, even in the case of a 'cold' peace. Two camps are emerging in the United States at the moment: one in favour of a freeze of the conflict—but not willing to give up on somehow including Ukraine in the NATO security network—, the other in favour of continuing the war and full military and economic support for Kiev. The Biden administration seems to be leaning towards the latter position, which does not exclude a convergence with the former in terms of medium-term objectives, but not before, probably, a further escalation of the conflict (missile attacks on Russian territory, as Kiev would like?). Moscow for its part cannot stop at this point before having ensured the 'failure' of the Ukrainian state, such as to make its NATO membership impossible. But it remains to be seen whether it has the resources to do this or will have to settle for an 'ugly victory'. Ultimately, barring a sudden collapse of either side, the war is expected to drag on through 2024 pending at least the outcome of US presidential elections.

This does not detract from the fact that Washington is faced with a tangle of problems that are not easy to solve: on the one hand, how to pull out of the conflict at some point without it appearing as a defeat; on the other hand, how to continue to put pressure on Russia and thus weaken China's flank. Weighing on all this is the potential loss of international prestige, which may not be limited only to non-NATO countries, if it is true that for Washington's allies (including the EU), the warning once expressed by Kissinger still applies: to align oneself with the American empire means voting oneself, sooner or later, to be the sacrificial lamb. Then there is the need to rethink the model of asymmetrical warfare followed up to now, based on absolute military and technological primacy in the battlefield operated by the least possible number of soldiers on the ground—essential for a home front that has hitherto been hostile to heavy war commitments—and, more generally, the urgent need to develop a Grand Strategy. Problems at once strategic, industrial and socio-political.

In all this, China has followed a line of consistent firmness vis-à-vis Washington, providing substantial support to Moscow, and seeking consensus in the global South coherently with its 'reformist' call for a multipolar international order. In February 2023, Beijing released its 'position paper' on the war in Ukraine for the activation of a path of negotiation to achieve peace, while affirming that it did not want to pull the chestnuts of the real perpetrator of the conflict out of the fire ("whoever started the trouble should end it").[40] It is no

---

40  Ministry of Foreign Affairs of the People's Republic of China, "China's Position on the Political Settlement of the Ukraine Crisis". 24 February 2023, accessed 3 March 2023 https://www.fmprc.gov.cn/eng/zxxx_662805/202302/t20230224_11030713.html.

coincidence that Xi Jinping himself visited Moscow in March. In the following months, Chinese diplomacy worked on reviving the international importance of the Brics countries, which had been somewhat tarnished in recent years. In the meantime, Beijing had to take note that the NATO summit in Vilnius, in full delusion of omnipotence, clearly pointed to China as the enemy.[41] This confirms the perception of US efforts to form "NATO-like military alliances in the Asia-Pacific"[42] and, at the same time, the view shared by the party-state leadership, but widespread in Chinese public opinion, that a Russian defeat in Ukraine would leave China alone to confront the US and open up a more direct confrontation in East Asia. The popularity gained by the term *Meixifang* (i.e. US and the West) is very telling in this regard. The urgency of a more pronounced international projection by China is on the cards.

## 4  China: the Domestic Picture

Before addressing this aspect, let us pause briefly on China's domestic situation.

At the time of our writing, there is much insistence in the West on the 'end of the Chinese miracle', attributing it essentially to the investment-consumption imbalance and the constraints imposed on private enterprise by the political command of the economy.[43] The criticism is by no means new

---

41  NATO, Vilnius Summit Communiquè, 11 July 2023, accessed 13 September 2023 https://www.nato.int/cps/en/natohq/official_texts_217320.htm: "24. [...] We are working together responsibly, as Allies, to address the systemic challenges posed by the PRC to Euro-Atlantic security and ensure NATO's enduring ability to guarantee the defence and security of Allies. We are boosting our shared awareness, enhancing our resilience and preparedness, and protecting against the PRC's coercive tactics and efforts to divide the Alliance. We will stand up for our shared values and the rules-based international order, including freedom of navigation".

42  China's Minister of National Defense Li Shangfu, "20th Asia Security Summit—The Shangri-La Dialogue—Fifth Plenary Session", The 20th IISS-Shangri-La Dialogue, 4 June 4 2023, accessed 16 September 2023 https://www.iiss.org/globalassets/media-library--content--migration/files/shangri-la-dialogue/2023/final-transcripts/p-5/general-li-shangfu-state-councilor-minister-of-national-defense-china---as-delivered.pdf.

43  Adam Posen, *The End of China's Economic Miracle. How Beijing's Struggles Could Be an Opportunity for Washington*, Foreign Affairs, Sepyember-October 2023, accessed 15 September 2023 https://www.foreignaffairs.com/china/end-china-economic-miracle-beijing-washington?utm_medium=promo_email&utm_source=special_send&utm_campaign=China_Economic_Prospects&utm_content=20230802&utm_term=promo-email-prospects.

and converges with the narrative that is prevailing in the Biden administration.[44] Let us note in passing that a different reading of the same data on the Chinese economy is possible.[45] But this is not the point. It is not a question of denying the criticalities of Chinese economic growth, already analysed in this volume—the decline in private investment and the reappearance of the real estate bubble—but of putting them in the correct context. On the one hand, it would be strange if, with the slowdown in global demand, there were no spillover effect on Chinese exports, and on private enterprise in particular. On the other, Beijing's overall deleveraging policy and the refinement of its industrial policy, which are closely linked, should be considered as a framework.

On the first front, already in the aftermath of the 2015–16 financial crisis the central authorities embarked on a gradual policy of liquidity reduction after the huge fiscal stimulus of 2009. Hence the slowdown in lending by both the shadow banking system and local governments, whose indebtedness exceeds that of the central government by almost four times, and whose diminishing returns are compounded by declining local revenues due to diminishing sales of land-use rights for the construction industry.[46] The aim is to gradually replace local debt with sovereign debt by making local authorities more dependent and controlled, and credit allocation more efficient. Something similar applies to the central government's attitude towards the recently rekindled real estate bubble. This too is paradoxically the by-product of the deleveraging campaign (see the tighter regulation of August 2020), which led some real estate holding companies to finance further construction projects by selling houses directly to buyers before their completion, following Ponzi-finance type of schemes. To the dismay of Western analysts, the ensuing bankruptcies or near-bankruptcies—far from representing China's Lehman moment (without securitisation and significant foreign exposure?!)—are for the authorities "the price of disciplining the property sector as a whole and reducing its weight

---

44  James Galbraith, "China in Decline? New US Narrative Is Geared towards 2024 Election", *South China Morning Post*, 18 August 2023, accessed 12 September 2023 https://www.scmp.com/comment/opinion/article/3231483/china-decline-new-us-narrative-geared-towards-2024-election.

45  Nicholas Lardy, "How serious is China's economic slowdown?", PIIE, 17 August 2023, accessed 29 August 2023 https://www.piie.com/blogs/realtime-economics/how-serious-chinas-economic-slowdown.

46  Macropolo, "China's Debt Hangover", Blog, December 2022, accessed 12 January 2023 https://macropolo.org/digital-projects/china-local-debt-hangover-map/?utm_source=MacroPolo&utm_campaign=44ad1c3dab-EMAIL_CAMPAIGN_2018_11_27_04_41_COPY_01&utm_medium=email&utm_term=0_791224187b-44ad1c3dab-438868821.

in the broader economy."⁴⁷ Besides, they also represent the push for a transition to a different model for the property industry as well, as explicitly stated by the CCP leadership.⁴⁸ In short, the reduction of financial risk under tighter central political supervision is fundamental to China's strategy of an overall rebalancing of the growth model followed so far.⁴⁹

In this regard, it should be noted that the industrial strategy itself is not standing still but subject to important adjustments, particularly in response to the growing constraints posed by the chip war. In a nutshell, an attempt at greater centralisation of technological investments can also be observed on this level, which overcomes the previous model of decentralised wild competition that proved to be very costly and not always efficient. From purely quantitative GDP growth, there is thus a shift towards targeted qualitative objectives.⁵⁰ Signs of this are: the inclusion of more technocrats in the CCP Politburo—following the 20th CCP Congress in October 2022—as well as at provincial level; the creation of a Central Commission for Technological Development at the CCP Politburo (March 2023); within this framework, a new stimulus for private enterprises after the regulatory tightening of previous years; the internal debate within the party on the need not to play investment against consumption and not to unbalance the domestic market.⁵¹ In short, within the limits set by the given conditions and the position in the international division of labour, a serious attempt seems to be underway in China, at least in the high-end production sectors, towards an intensive development based on forms of extraction of relative surplus value, albeit hybridised with more backward forms. Will the class struggle also be able to cope with this?⁵²

---

47   Nathan Sperber, *Forecasting China?*, september 8, 2023, New Left Review Sidecar, accessed 16 September 2023 https://newleftreview.org/sidecar/posts/forecasting-china.
48   Zichen Wang and Jinhao Bai, "Central Economic Work Conference 2022", *Pekingnology* Blog, 16 December 2022, accessed 13 March 2023 https://www.pekingnology.com/p/full-text-and-analysis-central-economic.
49   As also witnessed by the creation of a new Central Finance Commission in March 2023, not within the State Council, but directly within the CCP Central Committee.
50   Ruihan Huang, A.J. Cortese, "Nanometers over GDP: Can Technocrat Leaders Improve China's Industrial Policy?", Macropolo, 23 May 2023, accessed 23 August 2023 https://macropolo.org/analysis/technocrat-leaders-china-industrial-policy/?utm_source=MacroPolo&utm_campaign=95f36962d2-EMAIL_CAMPAIGN_2018_11_27_04_41_COPY_01&utm_medium=email&utm_term=0_791224187b-95f36962d2-438868821.
51   Xinyi Qu, Jia Yuxuan, and Zichen Wang, "Study Times op-ed Shoots Down New Policy Options", *Pekingnology* Blog, 20 August 2023, accessed 28 August 2023 https://www.pekingnology.com/p/study-times-op-ed-shoots-down-new.
52   Chuang, "China FAQ. Isn't China the world's sweatshop?", *Chuang* blog, 22 May 2023, accessed 3 September 2023 https://chuangcn.org/2023/05/china-faq-sweatshop/.

## 5   A Global Reformism?

The main novelties of the past year regarding China concern, as anticipated, mainly its external projection.

First of all, towards the Middle East. While Chinese BRI investment has remained more or less constant in relation to GDP since 2016, since 2022 the biggest flow has been towards the Middle East in the energy sector.[53] Xi Jinping's visit to Riyadh and his meeting with the Gulf Cooperation Council countries in December 2022 have increased joint projects, with a plan to harmonise the Saudi *Vision 2030* with the BRI, the revival of the petro-yuan plan as well as a free trade agreement with the countries in the area.[54] On a more strictly geopolitical level, and in some ways sensational, there was the signing in Beijing of the agreement between Iran and Saudi Arabia, for decades fierce enemies under careful US direction. The agreement provides for the full restoration of diplomatic relations, a commitment to the stabilisation of Syria and Afghanistan and to the cessation the Yemeni conflict, besides the intention to cooperate within OPEC also on the safety of maritime traffic in the Persian Gulf. It cannot be ruled out that this development could also be a prelude to an agreement on the Iranian nuclear issue. This would be, and is in fact, a severe blow to Washington's hegemony in the Middle East, in view of Saudi Arabia's historical role as a pro-US bastion, a change in the strategic situation in the area and a first clear affirmation of Beijing's geopolitical weight.[55] In the meantime, Saudi Arabia reduced its purchase of US bonds to 2016 levels for fear of future possible sanctions.

On a broader scale, in August 2023 the 15th Brics summit has taken place in Johannesburg. Let us look at the main results:

- to the surprise of Western observers, an enlargement of the organisation to six new countries was decided: Argentina, Ethiopia, Egypt, the United Arab Emirates, Iran and Saudi Arabia.

---

53   Christoph Nedopil, "China Belt and Road Initiative (BRI) Investment Report H1 2022", Green Finance & Development Center, FISF Fudan University, Shanghai, July 2022, accessed 23 August 2023 https://greenfdc.org/wp-content/uploads/2022/07/GFDC-202 2_China-Belt-and-Road-Initiative-BRI-Investment-Report-H1-2022.pdf.

54   Vivian Nereim, "China and Saudi Arabia Sign Strategic Partnership as Xi Visits Kingdom", *The New York Times*, 8 December 2022, accessed 12 January 2023 https://www.nytimes.com /2022/12/08/world/middleeast/china-saudi-arabia-agreement.html.

55   David Ignatius, "How China Is Heralding the Beginnings of a Multipolar Middle East", *The Washington Post*, 16 March 2023, accessed 23 August 2023 https://www.washingtonp ost.com/opinions/2023/03/16/china-saudi-arabia-iran-middle-east-change/.

- the Beijing-Moscow axis was strengthened, in favour of a qualified but broader enlargement than India would have liked, and the contextual inclusion of Iran and Saudi Arabia.
- the push for a reform of global economic governance in a truly multilateral direction, more favourable to the demands of the Global South and less subordinate to US policy and dollar dominance, has regained momentum.[56]
- thanks to their growing political prestige and economic influence, BRICS + can thus act as a catalyst towards a comprehensive reform of the international order led by actors outside of the Western bloc.
- On the financial and monetary level, there have been further steps towards conducting bilateral trade and investments in local currencies. This is by no means a common currency, which would be unfeasible at present. It is about giving a more decisive course to the shared desire to reduce dependence on the dollar as a means of international payment and to circumvent the increasingly frequent Western sanctions. In this respect, the concentration of oil producers in the BRICS + (more than 40% of world production) should not be underestimated.

The persistent heterogeneity of the members is a fact: BRICS + do not represent a true political bloc, let alone a security alliance. Moreover, the attitude of these countries—apart from today's Russia and, increasingly, China—is not anti-Western. It is rather a posture of multi-alignment. The other members, each with their own interests and peculiarities, aim at increasing their bargaining power with the West on issues such as technology transfer, armaments, terms of trade agreements, price of raw materials, and possible debt restructuring. India in particular seems willing to openly play on several tables, as is evident with respect to the Ukrainian conflict, without conceding anything to Beijing on a geopolitical and economic level. This does not detract from the fact that even so, the BRICS + could become a thorn in the side of the United States to the extent that they could begin to undermine its the quasi-monopoly of its currency on global trade transactions.[57]

All this would not be possible without the essential role of Beijing. To start with, thanks to China, bilateral trade between BRICS countries has increased

---

56 Steven Erlanger, David Pierson, Linsey Chutel, "Iran, Saudi Arabia and Egypt Invited to Join Emerging Nations Group", *The New York Times*, 24 August 2023, accessed 29 August 2023 https://www.nytimes.com/2023/08/24/world/europe/brics-expansion-xi-lula.html.

57 Piero Pagliani, "Brics + o bric-à-brac?", *Sinistrainrete*, 2 September 2023, accessed 12 September 2023 https://www.sinistrainrete.info/geopolitica/26251-piero-pagliani-brics-o-bric-a-brac.html.

significantly, especially with Brazil and Russia.[58] Consequently, the mutual use of local currencies has been further boosted. Furthermore, the yuan has started to be traded between and beyond the BRICS countries, in Asia, Africa and Latin America and for oil and gas purchases.[59] This is made possible by bilateral swap lines between central banks, by which Beijing compensates for the yuan's low international liquidity amount due to capital account restrictions.[60] In particular, as a result of Western sanctions, the yuan has become Russia's de facto reserve currency and the one most traded on the Russian currency and bond market. Finally, heavy purchases of gold, mainly by China, Russia and India, have continued since 2022, partially replacing the dollar as a central bank reserve both in view of the sanctions risk and persistent inflation in global markets.[61] For Beijing, this serves to give a more solid basis to the internationalisation process of the yuan. It is no coincidence that in 2023 the yuan, for the first time, came to surpass the dollar in bilateral international payments.[62]

In short, the 'reformist' challenge to the West continues to make headway.

## 6   The Crisis to Come

At the time of writing, the world economic situation is turning to the worst, having gone through violent ups and downs between '21 and '23: pandemic,

---

58    Marco Fernandes, "Brics gain new chances to improve global development", *AsiaTimes*, 13 April 2023, accessed 23 May 2023 https://asiatimes.com/2023/04/brics-gains-new-chance-to-improve-global-development/.

59    See the agreement between China National Offshore Oil Corp (CNOOC) and France's TotalEnergies in March 2023, representing the first purchase of liquefied natural gas in yuan: Neils Christensen, "China settled its first LNG trade in yuan", *Kitco News*, 29 March 2023, accessed 3 April 2023 https://www.kitco.com/news/2023-03-29/China-settled-its-first-LNG-trade-in-yuan-but-gold-remains-the-bigger-winner-in-the-global-de-dollarization-trend.html.

60    Hector Perez-Saiz and Longmei Zhang, "Renminbi Usage in Cross-Border Payments: Regional Patterns and the Role of Swaps Lines and Offshore Clearing Banks", IMF Working Paper, 31 March 2023, accessed 3 April 2023 https://www.imf.org/en/Publications/WP/Issues/2023/03/31/Renminbi-Usage-in-Cross-Border-Payments-Regional-Patterns-and-the-Role-of-Swaps-Lines-and-531684.

61    Marc Jones, "Countries repatriating gold in wake of sanctions against Russia", Reuters, 10 July 2023, accessed 12 August 2023 https://www.reuters.com/business/finance/countries-repatriating-gold-wake-sanctions-against-russia-study-2023-07-10/.

62    Noriyuki Doi and Saki Akita, "Yuan exceeds dollar in China's bilateral trade for first time", *Nikkei ASIA*, 24 July 2023, accessed 12 August 2023 https://asia.nikkei.com/Business/Markets/Currencies/Yuan-exceeds-dollar-in-China-s-bilateral-trade-for-first-time.

(relative) post-pandemic rebound, slowdown. It is true that the US has so far not entered recession, as was expected, probably also thanks to the huge stimulus programme provided by Trump and Biden. But the German economy is in a technical recession, dragging behind it the slowdown of the entire eurozone. And a slowdown in global demand and production is expected, which may this time also involve China, unlike in the GFC.

To conclude this update, we would like to briefly mention two more than merely cyclical aspects, closely connected.

The first is the reappearance, after several decades, of inflation in Western economies, dating from 2021 (before, it should be noted, the outbreak of the Ukrainian conflict). While in summer 2023 the phenomenon seems to have partially abated, in reality the cooling down only applies to the part defined by academic economists as 'volatile' (as if energy and food prices were secondary!), while the so-called 'core' inflation persists. In all events, producer and commodity prices are unlikely to fall back to pre-pandemic levels. Now, albeit through gritted teeth, part of the financial and academic establishment has recognised that one of the main contributing factors is, partly as a result of the opportunity provided by supply-side bottlenecks in the post-pandemic recovery, the increased price-setting power of national and international oligopolies, while the so-called wage-price spiral has hardly occurred.[63] It is important to emphasise even if it is not possible to develop the argument here, that the recent inflationary dynamic is rooted in a general fall in the profitability of capital, which is unevenly distributed through the price mechanism between oligopolies and sectors more open to competition through a stratified equalisation of the rate of profit.[64] The former can maintain profitability without changing the organic composition of capital or the rate of exploitation but only at the expense of other sectors and enterprises, without a real increase in the overall mass of surplus value. Also contributing to this trend is the credit mechanism, which in the decades of globalisation has seen the hinge between national currency and private liquidity, mostly denominated in dollars, lengthen enormously (so-called financialisation). While allowing a postponement of the overproduction crisis, it also tends to aggravate it by postponing the painful choice of drastic solutions. In the meantime, inflation has an important implication for the West: it erodes the real wages of the

---

63  Weber, Isabella M. and Evan Wasner, "Sellers' Inflation, Profits and Conflict: Why can Large Firms Hike Prices in a Emergency?" Economics Department Working Paper Series 340, February 2023. University of Massachussetts Amherst, accessed 3 March 2023 https://doi.org/10.7275/cbv0-gv07.

64  Bruno Astarian, Ferro Robert, *Le Ménage à trois de la lutte des classes*, 323–24.

proletariat, as well as the incomes of the middle classes, contributing decisively to the breakdown of the post-Fordist social compromise (upward globalisation), which, albeit with considerable shake-ups, has held up even in the post-GFC decade. Looking ahead, this will prove crucial for a reemergence of social conflict in imperialist countries, although not in the forms of the historical labour movement.[65]

Against this backdrop, and here we come to the second point, is also the gradual change of monetary policy by the US Federal Reserve (closely followed by the ECB) from Quantitative Easing (QE) to Quantitative Tightening (QT). With QE, the central banks of the Western bloc essentially monetised the debt of the financial system shaken by the 2008 crisis through a colossal programme of government bond purchases and interest rates kept very low, which also allowed the continuous (albeit very diverse) rises in stock market securities. With the pandemic crisis, this was repeated by guaranteeing the bailout of (even so-called zombies) companies. Now, since the peak in April 2022 total financial assets held by the Fed have dropped by $864 billion to a value of $8.10 trillion in August 2023 (or 15.2% of total outstanding US Treasury securities).[66]

It is still a significantly increased amount compared to $2 trillion Treasuries in the aftermath of the GFC. This makes the central bank's arms blunt by weakening its ability to control money and credit, with the effect of further inflating the debt bubble. Not only: a QE policy can only lead in the long run to a weakening of the dollar in global markets, all the more so given the signs of disaffection with the US currency by the non-Western world. In fact, what we have called "dollar fatigue" has not abated, nor has Washington's worsening debt position: national debt over $32 trillion, doubled since the start of the GFC; a negative net international investment position of more than 16 trillion dollars; a (still limited) contraction in the dollar's share as a reserve currency (58% of the total in 2022, the lowest value since 1995)[67]; a reduction in US government debt securities held by the Chinese Central Bank and others.[68] In addition, there is the growing intolerance of the domestic capital fractions

---

65   I have dealt with this topic in Raffaele Sciortino, *I dieci anni*, chapter 3.
66   Wolf Richter, "Fed Balance Sheet QT", *Wolf Street*, 7 September 2023, accessed 13 September 2023 https://wolfstreet.com/2023/09/07/fed-balance-sheet-qt-105-billion-in-august-864-billion-from-peak-to-8-1-trillion-lowest-since-july-2021/.
67   Naomi Rovnick and Libby George, "The end of King Dollar?", Reuters, 25 May 2023, accessed 3 June 2023 https://www.reuters.com/markets/currencies/end-king-dollar-forces-play-de-dollarisation-2023-05-25/.
68   CEIC, China's Holding of US Treasury Securities 2000–2023, accessed 13 September 2023 https://www.ceicdata.com/en/china/holdings-of-us-treasury-securities/holdings-of-us-treasury-securities.

linked to interest-bearing loans, which have accepted the low rates due to QE for years both because of the post-2008 emergency situation and because they were compensated by selling government bonds and through stock market rallies for the credit crunch in a stagnating economy. Now, however, the drop in profits is more acute.

Consequently, the allocation of the growing US foreign debt and the risk of a weakening dollar demanded for the Fed to raise interest rates. And it is no coincidence that, as already happened in 2022, the dollar strengthened through rate differentials against both the euro and the yuan due to the 'safe haven' effect following the outbreak of the Ukrainian conflict.[69]

It must be said, however, that rate increases are still modest compared to real inflation. Even so, they have caused considerable criticalities in the United States. In addition to rising interest expenses for the national debt, regional banks have suffered or are suffering from the hike—see the bankruptcy of Silicon Valley Bank and Signature Bank in March 2023 due to the devaluation of government bonds held as assets.[70] The same holds for commercial real estate, due to the fall in prices associated with expansive mortgage lending, and for businesses, due to the increased cost of financing. Criticalities, however, that also encourage capital centralisation processes.

Despite the propaganda of self-legitimation, the Fed's new monetary policy is therefore not really aiming at combating inflation, but at preserving the global command of the dollar without making decisive turns. In fact, only a sharp rise in rates like the Volcker choc could stop the phenomenon by inducing a hard recession. On the other hand, letting inflation run involves high risks: weakening of the dollar, financial instability, risk of a wage run-up: all in the context of rising international geopolitical tensions. Hence the dilemma for western central banks, which will only become more acute if the conditions remain as indicated.

We are not yet at the point of maturity of a drastic turn, one in which a massive devaluation of surplus capital by the leading fractions of US capital and state could open the way to a thorough capitalist restructuring with the

---

69 "China's State Banks Seen Selling Dollars for Yuan", Reuters, 17 August 2023, accessed 12 September 2023 https://www.reuters.com/markets/currencies/chinas-major-state-banks-sell-dollars-yuan-london-ny-hours-sources-2023-08-17/.

70 Uninsured deposits at the two failed institutions were immediately guaranteed while Fed providing liquidity through a new Bank Term Funding Program to prevent bank runs: Board of Governors of the Federal Reserve System, "Bank Term Funding Program", last update: 12 September 2023, accessed 14 September 2023 https://www.federalreserve.gov/financial-stability/bank-term-funding-program.htm.

generalisation of a new standard of value and the reconfiguration of class relationships. When it will occur, however, it will not be able to avoid a deepening of the clash that has just begun between the US and China, and will also reignite all the tensions between the West and the South, and within the West itself, as well as class conflict on a global scale. It will then be seen whether the gap between the structure of world accumulation and the margins for a US Grand Strategy can be bridged or whether it will open up the disarticulation of the world capitalist system.

# Bibliography

Abeliansky, Ana L. and Inmaculata Martínez-Zarzoso. "The relationship between the Chinese 'going out' strategy and international trade." *Economics E-Journal*, Vol. 13, 2019–21 (March 11, 2019): 1–18. DOI: 10.5018/economics-ejournal.ja.2019-21.

Aglietta, Michel, Guo Bai and Camille Macaire. *La course à la suprématie monétaire mondiale*. Paris: Éditions Odile Jacob, 2022.

Ahmed, Salman, Rozlyn Engel, Wendy Cutler, Douglas Lute, Daniel M. Price, David Gordon, Jennifer Harris (eds.) et al. *Making U.S. Foreign Policy Work Better for the Middle Class*. Washington, DC: Carnegie Endowment for International Peace, 2020. https://carnegieendowment.org/files/USFP_FinalReport_final1.pdf.

Ahn, JaeBin, Benjamin Carton, Ashique Habib, Davide Malacrino, Dirk Muir, and Andrea Presbitero. "Geoeconomic Fragmentation and Foreign Direct Investment." *IMF World Economic Outlook: A Rocky Recovery*, April 2023, Chapter 4.

Akira, Hayami. *Japan's Industrious Revolution: Economic and Social Transformations in the Early Modern Period*. Tokyo: Springer, 2015.

Akkemik, K. Ali and Murat Yülek. "'Made in China 2025' and the Recent Industrial Policy in China" in *Designing Integrated Industrial Policies*, vol. 1: *For Inclusive Development in Asia*, edited by Shigeru Th. Otsubo and Christian S. Otchia. London: Routledge, 2020.

Alfaro, Laura and David Chor. "Global Supply Chains: the Looming "Great Reallocation"." Working paper 31661. *National Bureau of Economic Research (NBER)*. Cambridge, MA, September 2023. https://www.nber.org/system/files/working_papers/w31661/w31661.pdf.

Allen, Gregory C. "Choking off China's Access to the Future of AI." Center for Strategic and International Studies. 11 October 2022. https://www.csis.org/analysis/choking-chinas-access-future-ai.

Alshareef, Salam. "The Gulf's shifting geoeconomy and China's structural power: From the petrodollar to the petroyuan?" *Competition & Change* 27 (2), 2022: 380–401. DOI: 10.1177/10245294221095222.

Alves, Carolina. "Fictitious Capital, the credit system, and the particular case of government bonds in Marx". *New Political Economy*, Vol. 28, No. 3, 2023: 398–415. https://doi.org/10.1080/13563467.2022.2130221.

Amighini, Alessia. "Cina: i freni alla corsa del Dragone." [China: The Brakes on the Dragon's Race] Istituto per gli Studi di Politica Internazionale (ISPI). 5 August 2021. https://www.ispionline.it/it/pubblicazione/cina-i-freni-alla-corsa-del-dragone-31336.

Amighini, Alessia (ed.). "China after COVID-19: Economic Revival and Challenges to the World." *ISPI*. 5 August 2021. https://www.ispionline.it/en/publication/china-after-covid-19-economic-revival-and-challenges-world-30780.

Amin, Samir. "China 2013." *Monthly Review* 64, 10 (March 2013). https://doi.org/10.14452/MR-064-10-2013-03_3.

Anderson, Grey. "Strategies of Denial". *New Left Review Sidecar*, June 15, 2023. https://newleftreview.org/sidecar/posts/strategies-of-denial.

Andreas, Joel, Sunila S. Kale, Michael Levien and Qian Forrest Zhang. "Rural land dispossession in China and India." *The Journal of Peasant Studies*, 47, 6 (2020): 1109–1142. DOI: 10.1080/03066150.2020.1826452.

"Die Ängste des 'Exportweltmeisters'." *German-Foreign-Policy.com*. 9 August 2021. https://www.german-foreign-policy.com/news/detail/8682/.

Antràs, Pol. "De-globalisation? Global Value Chains in the Post-COVID-19 Age." In *Central Banks in a Shifting World: Conference Proceedings—ECB Forum on Central Banking, 11–12 November 2020*, edited by European Central Bank, 28–80. Frankfurt: European Central Bank, 2021. https://data.europa.eu/doi/10.2866/268938.

Arrighi, Giovanni. *Adam Smith in Beijing: Lineages of the Twenty-first Century*. London: Verso, 2007.

Arrighi, Giovanni. *The Long Twentieth Century*. London: Verso, 1994.

Arslanalp, Serkan, Barry J. Eichengreen, and China Simpson-Bell. "The Stealth Erosion of Dollar Dominance: Active Diversifiers and the Rise of Nontraditional Reserve Currencies." IMF Working Paper No. WP/2022/058. IMF, Washington, DC. 24 March 2022. https://www.imf.org/en/Publications/WP/Issues/2022/03/24/The-Stealth-Erosion-of-Dollar-Dominance-Active-Diversifiers-and-the-Rise-of-Nontraditional-515150.

ASEAN. "ASEAN Hits Historic Milestone with Signing of RCEP." News release, 15 November 2020. https://asean.org/asean-hits-historic-milestone-with-signing-of-rcep/.

Astarian, Bruno. *Luttes de classes dans la Chine des réformes (1978–2009)*. La Bussière: Acratie, 2009.

Astarian, Bruno and Robert Ferro. *Le ménage à trois de la lutte des classes: classe moyenne salariée, prolétariat et capital*, Toulouse: l'Asymétrie, 2019.

Astarian, Bruno and Robert Ferro. "Accouchement difficile—Épisode 3 : Peut-on mettre une crise au congélateur ?" *Hic Salta—Communisation*. April 2021. http://www.hicsalta-communisation.com/accueil/accouchement-difficile-episode-3-peut-on-mettre-une-crise-au-congelateur.

Atlantic Council. *The Longer Telegram. Towards a New American China Strategy*. Washington, DC: Atlantic Council, 2021. https://www.atlanticcouncil.org/content-series/atlantic-council-strategy-paper-series/the-longer-telegram/.

Aufheben. "Class Conflicts in the Transformation of China." *Aufheben* journal, issue 16 (2008): 1–52. https://libcom.org/article/class-conflicts-transformation-china.

Balasz, Étienne. *Chinese Civilization and Bureaucracy; Variations on a Theme*. Translated by H. M. Wright. New Haven: Yale University Press, 1964.

Baldor, Lolita C. "Esper: US to Soon Put Intermediate Range Missile in Asia." *Military Times*. 4 August 2019. https://www.militarytimes.com/news/pentagon-congress/2019/08/04/esper-us-to-soon-put-intermediate-range-missile-in-asia/.

Baldwin, Rebecca and Richard Freeman. "Trade Conflict in the Age of COVID-19." *VoxEU* (Centre for Economic Policy Research). 22 May 2020. https://voxeu.org/article/trade-conflict-age-covid-19.

Baldwin, Richard. *The Globotics Upheaval: Globalization, Robotics and the Future of Work*. London: Weidenfeld & Nicolson, 2019.

Baldwin, Richard. "The peak globalisation myth: Part 1." *VoxEU*. 31 August 2022. https://cepr.org/voxeu/columns/peak-globalisation-myth-part-1.

Bank for International Settlements. *US Dollar Funding: an International Perspective*. Geneva: Bank for International Settlements, June 2020. https://www.bis.org/publ/cgfs65.pdf.

Barker, Tyson. "Withstanding the Storm: The Digital Silk Road, COVID-19 and Europe's Options" in Amighini, Alessia (ed.). "China after COVID-19: Economic Revival and Challenges to the World." *ISPI*. 5 August 2021: 108–38. https://www.ispionline.it/en/publication/china-after-covid-19-economic-revival-and-challenges-world-30780.

Barklie, Glenn. "China's FDI decline: Why are foreign companies decreasing their dependency on Asian giant?" Investment Monitor. 16 February 2023. https://www.investmentmonitor.ai/insights/chinas-fdi-decline-foreign-companies-covid-geopolitics/.

Bateman, John. "The Fevered Anti-China Attitude in Washington Is Going to Backfire." *Politico*. 15 December 2022. https://www.politico.com/news/magazine/2022/12/15/china-tech-decoupling-sanctions-00071723.

Beattie, Alan. "Coronavirus-Induced Reshoring Is Not Happening." *Financial Times*. 30 September 2020. https://www.ft.com/content/e06be6a4-7551-4fdf-adfd-9b20feca353b.

Beckley, Michael. "China's Century? Why America's Edge Will Endure." *International Security* 36, 3 (Winter 2011/12): 41–78.

Beeson, Mark. "Geoeconomics with Chinese Characteristics: The BIS and China's Evolving Grand Strategy." *Economic and Political Studies* 6, 3 (2018): 240–56. https://doi.org/10.1080/20954816.2018.1498988.

Bello, Walden and John Feffer. "Chain-Gang Economics." *Foreign Policy in Focus*. 30 October 2006. https://fpif.org/chain-gang_economics/.

Bergère, Marie-Claire. *Capitalismes et capitalistes en Chine*. Paris: Perrin, 2007.

Berndt, Christian. "Uneven Development, Commodity Chains and the Agrarian Question." *Progress in Human Geography* (2018): 1–14. https://journals.sagepub.com/pb-assets/cmscontent/PHG/Uneven_development-1520613548130.pdf.

Bernstein, Henry. "Some Reflections on Agrarian Change in China." *Journal of Agrarian Change* 15, 3 (2015): 454–77. https://doi.org/10.1111/joac.12116.

Bhadrakumar, M. K. "US' Coercive Diplomacy with Saudi Arabia." *Indian Punchline* (author's blog). 6 May 2022. https://www.indianpunchline.com/us-coercive-diplomacy-with-saudi-arabia/.

Bhusari, Mrugank and Maia Nikoladze. "Russia and China: Partners in Dedollarization." Atlantic Council blog. 18 February 2022. https://www.atlanticcouncil.org/blogs/econographics/russia-and-china-partners-in-dedollarization/.

Blanchette, Jude. "Xi's Gamble: The Race to Consolidate Power and Stave Off Disaster." *Foreign Affairs*. 22 July 2021. https://www.foreignaffairs.com/articles/china/2021-06-22/xis-gamble.

Bleek, Philipp C. "Nuclear Posture Review Leaks; Outlines Targets, Contingencies." News release, Arms Control Association, April 2002. https://www.armscontrol.org/act/2002-04/press-releases/nuclear-posture-review-leaks-outlines-targets-contingencies.

Board of Governors of the Federal Reserve System. "Bank Term Funding Program." Last update: 12 September 2023. https://www.federalreserve.gov/financial-stability/bank-term-funding-program.htm.

Bonnefond, Céline, Matthieu Clément, and François Combarnous. "In Search of the Elusive Chinese Urban Middle Class: An Exploratory Analysis." *Post-Communist Economies* 27 (2015): 41–59. https://doi.org/10.1080/14631377.2015.992223.

Bonvillian, William B. "US Manufacturing Decline and the Rise of New Production Innovation Paradigms." OECD. Paris, 2016. https://www.oecd.org/innovation/us-manufacturing-decline-and-the-rise-of-new-production-innovation-paradigms.htm.

Bordiga, Amadeo. *Mai la merce sfamerà l'uomo* [*Never Will the Commodity Feed Man*]. 1953–4. Milano: Ed. Iskra, 1979.

Bordiga, Amadeo. *Spazio contro cemento*, in *Drammi gialli e sinistri della moderna decadenza sociale* [*Mystery dramas of modern social decadence*]. Milano: Ed. Iskra, 1978.

Bordiga, Amadeo. *Lotta di classi e di stati nel mondo dei popoli non bianchi* [*Class and States Struggles in the World of Non-White Peoples*]. Napoli: La Vecchia Talpa, 1972 (first published in 1958).

Bordiga, Amadeo. *Proprietà e capitale* [*Ownership and Capital*]. *1948–52*. Milano: Ed. Iskra, 1980.

Borger, Julian. "Pentagon Chief's Russia Remarks Show Shift in US's Declared Aims in Ukraine." *The Guardian*. 25 April 2022. https://www.theguardian.com/world/2022/apr/25/russia-weakedend-lloyd-austin-ukraine.

Borin, Alessandro and Michele Mancini, "Measuring What Matters in Global Value Chains and Value-Added Trade." Policy Research Working Paper 8804. World Bank, Washington, DC, 2019. https://documents1.worldbank.org/curated/en/639481554384583291/pdf/Measuring-What-Matters-in-Global-Value-Chains-and-Value-Added-Trade.pdf.

Bown, Chad. "Four Years into the Trade War, Are the US and China Decoupling?" PIIE (Peterson Institute for International Economics). 20 October 2022. https://www.piie.com/blogs/realtime-economics/four-years-trade-war-are-us-and-china-decoupling.

Bown, Chad. "US-China Trade War Tariffs: An Up-to-Date Chart." PIIE. 6 April 2023. https://www.piie.com/research/piie-charts/us-china-trade-war-tariffs-date-chart.

Bradanini, Alberto. *Cina. L'irresistibile ascesa.* Roma: Sandro Teti Editore 2022.

Brandt, Loren, John Litwack, Elitza Mileva, Luhang Wang, Yifan Zhang, and Luan Zhao. "China's Productivity Slowdown and Future Growth Potential." Policy Research Working Paper 9298. World Bank, Washington, DC. June 2020. https://elibrary.worldbank.org/doi/epdf/10.1596/1813-9450-9298.

Bräutigam, Deborah. "U.S. Politicians get China in Africa All Wrong." *The Washington Post.* 12 April 2018. https://www.washingtonpost.com/news/theworldpost/wp/2018/04/12/china-africa/.

Bräutigam, Deborah and Kevin Gallaghe. "Bartering Globalization: China's Commodity-Backed Finance in Africa and Latin America." *Global Policy* 5, 3 (2014): 346–52. https://doi.org/10.1111/1758-5899.12138.

Bremmer, Ian. *The End of the Free Market: Who Wins the War Between States and Corporations?* London: Portfolio 2010.

Brown, Alexander, Jacob Gunter, and Max J. Zenglein. "Course Correction. China's Shifting Approach to Globalisation." *Merics China Monitor.* 19 October 2021. https://merics.org/sites/default/files/2021-10/MERICS-ChinaMonitor_Globalization_2021-10-13.pdf.

Brunhoff, Suzanne de. *Marx on money.* New York: Urizen Books, 1976.

Brunhoff, Suzanne de. *The state, capital and economic policy.* London: Pluto Press, 1978.

Brzezinski, Zbigniew. *The Grand Chessboard: American Primacy and its Geostrategic Imperatives.* New York: Basic Books, 1997.

Brzezinski, Zbigniew. "Toward a Global Realignment." *The American Interest* 11, 6 (17 April 2016). https://www.the-american-interest.com/2016/04/17/toward-a-global-realignment/.

Bukharin, Nikolai. *Imperialism and World Economy.* New York: Monthly Review Press Classics, 1929.

Butollo, Florian. *The End of Cheap Labour? Industrial Transformation and "Social Upgrading" in China.* Frankfurt: Campus Verlag, 2014.

Butollo, Florian and Tobias ten Brink. "Challenging the Atomization of Discontent: Patterns of Migrant-Worker Protest in China during the Series of Strikes in 2010." *Critical Asian Studies* 44, 3 (2012): 419–40. https://doi.org/10.1080/14672715.2012.711978.

Cai, Jane. "Property Tax Concerns for China's Homeowners, Buyers amid Xi Jinping's Common Prosperity Drive." *South China Morning Post*. 23 November 2021. https://www.scmp.com/economy/china-economy/article/3156951/property-tax-concerns-chinas-homeowners-buyers-amid-xi.

Campbell, Kurt M. and Rush Doshi. "How America Can Shore Up Asian Order: A Strategy for Restoring Balance and Legitimacy." *Foreign Affairs*. 12 January 2021.

Carchedi, Guglielmo and Michael Roberts, "The Economics of Modern Imperialism." *Historical Materialism* 29, 4 (2021): 23–69. https://doi.org/10.1163/1569206X-12341959.

Carter, Lance. "Auto Industry Strikes in China." *Insurgent Notes*. October 2010. http://insurgentnotes.com/2010/10/auto-industry-strikes-in-china/.

Case, Anne and Angus Deaton. *Death of Despair and the Future of Capitalism*. Princeton, NJ: Princeton University Press, 2020.

CEIC. "China's Holding of US Treasury Securities 2000–2023." https://www.ceicdata.com/en/china/holdings-of-us-treasury-securities/holdings-of-us-treasury-securities.

Cesaroni, Claudio. "Non solo Evergrande." *ISPI*. 18 November 2021. https://www.ispionline.it/it/pubblicazione/non-solo-evergrande-32378.

Chan, Anita. *China's Workers under Assault*. London: Routledge, 2001.

Chan, Anita. "Labor Unrest and the Role of Unions." *China Daily*. 18 June 2010.

Chan, Jenny. "The Collective Resistance of China's Industrial Workers", in Maurizio Atzeni, Immanuel Ness (eds.), *Global Perspectives on Workers' and Labour Organizations*: 107–25. Singapore: Springer, 2018.

Chan, Jenny and Pun Ngai. "Suicide as Protest for the New Generation of Chinese Migrant Workers: Foxconn, Global Capital, and the State." *Asia-Pacific Journal: Japan Focus* 37, 2.10 (2010), article ID 3408. https://apjjf.org/-Jenny-Chan/3408/article.html.

Chan, Jenny and Mark Selden. "The Labour Politics of China's Rural Migrant Workers." *Globalizations* 14, 2 (2017): 259–71. https://doi.org/10.1080/14747731.2016.1200263.

Chan, Kam Wing and Li Zhang. "The *Hukou* System and Rural-Urban Migration in China: Processes and Changes." *China Quarterly* 160 (1999): 818–55. https://doi.org/10.1017/S0305741000001351.

Chen, Aizhu. "Russia, China Agree 30-Year Gas Deal via New Pipeline, to Settle in Euros." *Reuters*, 4 February 2022. https://www.reuters.com/world/asia-pacific/exclusive-russia-china-agree-30-year-gas-deal-using-new-pipeline-source-2022-02-04/.

Chen, Chih-Jou Jay. "Peasant protests over land seizures in rural China." *The Journal of Peasant Studies*, 47, 6 (2020):1327–47. DOI: 10.1080/03066150.2020.1824182.

Chen, Gang. "Consolidating Leninist Control of State-Owned Enterprises: China's State Capitalism 2.0" in *China's Political Economy in the Xi Jinping Epoch: Domestic and Global Dimensions*, edited by Lowell Dittmer. Singapore: World Scientific, 2021: 43–60. https://doi.org/10.1142/9789811226588_0002.

Chen, Guidi and Wu Chutao. *Will the Boat Sink the Water? The Life of China's Peasants*. New York: Publicaffairs, 2003.

Cheney, Clayton T. "The digital silk road: Understanding Chinas technological rise and the implications for global governance" in *Research Handbook on the Belt and Road Initiative*, ed. J. C. Liow, H. Liu, and G. Xue: 88–101. Cheltenham: Edward Elgar Publishing, 2021.

Cheng, Evelyn. "Here's what the U.S. Hopes China Will Do after Raimondo's Trip." CNBC. 30 August 2023. https://www.cnbc.com/2023/08/30/heres-what-the-us-hopes-china-will-do-after-raimondos-trip.html.

Cheng, Hong, Ruixue Jia, Dandan Li, and Hongbin Li. "The Rise of Robots in China." *Journal of Economic Perspectives* 33, 2 (2019): 71–88. https://pubs.aeaweb.org/doi/pdfplus/10.1257/jep.33.2.71.

Cheng, Li. "Chinese Scholarship on the Middle Class: From Social Stratification to Political Potential" in Cheng, Li (ed.), *China's Emerging Middle Class: Beyond Economic Transformation*. Washington, DC: Brookings Institution Press, 2010: 55–83.

Cheng, Li. "Characterizing China's Middle Class: Heterogeneous Composition and Multiple Identities" in Cheng, Li (ed.), *China's Emerging Middle Class: Beyond Economic Transformation*. Washington, DC: Brookings Institution Press, 2010: 135–56.

Chi, Ch'ao Ting. *Key Economic Areas in Chinese History*. London: Routledge, 2019 (first published in 1936).

China Center, U.S. Chamber of Commerce. *Understanding U.S._China Decoupling: Macro Trends and Industry Impacts*. 2021 (https://www.uschamber.com/sites/default/files/024001_us_china_decoupling_report_fin.pdf).

"China Eases Mortgage Down Payment to 20% for First Homes." *US-China Business Council*. 2023. https://www.uschina.org/china-hub/china-eases-mortgage-down-payment-20-first-homes.

"China Oil Imports from Russia Surge amid Ukraine War Sanctions." *Al Jazeera*. 20 June 2022. https://www.aljazeera.com/economy/2022/6/20/china-oil-imports-from-sanctioned-russia-skyrocket-surpass-saudi.

China's Minister of National Defense Li Shangfu. "20th Asia Security Summit—The Shangri-La Dialogue—Fifth Plenary Session." The 20th IISS-Shangri-La Dialogue. 4 June 2023. https://www.iiss.org/globalassets/media-library---content--migration/files/shangri-la-dialogue/2023/final-transcripts/p-5/general-li-shangfu-state-councilor-minister-of-national-defense-china---as-delivered.pdf.

"China's State Banks Seen Selling Dollars for Yuan." Reuters. 17 August 2023. https://www.reuters.com/markets/currencies/chinas-major-state-banks-sell-dollars-yuan-london-ny-hours-sources-2023-08-17/.

"China Will Not Expand Its Property Tax Trial This Year." *Bloomberg News*. 16 March 2022. https://www.bloomberg.com/news/articles/2022-03-16/china-will-not-expand-its-property-tax-trial-this-year-l0tex2zh.

Christensen, Neils. "*China settled its first LNG trade in yuan.*" *Kitco News*. 29 March 2023. https://www.kitco.com/news/2023-03-29/China-settled-its-first-LNG-trade-in-yuan-but-gold-remains-the-bigger-winner-in-the-global-de-dollarization-trend.html.

Chuang Collective. "Sorghum & Steel. The Chinese Developmental Regime and the Forging of China." *Chuang*, issue 1, 2016. https://chuangcn.org/journal/one/sorghum-and-steel/.

Chuang Collective. "Gleaning the Welfare Fields. Rural Struggles in China since 1959." *Chuang*, issue 1, 2016. https://chuangcn.org/journal/one/gleaning-the-welfare-fields/.

Chuang Collective. "Red Dust: The Transition to Capitalism in China." *Chuang*, issue 2, 2018. https://chuangcn.org/journal/two/red-dust/.

Chuang Collective. "The Changing Geography of Chinese Industry: Data Brief." *Chuang* blog, 5 August 2019. https://chuangcn.org/2019/08/the-changing-geography-of-chinese-industry-data-brief/.

Chuang Collective. "Free to Move, Forced to Move: The Present State of the Hukou System." *Chuang* blog, 18 May 2020. https://chuangcn.org/2020/05/free-to-move/.

Chuang Collective. "Measuring the Profitability of Chinese Industry: Data Brief." *Chuang* blog, 21 June 2020. https://chuangcn.org/2020/06/measuring-profitability/.

Chuang Collective. "China FAQ. Isn't China the world's sweatshop?" *Chuang* blog. 22 May 2023. https://chuangcn.org/2023/05/china-faq-sweatshop/.

Cok, Cagan. "ASML Hit with New Dutsch Limits on Chip Gear Export to China." *Bloomberg*. 30 June 2023. https://www.bloomberg.com/news/articles/2023-06-30/dutch-publish-new-limits-on-asml-s-chip-gear-exports-to-china.

The Conference Board. "Global Productivity Growth Extends Slowing Trend." 3 May 2021. https://www.conference-board.org/topics/natural-disasters-pandemics/global-productivity.

Congressional Research Service. *Semiconductors: U.S. Industry, Global Competition, and Federal Policy*. 26 October 2020. https://crsreports.congress.gov/product/pdf/R/R46581.

Conte, Niccolò. "Charted: America's Import Reliance of Critical Minerals." *Visual Capitalist*. 4 August 2023. https://elements.visualcapitalist.com/americas-import-reliance-of-critical-minerals-charted/.

Council on Foreign Relations. "Assessing China's digital silk road initiative." 2021. https://www.cfr.org/china-digital-silk-road/.

Ctpost. "Sen. Blumenthal (opinion): 'Zelensky doesn't want or need our troops. But he deeply and desperately needs the tools to win.'" 29 August 2023. https://www.ctpost.com/opinion/article/sen-blumenthal-opinion-ukraine-tip-spear-18335871.php.

Cunningham, Fiona S. "Cooperation under Asymmetry? The Future of US-China Nuclear Relations." *Washington Quarterly* 44, 2 (2021): 159–80. https://doi.org/10.1080/0163660X.2021.1934253.

Dadush, Uri. "The Impact of the New Asian Trade Mega-Deal on the European Union." Bruegel blog. 19 November 2020. https://www.bruegel.org/blog-post/impact-new-asian-trade-mega-deal-european-union.

Dahlman, Abigal and Mary E. Lovely. "US-led effort to diversify Indo-Pacific supply chains away from China runs counter to trends." PIIE. 6 September 2023. https://www.piie.com/blogs/realtime-economics/us-led-effort-diversify-indo-pacific-supply-chains-away-china-runs-counter?utm_source=update-newsletter&utm_medium=email&utm_campaign=piie-insider&utm_term=yyyy-mm-dd.

Davies, Sally and Christopher Kent. "US Dollar Funding: An International Perspective." Working Group, CGFS Papers 65. Basel: Bank for International Settlements, June 2020. https://www.bis.org/publ/cgfs65.pdf.

Davis, Daniel. "The Hard Reality." 1945 Blog. 7 September 2023. https://www.19fortyfive.com/2023/08/the-hard-reality-ukraines-last-gasp-offensive-has-failed/.

Davis, Stuart and Immanuel Ness (eds.). *Sanctions as War: Anti-Imperialist Perspectives on American Geo-Economic Strategy*. Leiden: Brill, 2022.

Day, Alexander F. *The Peasant in Postsocialist China: History, Politics and Capitalism*. Cambridge: Cambridge University Press, 2013.

De Guzman, Chad. "U.S. and Philippines Announce New Sites for Military Cooperation." *Time*. 4 April 2023. https://time.com/6268379/philippines-us-military-bases-china/.

Di Conzo, Dario. "The AIIB in the Post-Pandemic World." T.Note 85. Turin World Affair Institute, 16 July 2020. https://www.twai.it/journal/tnote-85/.

DiPippo, Gerard, Ilaria Mazzocco, Scott Kennedy, and Matthew P. Goodman. "Red Ink: Estimating Chinese Industrial Policy Spending in Comparative Perspective." Washington, DC: *Center for Strategic and International Studies*, 2022. https://www.csis.org/analysis/red-ink-estimating-chinese-industrial-policy-spending-comparative-perspective.

Di Stefano, Erica. "COVID-19 and Global Value Chains." Occasional Papers No. 618. Rome: Banca d'Italia, April 2021. https://www.bancaditalia.it/pubblicazioni/qef/2021-0618/index.html.

Doi, Noriyuki and Saki Akita. "Yuan exceeds dollar in China's bilateral trade for first time." *Nikkei ASIA*. 24 July 2023. https://asia.nikkei.com/Business/Markets/Currencies/Yuan-exceeds-dollar-in-China-s-bilateral-trade-for-first-time.

Dooley, Michael P., David Folkerts-Landau, and Peter Garber. "An essay on the revived Bretton Woods system". Working Paper 9971. *NBER*. September 2003. https://www.nber.org/papers/w9971.pdf.

Doshi, Rush. *The Long Game: China's Grand Strategy to Displace American Order.* New York: Oxford University Press, 2021.

Dou, Eva. "New Phone Sparks Worry China Has Found a Way Around U.S. Tech Limits." *The Washington Post.* 2 September 2023. https://www.washingtonpost.com/technology/2023/09/02/huawei-raimondo-phone-chip-sanctions/.

Dunn, Gibson. "China's 'Blocking Statute'—New Chinese Rules to Counter the Application of Extraterritorial Foreign Laws." 13 January 2021. https://www.gibsondunn.com/wp-content/uploads/2021/01/chinas-blocking-statute-new-chinese-rules-to-counter-the-application-of-extraterritorial-foreign-laws.pdf.

Durand, Cédric. "La période qui s'ouvre pourrait être celle d'une longue crise financière au ralenti." *Le Monde.* 24 March 2023.

"Dutch to restrict semiconductor tech exports to China, joining US effort." *CNN.* 8 March 2023. https://edition.cnn.com/2023/03/08/tech/dutch-china-chips-ban-hnk-intl/index.html.

Edel, Charles. "A Fault Line in the Pacific: The Danger of China's Growing Sway Over Island Nations." *Foreign Affairs*, 3 June 2022. https://www.foreignaffairs.com/articles/china/2022-06-03/fault-line-pacific.

Elvin, Mark. "Why China Failed to Create an Endogenous Industrial Capitalism: A Critique of Max Weber's Explanation." *Theory and Society* 13, 3 (1984): 379–91. http://www.jstor.org/stable/657457.

Engelke, Peter and Emily Weinsten. "Global Strategy 2023: Winning the tech race with China." Atlantic Council Strategy Paper Series. 27 June 2023. https://www.atlanticcouncil.org/content-series/atlantic-council-strategy-paper-series/global-strategy-2023-winning-the-tech-race-with-china/.

Erlanger, Steven, David Pierson and Linsey Chutel. "Iran, Saudi Arabia and Egypt Invited to Join Emerging Nations Group." *The New York Times.* 24 August 2023. https://www.nytimes.com/2023/08/24/world/europe/brics-expansion-xi-lula.html.

Ernst, Dieter. "Competing in Artificial Intelligence Chips: China's Challenge amid Technology War." *Centre for International Governance Innovation*, 2020. https://www.cigionline.org/publications/competing-artificial-intelligence-chips-chinas-challenge-amid-technology-war/.

European Commission. "EU-US Trade and Technology Council Inaugural Joint Statement." 29 September 2021. https://ec.europa.eu/commission/presscorner/detail/en/STATEMENT_21_4951.

Evenett, Simon J. and Johannes Fritz, "*The* 27th Global Trade Alert—Advancing Sustainable Development With FDI: Why Policy Must Be Reset." London: *Centre for Economic Policy Research,* 2021. https://www.globaltradealert.org/reports/75.

Every, Michael and Michael Magdovitz. *"Biblical, Lean, and Mean."* Utrecht: Rabobank—RaboResearch Global Economics & Markets, 17 March 2021. https://research.rabobank.com/markets/en/detail/publication-detail.html?id=291426.

Fajgelbaum, Pablo, Pinelopi K. Goldberg, Patrick J. Kennedy, Amit Khandelwal, and Daria Taglioni. "The US-China Trade War and Global Reallocations." Working Paper 29562. NBER. 2023.

Fajgelbaum, Pablo D., and Amit K. Khandelwal. 2022. "The Economic Impacts of the US–China Trade War." *Annual Review of Economics* 14: 205–28. https://doi.org/10.1146/annurev-economics-051420-110410.

Fajgelbaum, Pablo, Pinelopi K. Goldberg, Patrick J. Kennedy, Amit Khandelwal, and Daria Taglioni. "The US-China Trade War and Global Reallocations." Working Paper No. 29562. NBER. 2023.

Fasulo, Filippo. "Strategie Globali: Indo-Pacifico, mare loro?" *ISPI*. 22 September 2021. https://www.ispionline.it/it/pubblicazione/strategie-globali-indo-pacifico-mare-loro-31743.

"Federal Deficit and Debt: October 2022." Peter G. Peterson Foundation. https://www.pgpf.org/the-current-federal-budget-deficit/budget-deficit-october-2022.

Feng, Kaidong, Yin Li, and William Lazonick (eds.). "Transforming China's Industrial Innovation in the New Era." Special feature, *China Review* 22, 1 (February 2022): 1–353.

Feng, Weijiang. "The Theoretical Foundations of the Global Security Initiative: The Holistic View of National Security." *Interpret: China*. Originally published 16 June 2022 at Chinese Academy of Social Sciences. https://interpret.csis.org/translations/the-theoretical-foundation-of-the-global-security-initiative-the-holistic-view-of-national-security/.

Fernandes, Marco. "Brics gain new chances to improve global development." *AsiaTimes*. 13 April 2023. https://asiatimes.com/2023/04/brics-gains-new-chance-to-improve-global-development/.

Financial Times Editorial Board. "China's emerging Belt and Road debt crisis." *Financial Times*. 2022. https://www.ft.com/content/eb2d89f6-afd1-491e-b753-863e9727f6de.

Foda, Karim. *The Productivity Slump: A Summary of the Evidence*. Washington, DC: Brookings Institution, 2016.

Frankopan, Peter. *The Silk Roads: A New History of the World*. Bloomsbury, London, 2015.

Freund, Caroline, Aaditya Mattoo, Alen Mulabdic, and Michele Ruta. "Is US Trade Policy Reshaping Global Supply Chains?" Paper presented at the IMF Conference on Geoeconomic Fragmentation, May 2023.

Freymann, Eyck and Brian Y. S. Wong. "Young People in China Are Losing Faith in the West." *Foreign Policy Magazine*, 22 March 2021. https://foreignpolicy.com/2021/03/22/racist-attack-asian-americans-china-lost-faith-west/.

Friedman, George. "Lo Spazio serve a farci la guerra." *Limes. Rivista Italiana di Geopolitica.* December 2021. https://www.limesonline.com/cartaceo/lo-spazio-serve-a-preparare-le-guerre-di-domani.

Friedmann, Harriet. "International Regimes of Food and Agriculture since 1870", in *Peasants and Peasant Societies: Selected Readings,* edited by Teodor Shanin, 2nd ed. Oxford: Basil Blackwell, 1987: 258–76 (1st ed., Harmondsworth: Penguin, 1971).

Fuest, Clemens, Felix Hugger, Samina Sultan, and Jing Xing. "Chinese Acquisitions Abroad: Are They Different?" Working Paper No. 7585. Munich: Center for Economic Studies & Ifo Institute (*CESifo*), April 2019. https://www.econbiz.de/Record/chinese-acquisitions-abroad-are-they-different-fuest-clemens/10011992349.

Fun, Haishan and Nada Hamadeh. "New Results from the International Comparison Program Shed Light on the Size of the Global Economy." *World Bank blog,* 19 May 2021. https://blogs.worldbank.org/opendata/new-results-international-comparison-program-shed-light-size-global-economy.

Galbraith, Andrew. "Explainer: Foreign Access to China's $16 Trillion Bond Market." Reuters, 23 September 2020. https://www.reuters.com/article/china-bonds-market/explainer-foreign-access-to-chinas-16-trillion-bond-market-idUSKCN26E0UE.

Galbraith, James. "China in Decline? New US Narrative Is Geared towards 2024 Election." *South China Morning Post.* 18 August 2023. https://www.scmp.com/comment/opinion/article/3231483/china-decline-new-us-narrative-geared-towards-2024-election.

Garcia Herrero, Alicia. "Resilience of Global Supply Chain: Facts and Implications." Working Paper 1398. Tokyo: Asian Development Bank Institute, 2023. https://doi.org/10.56506/UKPK2510.

Garcìa-Herrero, Alicia and Junyu Tan. "Deglobalisation in the context of Us-China decoupling." Policy Contribution 2020/21. Bruegel. 21 December 2020. https://www.bruegel.org/sites/default/files/wp_attachments/PC-21-2020-211220.pdf.

Gaulard, Mylène. "Changes in the Chinese Property Market: An Indicator of the Difficulties Faced by Local Authorities." Translated by Will Thornely. *China Perspectives* 2 (2013): 3–14. https://doi.org/10.4000/chinaperspectives.6143.

Gaulard, Mylène. *Karl Marx à Pékin : Les racines de la crise en Chine capitaliste.* Paris: Demopolis, 2014.

Gereffi, Gary. 2018. *Global value chains and development: Redefining the contours of 21st century capitalism.* Cambridge: Cambridge University Press.

Gernet, Jacques. *A History of Chinese Civilization.* Cambridge: Cambridge University Press, 1995.

"Die Geschäftsgrundlage der deutschen industrie." German-Foreign-Policy.com. 18 October 2021. https://www.german-foreign-policy.com/news/detail/8735/.

Gilli, Andrea and Mauro Gilli. "Why China Has Not Caught Up Yet: Military-Technological Superiority and the Limits of Imitation, Reverse Engineering, and

Cyber Espionage." *International Security* 43, no. 3 (2019): 141–89. https://doi.org/10 .1162/isec_a_00337.
Goldman, David P. "China's Digital Yuan Displaces the Dollar." *Asia Times*, 21 April 2021. https://asiatimes.com/2021/04/chinas-digital-yuan-displaces-the-dollar/.
Goodman, David S. G "Middle Class China: Dreams and Aspirations." *Journal of Chinese Political Science* 19 (2014): 49–64.
Green, Brendam R. and Caitlin Talmadge. "The Consequences of Conquest. Why Indo-Pacific Power Hinges on Taiwan." *Foreign Affairs*. July-August 2022. https://www.for eignaffairs.com/articles/china/2022-06-16/consequences-conquest-taiwan-indo -pacific.
Grieger, Gisela. "China's Maritime Silk Road Initiative Increasingly Touches the EU." Briefing paper. *European Parliamentary Research Service*. March 2018. https://www .europarl.europa.eu/RegData/etudes/BRIE/2018/614767/EPRS_BRI(2018)614767 _EN.pdf.
Guidi, Alberto. "Poli manifatturieri: geo-rivoluzione in corso." *ISPI*. 21April 2023. https://www.ispionline.it/it/pubblicazione/poli-manifatturieri-geo-rivoluzione-in -corso-123781.
Guidi, Alberto and Davide Tentori. "L'anno di Biden in 13 grafici." *ISPI*. 5 November 2021. https://www.ispionline.it/it/pubblicazione/lanno-di-biden-13-grafici-32268.
Gulati, Ashok and Shenggen Fan. *The Dragon and the Elephant: Agricultural and Rural Reforms in China and India*. Baltimore, MD: John Hopkins University Press, 2007.
Gürel, Burak. "Semi-private Landownership and Capitalist Agriculture in Contemporary China." *Review of Radical Political Economics* 51, 4 (2019): 650–69. https://doi.org/10 .1177/0486613419849683.
Gürel, Burak and Mina Kozluca. "Chinese Investment in Turkey: The Belt and Road Initiative, Rising Expectations, Ground Realities." *European Review* 30, 6 (2022): 806–34. https://doi.org/10.1017/S1062798721000296.
Haasbroek, Michiel. "A Glimpse into China's Changed Financial Sector." Mercator Institute for China Studies (*MERICS*). 15 July 2020. https://merics.org/en/comm ent/glimpse-chinas-changed-financial-sector.
Hanania, Richard. "The Inevitable Rise of China: U.S. Options with Less Indo-Pacific Influence." *Defense Priorities*. 26 May 2021. https://www.defensepriorities.org/exp lainers/the-inevitable-rise-of-china-us-options-with-less-indo-pacific-influence.
Hao, Qi and Li Zhongjin. "Giovanni Arrighi in Beijing: Rethinking the Transformation of the Labor Supply in Rural China During the Reform Era". Working paper 455. *Political Economy Research Institute*. February 2018. https://doi.org/10.7275/27274276.
Hao Ren et al. "Factory Stories: On the Conditions and Struggles in Chinese Workplaces." 2012–15. http://www.gongchao.org/en/factory-stories/.

Harrison, Bennett and Barry Bluestone. *Deindustrialization of America: Plant Closings, Community Abandonment and the Dismantling of Basic Industry*. New York: Basic Books, 1984.

Hart-Landsberg, Martin and Paul Burkert. *China and Socialism: Market Reforms and Class Struggle*. New York: Monthly Review Press, 2005.

Hayami, Akira. *Japan's Industrious Revolution: Economic and Social Transformations in the Early Modern Period*. Tokyo and London: Springer, 2015.

He, Alex. "What Do China's High Patent Numbers Really Mean?" *Centre for International Governance Innovation*. 20 April 2021. https://www.cigionline.org/articles/what-do-chinas-high-patent-numbers-really-mean/.

He, Xuefeng. "The Question of Land Privatisation in China's Urban-Rural Integration." *China Left Review*, 1, 2006.

Herrera, Rémy and Zhiming Long. "Capital Accumulation, Profit Rates and Cycles in China from 1952 to 2014." *Journal of Innovation Economics & Management*, vol. 23, 2, 2017: 59–82.

Herrera, Rémy and Zhiming Long. *La Chine est-elle capitaliste?* Paris: Éditions Critiques, 2019.

Herrera, Rémy and Zhiming Long. *Dynamique de l'économie chinoise : croissance, cycles et crises de 1949 à nos jours*. Paris: Éditions Critiques, 2021.

Hille, Kathrin. "The Great Uncoupling: One Supply Chain for China, One for Everywhere Else." *Financial Times*. 3 October 2020. https://www.ft.com/content/40ebd786-a576-4dc2-ad38-b97f796b72a0.

Hille, Kathrin. "China Builds Coalition to Counter America's 'Barbaric and Bloody' Leadership." *Financial Times*. 22 May 2022. https://www.ft.com/content/377cdb02-8a45-4ba2-b6ee-88620eb48f0b.

Hillman, Jonathan E. *The Digital Silk Road: China's quest to wire the world and win the future*. London: Profile Books, 2021.

Hoekman, Bernard (ed.). *The Global Trade Slowdown: A New Normal?*. London: Centre for Economic Policy Research, 2015. https://cepr.org/system/files/publication-files/60235-the_global_trade_slowdown_a_new_normal.pdf.

Holz, Carsten A. "Industrial Policies and the Changing Patterns of Investment in the Chinese Economy." *China Journal* 81 (2018). https://doi.org/10.1086/699877.

Horn, Sebastian, Brad Parks, Carmen M. Reinhart and Christoph Trebesch. "China as international lender of last resort." Working Paper 124. *Aiddata*. 2023.

Horn, Sebastian, Carmen M. Reinhart and Christoph Trebesch. "China's Overseas Lending." Working Paper 26050. NBER. July 2019. http://www.nber.org/papers/w26050.

Horn, Sebastian, Carmen M. Reinhart and Christoph Trebesch. "How Much Money Does the World Owe China?" *Harvard Business Review*. 26 February 2020. https://hbr.org/2020/02/how-much-money-does-the-world-owe-china.

Horn, Sebastian, Carmen M. Reinhart and Christoph Trebesch. "China's overseas lending and the war in Ukraine." *VoxEU*. 11 April 2022. https://cepr.org/voxeu/columns/chinas-overseas-lending-and-war-ukraine.

Hou, Aijun. "Le dieci lezioni che la Cina ha appreso dal crollo dell'URSS." *Limes*. 13 December 2021. https://www.limesonline.com/cartaceo/le-dieci-lezioni-che-la-cina-ha-appreso-dal-crollo-dellurss.

Howell, Jude and Jane Duckett. "Reassessing the Hu-Wen Era: A Golden Age or Lost Decade for Social Policy in China?" *China Quarterly* 237 (2019): 1–14. https://doi.org/10.1017/S0305741018001200.

Howell, Michael J. *Capital Wars. The Rise of Global Liquidity*. London: Palgrave Macmillan, 2020.

Hruby, Aubrey. "Dispelling the Dominant Myths of China in Africa." *Atlantic Council* blog. 3 September 2018. https://www.atlanticcouncil.org/blogs/new-atlanticist/dispelling-the-dominant-myths-of-china-in-africa/.

Hu, Wei. "Possible Outcomes of the Russo-Ukrainian War and China's Choice." Translated by Jiaqi Liu, *U.S. China Perception Monitor* (published by the Carter Center). 12 March 2022. https://uscnpm.org/2022/03/12/hu-wei-russia-ukraine-war-china-choice/.

Huang, Philip C. *The Peasant Family and Rural Development in the Yangzi Delta, 1350–1988*. Stanford, CA: Stanford University Press, 1990.

Huang, Philip C., Gao Yuan, and Yusheng Peng. "Capitalization without Proletarianization in China's Agricultural Development." *Modern China* 38, 2 (2012): 139–73. https://doi.org/10.1177/0097700411435620.

Huang, Ruihan and Joshua Henderson. "Is There a Method Behind China's Tech Crackdown Madness?" *Macro Polo* (Paulson Institute). 21 October 2021. https://macropolo.org/china-tech-crackdown-software-hardware/?rp=m.

Huang, Ruihan and AJ Cortese. "Nanometers over GDP: Can Technocrat Leaders Improve China's Industrial Policy?" *Macro Polo*. 23 May 2023. https://macropolo.org/analysis/technocrat-leaders-china-industrial-policy/?utm_source=MacroPolo&utm_campaign=95f36962d2-EMAIL_CAMPAIGN_2018_11_27_04_41_COPY_01&utm_medium=email&utm_term=0_791224187b-95f36962d2-438868821.

Huang, Tianlei. "Why China Still Needs Hong Kong." PIIE. 15 July 2019. https://www.piie.com/blogs/china-economic-watch/why-china-still-needs-hong-kong.

Huang, Tianlei and Nicholas R. Lardy. "China is Too Tied to the Global Economy to Risk Helping Russia." PIIE. 15 March 2022. https://www.piie.com/blogs/realtime-economic-issues-watch/china-too-tied-global-economy-risk-helping-russia.

Huang, Yiping. "Understanding China's Belt & Road Initiative: Motivation, Framework and Assessment." *China Economic Review* 40 (2016): 314–21. https://doi.org/10.1016/j.chieco.2016.07.007.

Hudson, Michael. *Super Imperialism: The Economic Strategy of American Empire*. New York: Holt, Rinehart and Winston, 1972.

Hufbauer, Gary Clyde, Megan Hogan, and Yilin Wang. "For Inflation Relief, the United States Should Look to Trade Liberalization." Policy Briefs 22–4. PIIE. March 2022. https://www.piie.com/publications/policy-briefs/inflation-relief-united-states-should-look-trade-liberalization.

Hufbauer, Gary Clyde and Megan Hogan. "CHIPS Act Will Spur US Production but Not Foreclose China." PIIE. October 2022. https://www.piie.com/sites/default/files/2022-10/pb22-13.pdf.

Hung, Ho-Fung 2022. *Clash of empires: From 'Chimerica' to the 'new cold war'*. Cambridge, UK: Cambridge University Press.

Hung, Ho-Fung. "America's Head Servant? The PRC's Dilemma in the Global Crisis." *New Left Review* 60 (Nov/Dec 2009): 5–25. https://newleftreview.org/issues/ii60/articles/ho-fung-hung-america-s-head-servant.

Huntington, Samuel. *The Clash of Civilizations and the Remaking of World Order*. New York: Simon & Schuster, 1996.

Huopytari, Mikko, Jacob Gunter, Carl Hayward, Max J. Zenglein, John Lee, Rebecca Arcesati, Caroline Meinhardt, Ester Cañada Amela, and Tom Groot Haar. *Decoupling: Severed Ties and Patchwork Globalisation*. Beijing: European Union Chamber of Commerce in China; Berlin: Mercator Institute for China Studies (MERICS). 14 January 2021. https://merics.org/en/report/decoupling-severed-ties-and-patchwork-globalisation.

Ignatius, David. "How China Is Heralding the Beginnings of a Multipolar Middle East." *The Washington Post*. 16 March 2023. https://www.washingtonpost.com/opinions/2023/03/16/china-saudi-arabia-iran-middle-east-change/.

ILO, *Global Wage Report 2008/9—Minimum Wages and Collective Bargaining: Towards Policy Coherence*. 2008. https://www.ilo.org/wcmsp5/groups/public/---dgreports/---dcomm/documents/publication/wcms_100786.pdf.

IMF. *World Economic Outlook 2023. A Rocky Recovery*. Washington, DC: IMF Publication Services, 2023. https://www.imf.org/en/Publications/WEO/Issues/2023/04/11/world-economic-outlook-april-2023.

IMF. *Geoeconomic fragmentation and the future of multilateralism*. Washington, DC: IMF Publication Services, 2023.

Information Office of the State Council, The People's Republic of China. *China's National Defence in 2010*. Beijing. March 2011. https://www.fmprc.gov.cn/mfa_eng/wjb_663304/zzjg_663340/jks_665232/kjfywj_665252/201104/t20110402_599668.html.

Intan Suwandi, R. Jamil Jonna, and John Bellamy Foster, "Global Commodity Chains and the New Imperialism." *Monthly Review* 70, no. 10 (March 2019): 1–24.

ISPI. "Global Watch: Speciale Geoeconomia n.72." 24 September 2021. https://www.ispionline.it/it/pubblicazione/global-watch-speciale-geoeconomia-n72-31775.

ISPI. "The Gulf and China: A Broadening Partnership?" ISPI MED This Week. 14 January 2022. https://www.ispionline.it/en/publication/gulf-and-china-broadening-partnership-32872.

Italian Trade Agency. "Il mercato dei macchinari in Cina." March 2020. https://www.ucimu.it/fileadmin/public/Documenti_PDF/IL_MERCATO_DEI_MACCHINARI_IN_CINA_01.pdf.

Iwamoto, Kentaro. "Indo-Pacific Economic Framework is not a FTA: 5 Things to Know." *Nikkei Asia.* 19 May 2022. https://asia.nikkei.com/Politics/International-relations/Biden-s-Asia-policy/Indo-Pacific-Economic-Framework-is-not-an-FTA-5-things-to-know.

Jamrisko, Michelle. "China No Match for Japan in Southeast Asia Infrastructure Race." BQ *Prime* (Bloomberg). 25 June 2019. https://www.bloombergquint.com/china/china-no-match-for-japan-in-southeast-asia-infrastructure-race.

Javorcik, Beata, Lucas Kitzmueller, Helena Schweiger, and Muhammed Yildirim. "Economic Costs of Friend-Shoring." EBRD Working Paper No. 274. London: Centre for Economic Policy Research, 2022. https:// cepr .org/publications/ dp17764.

Johnson, Robert C. and Guillermo Noguera. "A Portrait of Trade in Value-Added over Four Decades." *Review of Economics and Statistics* 99, 5 (2017): 896–911.

Jones, Marc. "Countries repatriating gold in wake of sanctions against Russia." Reuters. 10 July 2023. https://www.reuters.com/business/finance/countries-repatriating-gold-wake-sanctions-against-russia-study-2023-07-10/.

Kaplan, Stephen B. "The Rise of Patient Capital: The Political Economy of Chinese Global Finance." Working paper, IIEP-WP-2018-2. Institute for International Economic Policy, Elliott School of International Affairs, George Washington University. July 2018. https://www2.gwu.edu/~iiep/assets/docs/papers/2018WP/KaplanIIEP2018-2.pdf.

Kašin, Vasily. "La russia cosmica non rinuncia alla Cina." [Cosmic Russia Will not Give Up on China] *Limes.* December 2021.

Kearney. "The 2021 Foreign Direct Investment (FDI) Confidence Index". 2021. https://www.kearney.com/foreign-direct-investment-confidence-index/2021-full-report.

Kearney. "America is Ready for Reshoring. Are You?" 2022. https://www.kearney.com/service/operations-performance/us-reshoring-index.

Kennan, George F. "The Sources of Soviet Conduct." *Foreign Affairs*, 1947.

Kennedy, Scott and Jude Blanchette (eds.). *Chinese State Capitalism: Diagnosis and Prognosis.* Washington, DC: Center for Strategic and International Studies, October 2021.

Kim, Jaewon and Cheng Ting-Fang. "Samsung and SK Hynix face China dilemma from U.S. export controls." *Nikkei Asia.* 25 October 2022. https://asia.nikkei.com/Business/Tech/Semiconductors/Samsung-and-SK-Hynix-face-China-dilemma-from-U.S.-export-controls.

King, Sam. *Imperialism and the Development Myth*. Manchester: Manchester University Press, 2021.

Knizek, Claudio, Frank Jenner, and Sven Dharmani. "Why global industrial supply chains are decoupling." EY. 2022. https://www.ey.com/ en_cn/automotive-transportation/why-global-industrial-supply-chains-are-decoupling.

Korin, Anne and Gal Luft. *De-dollarization: The Revolt Against the Dollar and the Rise of a New Financial World Order*. Independently published, 2019.

Kratz, Agatha, Max J. Zenglein, and Gregor Sebastian. "Chinese FDI in Europe: 2020 Update: Investment Falls to 10-Year Low in an Economically and Politically Challenging Year." Berlin: MERICS and Rhodium Group, 16 June 2021. https://merics.org/en/report/chinese-fdi-europe-2020-update.

Kremlin. "Joint Statement of the Russian Federation and the People's Republic of China on the International Relations Entering a New Era and the Global Sustainable Development". 4 February 2022. http://en.kremlin.ru/supplement/5770.

Lardy, Nicholas R. "Foreign Investments into China are Accelerating." PIIE. 22 July 2021. https://www.piie.com/blogs/china-economic-watch/foreign-investments-china-are-accelerating-despite-global-economic?utm_source=update-newsletter&utm_medium=email&utm_campaign=piie-insider&utm_term=2021-07-28.

Lardy, Nicholas R. "How serious is China's economic slowdown?" PIIE. 17 August 2023. https://www.piie.com/blogs/realtime-economics/how-serious-chinas-economic-slowdown.

Lardy, Nicholas R. and Tianlei Huang. "Rising Foreign Investment in Chinese Stocks and Bonds Shows Deepening Financial Integration." PIIE. 6 July 2020. https://www.piie.com/research/piie-charts/rising-foreign-investment-chinese-stocks-and-bonds-shows-deepening-financial.

Lee, Amanda. "China Debt: How Big Is It and Who Owns It?" *South China Morning Post*. 19 May 2020. https://www.scmp.com/economy/china-economy/article/3084979/china-debt-how-big-it-who-owns-it-and-what-next.

Lee, Amanda. "China's Forex Reserves Fall by US$26 Billion Amid Ongoing Capital Outflows Following Russian Invasion of Ukraine." *South China Morning Post*. 7 April 2022. https://www.scmp.com/economy/economic-indicators/article/3173454/chinas-forex-reserves-fall-us25-billion-amid-ongoing.

Lee, Ching Kwan. *Against the Law: Labor Protests in China's Rustbelt and Sunbelt*. Berkeley: University of California Press, 2007.

Lee, John and Jan-Peter Kleinhans. "Mapping China's Semiconductor Ecosystem in Global Context: Strategic Dimensions and Conclusions." Berlin: MERICS and Stiftung Neue Verantwortung. 30 June 2021. https://merics.org/en/report/mapping-chinas-semiconductor-ecosystem-global-context-strategic-dimensions-and-conclusions.

Lee, John and Jan-Peter Kleinhans. "Mapping China's Place in the Global Semiconductor Industry." *MERICS*. 14 September 2021. https://merics.org/en/comment/mapping-chinas-place-global-semiconductor-industry.

Lee-Makiyama, Hosuk. "US Sanctions Against Chinese 5G: Inconsistencies and Paradoxical Outcomes." European Centre for International Political Economy. October 2021. https://ecipe.org/blog/us-sanctions-against-chinese-5g/.

Le Mons Walker, Kathy. "'Gangster Capitalism' and Peasant Protest: The Last Twenty Years." *Journal of Peasant Studies* 33, 1 (2006): 1–33. DOI: 10.1080/03066150600624413.

Lenin, Vladimir. *Capitalism in Agriculture*, 1899. https://www.marxists.org/archive/lenin/works/1899/agriculture/index.htm.

Lenin, Vladimir. *The Agrarian Question in Russia at the Close of the 19th Century*, 1908. https://www.marxists.org/archive/lenin/works/1908/agrquest/vii.htm.

Lenin, Vladimir. *Imperialism: The Highest Stage of Capitalism*, 1916. https://www.marxists.org/archive/lenin/works/1916/imp-hsc/imperialism.pdf.

Lenin, Vladimir. *Imperialism and the Split in Socialism*, 1916. https://www.marxists.org/archive/lenin/works/1916/oct/x01.htm.

Leonard, Mark. *What Does China Think?* New York: PublicAffairs, 2008.

Lerche, Jens. "Agrarian Crisis and Agrarian Questions in India." *Journal of Agrarian Change* 11, 1 (2011): 104–18. https://doi.org/10.1111/j.1471-0366.2010.00295.x.

Levine, Nathan. "Why America Leaving the INF Treaty is China's New Nightmare." *National Interest*. 22 October 2018. https://nationalinterest.org/blog/buzz/why-america-leaving-inf-treaty-chinas-new-nightmare-34087.

Li, Aixin and Bai Yunyi. "Russia-Ukraine Conflict Can Be Regarded as a 'Preview' of US' Possible Acts in Asia: Zheng Yongnian." *Global Times*. 17 March 2022. https://www.globaltimes.cn/page/202203/1255162.shtml.

Li, Minqi. *The Rise of China and the Demise of the Capitalist World Economy*. New York: Monthly Review Press, 2008.

Li, Minqi. "China: Imperialism or Semi-Periphery?" *Monthly Review* 73, 3 (Jul/Aug 2021). https://monthlyreview.org/2021/07/01/china-imperialism-or-semi-periphery/.

Li, Wei. "Towards Economic Decoupling? Mapping Chinese Discourse on the China–US Trade War." *Chinese Journal of International Politics* 12, 4 (2019): 519–56. https://doi.org/10.1093/cjip/poz017.

Li, Yin. *China's Drive for the Technology Frontier: Indigenous Innovation in the High-Tech Industry*. London: Routledge, 2023.

Li, Yuxuan, Weifeng Zhang, Lin Ma, Liang Wu, Jianbo Shen, William J. Davies, Oene Oenema, Fusuo Zhang, Zhengxia Dou. "An Analysis of China's Grain Production: Looking Back and Looking Forward." *Food and Energy Security* 3, 1 (2014): 19–32, https://doi.org/10.1002/fes3.41.

Lieven, Anatol. "Don't Kick the Can." 7 January 2022. https://responsiblestatecraft.org/2022/01/07/dont-kick-the-can-two-key-us-proposals-for-upcoming-russia-talks/.

Lin, Bonny. "The China-Russia Axis Takes Shape." *Foreign Policy*. 11 September 2023. https://foreignpolicy.com/2023/09/11/china-russia-alliance-cooperation-brics-sco-economy-military-war-ukraine-putin-xi/?utm_source=Sailthru&utm_medium=email&utm_campaign=Editors%20Picks%20-%2009122023&utm_term=editors_picks#cookie_message_anchor.

Lind, Michael. *The New Class War*. London: Atlantic Books, 2020.

Lockett, Hudson and Thomas Hale. "Global Investors Place Rmb1tr Bet on China." *Financial Times*. 14 December 2020. https://www.ft.com/content/d9ac222d-90d8-4570-b89e-a99f1bd4829b.

Lovely, Mary E. "The State of U.S.-China Relations Heading into 2021-" Prepared statement for the hearing on US-China Relations at the Chinese Communist Party's Centennial held before the US-China Economic and Security Review Commission, 28 January 2021, PIIE. https://www.piie.com/sites/default/files/documents/lovely2021-01-28testimony.pdf.

Lovely, Mary. "US Re-engagement: Is a Framework That Builds out China Realistic?" *East Asian Forum Quarterly* 14, 1 (2022). https://www.piie.com/commentary/speeches-papers/us-re-engagement-framework-builds-out-china-realistic.

Lukin, Alexander. *China and Russia. The New Rapprochement*. Cambridge: Polity, 2018.

Lund, Susan, James Manyika, Jonathan Woetzel, Jacques Bughin, Mekala Krishnan, Jeongmin Seong, and Mac Muir. *Globalization in Transition: The Future of Trade and Value Chains*. New York: McKinsey Global Institute, 2019. https://www.mckinsey.com/featured-insights/innovation-and-growth/globalization-in-transition-the-future-of-trade-and-value-chains.

Macro Polo. "China's Debt Hangover." *Macro Polo* Blog. December 2022. https://macropolo.org/digital-projects/china-local-debt-hangover-map/?utm_source=MacroPolo&utm_campaign=44ad1c3dab-EMAIL_CAMPAIGN_2018_11_27_04_41_COPY_01&utm_medium=email&utm_term=0_791224187b-44ad1c3dab-438868821.

Mahbubani, Kishore. *Has China Won? The Chinese Challenge to American Primacy*. New York: PublicAffairs, 2020.

Mahbubani, Kishore. "In Asia, China's Long Game Beats America's Short Game." *Foreign Policy Magazine*. 12 December 2021. https://foreignpolicy.com/2021/12/12/china-us-asean-trade-geopolitics/.

Mandel, Ernest. *Europe vs. America: Contradictions of Imperialism*. New York: Monthly Review Press, 1970.

Marx, Karl and Friedrich Engels. *The German Ideology*. 1845–6 (first edited 1932).

Marx, Karl. *Capital: critique of political economy, Vol III*. Trans. D. Fernbach. New York: Penguin Classics, 1991.

Mateè, Aaron. "John Mearsheimer: Ukraine War Is a Long Term Danger." *The Grayzone* Blog. 30 July 2023. https://thegrayzone.com/2023/07/30/john-mearsheimer-ukraine-war-is-a-long-term-danger/.

McGee, Patrick. "How Apple tied its fortunes to China." *Financial Time*. 17 January 2023. https://www.ft.com/content/d5a80891-b27d-4110-90c9-561b7836f11b.

Mearsheimer, John J. *The tragedy of great power politics*. New York: ww Norton and Company, 2001.

MEE staff. "Saudi Arabia Considers Accepting Yuan Instead of Dollars for Oil Sales, Report Says." *Middle East Eye*. 15 March 2022. https://www.middleeasteye.net/news/saudi-arabia-considers-accepting-yuan-instead-dollars-oil-sales.

Meisner, M. *Mao's China and after: A History of the People's Republic*. (*Third edition*). New York: Free Press, 1999.

Milanović, Branko. *Global Inequality: A New Approach for the Age of Globalization*. Cambridge, MA: Belknap Press of Harvard University Press, 2016.

Miller, Chris. *Chip War: The Fight for the World's Most Critical Technology*. New York; London: Simon & Schuster, 2022.

Mingey, Matthew and Agatha Kratz. "China's Belt and Road: Down But Not Out." Research Note. Rhodium Group. 4 January 2021. https://rhg.com/research/bri-down-out/.

Ministry of Foreign Affairs of the People's Republic of China. "China's Position on the Political Settlement of the Ukraine Crisis." 24 February 2023. https://www.fmprc.gov.cn/eng/zxxx_662805/202302/t20230224_11030713.html.

Mohamed, Edna. "New Evidence Shows Saudi Arabia Building Ballistic Missiles with China's Help." *Middle East Eye*. 23 December 2021. https://www.middleeasteye.net/news/saudi-arabia-china-building-ballistic-missiles-images.

National Security Commission on Artificial Intelligence. *Final Report*. March 2021. https://www.nscai.gov/wp-content/uploads/2021/03/Full-Report-Digital-1.pdf.

"La Nato promette l'artiglieria." *Il Fatto Quotidiano*. 16 June 2022: 2.

NATO. 2022 Strategic Concept. Adopted at the Madrid Summit, 29–30 June 2022. https://www.nato.int/strategic-concept/index.html.

NATO. Vilnius Summit Communiquè. 11 July 2023. https://www.nato.int/cps/en/natohq/official_texts_217320.htm.

NATO. "Secretary General Jens Stoltenberg at the joint meeting of the Committee on Foreign Affairs (AFET) and the Subcommittee on Security and Defense (SEDE) of the European Parliament." 7 September 2023. https://www.reportdifesa.it/nato-secretary-general-jens-stoltenberg-at-the-joint-meeting-of-the-committee-on-foreign-affairs-afet-and-the-subcommittee-on-security-and-defense-sede-of-the-european-parliament/.

Naughton, Barry. *The Chinese Economy: Transitions and Growth*. Cambridge, MA; London: MIT Press, 2007.

Nedopil, Christoph. *China Belt and Road Initiative (BRI) Investment Report H1 2022*. Shanghai: FISF Fudan University—Green Finance & Development Center. July

2022. https://greenfdc.org/wp-content/uploads/2022/07/GFDC-2022_China-Belt-and-Road-Initiative-BRI-Investment-Report-H1-2022.pdf.

Neel, Phil A. *Hinterland: America's New Landscape of Class and Conflict.* London: Reaktion Books, 2018.

Nereim, Vivian. "China and Saudi Arabia Sign Strategic Partnership as Xi Visits Kingdom." *The New York Times.* 8 December 2022. https://www.nytimes.com/2022/12/08/world/middleeast/china-saudi-arabia-agreement.html.

Neusüss, Christel, Bernhard Blanke, and Elmar Altvater. "Kapitalistischer Weltmarkt und Weltwährungskrise." PROKLA. *Zeitschrift für kritische Sozialwissenschaft* 1, 1 (1971): 5–116. https://doi.org/10.32387/prokla.vii1.1223.

Neusüss, Christel. *Imperialismus und Weltmarktbewegung des Kapital.* Erlangen: Politladen 1972.

Nicolaus, Martin. "The Universal Contradiction." *New Left Review* 59 (Jan/Feb 1970): 3–18. https://newleftreview.org/issues/i59/articles/martin-nicolaus-the-universal-contradiction.

Nogueira, Isabela, João V. Guimarães, and João P. Braga. "Inequalities and capital accumulation in China". *Brasilian Journal of Political Economy,* 39, 3, (2019): 449–69. https://doi.org/10.1590/0101-35172019-2929.

Norfield, Tony. "Finance, the Rate of Profit and Imperialism." Paper delivered to Wape conference. Paris, July 2012. https://dokumen.tips/documents/public-debt-finance-and-imperialism.html?page=28.

Norfield, Tony. "T-Shirt Economics: Labour in the Imperialist World Economy," in *Struggle in a Time of Crisis,* eds. Nicolas Pons-Vignon and Mbuso Nkosi. London: Pluto, 2015.

Obstfeld, Maurice. "Global Dimensions of US Monetary Policy." *International Journal of Central Banking* 16(1), 2020: 73–132.

OECD. *U.S. Manufacturing Decline and the Rise of New Production Innovation Paradigms.* Paris, 2016.

OECD. "OECD Business and Finance Outlook 2018—China's Belt and Road Initiative in the Global Trade, Investment and Finance Landscape." Paris, 2018. https://www.oecd.org/finance/Chinas-Belt-and-Road-Initiative-in-the-global-trade-investment-and-finance-landscape.pdf.

OECD. "FDI in Figures." Paris, October 2021. https://www.oecd.org/investment/investment-policy/FDI-in-Figures-October-2021.pdf.

Office of the US Trade Representative—Executive Office of the President. "Remarks As Prepared for Delivery of Ambassador Katherine Tai Outlining the Biden-Harris Administration's 'New Approach to the U.S.-China Trade Relationship'." 4 October 2021. https://ustr.gov/about-us/policy-offices/press-office/speeches-and-remarks/2021/october/remarks-prepared-delivery-ambassador-katherine-tai-outlining-biden-harris-administrations-new.

Olander, Eric. "Five Reasons Why Chinese Private Investment is Flowing into Africa." China Global South Project. 6 April 2021. https://chinaglobalsouth.com/2021/04/06/five-reasons-why-chinese-private-investment-is-flowing-into-africa/.

O'Leary, Brendan. *Asiatic Mode of Production: Oriental Despotism, Historical Materialism, and Indian History*. Oxford: Basic Blackwell, 1989.

Overholt, William. "Renminbi Internationalisation Deferred." Official Monetary and Financial Institutions Forum. 15 May 2020. https://www.omfif.org/2020/05/renminbis-limited-internationalisation/.

Pagliani, Piero. "Brics + o bric-à-brac?" *Sinistrainrete*. 2 September 2023. https://www.sinistrainrete.info/geopolitica/26251-piero-pagliani-brics-o-bric-a-brac.html.

Palmer, Alex. "An Act of War: Inside America's Silicon Blockade Against China." *The New York Times Magazine*. 12 July 2023. https://www.nytimes.com/2023/07/12/magazine/semiconductor-chips-us-china.html.

Panitch, Leo and Samuel Gindin. *The making of global capitalism: The political economy of American empire*. New York: Verso, 2012.

Pascucci, Angela. *Potere e società in Cina. Storie di resistenza nella grande trasformazione* [*Power and Society in China: Stories of Resistance in the Great Transformation*]. Roma: Il Manifesto, 2013.

Pearson, Margaret. M., Meg Rithmire, and Kellee S. Tsai. "China's party-state capitalism and international backlash: From independence to insecurity." *International Security* 47 (2), 2022:135–76. DOI: 10.1162/isec_a_00447.

Perez-Saiz, Hector and Longmei Zhang. "Renminbi Usage in Cross-Border Payments: Regional Patterns and the Role of Swaps Lines and Offshore Clearing Banks." IMF Working Paper. 31 March 2023. https://www.imf.org/en/Publications/WP/Issues/2023/03/31/Renminbi-Usage-in-Cross-Border-Payments-Regional-Patterns-and-the-Role-of-Swaps-Lines-and-531684.

Perry, Elisabeth and Mark Selden (eds.). *Chinese Society. Change, Conflict and Resistance*. London: Routledge, 2003.

Petri, Peter A. and Michael G. Plummer. "East Asia Decouples from the United States: Trade War, COVID-19, and East Asia's New Trade Blocs." Working Paper 20-9, PIIE. June 2020. https://www.piie.com/publications/working-papers/east-asia-decouples-united-states-trade-war-covid-19-and-east-asias-new.

Pomeranz, Kenneth. *The Great Divergence: China, Europe, and the Making of the Modern World Economy*. Princeton, NJ: Princeton University Press, 2000.

Posen, Adam. "The End of China's Economic Miracle. How Beijing's Struggles Could Be an Opportunity for Washington." *Foreign Affairs*. September-October 2023. https://www.foreignaffairs.com/china/end-china-economic-miracle-beijing-washington?utm_medium=promo_email&utm_source=special_send&utm_campaign=China_Economic_Prospects&utm_content=20230802&utm_term=promo-email-prospects.

Pouch, Thierry and Jean-Marc Chaumet. *La Chine au risque de la dépendance alimentaire*. Rennes: Presses universitaires de Rennes, 2017.

Poulantzas, Nicos. "L'internationalisation des rapports capitalistes et l'Etat-nation." *Les Temps Modernes* 319 (February 1973): 1456–1500.

Prasad, Eswar. *The Dollar Trap: How the U.S. Dollar Tightened its Grip on Global Finance*. Princeton, NJ: Princeton University Press, 2014.

Prasad, Eswar. *Gaining Currency: The Rise of the Renminbi*. Oxford: Oxford University Press, 2017.

Prasad, Eswar S. "Why China No Longer Needs Hong Kong." *New York Times*. 3 July 2019. https://www.nytimes.com/2019/07/03/opinion/hong-kong-protest.html.

Prashad, Vijay. "US Doing Its Best to Lock China Out of Latin America." *Asia Times*. 4 November 2020. https://asiatimes.com/2020/11/us-doing-its-best-to-lock-china-out-of-latin-america/.

President of the Russian Federation. "Joint Statement of the Russian Federation and the People's Republic of China on the International Relations Entering a New Era and the Global Sustainable Development." 4 February 2022. http://en.kremlin.ru/supplement/5770.

Pringle, Tim. "What do Labour NGOs in China Do?" *Asia Dialogue*. 17 October 2016. https://theasiadialogue.com/2016/10/17/what-do-labour-ngos-in-china-do/.

Pun Ngai. *Migrant Labour in China: Post-Socialist Transformations*. Cambridge: Polity Press, 2016.

Pun Ngai and Lu Huilin. "Unfinished Proletarianization: Self, Anger, and Class Action among the Second Generation of Peasant-Workers in Present-Day China." *Modern China* 36, 5 (2010): 493–519. https://doi.org/10.1177/0097700410373576.

Qiao, Liang and Wang Xiangsui. *Unrestricted Warfare*. Beijing: PLA Literature and Arts. Publishing House, 1999.

Qiao, Liang. *Empire Arc: America and China at the Ends of Parabola* [in Chinese]. Hong Kong: Changjiang Literature Press, 2016.

Qu Xinyi, Jia Yuxuan, and Zichen Wang. "Study Times op-ed shoots down new policy options." *Pekingnology*. August 20, 2023. https://www.pekingnology.com/p/study-times-op-ed-shoots-down-new.

Rajah, Roland, and Alyssa Leng. "Chart of the week: Global trade through a US-China lens." *The Interpreter*. 18 December 2019. https://www.lowyinstitute.org/the-interpreter/chart-week-global-trade-through-us-china-lens.

Ranasinghe, Dhara. "Global Debt is Fast Approaching Record $300 Trillion—IIF." *Reuters*. 14 September 2021. https://www.reuters.com/business/global-debt-is-fast-approaching-record-300-trillion-iif-2021-09-14/.

Reddy, D. Narasimha. "The Agrarian Question and the Political Economy of Agrarian Change in India." R. S. Rao Memorial Lecture delivered to the University of Hyderabad. 17 June 2016.

Reinhart, Carmen, Christoph Trebesch, and Sebastian Horn. "China's Overseas Lending and the War in Ukraine." *VoxEU*. 11 April 2022. https://cepr.org/voxeu/columns/chinas-overseas-lending-and-war-ukraine.
Rhodium Group. National Committee on U.S.-China Relations. "Two-Way Street." September 2020. https://publications-research.s3-us-west-2.amazonaws.com/RHG_TWS+1H+2020+Report_25Sept2020.pdf.
Rhodium Group. National Committee on U.S.-China Relation. "US-China Financial Investment: Current Scope and Future Potential." January 2021. https://rhg.com/wp-content/uploads/2021/01/US-China-Financial-Investment_25Jan2021-2.pdf.
Rhodium Group. "China's Belt and road: Down but not Out". January 2021.
Richter, Felix. "BYD and Tesla Dominate Global EV Sales." *Statista*. 5 September 2023. https://www.statista.com/chart/30758/most-popular-plug-in-electric-car-brands/?utm_source=Statista+Newsletters&utm_campaign=a0f3d19od3-All_InfographTicker_daily_COM_PM_KW35_2023_Th_COPY&utm_medium=email&utm_term=0_662f7ed75e-a0f3d190d3-350249006.
Ringstrom, Anna and Terje Solsvik. "North Stream Leaks Confirmed as Sabotage, Sweden Says." Reuters. 18 November 2022. https://www.reuters.com/world/europe/traces-explosives-found-nord-stream-pipelines-sweden-says-2022-11-18/.
Rittenhouse Green, Brendan and Caitlin Talmadge. "The Consequences of Conquest: Why Indo-Pacific Power Hinges on Taiwan." *Foreign Affairs*. 16 June 2022. https://www.foreignaffairs.com/articles/china/2022-06-16/consequences-conquest-taiwan-indo-pacific.
Roberts, Michael. "The Roaring Twenties Repeated?" Author's blog. 18 April 2021. https://thenextrecession.wordpress.com/2021/04/18/the-roaring-twenties-repeated/.
Roberts, Michael. "Profits Call the Tune." Author's blog. 17 June 2021. https://thenextrecession.wordpress.com/2021/06/17/profits-call-the-tune-2/.
Roberts, Michael. "China's Crackdown on the Three Mountains." Author's blog. 8 August 2021. https://thenextrecession.wordpress.com/2021/08/08/chinas-crackdown-on-the-three-mountains/.
Rogoff, Kenneth and Yuanchen Yang. "Peak China Housing." Working Paper 27697. NBER. August 2020. http://www.nber.org/papers/w27697.
Romm, Tony. "Senate Approves Sprawling $250 Billion Bill to Curtail China's Economic and Military Ambitions." *The Washington Post*. 8 June 2021. https://www.washingtonpost.com/us-policy/2021/06/08/senate-china-science-technology.
Rovnick, Naomi and Libby George. "The End of King Dollar?" Reuters. 25 May 2023. https://www.reuters.com/markets/currencies/end-king-dollar-forces-play-de-dollarisation-2023-05-25/.
Rowthorn, Robert E. "Imperialism in the Seventies: Unity or Rivalry?" *New Left Review* 69 (1971): 59–83.

Rozelle, Scott, Yiran Xia, Dimitris Friesen, Bronson Vanderjack, and Nourya Cohen. "Moving Beyond Lewis: Employment and Wage Trends in China's High- and Low-Skilled Industries and the Emergence of an Era of Polarization". Presidential address for the 2020 Association for Comparative Economic Studies Meetings. *Comparative Economic Studies* 62 (2020): 555–89. https://doi.org/10.1057/s41294-020-00137-w.

Ruckus, Ralf. *The Communist Road to Capitalism*. Oakland, CA: PM Press, 2021.

Ruta, Michele, Matias Herrera Dappe, Somik Lall, Chunlin Zhang, Cristina Constantinescu, Mathilde Lebrand, Alen Mulabdic et al. *Belt and Road Economics: Opportunities and Risks of Transport Corridors*. Washington, DC: World Bank and International Bank for Reconstruction and Development, 2019. https://www.worldbank.org/en/topic/regional-integration/publication/belt-and-road-economics-opportunities-and-risks-of-transport-corridors.

Salinger, Jerome David. *For Esmé—with Love and Squalor and Other StoriesI*. London: Penguin Books, 1986.

Sargent, Daniel J. *Superpower transformed: The remaking of American foreign relations in the 1970s*. Oxford: Oxford University Press, 2015.

Sargeson, Sally. "The Demise of China's Peasantry as a Class." *Asia-Pacific Journal: Japan Focus* 14, 13.1 (2016). https://apjjf.org/2016/13/Sargeson.html.

Schindler, Seth, Ilias Alami, Jessica DiCarlo, Nicholas Jepson, Steve Rolf, Mustafa Kemal Bayırbağ, Louis Cyuzuzo, Meredith DeBoom, Alireza F. Farahani, Imogen T. Liu, Hannah McNicol, Julie T. Miao, Philip Nock, Gilead Teri, Maximiliano Facundo Vila Seoane, Kevin Ward, Tim Zajontz & Yawei Zhao. "The Second Cold War: US-China Competition for Centrality in Infrastructure, Digital, Production, and Finance Networks." *Geopolitics*. 7 September 2023. https://www.tandfonline.com/doi/full/10.1080/14650045.2023.2253432. DOI: 10.1080/14650045.2023.2253432.

Schmalz, Stefan. "The Three Stages of Chinese Capital Export." *Journal für Entwicklungspolitik* 35 (2019): 17–38. doi: 10.20446/JEP-2414-3197-35-3-17.

Schmalz, Stefan, Brandon Sommer and Xu Hui. "The Yue Yuen Strike: Industrial Transformation and Labour Unrest in the Pearl River Delta." *Globalizations* 14, 2 (2017): 1–13. https://doi.org/10.1080/14747731.2016.1203188.

Schmalzer, Sigrid. "Toward a Transnational, Trans-1978 History of Food Politics in China: An Exploratory Paper." *The PRC History Review* 3, 1 (2018): 1–14. http://prchistory.org/wp-content/uploads/2017/11/Schmalzer.pdf.

Sciortino, Raffaele. "Il dibattito sulla globalizzazione: dagli anni Novanta ai segnali di crisi." Working paper open access. Trieste: Asterios, 2010. http://www.asterios.it/sites/default/files/Il%20dibattito%20sulla%20globalizzazione.pdf.

Sciortino, Raffaele. *Un passaggio oltre il bipolarismo. Il rapprochement sino-americano 1969–1972* [A transition beyond bipolarity. The Sino-American Rapprochement 1969–1972]. Bologna: I libri di Emil, 2012.

Sciortino, Raffaele. "Chicken Game: Eurocrisis Again." *Insurgent Notes: Journal of Communist Theory and Practice*. 3 June 2012. http://insurgentnotes.com/2012/06/chicken-game-eurocrisis-again/.

Sciortino, Raffaele. *I dieci anni che sconvolsero il mondo. Crisi globale e geopolitica dei neopopulismi* [The Ten Years that Shocked the World. Global Crisis and the Geopolitics of Neo-populisms]. Trieste: Asterios, 2019.

Sciortino, Raffaele. "Pandemic Crisis and Phase Changes." *Platforms, Populisms, Pandemics and Riots*. 2 October 2020. https://projectpppr.org/pandemics/pandemic-crisis-and-phase-changes.

Seaman, John. "China and the New Geopolitics of Technical Standardization." *Notes de l'Ifri*. 27 January 2020. https://www.ifri.org/en/publications/notes-de-lifri/china-and-new-geopolitics-technical-standardization.

Selden, Mark and Jieh-min Wu. "Chinese State, Incomplete Proletarianization and Structures of Inequality in Two Epochs." *Asia-Pacific Journal: Japan Focus* 9, 5.1 (January, 2011). https://apjjf.org/2011/9/5/Mark-Selden/3480/article.html.

Semiconductor Industry Association. *2020 SIA Factbook*. Washington, DC: April 2020. https://www.semiconductors.org/wp-content/uploads/2020/04/2020-SIA-Factbook-FINAL_reduced-size.pdf.

Semiconductor Industries Association. *2022 State of the U.S. Semiconductors Industry*. Washington, DC: 2023. https://www.semiconductors.org/wp-content/uploads/2022/11/SIA_State-of-Industry-Report_2022.pdf.

Sharp, Alexandra. "U.S., South Korea, Japan Bolster Ties at Camp David Summit." *Foreign Policy*. 18 August 2023. https://foreignpolicy.com/2023/08/18/camp-david-summit-us-japan-south-korea-china-commitment-consult-military-drills/?tpcc=recirc_latest062921.

Shear, Michael D. "Biden Describes China as a Time Bomb Over Economic Problems." *New York Times*. 11 August 2023. https://www.nytimes.com/2023/08/11/us/politics/biden-china-criticism-economy.html.

Sheehan, Matt. "China Technology 2025: Fragile Tech Superpower." Macro Polo (Paulson Institute). 26 October 2020. https://macropolo.org/analysis/china-technology-forecast-2025-fragile-tech-superpower.

Sheng, Yu, Ligang Song and Qing Yi. "Mechanisation Outsourcing and Agricultural Productivity for Small Farms: Implications for Rural Land Reform in China", in *China's New Sources of Economic Growth*, vol. 2: *Human Capital, Innovation and Technological Change*, edited by Ligang Song, Ross Garnaut, Cai Fang, and Lauren Johnston. Acton: Australian National University Press, 2017: 289–313.

Silver, Beverly J. and Lu Zhang. "China as an Emerging Epicenter of World Labor Unrest", in *China and the Transformation of Global Capitalism*, edited by Ho-Fung Hung. Baltimore, MD: John Hopkins University Press, 2009: 174–87.

Simes, Dimitri. "China and Russia Ditch Dollar in Move Toward 'Financial Alliance'." *Nikkei Asia*. 6 August 2020. https://asia.nikkei.com/Politics/International-relations/China-and-Russia-ditch-dollar-in-move-toward-financial-alliance.
Singh, Ajit. "The Myth of 'Debt-Trap Diplomacy' and Realities of Chinese Development Finance." *Third World Quarterly* 42, 2 (2020): 239–53. https://doi.org/10.1080/01436597.2020.1807318.
Smith, John. "Imperialism and the Law of Value." *Global Discourse* 2, 1 (2011). http://global-discourse.com/contents (website no longer functional).
Smith, John. *Imperialism in the Twenty-First Century: Globalization, Super-Exploitation, and Capitalism's Final Crisis*. New York: Monthly Review Press, 2016.
So, Alvin Y. *Class and class conflict in post-socialist China*. Hong Kong: Hong Kong University of Science and Technology, 2013.
Sofri, Gianni. *Il modo di produzione asiatico*. Torino: Einaudi, 1969.
Sohn, Jiyoung and Yang Jie. "China's New Chip Ban on Micron." *The Wall Street Journal*. 22 May 2023. https://www.wsj.com/articles/chinas-new-chip-ban-on-micron-puts-south-korea-in-a-delicate-spot-21ce5259.
Soros, George. "Will Trump Sell Out the U.S. on Huawei?" *Wall Street Journal*. 9 September 2019. https://www.wsj.com/articles/will-trump-sell-out-the-u-s-on-huawei-11568068495.
Sperber, Nathan. "Party and State in China. Beyond the Soviet Model." *New Left Review*, 142, July-Aug 2023: 29–53.
Sperber, Nathan. "Forecasting China?" *New Left Review Sidecar*. 8 September 2023. https://newleftreview.org/sidecar/posts/forecasting-china.
Sprout, Harold Hance and Margaret Sprout. *Man-Milieu Relationship Hypotheses in the Context of International Politics*. Princeton, NJ: Center of International Studies, 1956.
Starosta, Guido. "Global Commodity Chains and the Marxian Law of Value." *Antipode*, 42, 2 (2010): 433–465. DOI: 10.1111/j.1467-8330.2009.00753.x.
Starrs, Sean. "American Economic Power Hasn't Declined—It Globalized!" *International Studies Quarterly* 57, 4 (2013): 817–30.
Starrs, Sean. "The Chimera of global Convergence." *New Left Review*, 87, May/June 2014: 81–96. https://newleftreview.org/issues/ii87/articles/sean-starrs-the-chimera-of-global-convergence.
State Council Information Office of China. "China's International Development Cooperation in the New Era." White paper, 10 January 2021, posted in English at the Xinhua News Agency website. https://english.www.gov.cn/archive/whitepaper/202101/10/content_WS5ffa6bbbc6d0f72576943922.html.
Stavridis, James. "If the US Went to War with China, Who Would Win?" Asia *Nikkei*. 30 May 2021. https://asia.nikkei.com/Opinion/If-the-US-went-to-war-with-China-who-would-win.

"The Steam Has Gone Out of Globalisation." *Economist.* 24 January 2019. https://www.economist.com/leaders/2019/01/24/the-steam-has-gone-out-of-globalisation.

Steil, Benn and Benjamin Della Rocca. "Is China Helping Russia Hide Money? The Kremlin May Have Stashed Billions in Offshore Accounts." *Foreign Affairs.* 21 March 2022. https://www.foreignaffairs.com/articles/ukraine/2022-03-21/china-helping-russia-hide-money.

Sun, Irene Yuan, Kartik Jayaram, and Omid Kassiri. *Dance of Lions and Dragons: How are Africa and China Engaging, and How Will the Partnership Evolve?* New York: McKinsey Global Institute, 2017. https://www.mckinsey.com/~/media/mckinsey/featured%20insights/middle%20east%20and%20africa/the%20closest%20look%20yet%20at%20chinese%20economic%20engagement%20in%20africa/dance-of-the-lions-and-dragons.ashx#:~:text=Chinese%20%E2%80%9Cdragons%E2%80%9D%E2%80%94%20firms%20of%20every%20size%20and%20sector%E2%80%94,economies%20are%20often%20referred%20to.

Swift. *RMB Tracker: Monthly Reporting and Statistics on Renminbi (RMB) Progress Towards Becoming an International Currency.* La Hulpe, Belgium. Updated November 2021. https://www.swift.com/swift-resource/251736/download.

Tang, Frank. "China Estimates Shadow Banking Worth US$12.9 Trillion as it Moves to Clean Up High-Risk Sector." *South China Morning Post.* 7 December 2020. https://www.scmp.com/economy/china-economy/article/3112892/china-estimates-shadow-banking-worth-us129-trillion-it-moves?module=hard_link&pgtype=article.

ten Brink, Tobias. *Chinas Kapitalismus.* Frankfurt a.M.: Campus Verlag 2.

Thompson, Edward P. "The Moral Economy of the English Crowd in the Eighteenth Century." *Past & Present* 50, 1 (1971): 76–136. https://doi.org/10.1093/past/50.1.76.

Tobita, Rintaro. "US calls out Japan and Netherlands over China chip curbs." *Asia Nikkei.* 6 November 2022. https://asia.nikkei.com/Business/Electronics/U.S.-calls-out-Japan-and-Netherlands-over-China-chip-curbs.

Tooze, Adam. *Crashed: How a Decade of Financial Crises Changed the World.* London: Penguin, 2018.

Tooze, Adam. "The World is at Financial War." *New Statesman.* 2 March 2022. https://www.newstatesman.com/ideas/2022/03/ukraine-the-world-is-at-financial-war.

Tooze, Adam. "Chartbook-Unhedged Exchange: China under Pressure, a Debate." *Substack.* 24 March 2022. https://adamtooze.substack.com/p/chartbook-unhedged-exchange-china?s=r.

Townsend, Erik. *Beyond Blockchain: the Death of the Dollar and the Rise of Digital Currency.* Independently published, 2018.

Trotsky, Leon. *The Permanent Revolution.* 1929. https://www.marxists.org/archive/trotsky/1931/tpr/pr-index.htm.

Tyler Durden (pseudonym). "Whispers of Yuan Devaluation After Biggest Weekly Plunge Since 2015." *ZeroHedge.* 22 April 2022. https://www.zerohedge.com/markets/whispers-yuan-devaluation-after-biggest-weekly-plunge-2015 (archived).

UNCTAD. *World Investment Report 2018—Investment and New Industrial Policies.* UNCTAD/WIR/2018. https://unctad.org/system/files/official-document/wir2018_en.pdf.

UNCTAD. *World Investment Report 2019—Special Economic Zones.* UNCTAD/WIR/2019. https://unctad.org/publication/world-investment-report-2019.

UNCTAD. *World Investment Report 2020—International Production Beyond the Pandemic.* UNCTAD/WIR/2020. https://unctad.org/system/files/official-document/wir2020_en.pdf.

UNCTAD. *Trade and Development Report 2020—From Global Pandemic to Prosperity For All: Avoiding Another Lost Decade.* UNCTAD/TDR/2020. https://unctad.org/system/files/official-document/tdr2020_en.pdf.

UNCTAD. *Global Trade Update.* UNCTAD/DITC/INF/2021/2. May 2021. https://unctad.org/system/files/official-document/ditcinf2021d2_en.pdf.

UNCTAD. *World Investment Report 2021—Investing in Sustainable Recovery.* UNCTAD/WIR/2021. https://unctad.org/system/files/official-document/wir2021_en.pdf.

UNCTAD. *Global Investment Trends Monitor, No. 40.* UNCTAD/DIAE/IA/INF/2021/3. 19 January 2022. https://unctad.org/system/files/official-document/diaeiainf2021d3_en.pdf.

UNCTAD. "Global Foreign Direct Investment Rebounded Strongly in 2021, but the Recovery is Highly Uneven." 19 January 2022. https://unctad.org/news/global-foreign-direct-investment-rebounded-strongly-2021-recovery-highly-uneven.

UNCTAD. *World Investment Report 2022—International Tax Reforms and Sustainable Investment.* UNCTAD/WIR/2022. https://unctad.org/system/files/official-document/wir2022_en.pdf.

UNCTAD. *Global Trade Update June 2023.* UNCTAD/DITC/INF/2023/2. February 2023. https://unctad.org/system/files/official-document/ditcinf2023d2_en.pdf.

UNCTAD. *World Investment Report 2023: Investing in Sustainable Enegy for All.* UNCTAD/WIR/2023. https://unctad.org/system/files/official-document/wir2023_en.pdf.

United Nations—Department of Economic and Social Affairs. *World Economic and Social Survey 2010: Retooling Global Development.* E/2010/50/Rev. 1, ST/ESA/330. New York, 2010. https://www.un.org/en/development/desa/policy/wess/wess_current/2010wess.pdf.

"Unruhen in China." Editorial. *Wildcat,* issue 80 (December 2007): 2–10.

US Department of Commerce—Bureau of Economic Analysis. "U.S. International Investment Position, Fourth Quarter and Year 2021." News release. BE 22–12. 29 March 2022. https://www.bea.gov/news/2022/us-international-investment-position-fourth-quarter-and-year-2021.

BIBLIOGRAPHY

US Department of Defense. *Summary of the 2018 National Defense Strategy of the United States of America*. 2018. https://dod.defense.gov/Portals/1/Documents/pubs/2018-National-Defense-Strategy-Summary.pdf.
US Department of Defense. *Nuclear Posture Review*. February 2018. https://media.defense.gov/2018/Feb/02/2001872886/-1/-1/1/2018-NUCLEAR-POSTURE-REVIEW-FINAL-REPORT.PDF.
US Department of Defense. *Indo-Pacific Strategy Report: Preparedness, Partnerships, and Promoting a Networked Region*. 1 June 2019. https://media.defense.gov/2019/Jul/01/2002152311/-1/-1/1/DEPARTMENT-OF-DEFENSE-INDO-PACIFIC-STRATEGY-REPORT-2019.PDF.
US Department of Defense. "DoD Concludes 2021 Global Posture Review." News release. 29 November 2021. https://www.defense.gov/News/Releases/Release/Article/2855801/dod-concludes-2021-global-posture-review/.
US Department of State—Bureau of East Asian and Pacific Affairs. *A Free and Open Indo-Pacific: Advancing a Shared Vision*. 3 November 2019. https://www.state.gov/a-free-and-open-indo-pacific-advancing-a-shared-vision/.
US Department of State. "U.S. Position on Maritime Claims in the South China Sea." News release, 13 July 2020. https://2017-2021.state.gov/u-s-position-on-maritime-claims-in-the-south-china-sea/.
US Department of State—Office of the Secretary of State. *The Elements of the China Challenge*. November 2020, revised December 2020. https://www.state.gov/wp-content/uploads/2020/11/20-02832-Elements-of-China-Challenge-508.pdf.
US Department of State. "The Clean Network." 2020. https://www.state.gov/the-clean-network/ (page now archived).
US Department of State. "The Administration's Approach to the People's Republic of China." Speech by Antony J. Blinken. 26 May 2022. https://state.gov/the-administrations-approach-to-the-peoples-republic-of-china/.
US Department of Treasury. "Remarks by Secretary of the Treasury Janet L. Yellen on the U.S.—China Economic Relationship at Johns Hopkins School of Advanced International Studies." 20 April 2023. https://home.treasury.gov/news/press-releases/jy1425.
"U.S. Tech Restrictions." *CGTN*. 28 August 2023: interview with David Paul Goldman. https://news.cgtn.com/news/2023-08-28/U-S-tech-restrictions-impact-reasons-for-a-potential-tech-war-loss-1mCHAqKLOUo/index.html.
van der Ploeg, Jan Douwe and Jingzhong Ye (eds.). *China's Peasant Agriculture and Rural Society: Changing Paradigms of Farming*. London: Routledge, 2016.
Varas, Antonio, Raj Varadarajan, Jimmy Goodrich, and Falan Yinug. "Government Incentives and U.S. Competitiveness in Semiconductor Manufacturing." *Semiconductor Industry Association and Boston Consulting Group*. September 2020.

https://www.semiconductors.org/wp-content/uploads/2020/09/Government-Inc entives-and-US-Competitiveness-in-Semiconductor-Manufacturing-Sep-2020.pdf.

Varas, Antonio, Raj Varadarajan, Ramiro Palma, Jimmy Goodrich, and Falan Yinug. "Strengthening the Global Semiconductor Supply Chain in an Uncertain Era." *Boston Consulting Group*. 1 April 2021. https://www.bcg.com/publications/2021 /strengthening-the-global-semiconductor-supply-chain.

Varoufakis, Yanis. *The Global Minotaur: America, Europe and the Future of the Global Economy*. London: Zed Books, 2011.

Veltmeyer, Henry and Raúl Delgado Wise, "The Agrarian Question Today", in *Critical Development Studies: An Introduction*. Rugby, UK: Practical Action, 2018: 67–93.

von Braunmühl, Claudia. "Weltmarktbewegung des Kapitals, Imperialismus und Staat" in *Probleme einer materialistischen Staatstheorie*, edited by Claudia von Braunmühl, Klaus Funken, Mario Cogoy, and Joachim Hirsch. Frankfurt: Argument Verlag, 1973.

Voxeu. "*The Global Trade Slowdown: A New Normal?*" Cepr. 2015.

Wang, Dan. "China's Sputnik Moment? How Washington Boosted Beijing's Quest for Tech Dominance." *Foreign Affairs*. 29 July 2021.

Wang, Kan. "Collective Awakening and Action of Chinese Workers: The 2010 Auto Workers' Strike and its Effects." *Sozial.Geschichte Online* 6 (2011): 9–27. https://duep ublico2.uni-due.de/servlets/MCRFileNodeServlet/duepublico_derivate_00029 001/03_WangKan_Strike.pdf.

Wang, Jisi. "'Marching Westwards': The Rebalancing of China's Geostrategy." *IISS Report* No. 73. Peking University—Institute of International and Strategic Studies. 7 October 2012. http://en.iiss.pku.edu.cn/research/bulletin/1604.html.

Wang, Zhaohui and Zhiqiang Sun. "From Globalization to Regionalization: The United States, China, and the Post-COVID-19 World Economic Order." *Journal of China Political Science* 26 (2021): 69–87. https://www.researchgate.net/publicat ion/346467025_From_Globalization_to_Regionalization_The_United_States_Chi na_and_the_Post-Covid-19_World_Economic_Order.

Wang, Zichen and Jinhao Bai. "Central Economic Work Conference 2022." *Pekingnology* Blog. 16 December 2022. https://www.pekingnology.com/p/full-text-and-analy sis-central-economic.

Weber, Isabella M. *How China Escaped Shock Therapy. The Market Reform Debate*. Milton Park: Routledge 2021.

Weber, Isabella M. and Evan Wasner, "Sellers' Inflation, Profits and Conflict: Why can Large Firms Hike Prices in a Emergency?" Economics Department Working Paper Series 340. February 2023. University of Massachussetts Amherst. https://doi.org/10 .7275/cbvo-gvo7.

Wen, Tiejun. "Centenary Reflections on the 'Three Dimensional Problem' of Rural China." Translated by Petrus Liu. *Inter-Asia Cultural Studies* 2, no. 2 (2001): 287–95.

The White House. *Memorandum of Conversation*. 3 April 1949. https://nsarchive2.gwu .edu/nsa/DOCUMENT/200008/.

The White House. *National Security Strategy of the United States of America*. December 2017. https://trumpwhitehouse.archives.gov/wp-content/uploads/2017/12/NSS-Final-12-18-2017-0905.pdf.

The White House. *United States' Strategic Approach to the People's Republic of China*. May 2020. https://trumpwhitehouse.archives.gov/wp-content/uploads/2020/05/U.S.-Strategic-Approach-to-The-Peoples-Republic-of-China-Report-5.24v1.pdf.

The White House. Executive Order 14005. "Ensuring the Future is Made in America with All of America's Workers." 25 January 2021. https://www.whitehouse.gov/briefing-room/statements-releases/2021/06/08/fact-sheet-biden-harris-administration-announces-supply-chain-disruptions-task-force-to-address-short-term-supply-chain-discontinuities/#:~:text=The%20Federal%20Acquisition%20Regulatory%20Council,in%20manufactured%20products%20or%20component.

The White House. "Remarks by President Biden on America's Place in the World." 4 February 2021. https://www.whitehouse.gov/briefing-room/speeches-remarks/2021/02/04/remarks-by-president-biden-on-americas-place-in-the-world.

The White House. Executive Order 14017. "America's Supply Chains." 24 February 2021. https://www.whitehouse.gov/briefing-room/presidential-actions/2021/02/24/executive-order-on-americas-supply-chains/,.

The White House. Executive Order 13959. "Addressing the Threat from Securities Investments that Finance Certain Companies of the People's Republic of China." 3 June 2021. https://www.whitehouse.gov/briefing-room/presidential-actions/2021/06/03/executive-order-on-addressing-the-threat-from-securities-investments-that-finance-certain-companies-of-the-peoples-republic-of-china/.

The White House. "Building Resilient Supply Chains, Revitalizing American Manufacturing, and Fostering Broad-Based Growth." June 2021. https://www.whitehouse.gov/wp-content/uploads/2021/06/100-day-supply-chain-review-report.pdf.

The White House. 2021. *FACT SHEET: President Biden and G7 Leaders Launch Build Back Better World (B3W) Partnership*, June 12 2022. https://www.whitehouse.gov/briefing-room/statements-releases/2021/06/12/fact-sheet-president-biden-and-g7-leaders-launch-build-back-better-world-b3w-partnership/.

The White House. "Fact Sheet: Quad Leaders' Summit." 24 September 2021. https://www.whitehouse.gov/briefing-room/statements-releases/2021/09/24/fact-sheet-quad-leaders-summit.

The White House. *Indo-Pacific Strategy of the United States*. February 2022. https://www.whitehouse.gov/wp-content/uploads/2022/02/U.S.-Indo-Pacific-Strategy.pdf.

The White House. "Remarks by National Security Advisor Jake Sullivan on the Biden-Harris Administration's National Security Strategy." 12 October 2022. https://www.whitehouse.gov/briefing-room/speeches-remarks/2022/10/13/remarks-by-national-security-advisor-jake-sullivan-on-the-biden-harris-administrations-national-security-strategy/.

The White House. "Remarks by National Security Advisor Jake Sullivan on Renewing American Economic Leadership at the Brookings Institution." 27 April 2023. https://www.whitehouse.gov/briefing-room/speeches-remarks/2023/04/27/remarks-by-national-security-advisor-jake-sullivan-on-renewing-american-economic-leadership-at-the-brookings-institution/.

The White House. "Executive Order on Addressing United States Investments in Certain National Security Technologies and Products in Countries of Concern." 9 August 2023. https://www.whitehouse.gov/briefing-room/presidential-actions/2023/08/09/executive-order-on-addressing-united-states-investments-in-certain-national-security-technologies-and-products-in-countries-of-concern/.

White, Olivia, Jonathan Woetzel, Jeonmin Seong, and Tiago Devesa. *The complication of concentration in global trade*. Mckinsey. 12 January 2023. https://www.mckinsey.com/mgi/Our-Research/The-complication-of-concentration-in-global-trade?cid=other-eml-nsl-mip-mck&hlkid=2d6128a7e7a546fa9da2b228eeb5752c&hctky=12874489&hdpid=d44b5f86-27cd-4c36-8ae9-dda34b3493a8.

Willick, Jason. "Blow Up the Microchips? What a Taiwan Spat Says About U.S. Strategy." *The Washington Post*. 12 May 2023. https://www.washingtonpost.com/opinions/2023/05/12/microchips-us-taiwan-strategy/.

Woetzel, Jonathan, Yougang Chen, James Manyika, Erik Roth, Jeongmin Seong, and Jason Lee. *The China Effect on Global Innovation*. New York: McKinsey Global Institute, 2015.

Woetzel, Jonathan, Jeongmin Seong, Nick Leung, Joe Ngai, James Manyika, Anu Madgavkar, Susan Lund, and Andrey Mironenko. *China and the World: Inside the Dynamics of a Changing Relationship*. New York: McKinsey Global Institute, 1 July 2019. https://www.mckinsey.com/featured-insights/china/china-and-the-world-inside-the-dynamics-of-a-changing-relationship.

Wolf Richter. "US Trade Deficit in 2020 Worst since 2008." *Wolf Street*. 8 February 2021. https://wolfstreet.com/2021/02/08/us-trade-deficit-in-2020-worst-since-2008-goods-deficit-worst-ever-despite-first-ever-petroleum-surplus-services-surplus-drops-again/.

Wolf Richter. "Who Bought the $4.7 Trillion of Treasury Securities Added Since March 2020 to the Incredibly Spiking US National Debt?" *Wolf Street*. 17 May 2021. https://wolfstreet.com/2021/05/17/who-bought-the-4-7-trillion-of-treasury-securities-added-since-march-2020-to-the-incredibly-spiking-us-national-debt/.

Wolf Richter. "Update on US Dollar as Global Reserve Currency and the Impact of USD Exchange Rates & Inflation." *Wolf Street*. 2 April 2022. https://wolfstreet.com/2022/04/02/us-dollars-status-as-global-reserve-currency-drops-to-26-year-low-slowly-but-surely/.

Wolf Richter. "Who Bought the Incredibly Spiking US Government Debt, Now $30.4 Trillion in Treasury Securities?" *Wolf Street.* 19 May 2022. https://wolfstreet.com/2022/05/19/who-bought-the-incredibly-spiking-us-government-debt-now-30-4-trillion-in-treasury-securities/.

Wolf Richter. "Fed Balance Sheet QT." *Wolf Street.* 7 September 2023. https://wolfstreet.com/2023/09/07/fed-balance-sheet-qt-105-billion-in-august-864-billion-from-peak-to-8-1-trillion-lowest-since-july-2021/.

Wong, Sharnie and Francis Chan. "Yuan Could Globalize on Digital Currency, De-dollarization Steps." Bloomberg. 4 February 2021. https://www.bloomberg.com/professional/blog/yuan-could-globalize-on-digital-currency-de-dollarization-steps/.

World Bank—Development Research Center of the State Council, the People's Republic of China. "China 2030: Building a Modern, Harmonious, and Creative Society." Washington, DC: 2013. https://www.worldbank.org/content/dam/Worldbank/document/China-2030-complete.pdf.

World Bank. *Belt and Road Economics: Opportunities and Risks of Transport Corridors.* Washington, DC: 2019.

World Bank. *World Development Report 2020—Trading for Development in the Age of Global Value Chains.* Washington, DC: 2020. DOI: 10.1596/978-1-4648-1457-0.

World Bank, *China's Productivity Slowdown and Future Growth Potential.* Washington, DC: June 2020.

World Trade Organization. *Global Value Chain Development Report 2019—Technological Innovation, Supply Chain Trade and Workers in a Globalized World.* Report no. 136044. Geneva: WTO, 15 April 2019. https://www.wto.org/english/res_e/publications_e/gvcd_report_19_e.htm.

World Trade Organization. "World Trade Primed for Strong but Uneven Recovery after COVID-19 Pandemic Shock." News release 876. 31 March 2021. https://www.wto.org/english/news_e/pres21_e/pr876_e.htm.

World Trade Organization. *Global Trade Outlook.* Geneva: WTO, April 2023. https://www.wto.org/english/res_e/booksp_e/trade_outlook23_e.pdf.

Wu, Yanrui. *China's Economic Growth: A Miracle with Chinese Characteristics.* London; New York: Routledge Curzon, 2004.

Wu, Zhiheng, Guisheng Hou, and Baogui Xin. "Has the Belt and Road Initiative Brought New Opportunities to Countries Along the Routes to Participate in Global Value Chains?" *SAGE Open* 10, 1 (2020). https://doi.org/10.1177/2158244020902088.

Wübbeke, Jost, Mirjam Meissner, Max J. Zenglein, Jaqueline Ives, and Björn Conrad. "Made in China 2025: The Making of a High-Tech Superpower and Consequences for Industrial Countries." *MERICS Papers on China* No. 2. Berlin: MERICS. 12 August 2016. https://merics.org/en/report/made-china-2025.

Xi, Jinping. "Speech at the Symposium of Experts in Economic and Social Fields." Speech of 24 August 2020 delivered to a symposium of economist and sociologists on upcoming Fourteenth Five-Year Plan and published in Chinese by Xinhua News Agency; translated by Etcetera Language Group and published in English by the Center for Security and Emerging Technology on 30 September 2020. https://cset.georgetown.edu/publication/xi-jinping-speech-at-the-symposium-of-experts-in-economic-and-social-fields/.

Xi, Jinping. "Understanding the New Development Stage, Applying the New Development Philosophy, and Creating a New Development Dynamic." *Qiushi Journal* (English edition). Speech, 12 July 2021. https://www.chinadaily.com.cn/a/202107/12/WS60ec3e56a310efa1bd6614fb.html.

Xi, Jinping. "Full Text: Xi Jinping's Speech on Boosting Common Prosperity". *Caixin Global*. 19 October 2021. https://www.caixinglobal.com/2021-10-19/full-text-xi-jinpings-speech-on-boosting-common-prosperity-101788302.html.

Yan, Hairong and Chen Yiyuan. "Agrarian Capitalisation without Capitalism? Capitalist Dynamics from Above and Below in China." *Journal of Agrarian Change* 15, 3 (2015): 366–91. https://doi.org/10.1111/joac.12121.

Yan, Lang. "Some Thoughts on Foxconn and the Honda Strike." *Radical Notes*. June 2010. http://radicalnotes.org/2010/06/12/china-some-thoughts-on-foxconn-and-the-honda-strike/.

Yan, Xuetong. "China's Ukraine Conundrum: Why the War Necessitates a Balancing Act." *Foreign Affairs*. 2 May 2022. https://www.foreignaffairs.com/articles/china/2022-05-02/chinas-ukraine-conundrum.

Yeung, Henry Wai-Chung. *Interconnected worlds: Global electronics and production networks in East Asia*. Stanford: Stanford Business Books, 2022.

Yu, Sun. "China Meets Banks to Discuss Protecting Assets from US Sanctions." *Financial Times*. 30 April 2022. https://www.ft.com/content/45d5fcac-3e6d-420a-ac78-4b439e24b5de.

Zenglein, Max J. and Anna Holzmann. "Evolving Made in China 2025. China's Industrial Policy in the Quest for Global Tech Leadership." MERICS *Papers on China* No. 8, Berlin: MERICS, 2 July 2019. https://merics.org/en/report/evolving-made-china-2025.

Zhan, Shaohua. *The Land Question in China: Agrarian Capitalism, Industrious Revolution, and East Asian Development*. London: Routledge, 2019.

Zhan, Shaohua. "The Land Question in 21st Century China: Four Camps and Five Scenarios." *New Left Review* 122 (Mar/Apr 2020): 115–133. https://www.researchgate.net/publication/340730559_The_Land_Question_in_21st_Century_China_Four_Camps_and_Five_Scenarios.

Zhang, Hongzhou. "The U.S.-China Trade War: Is Food China's Most Powerful Weapon?" *Asia Policy* 15, 3 (2020): 59–86. DOI: 10.1353/asp.2020.0044.

Zhang, Jin. "The State, Capital and Peasantry in the Agrarian Transition of China: The Case of Guangxi Sugarcane Sector." PhD thesis. Wageningen University, 2019. https://doi.org/10.18174/471122.

Zhang, Lu. *Arbeitskaempfe in Chinas Autofabriken*. Wien-Berlin: Mandelbaum, 2018.

Zhang, Qian Forrest. "Class Differentiation in Rural China: Dynamics of Accumulation, Commodification and State Intervention." *Journal of Agrarian Change* 15, 3 (2015): 338–65. https://doi.org/10.1111/joac.12120.

Zhang, Qian Forrest and John A. Donaldson. "The Rise of Agrarian Capitalism with Chinese Characteristics: Agricultural Modernization, Agribusiness and Collective Land Rights." *China Journal* 60 (2008): 25–47.

Zhang, Qian Forrest and Zhanping Hu. "Rural China under the COVID-19 Pandemic: Differentiated Impacts, Rural–Urban Inequality and Agro-industrialization." *Journal of Agrarian Change* 21, 3 (2021): 591–603. https://doi.org/10.1111/joac.12425.

Zhang, Yu and Zhao Feng. "Saggio del plusvalore, Composizione del Capitale e Saggio del Profitto nell'Industria Manifatturiera Cinese: 1978–2004", in *Il mistero del dragone. La dinamica economica della Cina*, edited by Joel Andreas, Kam Wing Chan, Zhao Feng, Chloé Froissart, Hung Ho-Fung, Peter Nolan, Christine Peltier, Tim Pringle, and Zhang Yu. Trieste: Asterios, 2007: 216–40.

Zhang, Yugui. "US Wages Economic War to Maintain Global Supremacy." *China Daily*. 1 April 2022. http://www.chinadaily.com.cn/a/202204/01/WS6246c83da310fd2b29e54bb2.html.

Zhang, Yulin. "Land Grabs in Contemporary China". *Chuang* blog. 6 January 2015. https://chuangcn.org/2015/01/land-grabs-in-contemporary-china/, reposted from *Nao* journal; translated by Pancho Sanchez (originally published in Chinese in 2014).

Zhao, Minghao. "Is a New Cold War Inevitable? Chinese Perspectives on US–China Strategic Competition." *Chinese Journal of International Politics* 12, 3 (2019): 371–94. https://doi.org/10.1093/cjip/poz010.

Zheng, Bijian. "China's 'Peaceful Rise' to Great-Power Status." *Foreign Affairs*. 1 September 2005. https://www.researchgate.net/publication/272587685_China's_Peaceful_Rise_to_Great-Power_Status.

Zhou, Chao, Yunjian Liang, and Anthony Fuller. "Tracing Agricultural Land Transfer in China: Some Legal and Policy Issues." *Land* 10 (2021): 1–16. DOI: 10.3390/land10010058.

Zhou, Xiaochuan. "Reform The International Monetary System." 23 March 2009. University of South California—USC US-China Institute. https://china.usc.edu/zhou-xiaochuan-%E5%91%A8%E5%B0%8F%E5%B7%9D-reform-international-monetary-system-march-23-2009.

Zhun, Xu. "The Development of Capitalist Agriculture in China." *Review of Radical Political Economics* 49, 4 (2017): 591–98. https://doi.org/10.1177/0486613417717046.

Zhun, Xu and Ying Chen. "Spatial Shift in China's Labour Struggles: Evidence and Implication." *Journal of Labor and Society* 22, 1 (2019): 129–38. https://doi.org/10.1111/wusa.12397.

Zhun, Xu, Wei Zhang, and Minqi Li. "China's Grain Production", *Monthly Review* 66, 1 (1 May 2014). https://monthlyreview.org/2014/05/01/chinas-grain-production/.

Zou, Wei. "La metamorphose des enterprises rurales". *Perspectives chinois* 79 (September–October 2003): 18–31. https://www.persee.fr/doc/perch_1021-9013_2003_num_79_1_3142.

# Index

(*Please note: the words US, US dollar, China, and East Asia are not indexed because of their continuous recurrence in the text*).

Acheson, Dean   60n
Afghanistan   10, 41, 44, 53, 59n, 192, 261
Africa   109, 110, 178, 179n, 183n, 263
Agrarian question   5, 77, 90, 92n, 107
Akira, Hayami   80n
Algeria   173
Alibaba   144, 203
*America First*   34, 46, 56
American imperialism   35, 38, 206, 212
Anders, Günther   1
Anti-American   169, 205, 239, 240
Anti-Chinese   41–42, 47, 53–58, 63, 130, 185, 244, 246, 249, 251, 254
Anti-colonial   5–9, 78n, 81, 86
Anti-globalisation   34
Anti-imperialist   15, 17n, 38, 77, 84, 107, 132, 229, 234
Anti-western   5, 10, 262
April 5 Movement   112
Argentina   108, 200, 228n, 261
Arrighi, Giovanni   3, 74n, 87n, 106n, 236n
ASEAN   54–56, 173, 186–8, 218, 249, 253
Asia   13, 23–4, 26–8, 39–41, 45, 53, 56–7, 74, 85, 133, 148, 190, 192, 211, 216–7, 236, 245, 252, 263
Asian financial crisis   88, 103, 114, 135, 188
Asian Infrastructure Investment Bank (AIIB)   173, 192n
Asian mode of production   78–9
Asiatism   215
ASML   151, 246
Astarian, Bruno   19n, 30n, 95n, 106n, 112n, 131n, 264n
Asymmetry, asymmetrical   2, 4, 5, 13, 15, 39, 196, 217, 221, 225, 231, 233, 257
Atlanticism   35, 64–5
AUKUS   57, 254
Australia   44, 53, 57, 187, 189, 209, 219

Balasz, Étienne   79n, 80n
Bandung Conference   227
Belt and Road Initiative (BRI)   56, 143n, 173n, 174, 175n, 184, 261n

Biden, Joe   4, 35, 41, 45–53, 56, 57, 58, 61–3, 65, 67, 73, 74, 140, 182n, 186, 216, 220, 244–7, 249, 251, 254, 257, 259, 264
Bipolar system   10n, 15–6, 85n, 186n, 213, 218
Bordiga, Amadeo   1, 78, 79n, 82n, 91n, 162n, 232n
Borneo   53
Brazil   108, 173n, 185, 200, 228, 263
Bretton Woods system   3, 9–11, 73n, 211–3
Bretton Woods II   11, 73n, 211
BRICS   173, 200, 207, 228, 239, 256, 258, 261, 262, 263
Brussels   61, 62, 185
Brzezinski, Zbigniew   10n, 36n, 41, 60, 61

Camatte, Jacques   112n
Cambodia   187
Canada   189, 209
Capital flows   136, 194, 202, 203, 214, 230, 231, 232, 252
Capitalist accumulation   8, 13, 15, 74, 78, 132, 212, 254
Carchedi, Guglielmo   12n
Ch'ao, Ting Chi   79n
Chinese Communist Party (CCP)   77, 79–86, 92–7, 100, 108, 112–5, 118n, 125, 132–5, 140, 144, 167, 168, 260
Chinese revolution   77–82, 90
Chips and Science Act   35, 51, 245
Chip war   49–53, 260
Chuang collective   81n, 82n, 93n, 94n, 95n, 104n, 106n, 148n, 154, 260n
class struggle   2, 4, 5, 6, 18, 34, 37, 64, 76, 90, 110–2, 116n, 119, 130, 131–2, 144, 148, 238, 239, 241, 260
Clinton, Hillary   34
Coastal provinces   148n, 154, 168
Coercive diplomacy   40, 201n
Cold War   4, 37–9, 40, 59, 74, 107, 213
Collective ownership   82, 97
Collectivisation   83–4
Colonial   80, 232
Combined development   232n

Communes   83, 87, 91
Comprehensive and Progressive Trans-Pacific Partnership (CPTPP)   189
Containment   40, 41, 44, 45, 47, 53, 56, 60, 74, 171, 215, 227
Cooperatives   83, 97, 100, 106
COVID-19   20, 67, 71, 101, 162, 183, 202, 228
Cultural Revolution   9, 76, 84–85, 112–3
Current account deficit, US   248
Current account surplus, China   13, 134, 147

Danwei   115
de Brunhoff, Suzanne   233*n*
Debt crisis   160
Decentralisation   87
De-collectivisation   84, 88, 95
Decoupling   43, 45, 47–9, 53–4, 58, 114, 133, 140, 150, 152, 170–1, 189, 205, 208–11, 215, 220, 223, 237, 244–53
De-dollarisation   205–15
Deglobalisation   4, 20, 28, 32, 66, 170, 222, 241
Democracy Wall Movement   113
Deng, Xiaoping   10, 81*n*, 84, 86, 92, 113, 114, 130, 134, 135, 155, 167, 217, 225, 232
Department of Commerce (DoC)   208, 245
De-risking   246
Developing countries   24, 181, 204, 228
Diaoyu-Senkaku Islands   219
Didi   145
Digital currency, yuan   146, 171, 176, 199, 202–5, 209, 211
Digital economy, digitisation   25, 150
Digital Silk Road   171, 175, 204
Disengagement   44, 170
Division of labour, international   2, 3, 12, 25, 48, 73, 90, 117, 125, 131, 231, 232*n*, 235, 239, 260
Dragon-headed enterprises   99
Dual circulation   140–6, 178, 194, 208

East China Sea   218
Eastern Europe   41, 60*n*, 64, 89, 114, 224
Egypt   184*n*, 228*n*, 261
Elvin, Mark   80*n*
Emerging economies   12, 15, 231
Enterprise Law   114
Entity List   42, 49, 208
Environmental   13, 56, 101, 107, 109, 188
Ethiopia   179, 261

European Central Bank (ECB)   265
Europe, European Union (EU)   11, 14, 23, 27, 29, 35, 39, 41, 56, 59, 60, 61–5, 70, 74–5, 91, 106, 110, 113, 117, 143, 161, 171, 175, 181, 184, 185–7, 190, 191, 194, 200, 202, 207, 209, 210, 222, 233*n*, 236, 241, 245, 249, 252, 256
Evergrande   161–3
Existential challenge, China   6, 232
Exploitation   16, 29, 117, 121, 125, 127, 130, 131, 137, 148, 155, 238, 264
Exports, export sector   5, 13, 21, 25, 28, 42, 43, 48, 88, 90, 108, 117, 123, 134, 147, 159, 168, 175, 181, 187, 190, 198, 199, 209, 210, 218, 231, 249, 252, 253, 255, 259

Farmers   91, 98, 99, 101, 103, 155
Federal Reserve, US   10, 17, 20, 67, 70–2, 172, 196, 198, 199, 265
Ferro, Robert   19*n*, 30*n*, 264*n*
Fictitious capital   12, 17, 31, 89, 157, 236
Finance, financial imperialism   2, 6, 8, 11, 12, 13, 14, 22, 48, 67, 73, 89, 109, 133, 140, 145, 190, 194–6, 204, 206, 213, 214, 228, 237, 259
Financialisation   12, 14, 15, 18, 161, 264
Fiscal stimulus   67, 123, 156, 160, 259
Food self-sufficiency   84, 94, 101, 107–110
Fordist   8, 10, 49, 89
Foreign debt   68, 157, 266
Foreign direct investment (FDI)   22–4, 27, 28*n*, 29, 44, 179*n*, 180, 190, 198*n*, 249, 252
Foreign exchange reserves, China   138*n*, 199
Foreign Investment Law   142
Four modernisations   84
Foxconn   123–4
France   64, 226, 233*n*
Friendshoring   55, 247, 249, 251

*Gang of Four*   86*n*
Gaulard, Mylène   96*n*, 156*n*, 161*n*
Geo-economics   15
Geopolitics   3, 15, 17, 36, 36*n*, 37, 38, 46, 60, 61*n*, 73, 76, 86, 130, 194, 215
Georgia   59
Germany   20, 26, 27, 60, 61–5, 89, 139, 142, 149, 154, 171, 185, 186, 194, 207, 233*n*, 252, 253
Gernet, Jacques   80*n*

INDEX

Global financial crisis   1, 13, 21, 25, 30, 34, 103, 122, 134, 138, 147, 148, 154, 155, 172, 188, 211, 235, 251, 252
Globalisation   1–7, 14, 15, 18, 19, 20, 21, 22, 25, 28, 29, 32, 33, 34, 38, 40, 45, 46, 51, 53, 64, 74, 76, 89, 116, 117, 153, 156, 169, 170, 171, 172, 174, 192, 194, 196, 206, 222, 229, 236, 239, 240, 242, 244, 251, 264, 265
Global South   15, 180n, 222, 227–32, 256, 257, 262
Global supply chains   2, 28, 29, 126, 175, 252
Global value chains (GVCs)   5, 19, 25–8, 38, 118, 231, 249, 253
Gold standard   3, 9, 211, 214
Grand Strategy, US   4, 35, 36, 37, 73, 75n, 86, 237, 257, 267
*Great Chinese Famine*   84
*Great Leap Forward*   84, 107
Greenfield investments   23, 249, 252
Green New Deal   35
Gross domestic product (GDP), China   87
Gross domestic product (GDP), US   67
Guam   53
Gulf War   10
Guomindang   77

Hegemonic challenge   6, 227, 229, 235
Hegemonic successions   3
Hegemony, US   2, 5, 6, 11, 14, 17, 18, 36, 37, 38, 40, 41, 46, 53, 60, 70, 75, 89, 168, 206, 208, 210, 212, 213, 215, 217, 229, 230, 232, 254, 261
Honda   123, 124
Hong Kong   117, 137, 169, 201, 204
Hormuz, Straits of   173, 191
Household responsibility system   87, 98
Hu, Jintao   95, 100, 121, 217
Huawei   42, 50, 57, 63, 151, 185, 191, 208, 245, 251
Hudson, Michael   9n
Hukou   83n, 97, 101n, 102–4, 121, 137, 142, 164

Imperialism   2, 3, 5, 6, 8, 11, 119, 130, 131, 132, 133, 146, 156, 157, 169, 186, 195, 196, 206, 212, 229–43, 254
India   23, 44, 53–6, 80, 102n, 110, 173, 189, 206–8, 212, 222, 228, 262, 263
Indigenous innovation   139, 142
Indonesia   189, 219, 228n

Indo-Pacific   41, 44, 47, 53–7, 190, 192, 219, 221, 223, 224, 249
Indo-Pacific Economic Framework   56, 219
Inflation   10, 17, 69, 71, 74, 93, 109, 113, 123, 170, 198, 202, 212, 214, 230, 263–4, 266
Inflation Reduction Act   35, 63, 245
Inland, areas or regions   90, 127, 148, 178
Intellectual property   18, 188
Inter-bourgeois   2
Inter-capitalist   2, 171, 238, 240
Interest rates   10, 67, 68, 71, 72, 133, 135, 137, 162, 182, 183, 265, 266
Inter-firm trade   25
Internationalisation   8, 16, 25, 28, 89, 146, 176, 178, 194–215, 238, 263
International order   3, 9, 18, 20, 38, 41, 215, 217, 223, 228, 235, 244, 257, 262
International relations   1, 224, 239
International system   7, 19, 39, 65, 134, 213, 215
International Monetary Fund (IMF)   10, 154, 157, 174, 179, 198, 205, 252
inter-regional   148
Iran   10, 44, 173, 184–5, 191–2, 201, 206, 207, 210, 256, 261, 262
Iraq   10, 207, 210
Israel   193

Japan   11, 20, 24, 26, 44, 49, 53, 54, 55, 60n, 64n, 68, 75, 77, 78n, 80n, 82, 89, 92, 116, 132n, 136, 139, 147, 149, 154, 170, 185, 187, 188, 189, 190, 194, 219, 233, 236, 246, 252, 253, 254, 255
Joint Comprehensive Plan of Action (JCPOA)   191
Joint ventures   117

Kautsky, Karl   83n
King, Sam   13n, 148n
Kissinger, Henry   9, 10, 61, 85, 257
Korean War   48n, 81, 83
Kuwait   192
Kyrgyzstan   59

Labour Contracts Act   122
Labour Law   124
Labour struggles   72n, 124, 126
Land ownership   80n, 98
Land rent   81, 101–4, 109, 164

Land (use) rights   95–7, 103
Land transfers   99
Latin America   65, 108, 110, 173, 175, 185, 200, 263
Left, the   7, 14, 35, 241
Lenin, Vladimir   33, 36$n$, 79$n$, 81, 83$n$, 92, 101, 105, 110$n$, 232
Li, Minqi   94$n$, 118$n$
Liberal international order   30, 41
Libya   10, 173, 179$n$, 184, 185, 210
Lin, Biao   86$n$
Long   8, 14, 68$n$3, 73, 84, 131
Lukàcs, Georg   15
Luxemburg, Rosa   36$n$

Mackinder, Halford John   61
*Made in China 2025*   42, 138–40, 150, 151, 175, 218
Mahbubani, Kishore   39$n$, 75$n$, 187$n$
Malacca, Straits of   53, 173, 184
Malaysia   189, 219
Mandel, Ernest   64$n$, 233$n$
Mao, Zedong   9, 57, 77, 79$n$, 81, 84, 85, 87
Maoism, Maoist   76, 77, 83, 84, 86, 92, 95, 103, 106, 107, 110$n$, 112, 115, 141, 225, 235
Marx, Karl   2, 6$n$, 8, 12, 78, 79$n$, 81, 89, 91, 238
Marxism, marxist   2, 3, 64$n$, 78$n$, 79$n$, 110$n$, 232
Mass casualties   111
Merkel, Angela   62, 64, 186
Mexico   43, 189, 249
Middle classes   8, 14, 20, 30, 34, 39, 73, 111$n$, 130, 149, 164–9, 239, 240, 265
Middle East   41, 44, 54, 184$n$, 191–4, 201, 210, 211, 261
Migrant workers   104, 119, 121, 122, 124, 148
Moscow   5, 10, 35, 41, 55, 59–61, 65, 66, 85, 173, 200, 206, 208, 209, 213, 218, 222, 224, 226, 228, 255, 256, 257, 258, 262
Multinational corporations (MNCs)   11, 12, 21, 24, 25, 29, 42, 54, 62, 63, 109, 111, 114, 117, 118$n$, 120, 125, 131, 140, 233, 252, 253
Multipolar, multipolarism   6, 19, 134, 215, 217, 218, 224, 229, 239, 240, 257
Myanmar   184

National Defense Strategy   41
Nationalisation   77, 92, 101
National Security Strategy   41
Nation-state, Chinese   6
Naval power   226
Nearshoring   43, 251
Neo-colonial   234
Neoconservative   41
Neoliberal, Neoliberalism   13, 14, 15, 32, 179
Neo-Maoist   106
Neo-populism   7, 30, 35$n$, 73
Neusüss, Christel   233$n$
New Cold War   38
New Left, Chinese   106
Newly industrialised countries   25, 89
*New Silk Roads*   5, 54, 149, 170, 172–174, 184–5, 193, 200, 231
New Zealand   189, 219
Nicolaus, Martin   64$n$, 233$n$
Nixon, Richard   9, 11, 57, 85, 210
Nongmin   90
Nongmingong   97, 111, 119
Nord Stream   62, 207
Norfield, Tony   12$n$
North America   27
North Atlantic Treaty Organization (NATO)   54, 56, 58$n$, 59, 60$n$, 62, 65, 222, 223, 254–6, 258

Obama, Barack   34, 40, 41, 44, 53, 63, 191, 217
Offshoring   29
Offshore balancing   41
One China policy   57
Organization of the Petroleum Exporting Countries (OPEC)   11, 193, 210, 261
Outsourcing   14, 25

Pacific, Ocean   44, 57, 175, 209, 220, 226
Pakistan   173, 176, 184, 200, 206
Party-state   105, 133, 136, 138, 148, 156, 167, 168, 196, 229, 240, 258
Pearl River Delta   123
Peasants   77–83, 90–5, 96, 98, 99, 103, 106, 234
People's Liberation Army   225
Petrodollar   11, 12, 68, 208, 210, 211
Philippines   53, 189, 219, 254
*Pivot to Asia*   40, 41, 53
Plekhanov, Georgi   78$n$, 79$n$
Poulantzas, Nicos   233$n$

INDEX

Pound, British   16
Poverty   96, 153, 165
Primacy, US   38, 41, 247, 253, 257
Primitive accumulation   4, 81*n*, 82, 91, 103
Private sector   144, 150, 167, 203
Privatisation   14, 94, 96, 100, 114, 116
Production brigades   83
Productivity, China   83, 93, 95, 98, 103, 109, 112, 115, 118, 122, 125, 129, 138, 149, 153–6, 238
Profit rate   24
Proletarianisation   13, 14, 99, 102, 105, 120, 177
Property Law   97
Pun Ngai   102*n*, 120*n*, 123*n*
Putin, Vladimir   60, 206*n*, 224, 255

Qiao, Liang   18*n*, 225*n*, 229, 230*n*
Quadrilateral Security Dialogue (Quad)   53–7
Quantitative Easing   17, 71, 72, 133, 199, 265, 266
Quantitative Tightening   265

Rapprochement, Sino-US   3, 9, 36, 57, 65, 84, 85, 218, 220, 221
Reagan, Ronald   10, 39, 72, 73
Real estate   72, 146, 149, 154, 156, 157, 160–4, 170, 259, 266
Real socialism   20, 72, 89, 113
Rebalancing   131, 147, 148, 168, 218, 239, 260
Reform and Opening Up   84–8
Reformism   6, 14, 261
Regional Comprehensive Economic Partnership (RCEP)   187–9, 190, 204, 218, 249
Regionalisation   27, 28, 47, 194, 240
Renminbi yuan   5, 70, 146, 159, 160, 171, 194–205, 207–15, 218, 230, 263, 266
Research and development (R&D)   150, 253
Reserve currency   9, 16, 67, 192, 205, 206, 207, 214, 263, 265
Reshoring   28, 29, 42, 43, 46, 63, 237, 249
Revisionism, revisionist   38, 41, 84, 228
Riyadh   191*n*, 193, 261
Roberts, Michael   12*n*, 31*n*, 155*n*
Ruckus, Ralf   112*n*, 113*n*
Rural migrants   97, 103, 104, 115, 121–6
Russia   10, 36, 39, 41, 47, 55, 58, 59–65, 66, 78, 81, 85, 91, 108, 157, 172, 183–6, 192, 193, 194, 199, 200–1, 205–8, 209–11, 213, 222–4, 228, 230, 233, 236, 239, 256–8, 262, 263
Russian-Chinese   209, 212, 223
Ryukyu, islands   53

*Safe haven*   16, 266
Samsung   51*n*, 246, 249
Sanctions   17, 42, 48, 64, 65, 143, 157, 172, 173, 184, 191, 194, 199, 201, 205, 207, 208, 222, 230, 250, 256, 261–3
Saudi Arabia   173, 191–3, 201, 206, 207, 208, 210, 261, 262
Sciortino, Raffaele   8*n*, 10*n*, 19*n*, 35*n*, 59*n*, 61*n*, 85*n*, 111*n*, 186*n*, 208*n*, 265*n*
Semiconductor Manufacturer International Corporation (SMIC)   42, 151, 152
Semiconductors   42*n*, 52, 245, 250*n*
Semi-proletarianisation   84, 102–4, 105, 111, 119
Serbia   10
Service sector, China   123*n*, 129, 167
Shanghai   137, 162, 201
Shanghai Cooperation Organisation (SCO)   172, 207
Singapore   49, 136, 188, 189
Sino-Soviet   10, 81
Sino-US relationship   4, 19
SK hynix   246
Slowbalisation   20, 251
Smith, John   13*n*, 25*n*
Social compromise   5, 6, 13, 14, 112, 124, 133, 265
Social-democratic   5, 132, 164, 238
Socialism   76–8, 81, 88, 92*n*, 110, 144, 170
*Socialist accumulation*   4, 5, 13, 81, 118, 130
South China Sea   54, 189, 218, 219, 223, 227
South East Asia   43, 56, 173, 175, 176
South Korea   55, 58*n*, 108*n*, 136, 147, 188, 190, 200, 208, 246, 253, 254, 255
South-South   24, 182
Soviet Union   9, 10, 38, 39, 59, 61, 77, 78*n*, 82, 85
Special economic zones (SEZs)   88, 115, 116
Sri Lanka   184*n*
Stalin, Joseph   77, 79*n*
State-owned enterprises (SOEs)   88, 114–6, 125, 135, 136, 137, 167, 175

State ownership   135
Stoltenberg, Jens   60$n$, 255
Strategic triangle   5, 85, 218
Suleimani, Qassim   44, 191
Sullivan, Jake   247
Super imperialism   232, 236
Surplus value   5, 12, 13, 18, 19, 73, 75, 117, 118, 120, 125, 130, 131, 136, 154, 155, 190, 231, 234, 237, 238, 260, 264
SWIFT   195, 198, 199, 204, 205, 223
Syria   10, 44, 60, 179$n$, 184, 185, 192, 207, 210, 261

Taiwan   50, 53, 54, 57–9, 108$n$, 117, 124, 136, 151, 190, 218, 219, 220–2, 224, 249, 254
Taiwan Relations Act   58
Taiwan Semiconductor Manufacturing Co. (TSMC)   49, 51$n$, 151, 220, 249
Tehran   191, 193, 207, 208
Thailand   188, 204, 228$n$
Third World   10, 73, 84, 86, 90, 111, 228
*Thirty Glorious Years*   9
Tiananmen Square   93, 113
Tokyo Electron   246
Tooze, Adam   66$n$, 205
Trade unions, trade unionism   121, 125
Trade war   22, 42, 43, 45, 47, 139, 141, 208, 231
Transition to capitalism   78, 81$n$, 83$n$
Treasury bonds   13, 68, 69, 71, 199, 207, 231
Trotsky, Leon   78$n$, 79$n$
Trump, Donald   4, 22, 34, 35, 37, 40–5, 46, 48, 50, 53, 57, 58, 61, 63, 65, 67, 73, 140, 189, 191, 216, 218, 226, 244, 245, 250, 256, 264
Turkey   184, 206, 207, 208

Ukraine, Ukrainian conflict   35, 47, 58, 59–61, 63, 64, 65, 108, 156, 185, 186, 195, 200, 205, 207, 208, 220, 221, 22, 223, 224, 255, 257, 258
United Kingdom   57, 226
United Nations Conference on Trade and Development (UNCTAD)   22

Urbanisation   94, 99, 137, 142
US-China relations   2, 3, 45
US foreign policy   36

Venezuela   185, 201, 206, 210
Vietnam   9, 10, 39, 43, 85, 188, 189, 219, 249
Village collective ownership   97
Village and township enterprises   87, 93, 94, 116
*Volcker Shock*   10, 72, 266
von Braunmühl, Claudia   233$n$

Wall Street   11, 16, 17, 68, 72
Western Asia   191–4
Western imperialism   5, 90, 119, 130, 131, 132, 156, 157, 178, 241
Western, the West   1, 3, 8, 10, 12, 13, 14, 15, 18, 20, 24, 29, 47, 52, 60$n$, 63, 64, 65, 71, 76, 77, 81, 102, 110, 111, 113, 117, 118, 128, 130, 131, 132, 134, 145, 146, 148, 163, 164, 166, 167, 168, 169, 173, 176, 177, 188, 191, 194, 205, 210, 216, 221, 222, 223, 229, 233, 237, 252, 256, 258, 262, 263, 264, 265, 267
Working class   6, 12, 14, 19, 34, 65, 76, 77, 78, 82, 88, 111, 112, 113, 114, 119–26, 130, 131, 133, 168, 239, 240, 241
World Bank   137, 153, 154, 157, 165, 179, 182$n$
World economy   4, 46, 244, 247
World market   2, 4, 7, 8, 21$n$, 33, 38, 76, 78, 89, 114, 125, 209, 212, 215, 224, 229, 233, 234, 239, 240, 244, 253
World system   3, 75, 215, 229, 232$n$
World War I   78$n$, 81
World War II   6, 8, 9, 16, 37, 64, 73$n$, 81, 186, 213, 218, 232$n$

Xi, Jinping   37, 96, 100, 122, 134, 137, 138, 140, 160, 163, 173, 215, 216, 217, 224, 258, 261

Zhou, Enlai   86, 112
Zhou, Xiaochuan   66$n$
ZTE   208

www.ingramcontent.com/pod-product-compliance
Lightning Source LLC
Chambersburg PA
CBHW070611030426
42337CB00020B/3751